SLAVISTIC PRINTINGS AND REPRINTINGS

edited by

C. H. VAN SCHOONEVELD

Indiana University

108

'SUPERFLUOUS MEN'
AND THE
POST-STALIN 'THAW'

THE ALIENATED HERO IN SOVIET PROSE
DURING THE DECADE 1953-1963

by

THOMAS F. ROGERS
Brigham Young University

1972
MOUTON
THE HAGUE · PARIS

This book was made possible by a grant from the Brigham Young University.

LIBRARY OF CONGRESS CATALOG CARD NUMBER: 75-165148

Printed in The Netherlands by Mouton & Co., Printers, The Hague.

To   Michael Krupensky for the idea,
     David Korn for the encouragement,
     Dmitry Grigorieff for his indulgence

PREFACE

Alienation as a common vicissitude issue and a major theme in literature has persisted in the West up to the present day. It has also made a striking reappearance in Soviet prose fiction, particularly in the first decade since the death of Stalin. To determine, therefore, to what extent the alienation which Russian writers described during this period might reflect what is unique to life in contemporary Soviet society and to what extent that which is instead more universal (at least more universally Russian) is the general purpose of this investigation.

The prior literary tradition will first be examined in order to define the typical Russian 'alienated' protagonist and establish a basis of comparison for the analysis of Soviet literary heroes. The discussion of nineteenth-century 'superfluous men' is itself perhaps the most complete which has yet appeared on the subject. Similar character types which appeared in Soviet prose after the death of Stalin and the subsequent liberalization of the arts will be considered next — types which, for a variety of reasons, find themselves estranged from and often in disagreement with their fellows if not, frequently, their whole society.

The following study (1) establishes which representative protagonists of which representative authors fit this same general description; (2) analyzes the various thematic implications which underlie their depiction — the reasons for their estrangement; (3) assesses, by their narrative slant and the stylistic devices in their presentation, the degree to which these characters — as loners, non-conformists, rebels, 'dissonant voices' — receive the endorsement or condemnation of their respective authors; and, finally, (4) compares these characters, as a type, with others in the prior literary tradition — that of the nineteenth century, the pre-Soviet twentieth century, and early Soviet periods. In addition, the book's three appendices provide a valuable listing of critical reviews, relevant 'Thaw' works, and plot synopses.

The scope of my investigation is itself immense. It is doubtless, to cite

Harry Levin, "one of those projects which only youth could conceive and only age could complete".[1] Many of its assumptions — its selection of representative works and protagonists, particularly for the nineteenth century; its assessment of ultimate author bias — are unavoidably subjective. It is to be hoped however that the matter itself, the incidental observations, will compensate where premises and conclusions prove tentative or controversial. As a compendium, this study readily acknowledges and abundantly cites the conclusions already reached by prior critics. It does not always radically differ from, though it further substantiates, many of their findings. As an advance over preceding analyses it correlates a variety of topics in a highly comprehensive fashion — precedents, themes, biases, political repercussions, and, finally, the alignment of writers according to common tendencies. In other words it tests a number of critical views against its own rather statistical findings in diverse but integrated contexts. It subscribes, as it were, to a cubist-like, multi-dimensional critical vision. This is its special contribution.

The publication date of each work cited is given with its first mention in the text. Likewise, the given name or initials of each writer are generally indicated with the first reference to that writer and also later if necessary, to avoid confusion, e.g. Vsevolod Ivanov, A. Tolstoj. All translations are my own.

Provo, Utah   T.F.R.
June, 1971

---

[1] Harry Levin, *The Gates of Horn* (New York, Oxford University Press, 1966), p. v.

CONTENTS

PART FOUR: THE 'THAW' HERO AS BOTH THE OUTGROWTH OF A PRIOR LITERARY TRADITION AND A DISTINCTLY NEW CHARACTER CREATION

LIST OF TABLES

LIST OF ABBREVIATIONS

PERIODICALS AND ANTHOLOGIES

Al'manax:	*Al.*
Grani:	*Gr.*
Junost':	*Ju.*
Kultura: (Polish)	*Ku.*
Literaturnaja Moskva II:	*L.M. II.*
Literaturnaja Rossija:	*L.R.*
Molodaja gvardija:	*M.g.*
Moskva:	*Mo.*
Naš sovremennik:	*N.s.*
Nauka i religija:	*N.iR.*
Neva:	*Ne.*
Novyj mir:	*N.m.*
Oktjabr':	*Ok.*
Sovetskaja Rossija:	*S.R.*
Tarusskie stranicy:	*T.s.*
Teatr:	*Te.*
Znamja:	*Zn.*
Zvezda:	*Zv.*

WORKS OF FICTION

Ju. Kazakov	*Adam and Eve*:	*Adam*
A. Kuznecov	*Continuation of a Legend*:	*Legend*
B. Pasternak	*Doctor Živago*:	*Živago*
A. Solženicyn	*For the Good of the Cause*:	*For the Good*
N. Ždanov	*Journey Home*:	*Journey*
V. Nekrasov	*Kira Georgievna*:	*Kira*

Ju. Nagibin,	*Light in the Window*:	*Light*
A. Solženicyn	*Matrena's Home*:	*Matrena*
V. Dudincev	*Not by Bread Alone*:	*Bread*
A. Solženicyn	*One Day in the Life of Ivan Denisovič*:	*One Day*
D. Granin	*One's Own Opinion*:	*Opinion*
N. Pogodin	*Petrarch's Sonnet*:	*Sonnet*
V. Kaverin	*Quests and Hopes*:	*Quests*
Ju. Kazakov	*The Renegade*:	*Renegade*
V. Panova	*Seasons of the Year*:	*Seasons*
V. Tarsis	*Tale of a Bluebottle Fly*:	*Bluebottle*
I. Èrenburg	*The Thaw*:	*Thaw*
N. Aržak	*This is Moscow Speaking*:	*Moscow*
V. Aksenov	*Ticket to the Stars*:	*Ticket*
V. Tendrjakov	*The Trial*:	*Trial*
A. Terc	*The Trial Begins*:	*Trial Begins*

"There have unfortunately been very few separate attempts at a systematic survey of the motifs of one or the other literary trend or of the motifs of an individual writer. For the further successful development of historico-literary research, such surveys, and even 'dictionaries', indices of literary motifs, are absolutely indispensable."

Dmitrij Chizhevskij, *On Romanticism in Slavic Literature*, 1957.

"In dem Lärm und der Hast des politischen Geschehens unserer Tage wird der sich mehr in der Stille vollziehenden Entwicklung im geistigen Bereich im Osten meist nur wenig Beachtung geschenkt. Aber gerade sie dürfte, in historischen Zeiträumen gemessen, bedeutender sein als jede aufmerksam registrierte Äusserung Chruschtchows. Die Geschichte lehrt, dass sich auf lange Sicht anbahnende Wandlungen oft zuerst in der Literatur ankündigten."

Heinz Kersten, *Politische Meinung*, January, 1959.

INTRODUCTION

No one will question that Stalin's death appeared to mark a decisive turning point in Soviet literary affairs and initiated a period which, despite its fluctuations, offered writers decidedly more creative opportunity. The fact that newly published writers were once again a topic of controversy within the Soviet Union itself suggests a radical advance over the climate of affairs which had existed ever since Stalin's great purges in the thirties. Hence, the overt depiction of a character's social dissatisfactions — his alienation — was once more a possibility, and writers quickly took notice. The title of Èrenburg's novelette, *The Thaw*, whose first installment appeared just fourteen months after Stalin's demise, aptly characterized the new, encouraging atmosphere and soon served as the period's unofficial designation.

Although that label's range of application may be disputed, it is perhaps not inappropriate — in view of subsequently alternating 'thaws' and 'freezes' — to extend its reference to the whole period since the death of Stalin — particularly to the whole first decade, which is by now sufficiently in the past to merit an unhurried, objective assessment. Moreover, since that decade very little has appeared that is nearly so original or provocative as the numerous manifestations of the first ten years. The notable exceptions include the appearance, after decades of suppression, of Bulgakov's profound fantasy, *The Master and Margrita*, and the publication of Solženicyn's truly devastating anti-establishment satires, *Cancer Ward* and *The First Circle* — both by way of the underground. Nor have subsequent political developments been especially encouraging. It is therefore safe to conclude that the period here treated and the works it circumscribes delineate a movement that is already in the past and whose revival, though always possible, is far from certain.

The theme of alienation is also abundantly evident in verse written during the first post-Stalin decade. The present investigation has, all the same, been restricted to works of prose fiction in order to explore its

subject in terms of more fully developed plots and character confrontations. Of the earlier works which have proved useful for comparison
(Part I), two actually — Griboedov's *Woe from Wit* and Puškin's
Evgenij Onegin — are written in verse. The one is nevertheless a full-
length play, the other "a novel in verse".[1] As poetry they are, with their
well developed plots and subtle characterizations, obvious exceptions.

In a sense, its preoccupation with the ultimate bias of each particular
author is the book's principal concern. Indicative is the disproportionate
size of Part III (Chapter V) with its application of various oblique criteria
and its extensive probing of the author's slant toward his protagonist.
Such concern is truly warranted with respect to Russian, particularly
Soviet Russian writers. Accustomed as we are in the West to presume
an author's inviolable freedom of self-expression, we are all too apt to
forget the difficult incursions of Czarist censorship, which merely *proscribed*, and the far more insidious policies of *prescribed* writing and of
editorial overhaul in Soviet times.

If for a while we naively believed that, after Stalin, these policies had
altogether attenuated, the abrupt defection in 1969 of one of the authors
here surveyed and his subsequent exposé to the Western press[2] gave us
to know otherwise. His retraction of the suit which in 1965 he won
against a French firm for publishing an unauthorized but authentic
translation of the novelette, *Continuation of a Legend*, has become an
anomaly in the history of French justice. Apart from its novelty, however,
the incident dramatizes both the seriousness and the difficulty of deter-
mining just what may be an author's true aim. The present study's attempt
to ferret out the actual intent of Soviet authors may therefore be illusive.
But it will come nearer the truth than those based on more complacent
presuppositions.

As for the literary merit of the works here considered, there are those
who advise caution:

Of course, argument here is futile, since there are no recognized standards for
the measurement and comparison of aesthetic values. It is obviously only some
consensus of opinion — and in a future generation at that! — which can
'decide' the relative status of Solzhenitsyn, Evtushenko, and Abram Tertz. At
the moment we can only judge them from their impact on ourselves (and this
is of course highly personal), the apparent extent of their influence on contemporary readers (a poor guide!), and such like factors.[3]

---

[1]   Puškin's own designation.
[2]   Anatolij Kuznecov.
[3]   Max Hayward, "Solzhenitsyn's Place in Contemporary Soviet Literature", *Slavic
Review*, XXIII (September, 1964), 433.

Debatable as the case may still be for Soviet literature as a sufficiently free and objective art form, the matter of its socio-political, even polemical content is indisputable. This is in turn a frequent cause of dissatisfaction among Western critics. Because of its subject matter, some would doubtless consider the survey which follows an unworthy literary investigation. A number of respected critics have already dealt with such reservations, however, as follows. Gleb Struve:

If at present many of the published studies in the field of Soviet literature tend to be politically and socially oriented, the blame for this should fall on Soviet literature itself: its destinies are too closely interwoven with politics, and it is almost impossible to study it *qua* pure literature.[4]

Max Hayward:

In the case of Soviet literature, discussion of the political implications and context is unavoidable. ... In this respect Soviet literature in the post-Stalin era even seems to have a certain advantage over Western literature which, having broken loose from all conceivable bonds and restraints, now increasingly tends to concern itself with themes that are essentially trivial.[5]

George Gibian, who also suggests a possible "advantage" in the general Soviet orientation to literary content:

In Western Europe and the United States, some authors do study social and public themes, but a greater number of the significant and best authors concentrate on the fate of the individual, outside politics, office, factory — ignoring his links with society, delving into inter-personal and intra-personal matters. This may be a symptom of the depoliticization of the intellectual-artistic classes in the West; it may also be connected with the sense of purposelessness and loneliness of which our writers complain.[6]

Irving Howe, with particular reference to Solženicyn's *One Day in the Life of Ivan Denisovič*:

Only a Cretin could read such a book 'purely' in literary terms.[7]

Victor Erlich warns, however, that in studying and assessing Soviet writing Western critical standards ought to prevail: "To measure the performance of Soviet writers by other standards than the 'Western' ones

---

[4] Gleb Struve, "Western Writing in Soviet Literature", *Survey*, No. 50 (January, 1964), 143.
[5] Hayward, *Slavic Review*, 432.
[6] George Gibian, "Soviet Literature during the Thaw", *Literature and Revolution in Soviet Russia 1917-1962*, (ed.) Max Hayward & Leopold Labedz (London, Oxford University Press, 1963), 147.
[7] Irving Howe, "Predicaments of Soviet Writing", *The New Republic*, CXLVII (May 11, 1963), 19.

would be a sign of condescension rather than of understanding."[8]
F. D. Reeve seconds this view:

We know that not much of Soviet literature is up to our best standards. Often
we prefer to patronize its awkward but to us, flattering celebration of Wester-
ness.
    We are guilty of disservice to young Russian writers, to precisely those who
have been trying to make literature less and less political. Every time they take
a stand for themselves, our newspapers construe it as a political stand against
the Soviet regime; our papers make it into a political opposition and play into
the hands of the bureaucrats of literature. The art that is trying to be apolitical
is being forced into a political stance by dogmatists and sensationalists, by men
who have no real respect for literature at all.[9]

Vickery refers to this same phenomenon as the Western world's 'intellectual parlor game' which "consists in making use of Soviet literature to
point up the defects and vices of the 'Soviet system'".[10] Indeed a number
of critics have told of the resentment of Soviet writers at the political
sensation which American journalism often exploits or even manufactures
in its reportage of literary events in the USSR.[11]

    Western scholars must therefore tread a tenuous middle ground —
recognizing the ubiquitous political import of Soviet letters, yet assessing
them esthetically, not as documents. The effort should be rewarding,
whether or not its findings are only quasi-literary. Erlich maintains that
"while few literary manifestations of the post-Stalin 'thaw' will repay
close aesthetic analysis, many of them yield significant glimpses of the
human reality hidden by the bland official facade — of unauthorized
attitudes or hitherto unpublicized tracts of Soviet experience".[12] Marc
Slonim has in turn avowed that such investigation provides insight into
"not only the outward changes and adjustments which have taken place
since the Revolution" but also "those submarine spiritual and mental
currents which stir in the depths of the turbulent Russian sea and which

[8]   Victor Erlich, "Post-Stalin Trends in Russian Literature", *Slavic Review*, XXIII
(September, 1964), 406.
[9]   F. D. Reeve, "Writer vs. Bureaucrat in the Soviet Union", *The Atlantic Monthly*,
CCXIII (January, 1964), 73-74.
[10] Walter Vickery, *Political and Ideological Problems of Recent Soviet Literature*
(Bloomington, Indiana University Press, 1963), 167.
[11] For example, George Feiffer ("Brodsky: Reactions in Moscow", *The New Leader*,
XLVII (September 14, 1964)) and Mihajlo Mihajlov ("Why We Are Silent", *The New
Leader*, XLVIII (August 30, 1965)). It is also rumored that Solženicyn — in view of
the KGB's outright attempt to sell his later manuscripts to Western publishers and
make a case against him — either has not or must deny that he authorized the English
editions of *Cancer Ward* and *The First Circle*.
[12] Erlich, *Slavic Review*, 405.

may determine the future fate of the country and its people".[13] When, by Mehnert's 1963 estimate, the monthly yield of significant Soviet literary publications totals some 40,000 printed pages[14] — the possibility for such investigation is real enough and the promise its findings will bear significance, literary or other, seems assured.

[13] Marc Slonim, "The New Spirit in Russian Literature", *Soviet Literature: An Anthology*, (trans.) George Reavey (New York, Covici Friede Publishers, 1934), 13.
[14] Klaus Mehnert, *Humanismus in der jüngsten Sowjetliteratur?* (Mainz, Verlag der Akademie der Wissenschaften & der Literatur, 1963), 6.

PART ONE

ALIENATION IN THE PRIOR
RUSSIAN LITERARY TRADITION

I

LITERARY PRECEDENTS: PRE-SOVIET

CRITICAL INTIMATIONS

THE HAMLET FIGURE. — In January, 1860, I. S. Turgenev's provocative essay, "Hamlet and Don Quixote", appeared in the journal first founded by Puškin, *The Contemporary*. In this work — perhaps the first Russian study in comparative literature — Turgenev suggests that two fundamental, though mutually contradictory attitudes characterize human nature, one generally dominating the other. These attitudes are respectively typified by the two archetypal heroes, Hamlet and Don Quixote. While Quixote symbolizes idealism, particularly faith in eternal verities external to the believer and inspires an even sacrificial extension of one's self beyond one's self in behalf of others, the qualities of a Hamlet are — though rational — sceptical, introverted, and egoistic: "He is constantly preoccupied with his predicament rather than with his duty. ... Though vain, he lacks confidence; though greedy for life, he does not know what he seeks or why he is alive."[1]

As in *Don Quixote* Sancho Panza stands for the antithetical ordinary man, so in *Hamlet*, says Turgenev, does Shakespeare's Polonius. Turgenev approves Polonius' assessment of Hamlet as less insane than merely adolescent. The Hamlets, he says, are of no practical benefit to the mass of ordinary people: "They cannot lead, because they are going nowhere themselves. Therefore the Hamlets detest the crowd. How can one respect others if he does not respect himself?"[2] "Hamlet ... does not love, but only feigns that he loves — and he even does this rather nonchalantly."[3] Like Göthe's Mephistopheles, Hamlet negates, but does so because he questions the good. He "suspects its truth and sincerity and attacks it like some artificial good behind whose mask evil and falsehood

---

[1] I. S. Turgenev, "Gamlet i Don-Kixot", *Sovremennik*, XXV (January, 1860), 243.
[2] *Ibid.*, 246-247.
[3] *Ibid.*, 248.

still hide. ... But Hamlet's scepticism isn't mere indifference, and in this is to be found his significance and worth."[4] Turgenev warns, however, that in negation, as in fire, resides a destructive force that cannot always be controlled. He adds that the Hamlets remain indebted to the Don Quixotes. For the latter discover and produce that which, with their analysis, the former pick to pieces.

Clearly, Don Quixote has little in common with the theme of alienation.[5] If anything, he suggests its very opposite. Quite the contrary, however, as concerns the Hamlet figure, who remains perhaps its most fitting symbol.

"OBLOMOVŠČINA". — Probably the first to generalize about Russian Hamlets, however, was the young utilitarian critic, N. A. Dobroljubov, who published his famous "What is Oblomovism?" the year before that of Turgenev's essay in the same journal. He deals of course with the same phenomenon for which Turgenev had already coined a more comprehensive term — the 'superfluous man'.[6] Dobroljubov considers what he in turn calls the *Oblomovščina*[7] personality a "fundamental national type"[8] and traces it in literature as far back as Puškin's *Evgenij Onegin* (1823-1831). He attributes to this type, in a general sense, "complete inertness resulting from his [the character's] apathy toward everything that happens in the world. The cause of this apathy is partly due to his external situation, partly to the manner of his intellectual and moral development. His external situation is that of a gentleman."[9] Dobroljubov then explains that such gentlemen have grown indolent by being waited upon since childhood. They think that work is only for menials. They become overly demanding hence impractical in their expectations and unable to cope with real obstacles. They become frivolous and dependent on others:

A normal man only desires what he can achieve; consequently he directly accomplishes what he wishes. But Oblomov is unaccustomed to doing any-

---

[4]   *Ibid.*, 249-250.
[5]   Mathewson qualifies this interpretation, however, suggesting that, in their own way, the Don Quixotes are equally alienated. See p. 32.
[6]   From the title of Turgenev's story, first published in 1850 in *Otečestvennye zapiski* — "The Diary of a Superfluous Man".
[7]   The inspiration for this label is of course *Oblomov*, the novel by Gončarov, which had appeared in the four preceding issues of *Sovremennik*, those of January through April, 1859.
[8]   N. A. Dobroljubov, "Čto takoe Oblomovščina?", *Sovremennik*, XXIV (May 1859), quoted in N. A. Dobroljubov, *Izbrannye filosofskie proizvedenija* (Moscow, Gosudarstvennoe izdatel'stvo političeskoj literatury, 1948), I, 508.
[9]   *Ibid.*, 509.

thing and so is unable to determine what he can and cannot do. Hence he cannot seriously, *actively* wish for anything. His desires only take the form of 'it would be fine if this were done,' but he has no idea how. Therefore he likes to dream and dreads the moment when his dreams will come into contact with reality. So he tries to pass the responsibility to someone else, and if there is no one else, well then ....[10]

With an increased lack of confidence, the Oblomov type also acquires an excessive arrogance, even though he is a slave to everyone else — women, servants, *etc.* His main difficulty, however, says Dobroljubov, is that "he has been unable to understand the purpose of life in general. ... Having failed to comprehend his relationship to the world and to society, it follows that Oblomov can no longer understand his own life and so is burdened and wearied by all he has to do."[11] Thus he fails to follow through in acquiring an education, in public service, in social life, *etc.* Instead he becomes all the more indolent as well as cynical toward others.[12]

[10] *Ibid.*, 511.

[11] *Ibid.*, 515-516.

[12] This is the very aristocratic mentality which V. Bill, in paraphrasing V. O. Ključev-skij's *Kurs russkoj istorii*, ascribes to social developments in the Seventeenth and Eighteenth Centuries: "In the Seventeenth Century Western influence slowly pene-trated Russia but affected only the upper levels of the Muscovite state. With the exception of this refined social level, the whole society from top to bottom remained under the influence of concepts and traditions which had accumulated during the preceding two centuries. ... As of the Seventeenth Century, division and disharmony begin to take place in the spiritual, social, and intellectual life of the Russian people, affecting the following centuries. ... Toward the end of the Eighteenth Century the unity of Russian culture, which had already been shaken in the Seventeenth Century and even more violently under Peter the Great, is conclusively shattered. ... Society divides itself into two main groups, the free nobles and the enslaved peasants. A deep gulf divides them. The peasant masses continue to preserve their tie with the confession of the church, with their religious origins. The monastery remains their principal or only cultural center, while secular culture, based on Western European notions of free thinking, flourishes among the aristocracy. ... Foreign words and ideas freed Russian society from the obligation of thinking, just as the gratuitous labor of the serfs freed it from the necessity of working. Literature went in two directions: the idyll and the satire. It either lauded contemporary ideas or scourged the monstrous manifestations of contemporary life. Satire disparaged; the idyll exalted; both declaimed; neither reflected. ... The Russian noble was no longer on firm ground. He spoke French; read Voltaire, Montesquieu, Diderot, Rousseau; dressed in the latest Parisian fashion; and a French tutor instructed his children. But the French soil, from which he plucked the flowers of culture, was alien to him, while the Russian soil on which he stood brought forth no such blooms. Neither thought nor practical interests bound him to his native land. He was a Russian who passionately yearned to become a Frenchman. Constantly endeavoring to become one of the group in a society of strangers, he only became a stranger among his own. This division in Russian society cast a profound shadow on the whole subsequent Nineteenth Century." V. Tschebotarioff Bill, *The Russian People* (Chicago, The University of Chicago Press, 1965), 57-58, 77-79.

In all, Dobroljubov attributes this same Oblomov-like personality to the heroes of some seven complete novels: A. S. Puškin's *Evgenij Onegin*, Ju. M. Lermontov's *A Hero of Our Times* (1840), A. I. Gercen's *Whose Fault?* (1847), Turgenev's *Rudin* (1856), his *The Diary of a Superfluous Man* (1850), and also his *Prince Hamlet of Shchigrov District* (1852) — as well as, of course, to I. A. Gončarov's *Oblomov* (1859). He points out that Onegin, Rudin, Oblomov, and Tentetnikov (a character in N. V. Gogol''s *Dead Souls*, *II*) have all, at one time or another, been aspiring writers, while Bel'tov (Gercen's hero) hoped to be a painter. But they do not fulfill these ambitions. They even fail to complete their intended reading. Likewise, all but Onegin and Lermontov's Pečorin attempt government service (Rudin as a teacher), which they nonetheless soon abandon. All display a misanthropic conceit, and at least three — Onegin, Pečorin, and Rudin — abuse or even destroy their closest friends.

Where women are concerned, the Oblomovs prove not only cynical and deceptive, but cowardly and inferior. This blights the relationships between Onegin and Tat'jana, Bel'tov and Kruciferskaja, Rudin and Nataša, Pečorin and Mary, and Oblomov and Ol'ga. All four — Onegin, Pečorin, Rudin, and Oblomov — plead unworthiness as an excuse for not becoming faithful lovers. They debase themselves, says Dobroljubov, in order to be conciliated with praise. As an example he cites Onegin's posture of benevolence toward Tat'jana after first revealing to her his own self-styled inadequacies.

While clearly critical of the Oblomovs, Dobroljubov blames not so much individuals as their environment:

It is most probable that, under different conditions of life, in another society, Onegin would have been a truly admirable fellow, Pečorin and Rudin would have made significant contributions; and Bel'tov would have turned out to be a truly superior individual. And perhaps under different conditions of development both Oblomov and Tentetnikov would not have been such drones and would have found themselves some sort of useful activity.[13]

All in fact seem to sense their unexploited potential and to regret their wasted lives. Again Dobroljubov suggests what is perhaps deficient in the Oblomovs' way of life: "... there is nothing in life that they can consider a vital necessity, a shrine in their heart, a religion so organically grown a part of them that to remove it would be to deprive them of their life. Everything about them is SUPERFICIAL, nothing is rooted in their very nature."[14] (Emphasis mine.) Dobroljubov seems to believe that,

[13] Dobroljubov, *Sovremennik*, 525.
[14] *Ibid.*, 533.

although Oblomovism still characterizes Russian life, it no longer deceives others as it did previously. It is Ol'ga in fact — the woman of purpose and resolution — who represents for Dobroljubov Russia's future.

THE NINETEENTH CENTURY

OVERVIEW. — It is generally conceded that A. S. Griboedov and Puškin first derived the notion of a hypercritical, socially maladjusted protagonist from works published in the West. One of these, Benjamin Constant's *Adolphe* (1816), appears in fact on the book shelf in Onegin's study. Besides the phlegmatic Adolphe, Göthe's Werther (*The Sorrows of Young Werther*, 1774), Chateaubriand's René (*Génie du Christianisme*, 1802), Sénancour's Obermann (*Obermann*, 1804), and Byron's Childe Harold (*Childe Harold's Pilgrimage*, 1812) had each made his debut before the writing of either *Woe from Wit* (1824) or *Evgenij Onegin*. Especially influential were Byron's heroes. As Henry Gifford observes:

With Harold, and those other effigies, Conrad, Lara, Manfred and the rest, Byron brings a more lurid light onto the scene. He adds to the disillusion of René the scowl of Montoni, from Mrs. Radcliffe. It is with him that the demon motive begins to show itself. At the same time, he multiplies the points of conflict between the hero and society. The sense of sin, incestuous attachment, renegacy — all these are complications which deepen the hero's gloom. Byron exploited what others had half hewn .... He gave to despondent egotism, as Pushkin said, its romantic dress. Those that follow are all of Byron's school.

It is something of a relief that no more need be said of Byronic heroes in England, France and Germany. They were numerous indeed, but seldom so convincing as Childe Harold or Manfred, or even René. We must look to Russia if we wish henceforth to find living characters in that mould.[15]

Like Dobroljubov, Gifford attributes the superficial existence of subsequent Russian protagonists to conditions indigenous to the society of their own nation. He points for instance to: the creation of an original Russian problem hero as early as 1792 in N. M. Karamzin's *Poor Liza*; the aroused social concern which followed the Napoleonic invasion; the peculiar function of Russian letters as a vehicle for social criticism; and, consequently, the unusually specific reference in Russian works to a particular social milieu: "René and Adolphe move among a handful of grey figures in a world that is drained of colour and almost timeless. Not so Onegin, who starts his career in a meticulously described St.

[15] Henry Gifford, *The Hero of His Time* (London, Edward Arnold & Co., 1950), 17-18.

Petersburg, at the end of 1819, or Čackij, who is at odds with the diehards of a Moscow society that lives for us in every detail. These men are at the centre of Russian life."[16] Rufus Mathewson makes several further distinctions with respect to this type, which, as he asserts, "dominated Russian literature for a century".[17] Including the heroes of Turgenev, F. M. Dostoevskij, L. N. Tolstoj, and even A. P. Čexov, he suggests that all are united in terms of their common 'fallibility' and 'suffering':

Thus the Pechorins and Bazarovs, as well as the Stavrogins and Prince Andreis yet to come, are brothers beneath their ideological labels, and are, in turn, joined by the bond of suffering with the mock-heroic Onegins, Rudins, even with the quixotic Myshkin, and conceivably, at the far end of the scale of heroism, with the monstrous antihero of *Notes from the Underground.*

. . . .

The literary portraiture of the alienated man, on the other hand, was to reach new heights of complexity and richness in the years that followed the decade of controversy: *War and Peace, Anna Karenina, The Raw Youth,* and *The Brothers Karamazov* were yet to be written.

Chekhov carried the alienated man, in his mock-heroic aspect, to a kind of apotheosis, in response, perhaps, to the general antiheroic trend in modern European realism.[18]

Mathewson also distinguishes these heroes according to two characteristic dispositions — "men without hope" who "are successful in their rebellious search for annihilation" and "men of hope and good intentions" who "fail, in spite of themselves, to live as they plan to, or to fulfill the apparent promise of their lives".[19] (This latter type would appear to bear at least partial resemblance to the Don Quixote as well as to the Hamlet discussed by Turgenev.) With the first type Mathewson identifies Pečorin, Dostoevskij's Stavrogin (*The Possessed,* 1871-1872), and Tolstoj's Andrej Bolkonskij (*War and Peace,* 1869), while with the second — the successive heroes of Turgenev's three novels: *Rudin, A Nest of Gentlefolk* (1859), and *Fathers and Sons* (1862), i.e. Rudin, Lavreckij, and Bazarov. Both types, he adds, display "a disastrous alienation from other human beings and from purposeful activity".[20]

Commenting on Turgenev's "Hamlet and Don Quixote", Mathewson further argues that even the outright Don Quixotes — the positive heroes who occur from time to time during the same period and again in ever

---

[16]   *Ibid.,* 20.
[17]   Rufus W. Mathewson, Jr., *The Positive Hero in Russian Literature* (New York, Columbia University Press, 1958), 15.
[18]   *Ibid.,* 141-143.
[19]   *Ibid.,* 15-16.
[20]   *Ibid.,* 16.

increasing numbers after 1917 — are to some extent alienated also, estranged from a full emotional life as well as from a complete knowledge of good and evil: "Don Quixote's strength, then, *is* his weakness. His singleness of purpose requires that he be both deficient in understanding and limited in sensibility, to the degree that he has a well-developed capacity for self-delusion".[21] An equally valuable classification is proposed by the author and critic, A. I. Gercen, who, on the one hand, groups together Onegin, Pečorin, and the heroes of Turgenev — frustrated young nobles, disenchanted with the prevailing autocratic regime ("They are one and the same personality"[22]) — and, on the other hand, the oppressed petty civil servants and the victims of serfdom, who, he says, have subsequently provided a new direction to Russian literature. To this group he assigns Akakij Akakievič Bašmačkin, the hero of Gogol''s *The Overcoat* (1835), and various peasants who appear in Turgenev's *A Sportsman's Sketches* (1852) and in his short story, *Mumu* (1854). He might have added Puškin's Samson Vyrin (*The Station Master*, 1831), Dostoevskij's Devuškin (*Poor Folk*, 1846), and, eventually, Tolstoj's Platon Karataev, who appeared the year before Gercen's death in the first complete edition of *War and Peace*.

SELECTED CASES. — If, for purposes of generalization, we were to select a single representative superfluous hero created by each of the most prominent nineteenth-century Russian writers, the list might well include the following:[23]

Griboedov's Čackij (*Woe from Wit*).

Puškin's Eugene Onegin (*Evgenij Onegin*).

Lermontov's Pečorin (*A Hero of Our Times*).

Gogol''s Bašmačkin (*The Overcoat*).

Gončarov's Oblomov (*Oblomov*).

Turgenev's Bazarov (*Fathers and Sons*).

Dostoevskij's Ivan Karamazov (*The Brothers Karamazov*).

Tolstoj's Andrej Bolkonskij (*War and Peace*).

Čexov's Treplev (*The Sea Gull*, 1897).

[21] *Ibid.*, 138. One is reminded of the principal characters in Černiševskij's tendentious novel *What is to be Done?* (1863), one of whom, Lopuxov, is, as a revolutionary zealot, so devoid of self-interest that he deliberately leaves the scene, sensing that his wife, Vera, will be happier living with his good friend, Kirsanov.

[22] A. I. Gercen, "O romane iz narodnoj žizni v Rossii (Pis'mo k perevodčice 'Rybakov')", *Izbrannye proizvedenija* (Moscow, Izdatel'stvo 'Detskaja literatura', 1964), 370.

[23] These examples, while affording an adequate enough sample, could well be expanded to include appropriate protagonists from the works of N. S. Leskov, A. F. Pisemskij, M. E. Saltykov-Ščedrin, and others.

Analysis of each of the above discloses the following with respect to his distinctive nature and the sources of his alienation.

Čackij

Čackij's is essentially a liberal's protest against the conservatism of a previous era (eighteenth century), whose adherents, the gentry of his day, assume a variety of shapes but stand together, socially, in order to protect their mutual interests. There are: Famusov, the worshipper of rank, who fears learning and seeks to conserve his position by finding the proper suitor for his daughter — "a man to whom existing abuses and injustices have acquired all the sacred authority of cherished traditions, and who resents any attempt to curb or ameliorate them";[24] Skalozub, the military fop with vain, superficial views; the obsequious social climber, Molčalin, who does his superiors' bidding without respecting them; the slanderer, Zagoreckij; the Frenchified rake, Repetilov; and finally the ambivalent Sof'ja, who lacks discretion, candor, and constancy of feeling. In view of his circumstances, Čackij seems, as a 'superfluous' man, especially vindicated. Gifford, at least, argues that

... numerous though the ghosts are that haunt the cemetery where Oblomov lies, Chatsky is not among them.

Now, although Chatsky is at one with them in his injured vanity, and although, like Rudin, he is a fine orator, there is a real force and conviction in what he says, and he is never dazzled by his own words. Chatsky is a tribune; the rest are hypochondriacs, in a greater or less degree. They caught their infection from society, but they have no will to cure themselves.[25]

The very author of Oblomov has also made a similar distinction between Čackij, on the one hand, and Onegin and Pečorin, on the other.[26]

---

[24]   Ivan Spector, *The Golden Age of Russian Literature* (Caldwell, Idaho, The Caxton Printers, Ltd., 1952), 56.
[25]   Gifford, 152-153.
[26]   "Čackij is, as a personality, incomparably more outstanding and more intelligent than Onegin and Lermontov's Pečorin. He is a sincere and impassioned man of action, but they — parasites, amazingly endowed with great talents, like the morbid offspring of an outlived age ... detesting life's emptiness, aristocratic idleness, they submitted themselves to it and did not consider fighting with it or altogether avoiding it. Dissatisfaction and malice did not prevent Onegin from being a dandy, 'shining forth' at the theatre, the ball, the fashionable restaurant, flirting with young girls and seriously chasing after them in wedlock, nor Pečorin from vaunting his interesting ennui and indulging his indolence and malice between Princess Mary and Bèla, then describing his indifference toward them to the dull Maksim Maksimyč. ... Both grew weary, suffocated in their milieu, and did not know what they wanted. Onegin tried to read, but yawned and gave it up, because he and Pečorin only know the science of 'tender

Onegin

Unlike Čackij, Onegin never tries to reason with society. He is already too cynical. Even in the country he remains the indolent victim of a Byronic malaise. In a sense, however, Onegin, like Repetilov, plays an active role in that same superficial society with which both he and Čackij are theoretically so dissatisfied. As Leon Stilman suggests:

Let us also mention the features of Evgenij's nature that are indicated by his choice of books; he 'banished from disgrace' a very small number of works:
> By the singer of Giaour and Juan,
> In fact he had two or three other novels
> In which the age was reflected
> And the contemporary man
> Quite faithfully depicted.[27]

What is relevant here is not the nature of the age or of the contemporary man, but the fact that Evgenij 'banished from disgrace' particularly those works depicting the contemporary man; he could only find himself in these works, could only identify with the subject of a definite socio-historical moment, with the son of his own society and age.[28]

Why, as the unhealthy product of an artificial age, Evgenij first breaks Tat'jana's heart, then seeks her hand once she is a sophisticated socialite, is worth some speculation: is it not to some extent simply because such a conquest would yet flatter his wounded vanity?[29] And why does he insist on the duel with Lenskij? Is it not pride and the fear of being otherwise ridiculed by such as Zareckij? Again, unlike Čackij, it is Onegin, not the girl, who proves unworthy. Truly there is something of Aleko (Puškin's *The Gypsies*, 1823) in Evgenij, and, at least implicitly, the author serves him the same kind of censure which Aleko receives from Zemfira's father. Thus, D. S. Mirsky, speaking of "the classical attitude of Pushkin, of sympathy without pity for the man and of respect without reward for the woman", observes that "Onegin's irresponsible self-indulgence and fidelity to self subtly, inevitably, untheatrically undo

---

passion.' ... Čackij ..., on the other hand, had seriously prepared himself for activity. 'He writes brilliantly, translates,' Famusov says of him, and all affirm his fine intelligence. He has of course not traveled in vain, has studied, read, obviously set to work, associated with ministers, then moved on. ... He loves seriously, viewing Sof'ja as a future wife." I. A. Gončarov, "Miljon terzanij", *Literaturno-kritičeskie stat'i i pis'ma* (Leningrad, Gosudarstvennoe izdatel'stvo 'Xudožestvennaja literatura', 1938), 60.

[27] A. S. Puškin, *Evgenij Onegin*, Ch. VII, Strophe 22.

[28] Leon Stilman, "Problemy literaturnyx žanrov i tradicij v 'Evgenii Onegine' Puškina", *American Contributions to the Fourth International Congress of Slavicists* (The Hague, Mouton & Co., 1958), 348.

[29] *Ibid.*, 365.

him, while the calm self-command and resignation of Tatjana give her
that unquestionable halo of moral greatness which is forever associated
with her name...".[30] With equal subtlety and perhaps even greater
emphasis, German, who follows Onegin (*The Queen of Spades*, 1834), is
also punished by the nemesis which rewards his actions and drives him
insane.

Pečorin

In an earlier work by Lermontov, the play *Masquerade* (1835-1836), its
hero, Arbenin, declaims denunciatory monologues reminiscent of Čackij's
but, beyond this, becomes vengeful and lawless — which leads to his
destruction. In his own way, Pečorin is as much a rebel as Arbenin and
to the same extent distinct from and more complex than Čackij. Even
Onegin lacks the 'thirst for self-immolation'[31] which Mathewson ascribes
to Pečorin. Slonim adds that "unlike Onegin, the dandy who depends
on other people's opinions, Pečorin defies all social conventions; he is
'anarchically free', beyond good and evil. As Dostoevsky's Raskolnikov
or Ivan Karamazov later on, he discards the accepted moral values and
looks for his own truth".[32] Pečorin, furthermore, is revealed through a
multiplicity of viewpoints — Maksimyč's, the author's, and Pečorin's
own. He also has successive affairs with three separate women (four,
including Vera). None of them satisfies. His relationship with Bèla is
reminiscent of that experienced by Puškin's captive (*The Caucasian
Captive* (1821)), his encounter with the girl in Taman' like that of Aleko,
who intrudes among a less civilized but perhaps more civil group of
people. Likewise, his treatment of Mary resembles both Onegin's
flirtation with Ol'ga and his renunciation of Tat'jana.[33]

Why is Pečorin so spiteful? With exceptional candor he assesses his
own behavior:

"To arouse toward oneself the feeling of love, devotion and fear — isn't this
the first sign and the great triumph of power? To be the cause of someone's

[30]　D. S. Mirsky, *A History of Russian Literature from its Beginnings to 1900* (New
York, Vintage Books, Inc., 1958), 92.

[31]　Mathewson, p. 133.

[32]　Marc Slonim, *The Epic of Russian Literature* (New York, Oxford University Press,
1964), 121. Otherwise, there are considerable similarities in the stories of both
Onegin and Pečorin. As Gifford observes: "There is a declaration of love by the
heroine; a duel in which the hero ruthlessly kills a former friend; the hero refuses
marriage, and is driven out into the world to begin life over again." Gifford, 127.

[33]　Gifford notes that "Princess Mary combines the roles of both Larin sisters".
Gifford, 126-127.

suffering and joy, without having a positive right to be such — isn't this the sweet nourishment of our pride? And what is happiness? Satiated pride. If I could consider myself better, more powerful than everyone on earth, I would be happy."[34]

This leads him to conclude that: "I feel in myself this unquenchable thirst to swallow up everything I encounter; I regard the sufferings and joy of others only as they affect me, as the nutrient which sustains the forces of my soul."[35] Therefore Pečorin regards Mary as he would a freshly bloomed flower, meant to be plucked, to be imbibed for its fragrance, then discarded along the way. Likewise, he piques Grušnickij by courting Mary, not because he wishes to deceive her, not so much because he envies Grušnickij, as because, he tells himself,

"... it is the consequence of that nasty, but uncontrollable feeling that forces us to destroy the sweet delusions of one near to us, in order to have the petty pleasure of saying to him, when in despair he asks us what we should believe in: 'My friend, I had the same problem, but you see that I nonetheless sup, dine, and sleep in contentment and will, I hope, know how to die without shouts and tears.'"[36]

What therefore was with respect to Onegin a suspicion is in Pečorin an open avowal.

There is obviously a more personal explanation, related to his past, which accounts for Pečorin's state of mind. To this he also vaguely alludes while speaking to Mary. In his childhood, he says,

"I was deeply sensitive to good and evil: no one caressed, all abused me: I acquired unpleasant memories and became morose — while other children were gay and garrulous; I felt superior to them — and they debased me. Then I became envious. I was ready to love the whole world — but nobody understood me: and I learned how to hate. My colorless youth passed in a struggle between myself and society; I buried my finest feelings in the depth of my heart, where they died. I spoke the truth, but no one believed me: so I began to deceive; being well acquainted with life and the workings of society, I became an artificer in the science of life ..."[37]

As he sums it up, elsewhere: "If everyone had loved me, I would have found endless sources of love in myself. Evil begets evil; a first distress teaches one to appreciate the pleasure of tormenting another."[38]

---

[34] M. Ju. Lermontov, "Knjažna Meri", *Geroj našego vremeni.*
[35] *Ibid.*
[36] *Ibid.*
[37] *Ibid.*
[38] *Ibid.*

Pečorin emerges, unlike Čackij, well after the Decembrist defeat and, unlike Onegin, well into the reactionary regime of Nicholas I. Even more than Onegin's shooting of Lenskij, Pečorin's murder of Grušnickij may well be "a revenge on society. ... He lives in a tragic age. There can be no peace for him with that kind of society."[39] "It can be hardly contested that the social and political environment was largely responsible for Lermontov's pessimism and his feeling of futility, and that his Pečorin was the product of his times", says Slonim.[40] V. G. Belinskij likewise commiserates with Pečorin's situation, even commending his ability to be so dissatisfied, yet so honest with himself:

In judging a man one must consider the circumstances of his development and the sphere of life to which fate has consigned him.[41]

. . . .

Is Pečorin really happy about his disbelief? Is he really proud of it? Hasn't he suffered for it? ... Do you call him an egoist? — But doesn't he really detest and hate himself for it? Doesn't his heart thirst for pure and unqualified love? ... No, that is not egoism: egoism does not suffer, does not accuse itself, but is self-satisfied, pleased with itself. Egoism does not know torment; suffering is the lot of love alone.[42]

. . . .

This man does not bear his suffering indifferently, apathetically: he frantically chases after life, seeking it everywhere; he bitterly blames himself for his own delusions. Within him, unabated, deep questions resound, disquiet and torment him, and he seeks their solution in reflection: he spies upon every flutter of his heart, examines his every thought. He has made of himself the curious object of all his observations and, in order to be as sincere as possible in his confession, he not only frankly admits all his actual imperfections but also either imagines nonexistent ones or falsely interprets his most natural actions.[43]

Thus, with some, Pečorin's behavior finds at least partial vindication. Gifford is, for instance, as emphatic as Belinskij: "But, in a day when heroism is no longer possible, Pechorin remains a hero. He can endure and stand upright. He can pay the price of his own folly. ... It was a cry of negation, yet there are moments when a cry of negation is, in its way, an act of faith."[44] Slonim adds that "there was in Lermontov a constant

---

[39]   Gifford, 131.
[40]   Slonim, *The Epic of Russian Literature*, 120.
[41]   V. G. Belinskij, "Geroj našego vremeni", *Otečestvennye zapiski*, X (June, 1840), quoted in V. G. Belinskij, *Geroj našego vremeni, sočinenie M. Lermontova* (Moscow, Gosudarstvennoe izdatel'stvo Xudožestvennoj literatury, 1958), 85-86.
[42]   *Ibid.*, 85.
[43]   *Ibid.*, 88-89.
[44]   Gifford, 132.

quest for moral justification. His refusal to accept man, society, and the universal order was determined by his search for a higher finality, and this gives to his poetry a dynamic quality and a brilliance that enliven almost every line. This search for moral truth is even more manifest in his semiautobiographical prose narrative, *A Hero of Our Times.*"[45]

Bašmačkin

Bašmačkin is, as the pure recipient of others' oppression, distinct from the rest. But as a sub-type he has several successors among the characters of Dostoevskij, Tolstoj, and even Čexov (*e.g. The Death of a Government Clerk*, 1886) and is, as noted, to some degree anticipated in the plight of Puškin's Samson Vyrin. Sounding an even more universal note, however, Vladimir Nabokov provides a further, distinctive insight into Bašmačkin's alienated nature:

The essence of mankind is irrationally derived from the chaos of fakes which form Gogol's world. Akaky Akakyevich, the hero of *The Overcoat*, is absurd *because* he is pathetic, *because* he is human and *because* he has been engendered by those very forces which seem to be in such contrast to him.[46]

. . . .

Russian progressive critics sensed in him the image of the underdog and the whole story impressed them as a social protest. But it is something much more than that. The gaps and black holes in the texture of Gogol's style imply flaws in the texture of life itself. Something is very wrong and all men are mild lunatics engaged in pursuits that seem to them very important while an absurdly logical force keeps them at their futile jobs — this is the real 'message' of the story. In this world of utter futility, of futile humility and futile domination, the highest degree that passion, desire, creative urge can attain is a new cloak which both tailors and customers adore on their knees. I am not speaking of the moral point or the moral lesson. There can be no moral lesson in such a world because there are no pupils and no teachers: This world *is* and it excludes everything that might destroy it, so that any improvement, any struggle, any moral purpose or endeavor, are as utterly impossible as changing the course of a star. It is Gogol's world and as such wholly different from Tolstoy's world, or Pushkin's, or Chekhov's or my own. But after reading Gogol one's eyes may become gogolized and one is apt to see bits of his world in the most unexpected places. I have visited many countries, and something like Akaky Akakyevich's overcoat has been the passionate dream of this or that chance acquaintance who never had heard about Gogol.[47]

Although, as Slonim contends, "Gogol was never fully aware of the

---

[45]   Slonim, *The Epic of Russian Literature*, 119.
[46]   Vladimir Nabokov, *Nikolai Gogol* (New York, James Laughlin, 1944), 141-142.
[47]   *Ibid.*, 143-144.

social implications of his early works",[48] still a story like *The Overcoat* also vividly reflects the growth of urban Petersburg and the imperial bureaucracy with their increasing impersonality and consequent disregard for the low-status individual. The shortest of the nine works here discussed, it nonetheless made its author in the view of some "the greatest artist that Russia has produced".[49]

Oblomov

Oblomov, already discussed in the context of Dobroljubov's essay, is himself a former bureaucrat, self-retired. His very indolence is, according to Gifford, a "passion for liberty. ... Oblomov prided himself on not having to work, or make decisions".[50] Just as it took Belinskij to discover (or create) the social import in Gogol', likewise, "Goncharov", says Stilman, "discovered the 'significance' of *Oblomov* after Dobroljubov had pointed it out to him".[51] Stilman insists nonetheless that, more than an historically accurate reflection of a certain representative type of personality, Oblomov is essentially a work of introspection: "Goncharov was a genius of reminiscence, not an analyst of social change."[52] Hence, Oblomov "has more in common with some of the varieties of the 'neurotic personality of our time' than with romantic seekers of adventure, disillusioned Don Juans, or would-be reformers of his own age".[53]

Gončarov's own view of Oblomov may well have been ambivalent. As Gifford astutely observes: "When Oblomov is dead, Zakhar ends up as a beggar upon the streets. This grudging and yet spontaneous loyalty felt by Zakhar towards Oblomov was something that Goncharov fully understood. It typifies his own feelings about the old order. With his head he rejected it; with his heart he clung to it. And that is why he was incapable of fashioning the new man, and why Stolz had to be a foreigner."[54] That Gončarov elsewhere at least preferred an alienated 'man of action' to an alienated 'parasite' is evidenced by the favorable comparison of Čackij to both Onegin and Pečorin in his essay of 1872, "A Million Torments".[55]

---

[48]   Slonim, *The Epic of Russian Literature*, 168.
[49]   Nabokov, 140.
[50]   Gifford, 150.
[51]   Leon Stilman, "Oblomovka Revisited", *The American Slavic and East European Review*, VII (1948), 60.
[52]   *Ibid.*, 56.
[53]   *Ibid.*, 63.
[54]   Gifford, 158.
[55]   *Supra*, 34-35.

Bazarov

The remaining four heroes — Bazarov, Ivan Karamazov, Andrej Bolkonskij, and Treplev — are each something of a culmination, one of those at the end of a line of similar heroes previously created by each of their respective authors. They are also perhaps best understood in terms of their particular antecedents. Rudin, for instance, is one of Bazarov's older cousins. Both are devoted to the ideals of science and reform. Both are inferior to the women for whom they vie. Both lose their lives in the pursuit of vain, unrealizable utilitarian schemes. Rudin's death on the barriers is at least a kind of last noble gesture. Helen Muchnic contrasts him and Bazarov as follows:

> Rudin is Hamlet trying to be Don Quixote, a neurotic man, longing to be himself but not knowing what he is, and so unable to bring to life the great convictions with which he is on fire .... Rudin is a subtly drawn portrait of an egoist whom weakness of will — probably connected with sexual impotence — has made him what he is: a man so blind to others that he offends when he wishes to be most straight and open, and cannot see that his rhetorical gestures are efforts at self-justification. He is unconsciously hypocritical, and his preoccupation with himself is a perpetual and hopeless endeavor to reconcile what he desires to be with what he is.
>
> In the nihilist Bazarov we have a character who is almost a photographic negative of Rudin; what is black in one is white in the other, but they are both Don Quixotes reduced to tragedy through traits of Hamletism.[56] Bazarov's failure, TURGENEV WOULD HAVE US THINK, is one of intellect rather than of temperament. Unlike Rudin, Bazarov has a will of iron, but the idea for which he fights is, in Turgenev's interpretation, barbarous; he is crushed by the inhumanity of this idea as Rudin is defeated by want of feeling.[57] (Emphasis mine.)

Bazarov, whatever Turgenev's intentions, seems often ludicrous, so ironical is the discrepancy between his intentions and the actual turn of events. He disdains emotion, yet, unable to help himself, falls in love with Odincova, who then spurns him. Working on a cadaver for the improvement of his medical knowledge, i.e. for the betterment of human life, he unwittingly infects himself and dies. His retiscence to be affectionate or communicative with his parents, together with his opposition to the views of Arkadij's elders, suggests a further theme — the conflict between generations — from which the book itself derives its title. This conflict, a real one, also involves two opposing social theories, Westernism and

---

[56] Note Mathewson's distinction. *Supra*, 32.
[57] Helen Muchnic, *An Introduction to Russian Literature* (New York, E. P. Dutton Co., 1964), 114-115.

Slavophilism, which reached their fiercest clash in Turgenev's day.

Bazarov's stand against the older generation, his nihilistic assertions, his denial of both tradition and feeling are so extreme that they alienate even his disciple, Arkadij, and assume the features of a pose. Turgenev's view of him, like Gončarov's of Oblomov, was probably complex. The controversy which ensued in the wake of the novel's publication is indicative:

He is slandering the younger generation, shouted the radicals; he is too lenient toward the horrible Nihilists, contended the conservatives .... The revolutionaries called him an enemy of the people, while the reactionaries labeled him the obedient flunky of the Nihilists. In vain did he cite his realistic method and emphasize that 'To reproduce truth, the very reality of life, is the highest happiness for the writer, even if that truth does not coincide with his own sympathies.'[58]

It is well to remember that Turgenev was, by disposition, primarily an esthete. Critics generally testify to his artistic detachment. Speaking of the Russian revolutionary as a literary subject, Mathewson mentions that "Turgenev, Dostoevsky, Conrad, and others have found ... that he was indeed an excellent subject, provided he was kept at a distance, and shown in all his dimensions."[59] Mirsky adds that "*Fathers and Sons* is Turgenev's only novel where the social problem is distilled without residue into art, and leaves no bits of undigested journalism sticking out. Here the delicate and poetic narrative art of Turgenev reaches its perfection, and Bazarov is the only one of Turgenev's men who is worthy to stand by the side of his women."[60] Mathewson's incisive analysis further suggests the near neutrality in Turgenev's attitude toward Bazarov:

Bazarov, his own version of the radical personality, was a tragic figure precisely because of his involvement in what was to come. 'I dreamt of a dark, wild, large figure,' he wrote, 'half growing out of the soil, strong, malicious, honorable — and doomed all the same to perish because ... he stands on the threshold of the future.'[61] The source of the radicals' optimism became for Turgenev, since he did not share their faith in the rapid, upward evolution of things, the very source of Bazarov's undoing. The doctrinal motives which constitute Bazarov's commitment to the future become devalued and evaporate in the face of his present personal needs. Thus stripped of his ideals he is confronted with the last responsibility of all large men, of 'dying with dignity.'[62]

---

[58] Slonim, *The Epic of Russian Literature*, 260.
[59] Mathewson, 11.
[60] Mirsky, 203-204.
[61] Citing Turgenev's letter to K. K. Slučevskij, April 14, 1862.
[62] Mathewson, 121. Citing Turgenev's letter to A. A. Fet, September 14, 1862.

In view of Turgenev's characterization of Hamlet — "No, he won't fight with windmills, he doesn't believe in giants ... but he wouldn't attack them even if they actually existed. ... But, who knows, perhaps there is no truth just as there are no giants?"[63] — it is indeed unclear with which he would have classified Bazarov, with Hamlet or Don Quixote. Nor do the critics entirely agree as to Turgenev's ultimate achievement. While Slonim contends that "Bazarov himself is more than merely a man of the 'sixties; he is a national type, as fundamentally Russian as any previous literary hero".[64] Mirsky argues that "what Turgenev was in touch with were not the raw realities of Russian life, but only their reflection in the minds of his generation of intellectuals".[65]

Ivan Karamazov

If Bazarov's alienation stems in large part from his misplaced faith in reason, so too does that of Dostoevskij's Raskol'nikov (*Crime and Punishment*, 1866). The latter is, again, one of several similarly alienated heroes, conceived by the pen of the same author and leading, in due course, to Ivan Karamazov. Like Bazarov and the heroes of Tolstoj and Čexov, Ivan is better understood when compared with the kin who immediately precede him.

Ivan's evolution is traceable, in fact, to certain predecessors in Dostoevskij's earliest stories: *Poor Folk*, *The Double* (1846), *Mr. Proxačin* (1846), *The Landlady* (1847), *White Nights* (1848), and *Netočka Nezvanova* (1849). These stories' characters all have in common the qualities of what, in an 1847 feuilleton which remarkably anticipates Dobroljubov's essay of 1859, Dostoevskij himself describes as the "Dreamer":

Not infrequently, reality produces a burdensome, hostile impression upon the heart of the dreamer, and he rushes off to hide in his sacred, golden little corner, which in fact is often dusty, untidy, disarrayed, filthy. Little by little our prankster begins to avoid the crowd, to avoid any common interests, and gradually, imperceptibly his talent for real life begins to wane. It begins to appear natural to him that the pleasures obtained through his own fantasy are more complete, more luxurious, more pleasing than life itself.[66]

Even the dreamers Dostoevskij describes in the forties, before his exile, display a decided neurotic tendency; their morbidity becomes fully

---

[63] Turgenev, *Sovremennik*, XXV (January, 1860), 245.
[64] Slonim, *The Epic of Russian Literature*, 260-261.
[65] Mirsky, 207.
[66] F. M. Dostoevskij, feuilleton of June 15, 1847, *Peterburgskaja letopis'*, quoted in *Èpoxa* (Berlin, 1922), 74-75.

articulated, however, in the remarks and person of Dostoevskij's Underground Man (*Notes from the Underground*, 1864), who, asserting his individuality and freedom in the irrational, displays both masochistic and sadistic impulses.[67] Nikolaj Berdjaev interprets such behavior in more or less philosophical terms:

For Dostoevskij the *true realities* are not the fact of empirical, external phenomena, of customary existence, nor the fact of flesh and blood people. For him reality is the spiritual profundity of man, the fate of the human spirit. Reality is the relationship between man and God, man and the devil. Reality is the ideas by which man lives.[68]

. . . .

Dostoevskij is most concerned with man's destiny as a free agent, where freedom becomes willfulness. This is where human nature reveals its true self.[69]

The immediate impetus for Dostoevskij's philosophical concern, and that of his heroes, was doubtless those same conditions which so oppressed Gogol''s Bašmačkin.[70] It is therefore more than coincidence that both writers should have shown a predilection for Petersburg settings. Both managed, however, to elevate their subjects to a level of universal significance. Dostoevskij's formulation of the problem of self-will and human freedom bears implications that touch upon the whole western Judaeo-Christian ethical tradition as opposed to the scientific and deterministic traditions (either Communistic or Western positivist).

Such considerations underlie, to some degree, the 'self-lacerating' masochism of so many of his female characters: Netočka Nezvanova (*Netočka Nezvanova*), Nellie and Nataša (*The Humiliated and Insulted*, 1861), Nastas'ja Filipovna (*The Idiot*, 1869), Liza and Katja (*The Brothers Karamazov*). Such is also the ultimate import of the hostile (both destructive and self-destructive) behavior of Raskol'nikov and Stavrogin (*The Possessed*, 1871-1872) and of the doubts and self-incriminations of Ivan Karamazov. Ivan's transgression is less overt but, as a sin of omission, equally destructive,[71] and further compounded by his ethical

[67]   Robert Jackson calls the Underground Man, in fact, "the first, *fully conscious* representative of a line of little men, clerks, dreamers, poor folk, who appear in Russian literature". Robert Louis Jackson, *Dostoevsky's Underground Man in Russian Literature* (The Hague, Mouton & Co., 1958), 25.
[68]   Nikolaj Berdjaev, *Mirosozercanie Dostoevskago* (Paris, YMCA Press, 1968), 22.
[69]   *Ibid.*, 43.
[70]   Jackson, again, speaks of the Underground Man's rejection of a tyrannical reality "completely ruled by logic" and where "the individual is sentenced to oblivion by the very laws of nature". Jackson, 30.
[71]   Perhaps unwittingly, he has justified to Smerdjakov the latter's act of patricide. More consciously, he had left town so as not to prevent Smerdjakov from acting.

uncertainty. Like Raskol'nikov, he questions traditional morality, which seems to suppress freedom and foster its own evil: Raskol'nikov would both assert his unique individuality (his 'superiority' to other men) and simultaneously rid society of a malignancy — the pawnbroker. Ivan similarly questions an order which, like that of the Grand Inquisitor, exacts blind submission in exchange for security and a God whose world permits the torture of innocent children. But to do so is to begin to doubt the certainty of truth (as even Turgenev momentarily does[72]), and, for Dostoevskij, this inevitably leads to moral relativism. What, for instance, bothers Ivan most about his interview with the devil is his inability to determine whether or not the devil is his own hallucination. The logical next step is amorality, which, as in the case of Stavrogin, leads to eventual self-destruction.

Yet another aspect of alienation is implicit in the foregoing characters, as it is in Dostoevskij's thought as such. This is the slavophile "theme of the individual 'divorced from life' — from the life of the people, the soul, the national element...".[73] It is the same theme which Puškin had raised in *The Gypsies* and Lermontov in *Taman'*. It also provides a clue to Dostoevskij's own ultimate view of his heroes' alienation. Necessary, in a sense, as their experiences may seem to be for the insight that might ultimately save them, he is equally concerned about their salvation, as such. His views here take a rather topical, even political form and are frequently expressed in his journalistic writings (*Diary of a Writer*, 1873-1877, 1880-1881). They are intimately related to Dostoevskij's later slavophilism and his notion that the Russian intelligentsia will find its future and its strength by turning to the people (*narod*).

A further Dostoevskian character — like Rudin, ineffective and misunderstood, hence decidedly alienated — is in a category all his own. This is Prince Myškin (*The Idiot*), who also bears decided affinities to Don Quixote. Perhaps the subject of Puškin's verse — "There lived on the earth a poor knight" — was indeed his inspiration.[74] He is, in any event, one of the few truly successful literary creations at the same time so positive as to appear 'saintly',[75] even 'Christlike'.[76]

Many of Dostoevskij's major heroes are contrasted to an opposite personality type, or 'double' — thus creating further sympathy or

[72]   *Supra*, 43.
[73]   Jackson, 25.
[74]   Dmitrij Chizhevskij, *On Romanticism in Slavic Literature* (The Hague, Mouton & Co., 1957), 51-52.
[75]   Mirsky, 287.
[76]   Muchnic, 135.

aversion with respect to the central character. Hence, Goljadkin Senior and Goljadkin Junior (*The Double*), Raskol'nikov and Razumixin (*Crime and Punishment*), Myškin and Rogožin (*The Idiot*), Stavrogin and Petr Verxovenskij (*The Possessed*), and Ivan and his brothers, including Smerdjakov (*The Brothers Karamazov*).

Andrej Bolkonskij

Olenin, hero of Tolstoj's *Cossacks* (1863), continues the theme of civilized man rejected by more primitive, more natural peoples, hence estranged in a sense from his very origins, from what in life is most vital and fundamental. Olenin is both a modified Aleko and a Pečorin. His quest, like Pečorin's, ends unfulfilled. In his restlessness and sense of purpose-lessness, he is the progenitor of Andrej Bolkonskij, whose resemblance to him is partially explained by the fact that *Cossacks* was published in the very year that Tolstoj began to write *War and Peace*. Andrej's story goes a step farther, however, and involves a more philosophical dimension.

Andrej's dissatisfaction stems from his almost metaphysical need to identify with all creation. His vision of the sky, while he lies wounded at Austerlitz, gives him a sense of the eternal which makes the round of human affairs, even those of a Napoleon, seem futile and insignificant. This new understanding is stained with pessimism at the death of Andrej's wife, however; and only the youthful Nataša — herself a symbol of the good, innocent elemental life — can subsequently revive in him the hope of finding further satisfaction. His spiritual rehabilitation is also dramatized by the vision of an oak tree which, while appearing to be dead in the early spring, later acquires new foliage. Nataša's fickle attachment to the flirtatious Kuragin again disenchants Andrej, who enlists for the battle at Borodino, there to be mortally wounded. Before his death, however, he becomes reconciled with both the maimed and suffering Kuragin and then Nataša. He dies, having experienced compassion for and from others, and thereby discovers, at last, life's meaning.[77] In dying he is no longer alienated — though in a sense quite different from that which applies to Oblomov.

Two additional characters in the Tolstojan repertoire, though quite unlike Andrej, deserve additional mention for the kinds of alienation they tend to represent. These are Nexljudov (*Resurrection*, 1899) and Anna Karenina (*Anna Karenina*, 1875-1877). The former becomes

[77] Although this is essentially P'er Bezuxov's quest as well, the latter pursues it in a much more optimistic and whole-souled, hence much less alienated fashion.

remorseful when reminded of the young girl whose life he has ruined. His effort to assuage a guilty conscience seems nonetheless egotistical, hence still estranged from a genuine selflessness. As Mirsky observes, "It is not a revelation of inner light, but a cold decision to adapt himself to the moral law so as to escape the stings of conscience and acquire an inner peace."[78]

Anna Karenina, on the other hand, appears, like the lowly Bašmačkin, to be more the victim of circumstances, albeit circumstances applicable to all women of her time and station. As Spector explains:

It was imperative for the Russian woman of aristocratic origin to marry as soon as possible, with the question of love a minor problem to be settled as satisfactorily as possible after the wedding. Before marriage they met men in society under strained, artificial conditions that did not lead to a real knowledge of character .... In *Anna Karenina*, perhaps better than elsewhere, Tolstoy revealed the double moral standard for Russian men and women of the aristocracy.[79]

Anna's mistake — perhaps an evidence of her genuineness and magnanimity — is that, by traveling with Vronskij, she forces society to recognize what it knew already but was willing to close its eyes to — that she is an adulteress. Even Karenin is mostly concerned about the effect of her behavior on his social position. Anna's conflict involves the possibility of love as opposed to an empty life that conforms to hypocritical social conventions.

Other characters suggest further conflicts bordering on alienation:

In his novels he [Tolstoj] showed that the artificiality, restlessness, and boredom of the average noble demanded a far heavier price than he lavished on his own entertainment. Levin and Nekhludov bore witness to the serious problem of land management which faced the rural nobility, Karenin and Oblonsky to the political wire pulling necessary in order that the city official might not only retain his position, but secure a better one.[80]

Treplev

This same late aristocratic life of 'artificiality, restlessness and boredom' is essentially the subject matter both of Čexov's plays and a number of his stories. While *The Sea Gull* is not generally regarded as Čexov's finest dramatic achievement nor is Treplev necessarily his most provocative hero, the chief protagonists of the plays which follow, being women,

[78] Mirsky, 319.
[79] Spector, 219-220.
[80] *Ibid.*, 221.

lend themselves less successfully to comparison with the eight males discussed at length in the foregoing. As a Čexovian type, Treplev belongs to the category of sensitive gentlemen who are generally sinned against, either by circumstances or, more often, by their inability to adjust to them. This type includes Ivanov (*Ivanov*, 1889) and Vojnickij (*Uncle Vanja*, 1897) as well as a number of secondary characters, *e.g.* *The Sea Gull*'s Medvedenko and *The Three Sisters*' Andrej and Veršinin (1901).

Together with Veršinin, Treplev also fits another group of maudlin sentimentalists who may to some degree serve as mouthpiece for the playwright's social criticism and historical speculations. Their rambling speeches are seldom related to the immediate plot. They generally anticipate an improved distant future, though they lack the sense of urgency and the energy which characterize Turgenev's revolutionaries. Others of this type include *Uncle Vanja*'s Astrov and both Trofimov and Gaev of *The Cherry Orchard* (1904). Although a young man, Treplev seems as effete and out of touch with reality as many another of Čexov's principals, including Ol'ga, Maša, Irina (*The Three Sisters*), and Ranevskaja (*The Cherry Orchard*). He suffers from a universally Čexovian malady: "the mutual unintelligibility and strangeness of human beings, who cannot and do not want to understand each other".[81] Like Čexov's other 'sensitive gentlemen', Treplev is unsuccessful at love. Like Ivanov, he takes his own life.

Čexov's portrayal of such types — their exaggerated self-pity; their moodiness so seldom justified by actual circumstances — and the fact that he called *The Sea Gull* and other such plays 'comedies' suggest a decided satirical intent, however gentle, toward his subject matter.

General Characteristics

The foregoing discussion affords the following observations: Čackij, Onegin, Pečorin, and Andrej Bolkonskij are essentially bored with the meaningless round of social conventions to which, as aristocrats, each is subjected. In the case of each of the first three, the character's malaise reflects historical circumstances peculiar to his time. Gifford has, for instance, noted the following:

Molchalin thinks one has to depend on others, when one's rank is still low. Chatsky says, almost out loud, that Sofya must be mocking him, for how could she love such a man? In their dialogue two creeds have clashed: that of the

[81] Mirsky, 381.

new liberal Russia for which the Decembrists were working and that of the Russia which Nicholas I would bring into being.[82]

. . . .

Evgeny's first impulse is that of others among his generation who already show signs of *barin*'s uneasy conscience. He means to change things and lets off his peasants with a light *obrok*, which allows them, for a small payment yearly, to seek work elsewhere. This scandalizes his neighbours who proclaim him a most dangerous crank. He does nothing to conciliate them, but whenever he hears the rumble of their coaches along the high-road, he mounts his Don stallion at the back of the house and rides off. ... These middling gentry condemn Onegin much as their cousins in Moscow condemn Chatsky: he, too, is mad and a Freemason (Pushkin, like other liberals of the time, became one in the south).[83]

. . . .

Onega and Pechora are both rivers of northern Russia. So when, at the end of the 1830's, Lermontov chose the name Pechorin for his hero, he was hinting at a relationship with Onegin. Herzen, like many later critics, saw a family likeness between Chatsky, Onegin, and Pechorin. "Chatsky", he said, "is a *raisonneur*. Onegin, his elder brother. Lermontov's 'Hero of our time' is his younger brother." In point of fact, the younger brother belongs to a new generation, and his creator became the spokesman of the young men who grew up after the Decembrist rising ... he has qualities which stamp him as the man of a more advanced period than Onegin was — more advanced in suffering, if in nothing else.[84]

Among the young aristocratic intelligentsia, then, frustration and/or malaise are due not only to the hero's social conditioning (as with Onegin, Treplev, and perhaps Oblomov) but also to his superior ethical judgment and his consequent dissatisfaction with society's false and superficial values. In this respect, he is generally the object of his author's sympathy. In ensuing heroes the conflict occurs between thought and feeling, the expectations of reason and the seeming contradictions which nonetheless attend the experiences of real life (Bazarov, Ivan Karamazov, Andrej Bolkonskij). Still others as diverse as Oblomov and the Bašmačkin of Nabokov's interpretation are opposed as much by life itself as by a particular society. The author's attitude toward such protagonists is, because to some extent satirical, often complex and ambivalent.

At least half the protagonists surveyed are, in any event, realists, while the society or the universe they oppose are respectively deluded or, from the human standpoint at least, deceptive. Onegin, Bazarov, and Treplev are deluded, primarily, about themselves — each in his own distinct fashion. Čackij, Pečorin, Karamazov and Bolkonskij, however, all show

---

[82] Gifford, 40-41.
[83] *Ibid.*, 70-71.
[84] *Ibid.*, 102.

a peculiar self-awareness. Pečorin understands himself all too well as do Čackij the terms and conditions of society and Karamazov those of his very existence. In terms of their awareness and understanding, all behave with remarkable consistency. As literary characters they are, in other words, well motivated.

All resort to one or another means of escape: Čackij, who was so recently abroad, again leaves Moscow in the course of the play; Onegin acquires an estate in the country, which he later abandons after killing Lenskij; Pečorin roams from one setting to the other in the general area of the Caucasus; Oblomov escapes to his couch and daydreams; Bazarov steels himself against emotional disappointment by espousing a life of science and reason; Karamazov, in a sense, does the same thing in his effort to be free of moral responsibility for what happens to others, declaring that, if there is no God, then everything is permitted; Bolkonskij rushes off to the Napoleonic Wars to be free of society and his domestic situation; while Treplev writes incomprehensible dramas about life thousands of years hence. In a figurative sense, even Bašmačkin's new coat holds the illusion of a panacea for all his wretchedness.

A number retaliate as well as escape: Čackij with wit and Bazarov with invective; Onegin and Pečorin by teasing and shocking, then spitefully killing their respective rivals; Karamazov by failing to prevent his father's murder. Bašmačkin's death is both his escape and, if it is really his Ghost who later haunts the Petersburg streets,[85] his means of revenge. The rest — Oblomov, Bolkonskij, Treplev — are less rebellious in the roles they play — silent sufferers. Perhaps the only one who is a completely passive victim, however, whose personality and behavior do not in some way aggravate his predicament, is Bašmačkin.

---

[85]	According to Vladimir Nabokov: "The account of his ghost haunting the streets of St. Petersburg in search of the cloak of which he had been robbed and finally appropriating that of a high official who had refused to help him in his misfortune — this account, which to the unsophisticated may look like an ordinary ghost story, is transformed towards the end into something for which I can find no precise epithet. It is both an apotheosis and a *dégringolade*. ... A piece of most important information, the main structural idea of the story is here deliberately masked by Gogol (because all reality is a mask). The man taken for Akaky Akakyevich's cloakless ghost existed solely on the strength of his lacking a cloak, whereas now the policeman, lapsing into the queerest paradox of the story, mistakes for this ghost just the very person who was its antithesis, the man who had stolen the cloak. Thus the story describes a full circle: a vicious circle as all circles are, despite their posing as apples, or planets, or human faces." Nabokov, 146, 148-149. Nabokov presumes that both the important official and the policeman encounter the same individual at story's end. This individual is described, in the case of the policeman, as was the thief who had previously robbed Bašmačkin of his cloak, *i.e.* in terms of a great moustache and very large build.

Unlike Čackij, Bazarov, and Treplev — whose love is spurned — Onegin, Pečorin, and Oblomov, fearing for their independence, evade traditional attachments to women and the consequent responsibilities of married life. Bazarov tries to remain dispassionate, despite his true feelings, and Bolkonskij, in the first part of his story, regrets the tie to his wife. Onegin, Oblomov, and Bazarov contend with women of a greater sense of purpose and/or moral stamina. All are contrasted, moreover, to a generally more practical, more healthy, though often less admirable rival: Čackij to the sycophant, Molčalin; Onegin to the naive though well-intended Lenskij (perhaps at the end to the indomitable Tat'jana); Pečorin to the awkward, unscrupulous Grušnickij, as well as, earlier, to the kind-hearted, disenchanted Maksim Maksimyč; Bašmačkin to the aloof and impersonal Very Important Person; Oblomov to the business-like but colorless Štol'c; Bazarov to the less radical Arkadij; Karamazov to his brothers — the more impetuous Dmitrij and the more spiritual Aleša; Bolkonskij to the questing P'er Bezuxov; and Treplev to the cynical, unprincipled older writer, Trigorin. The number who are spurned in love and who, in turn, evade conjugal attachments is thus evenly divided, while the contrast with rivals generally favors the alienated individual — rivals appearing, while more practical, often less scrupulous or at least less idealistic.

As for the resolution of their woes, only two — Oblomov and Bolkonskij — are at all victorious: Oblomov, because he has managed to escape life while still alive, life itself being his principal adversary; Bolkonskij in spurts of reconciliation with that same life, but not conclusively until the very end. Otherwise, all are essentially failures: Čackij, Onegin, and Treplev spurned in love; Čackij forced to flee; Karamazov insane; Čackij considered insane; Pečorin so distraught that he is left crying over his dead horse and, later, rebuffed, so that he continues wandering; Bazarov and Treplev suicides, even if the former is an unwitting one; Bašmačkin an ignored and broken man who succumbs both to the cold and to the world's heedless indifference. Death comes as a kind of victory only for Oblomov, as a kind of neutral termination for Bolkonskij. None are reformed.

The table which follows compares the nine foregoing protagonists according to a number of categories, mostly as analyzed above. More or less opposite characteristics are represented by pairs of columns, the left-hand member of which tends to stand for a characteristic that would elicit sympathy or admiration by contrast with its opposite. A protagonist is rated only where the given characteristic is relevant or can be assessed. The ten pairs of columns represent the following opposed characteristics:

(1) opposition to vs. support of status quo;

(2) laudability vs. unjustifiability of hero's protest (*i.e.* whether or not his protest represents a realistic criticism of an either deceptive or deluded society and/or universe);

(3) self-understanding vs. self-delusion;

(4) resignation vs. engagement (a silent sufferer or unwitting victim vs. a hero whose action itself elicits or aggravates his alienation);

(5) rejection by the woman vs. the hero's own fickle behavior in a love situation;

(6) consistent resistance to the source of alienation vs. ultimate escapism;

(7) defense of others vs. exploitation of others as a means of retaliation;

(8) moral superiority vs. moral inferiority to foil (foils);

(9) minority protest vs. socially conditioned majority behavior or viewpoint;

(10) ultimate defeat vs. ultimate victory.

As the totals tend to indicate, the protagonists in question all oppose the status quo[86] and all resort to some form of escape. However, they are generally contrasted to foils in a favorable fashion. In the particular context of the works in which they appear, each opposes a situation or viewpoint upheld by the majority of his peers. The protest of earlier heroes tends to be more justifiable, that of later heroes either less so or at least more abstract and controversial. Most react in some retaliatory fashion, which itself intensifies their alienation. Their story's final outcome is mostly unsuccessful, even tragic. In other respects, their behavior is random and indicates no discernible pattern or trend. (Onegin in fact betrays a kind of ambivalence with respect to the characteristics represented in columns five and seven.)

To what then do these heroes react? What are the forces which they oppose or which oppress them? What are the ultimate issues? Clearly for Čackij — a most superficial, unprogressive social structure filled with hypocrisy and wanting worthwhile values. The same is true for Onegin, Pečorin, Bazarov, and Bolkonskij, although each is likewise personally tainted. The canker in each doubtless aggravates his outrage, also en-

---

[86] Treplev's attitude is less clear. His art, however, which is also his particular brand of escapism, tends to suggest that he seeks a break with the present in avant-garde forms and distant speculation.

TABLE 1

Comparison of Nineteenth-Century Alienated Heroes

Hero	1 pro-status quo	1 con-status quo	2 laudable protest	2 false protest	3 self-understanding	3 self-delusion	4 resigned	4 active	5 rejected	5 fickle	6 resists	6 escapes	7 defends	7 exploits	8 superior	8 inferior	9 minority	9 majority	10 defeated	10 victorious
Čackij		×	×		×			×	×			×			×		×		×	
Onegin		×	×			×		×		×		×	×	×		×	×		×	
Pečorin		×	×		×			×		×		×	×	×	×		×		×	
Bašmačkin		×	×				×					×			×		×		×	
Oblomov		×				×	×			×		×					×		×	
Bazarov		×		×		×		×	×			×		×			×			×
Karamazov		×		×	×		×		×			×					×		×	
Bolkonskij		×		×		×		×	×			×			×		×			×
Treplev				×	×				×			×					×		×	
Totals	0	8	4	4	4	4	3	5	5	3	0	9	2	3	4	1	9	0	7	2

larging his sensitivity and consciousness. If we discount Dobroljubov's polemical bias, Oblomov's adversary becomes completely internalized and is his own indolence. Likewise Treplev, although the product of a decadent way of life, is mostly self-deluded; as much as any rival, his own faded personality prevents his keeping Nina or becoming a successful writer. Bašmačkin either is, like the previous two, too petty and ineffectual a being to cope with even the rigors of normal life, or he is the helpless victim of a completely impersonal, totally inhuman social order, even universe — owing to the particular critic. To an extent both Pečorin and Bolkonskij vent their frustration at the behest of their authors' metaphysical preoccupations — Lermontov's obsession with demonic freedom, Tolstoj's with the futility of mind, ego, and artificiality and the necessity for resignation to elemental life and to death, its natural culmination. Doubtless the most purely philosophical of all is Ivan Karamazov, whose *idée fixe* is also Dostoevskij's — the universal question of human privilege *vs.* human accountability in man's interaction with the Divine.

THE EARLY TWENTIETH CENTURY

If in the first decades of the twentieth century any one nineteenth-century writer influences the depiction of alienation, it is Dostoevskij. Together with the critical assessments of N. K. Mixailovskij, Vladimir Solov'ev, and Vasilij Rozanov in the later nineteenth century, those of Dmitrij Merežkovskij, *Tolstoj and Dostoevskij* (1901); Lev Šestov, *Dostoevskij and Nietzsche: The Philosophy of Tragedy* (1903); and Vjačeslav Ivanov (collected as *Freedom and the Tragic Life* (1952)) suggest with what continued interest Dostoevskij was regarded at the turn of the century. Doubtless, the conditions which prevailed from then until 1917 — greater urban populations, exploitation of industrial labor, extremes of wealth, political instability — produced the same oppressive atmosphere, the same frustration and discouragement which bred Dostoevskij's Underground Man. Besides the protagonists of M. N. Albov and V. M. Garšin, which appear in the 1880's, Robert L. Jackson mentions the following 'Underground' heroes who come to the fore between 1900 and 1917:[87]

---

[87] Jackson, *Dostoevsky's Underground Man*. Jackson generally designates a work by genre, either as 'story' or 'novel' — hence the symbols "s" and "n".

TABLE 2

'Underground' Heroes Between 1900 and 1917

Year	Hero	Author	Work
1900	Sergej Petrovič	L. Andreev	*The Story of Sergej Petrovič* (s)
1902	Dr. Keržencev	L. Andreev	*Thought* (s)
1902	student	A. I. Kuprin	*River of Life* (s)
1904-05	all characters	V. Y. Brjusov	*Republic of the Southern Cross* (s)
1905	Romašev	A. I. Kuprin	*The Duel* (n)
1905	Peredonov	F. Sologub	*Petty Demon* (n)
1907	(hero)	L. Andreev	*Curse of the Demon* (s)
1908	memoirist	L. Andreev	*My Memoirs*
1910	Marakulin	A. M. Remizov	*Sisters in the Cross* (s)
1911-12	Naumov, Čiž	M. P. Arcybašev	*At the Last Boundary* (n)

Half of these (Sergej Petrovič, Marakulin, and Čiž) — as well as Glazkov and Aleksej Petrovič, the respective heroes of Albov's *Day of Reckoning* (s) and Garšin's *Night* (s) — end as suicides.

ASSESSMENT

Despite the foregoing observations, an author's attitude toward his protagonist is — in the case of nineteenth-century alienated heroes — an often complex and tenuous matter. Various critics attest to the difficulty. In his famous Puškin address Dostoevskij, for instance, saw a positive value in Onegin's anti-social behavior, "a longing for some universal ideal".[88] John Bayley in turn speaks of 'the Timon effect'[89] a special awareness of the good arrived at through negation — in such diverse characters as Shakespeare's Hamlet and Timon (*Timon of Athens*), Milton's Satan (*Paradise Lost*), Byron's heroes, and those of the Byronic Lermontov and the evil-fixated Dostoevskij. These authors doubtless intended for their heroes some such redeeming quality.

Charles Moser alludes to the ambiguities in Bazarov when he characterizes *Fathers and Sons* "an antinihilist novel in the sense that radicalism was central to the book and that the progressive characters in the

[88] F. M. Dostoevskij, speech before the Society of Lovers of Russian Literature, June 8, 1880, *Sobranie sočinenij*, X (Moscow, Gosudarstvennoe izdatel'stvo xudožestvennoj literatury, 1958), 451.
[89] John Bayley, *Tolstoy and the Novel* (New York, The Viking Press, 1966), 43.

novel were not treated from an unreservedly sympathetic point of view".[90] Citing an epigraph originally intended for the same novel as well as subsequent remarks by its author, Moser further argues that "Turgenev's basic attitude toward the younger generation and toward Bazarov as its representative was one of indecision."[91] Moser's explanation: "... in the case of Turgenev and Leskov, who were partial to their most important nihilistic heroes, their penchant for objectivity was such that they could not refrain from portraying the weak sides of the movement, an approach which it was difficult for the radicals to excuse".[92] Donald Davie's statement of the problem is more all-inclusive and also more adamant: "Lermontov's attitude to Pechorin, like Goncharov's attitude to Oblomov, like Turgenev's attitude to Bazarov, no comment can determine. At no point can it be said that Lermontov speaks through the mouth of Pechorin, or through the mouth of any other character. As a result we cannot say whether Lermontov, in making Pechorin the hero of the age, was or was not ironical."[93]

Perhaps least uncertain are Griboedov's approval of Čackij and Tolstoj's essential sympathy for Andrej. As Bayley argues with respect to all of Tolstoj's characters: "When their environment becomes unified and makes sense, it is a sinister thing: it makes sense *against* them, enters them to tell them they must die, and presents itself to them in a singular, coherent, and therefore insupportable form."[94] Thus life itself — its impermanence and mutability — dooms all men from the outset. Man can become reconciled to this inevitability but remains nevertheless pathetic.

Čexov's view, however, again poses a most delicate, difficult balance. Says D. S. Mirsky:

That man is good and lovable who makes no attempt (or only obviously absurd attempts) to counteract necessity, and the more sensitive and thin-skinned he is, the more he suffers in the act of submitting, the more he is lovable and good. He may writhe and wriggle, he may even struggle ineffectively — but fixity of purpose and steady resolution to act is unpardonable sin. The man who does not succumb to pinpricks is an insensible brute. The man who knows his mind and works his own way through the world may still be redeemed by failure and defeat, and if he at last succumbs, he may even become doubly

[90] Charles Moser, *Antinihilism in the Russian Novel of the 1860's* (The Hague, Mouton & Co., 1964), 65.

[91] *Ibid.*, 83.

[92] *Ibid.*, 183.

[93] Donald Davie, "Tolstoy, Lermontov, and Others", *Russian Literature and Modern English Fiction*, (ed.) Donald Davie (Chicago, U. of Chicago Press, 1965), 197.

[94] Bayley, 44.

worthy of the smilingly indulgent and contemptuous pity that is Chekhov's substitute for sympathy.[95]

Valid as this evaluation may be — and how true it is of Tolstoj — it ignores the possibility of volition and personal accountability as standards of Čexov's judgment. Discussing *Ivanov* (and suggesting Aristotle on the ideal tragic hero), A. P. Skaftymov contends that "'Chekhov felt it was important not to allow sympathy for Ivanov's pessimism, and, at the same time, not to make Ivanov morally at fault.'"[96] G. Berdnikov argues as follows: "... Ivanov reacts ... without feeling guilty and without active evil intent. But he lacks the will to oppose wrong actions, and so they are carried out."[97]

If Soviet critics tend to be deterministic, those in the West see it otherwise. Discussing *The Sea Gull*, Robert Louis Jackson speaks of Treplev's 'tragic flaw' — "his refusal to recognize his essential freedom and to accept the responsibility that it implies. ... Those characters in Chekhov who accept the notion of fate, of a force acting independently and capriciously outside of human will, seem to bear within themselves the element of defeat."[98] On *The Cherry Orchard*: "It is the merchant Lopakhin — no relier on chance or the help of others, but a man who lifts himself by his own bootstraps — who takes fate into his own hands and who triumphs."[99] Charles du Bos perhaps best sums up the complexity of Čexov's viewpoint: "... he conveys to us that they (his characters) cannot do otherwise and, at the same time, without ever stating it, makes us feel that at a given moment, at the start, they might have been different. He seems always to imply — and at the same time: 'It is no longer their fault — and yet it is their fault that it should no longer be their fault.'"[100]

Of all the writers here discussed, however, Gogol' and Dostoevskij are doubtless the most enigmatic and controversial. Nabokov's existentialist analysis of *The Overcoat*'s Bašmačkin has already been mentioned.[101] Although he considers Bašmačkin 'absurd', a 'mild lunatic', Nabokov

[95] D. S. Mirsky, "Chekhov and the English" (cited from *Monthly Criterion*, VI (October, 1927)), (ed.) Donald Davie (Chicago, U. of Chicago Press, 1965), 207-208.
[96] G. Berdnikov, "*Ivanov*: An Analysis" (citing A. P. Skaftymov, *Stat'i o russkoj literature* (Leningrad-Moscow, 1957), 51-63 (trans.) Joyce Vining), *Chekhov* (ed.) Robert Louis Jackson (Englewood Cliffs, N.J., Prentice-Hall, Inc., 1967), 93.
[97] Berdnikov, 95.
[98] Robert Louis Jackson, "Checkhov's *Seagull*", *Chekhov*, (ed.) Robert Louis Jackson (Englewood Cliffs, N.J., Prentice-Hall, Inc., 1967), 103, 105.
[99] *Ibid.*, 105.
[100] Charles du Bos, "The Chekhovian Sense of Life" (trans.) Leslie Jackson, *Chekhov* (ed.) Robert Louis Jackson (Englewood Cliffs, N.J., Prentice-Hall, Inc., 1967), 189.
[101] *Supra*, 39.

really condemns life itself, "this world of utter futility" more than Akakij, who is unavoidably this world's victim, "pathetic, *because* he is human and *because* he has been engendered by those very forces which seem to be in such contrast to him". This much — his wistful sympathy — Nabokov shares with those, like Belinskij, who first saw Gogol' as a critic of social institutions and a champion of the oppressed. Nabokov's pessimism is more abstract and universal, however, like that of Tolstoj and Čexov, as interpreted by Mirsky and the Soviet critics, Skaftymov and Berdnikov. Indeed Nabokov's view is even further removed from real social concern in its purely esthetic titillation, and for this Philip Rahv condemns it: "... Nabokov's Gogol is too pure to be true, too literary and abstract to be genuine. The poet who inserted into *Dead Souls* epic apostrophes to Holy Russia — apostrophes infused with messianic hope in which love and despair are inextricably mingled — was not a purist writing in a vein of exclusive subjectivity and dedicated to the tormenting refinements of his solitary dreams. He too, like all of Russia's great writers, suffered with his country and its people."[102]

On the other hand, Rozanov, Chizhevskij, and Setchkarev have taken an altogether opposite position:

... Gogol covers the poor Akaky Akakiyevich with scorn, according to the philosopher and the literary critic Vasily Rozanov, who was one of the first to attempt to revise the traditional view of Gogol. The hero's precarious situation is not in the least attributable to the "capitalistic structure of society," but to his own narrow intellectual horizon.... Akaky Akakiyevich's great passion for the little, insignificant thing — the overcoat — brings with it a gaping spiritual and ideational discrepancy, a precipitous falling from the heights into the depths, which Gogol manages to make clear both stylistically and compositionally. In his excellent essay on "The Overcoat," Dmitry Chizhevsky has investigated these connections. The extraordinarily frequent use of the word "even" (Russian *dazhe*) symbolizes the gap that exists between Akaky Akakiyevich's conception of the world and that of the reader. In the little world of Akaky Akakiyevich, the little is great, and through the constant repetition of this intensifying conjunction, which is not, however, always followed by the expected intensification and which in fact is apparently used at times without logical reason ... the difference in size is also made completely clear by stylistic means.[103]

Are Rozanov and his emigré successors stretching a point to defend the "'capitalistic structure of society'" against its socialist detractors? The

[102]   Philip Rahv, "Gogol as a Modern Instance" (cited from Philip Rahv, *Image and Idea* (New York, New Directions, 1949)), *Russian Literature and Modern English Fiction*, (ed.) Donald Davie (Chicago, University of Chicago Press, 1965), 243-244.
[103]   Vsevolod Setchkarev, *Gogol: His Life and Works* (New York, New York University Press, 1965), 218, 226.

dilemma thus posed brings to mind the similar quandry which Levin raises regarding Madame Bovary: "Emma's dreams are destined, at the touch of reality, to wither into lies. Is that a critique of her or of reality? If she suffers for her mistakes, shall we infer that those who prosper are being rewarded for their merits? If we cannot, we can hardly assume — with the novel's courtroom apologists — that it preaches a self-evident moral."[104]

As for Dostoevskij's Ivan Karamazov, N. Berdjaev and D. H. Lawrence have in turn advanced two classical though diametrically opposite arguments. Both arguments turn on the correct interpretation of the "Grand Inquisitor" episode, particularly of Christ's parting kiss; for Ivan is the intended author of this powerful tale and the attitude he therein ascribes to Christ should afford a clue to his own, if not to Dostoevskij's actual sympathies. Berdjaev unequivocally declares that Christ rejects the Inquisitor's harangue and that "Christ's failure to reply, his benign silence persuade and inspire far more...."[105] Lawrence as vehemently insists that "Jesus in the end gives the kiss of acquiescence to the Inquisitor, as Alyosha does to Ivan. ... So let the specially gifted few make the decision between good and evil, and establish the life-values against the money-values. And let the many accept the decision, with gratitude, and bow down to the few in the hierarchy. What is there diabolical or satanic in that?"[106] Dostoevskij himself might have provided the answer, as he did for Raskol'nikov, who learned to his grief how difficult it is to identify the 'specially gifted' and the 'extraordinary'. If Lawrence could only approve the Inquisitor's argument and Christ's 'acquiescence', most readers would — in view of subsequent twentieth-century totalitarianism — be hard pressed to concur with him or to uphold Ivan, if the Inquisitor's is indeed also Ivan's view. There are of course other ambiguities, which Berdjaev himself acutely recognizes: "... it is intriguing that the legend, which is a most powerful vindication of Christ, has been placed in the mouth of the atheist Ivan Karamazov. The legend is a riddle. It is never entirely clear with whom the legend's narrator sides, nor with whom the author. Our own human freedom is given much to decipher. But a legend about freedom should be addressed to freedom. Light kindles in darkness."[107]

---

[104] Levin, 263.
[105] Berdjaev, 196.
[106] D. H. Lawrence, "Preface to Dostoevsky's *The Grand Inquisitor*", *Selected Criticism* (ed.) Anthony Beal (New York, The Viking Press, Inc., 1956), 234, 241.
[107] Berdjaev, 195.

The complexities here surveyed indicate the difficulty of establishing the exact orientation of most of these writers to their respective heroes. Nevertheless, it may be worth conjecture, at least to the point of discerning certain tendencies. In view, for instance, of Bazarov's constant ineptitude and of certain moments bordering on parody, Turgenev appears, if anything, more critical than sympathetic. In view of Tolstoj's own lifelong spiritual restlessness, on the other hand, it is likely that his view of Andrej is, for the most part, sympathetic. As the mastermind of his father's parricide, Ivan Karamazov stands morally condemned, and in view of his nervous collapse and Aleša's last word to the young boys, Dostoevskij would appear to side eventually against Ivan.

On the other hand, to the extent that Ivan champions the principle of self-determination, Dostoevskij doubtless views him positively. It is likely, furthermore, that the dualisms of freedom and conformity, faith and agnosticism, *etc.* which so plague Ivan were never completely resolved for Dostoevskij either, much as he might have preferred to think otherwise. It is this contradiction, in fact, which has made him so lastingly profound, so useful to twentieth-century thought in the West. Indeed, although many if not most of the stories in question are clearly semi-autobiographical, their writers all generally maintain the same aloof, detached objectivity in their various portrayals. This is perhaps one of the hallmarks which so distinguish them as a school and also what complicates the question of their ultimate viewpoint.

A further clue nevertheless emerges from the contrast each author poses between his hero and his hero's rival, as well as by the unfortunate, if not calamitous fate that attends the conclusion of most heroes' stories. As previously noted, the rivals of Čackij, Pečorin, Bašmačkin, and Treplev are decidedly less sympathetic — while the reverse, at least in some respects, appears to be true of Bazarov and Ivan Karamazov. Lenskij's naivete may irritate the reader as it does Onegin, but he still seems far more pitiable than, say, the deceptively vengeful Grušnickij. Hence, Onegin's insistence on the duel renders him somehow less admirable than the same quality in Pečorin. Onegin is also more calculating, while Pečorin's actions seem both more impulsive and more profoundly regretted. Eventually Bolkonskij becomes magnanimously reconciled to his offender, Kuragin, and he never directly opposes his seeming rival, P'er Bezuxov. P'er does not, of course, really contest Nataša until after Andrej's death.

The foregoing contrasts, where they occur, tend therefore to qualify the preceding assumptions as to the authors' bias for or against their respective heroes. This very complexity can serve, nevertheless, as a criterion for comparing the latter with subsequent, particularly Soviet alienated, protagonists. Of equal importance, however, is the fact that — despite the ostensible diversity in these authors' attitudes toward their heroes as such — they nonetheless register a like social protest. Puškin's disapproval of Onegin in no way discounts his own disdain for the society which produced this dandy. One need but recall his poem modelled after Deržavin's "Monument" (1796), itself a paraphrase of Horace's "*Exegi Monumentum*" — "I raised a monument to myself unfashioned by human hands ..." (1836). Though a political conservative after his exile, Dostoevskij was also a bitter critic of both the philistinism and the revolutionary socialism which, in his *Diary of a Writer*, in *The Possessed*, and elsewhere he blamed for the formation of Raskol'nikovs, Stavrogins, and Ivan Karamazovs. Čexov, whose grandfather had been a serf, lucidly foresaw the decline of a lifeless, unresponsive aristocracy, while Tolstoj's hatred for prevailing institutions was notorious.

Their social protest is perhaps also registered in these authors' frequent inability to reform their heroes or make them, in the end, any the more efficacious. The works and characters already discussed, as well as others by these same writers, are especially illustrative. It is generally conceded, for instance, that Gogol''s Čičikov is unconvincingly reform-ed in *Dead Souls*, Part II; the plausibility of Raskol'nikov's reformation in the epilogue of *Crime and Punishment* is also frequently questioned. Both Dostoevskij's Myškin and Tolstoj's Levin (*Anna Karenina*) fail to achieve much of what, in behalf of others, they had originally intended. Both Myškin and Ivan Karamazov, in fact, go mad. Furthermore, as if sensing their inability to transform either Onegin or P'er Bezuxov into a "successful image of ideological virtue",[108] both Puškin and Tolstoj avoid making these heroes Decembrists, despite their original intention. Instead Tolstoj allows certain of his characters — *e.g.* Nataša (*War and Peace*) and Levin (*Anna Karenina*) — to fade into mundane old age by pure attrition.

Finally, a kind of positive quality can be read into these authors' social protest and, where it occurs, in each of their heroes'. As Mathew-son remarks with respect to the same nineteenth-century protagonists: "The superfluous man, it must be kept in mind, does not represent retrogressive values; rather, he opposes them inadequately; he is their victim, not their advocate."[109] Gifford concurs:

[108] Mathewson, 17.
[109] *Ibid.*

We know what happened to each one individually. Onegin may have perished in the Caucasus; Pechorin, it seems, died on his return from Persia; Rudin fell on a revolutionary barricade. But, supposing they had escaped these perils, what lay ahead? What was their goal, what was the last stage on that unhappy journey?

A haven of unpaved streets' wooden sidewalks, meagre gardens, and ditches overgrown with nettles. The long afternoons and sleepy dinners, the tranquillity and dead routine of the Vyborg side. Onegin had seen the endless vista of dinners and ceremonies: here was the same tedium, the same privilege. There would always be somebody like Pshenitsyna to tend the *barin* in his retirement. But these earlier heroes had revolted against that end. Each in his own way sought death, rather than death-in-life.[110]

Of those who seem critical of their heroes, Turgenev particularly poses a perplexing question. Why, with basically Western sympathies, would Turgenev not more prefer to commiserate with, if not idealize, the radical young Bazarov? Again, it is helpful to recall that, more than most of the others and by his own declaration, Turgenev was primarily a man of letters, a detached esthete, and only secondarily a man of political or otherwise utilitarian persuasion.

By contrast, the 'underground' types which follow Dostoevskij and which appear to provide the major trend in alienation before 1917 all appear to voice their creators' social protest. This is also the case throughout the 'twenties, with certain instances occurring as late as 1935.

[110]   Gifford, 152.

II

LITERARY PRECEDENTS: SOVIET

THE SOVIET 'UNDERGROUND MAN'

The Dostoevskian 'underground' mentality exerts a profound influence on successive writers until as late as the early 1930's. These are generally sympathetic toward their heroes' rebellion, which serves, as with Dostoevskij, to assert the hero's innate self-will. Jackson specifies the following, each of whom personifies such a protest:

TABLE 3

'Underground' Heroes After 1917

Year	Hero	Author	Work
1920	D-503	E. Zamjatin	*We* (n)
1924	Makarov	M. Gor'kij	*The Story of a Hero* (s)
1924	Petr Karazin	M. Gor'kij	*Karamora* (s)
1924	Elkov, Titus	L. Leonov	*The End of a Petty Man* (s)
1925	Kalafat	L. Leonov	*The Badgers* (n)
1925	Mixail Lykov	I. Èrenburg	*The Racketeer* (n)
1926	Kavalerov	Ju. Oleša	*Envy* (n)
1927	freckled man	A. Sobol'	*Memoirs of a Freckled Man* (s)
1927	Mitja Vekšin, Čikilev	L. Leonov	*The Thief* (n)
1927	Pavel Červakov	L. Leonov	*Untilovsk* (s)
1928	Andrej Pustynnov	L. Leonov	*Provincial Story* (s)
1930	Ožogov, Poltorak, Marija	B. Pil'njak	*The Volga Falls to the Caspian Sea* (n)
1930	Okromeškov	A. Vojnova	*Semi-Precious Stones* (n)
1932	Arsenij Skutarevskij	L. Leonov	*Skutarevskij* (n)
1933	Volodja Sofonov	I. Erenburg	*Out of Chaos* (n)
1935	Dudnilov, Poxvisnev	L. Leonov	*Road to the Ocean* (n)

Up to the very advent of strict Soviet censorship in the thirties, a high proportion of such heroes end as suicides. A number of others are either failures in love or, in desperation, indiscriminately resign themselves to a crude sexual relationship, often with an older, unattractive woman. Their outcome is again mostly tragic or unsuccessful. Jackson makes the following distinction, however, between 'Underground' types in works published during the first fifteen years of the Soviet period and those occurring before 1917:

> The "underground" themes ... were employed after 1917 not to uphold the ego with its tyrannical aspirations, or to give expression to a nihilistic despair, but rather to defend the individual himself; to protest against ideological and cultural conformity and the domination of rationalistic and utilitarian imperatives: to insist upon a morality in which the integrity of the individual is protected against arbitrary assaults of a relativistic class, political, collective morality.[1]

Leonov's Mit'ka Vekšin is an outstanding example of the 'underground' personality under Soviet conditions. Jackson proposes three subdivisions for this same type — downtrodden 'little men'; 'hypersensitive students and intellectuals'; and informers or provocateurs whose own moral deception and distortion of truth and logic often turn back upon them. A further breakdown of 'underground' types suggests the following thematic variations:

(1) rebellion via the atavistic destruction of others (occurring particularly in works published approximate to the Revolution of 1905, as in Sologub and Brjusov);

(2) rebellion via nihilism, the death wish, or actual self-destruction (as in Arcybašev and Leonov);

(3) anti-utopianism (as in Leonov and Zamjatin);

(4) yearning for the pre-Revolution past and for rural freedom (as in Pil'njak);

(5) the theoretician's contempt for and envy of the practical man of action (as in Oleša);

(6) confusion of truth and logic (as in Andreev).

'COMPLICATED' CHARACTERS

In an even more comprehensive, near definitive survey of Soviet literary characters prior to the death of Stalin, A. M. Van der Eng-Liedmeier subdivides the years 1917-1953 into four distinct periods: 1917-1929,

---

[1] Jackson, *Dostoevsky's Underground Man*, 149.

1929-1934, 1934-1941, and 1946-1953.[2] These periods respectively cover the following broad events: (1) War Communism and the New Economic Policy, (2) First Five-Year Plan, (3) further Five-Year Plans following the foundation of the Writers' Union, and (4) the post-war Five-Year Plans. Van der Eng-Liedmeier's analysis of the so-called 'complicated'[3] characters which appear during these years is especially pertinent to the subject of alienation:

TABLE 4

Representative 'Complicated' Characters (1917-1953)

Author Bias	Year	Hero	Author	Work

I. MORAL AND PSYCHOLOGICAL TYPES

A. *'Disillusioned Idealists'* (partly correspond to Jackson's 'hypersensitive students and intellectuals')
1917-1929

(+)	1922	Terentij Zabytij	A. Arosev	*Terentyj Zabytyj's Notes* (s)
(+)	1922	(woman revolutionary)	J. Libedinskij	*The Week* (n)
(+)	1925	Polja	F. Gladkov	*Cement* (n)
(+)	1925	(hero)	A. Tolstoj	*Sky-blue Cities* (s)
(+)	1928	Boris	A. Afinogenov	*The Eccentric* (p)
(+)	1928	(heroine)	A. Tolstoj	*The Adder* (s)
(+)	1929	(old worker)	L. Ovalov	*Chatter* (s)
(+)	1929	Ivan Ožogov	B. Pil'njak	*Mahogany* (s)

1929-1934

(+) (−)	1930	Ivan Ožogov	B. Pil'njak	*The Volga Falls to the Caspian Sea* (n)
(−)	1931	Raevskij	V. Kiršon	*Bread* (p)
(+)	1931	Korčagin, Debec	B. Levin	*Once There Were Two Comrades* (n)
(−)	1931	Nagul'nov	M. Šoloxov	*Virgin Soil Upturned* (n)

[2] Van der Eng-Liedmeier's omission of the Second World War years is intentional: "The characters we find in the fiction of this period are mostly represented as national heroes or as simple Russians but very rarely as typical Soviet men." A. M. Van der Eng-Liedmeier, *Soviet Literary Characters* (The Hague, Mouton & Co., 1959), 9.

[3] *Ibid.* The following table lists only those titles discussed in the body of Van der Eng-Liedmeier's text. (Still others are mentioned in her notes.) The symbols — "+" and "−" — serve to convey the author's essential approval or disapproval of the hero cited. Where, from Van der Eng-Liedmeier's discussion, an author's reaction appears mixed, ambiguous, or indeterminable, the symbol "(+) (−)" is used instead. A work's genre — whether novel, story, or play — is also indicated wherever mentioned by Van der Eng-Liedmeier.

Author Bias	Year	Hero	Author	Work

1934-1941

Author Bias	Year	Hero	Author	Work
(+)	1935	Ljubaša	F. Gladkov	*Ljubaša's Tragedy* (s)
(+)	1936	Krečet	A. Kornejčuk	*Platon Krečet* (p)
(+)	1938	Basov	Ju. Krymov	*The Tanker Derbent* (n)

1946-1953

Author Bias	Year	Hero	Author	Work
(+)	1947	(hero)	K. Simonov	*The Smoke of the Fatherland* (s)
(+)	1948-51	(Soviet citizens)	S. Babaevskij	*Light over the Land* (n)
(+)	1950	(Soviet citizens)	T. Tur-Pyr'ev	*The Family Lutonin* (p)
(+)	1952	(Soviet citizens)	V. Kočetov	*The Family Žurbin* (n)
(+)	1953	(woman architect)	S. Narin'jani	*The Anonymous Writer* (p)

B. '*Vacillating Intellectuals*' (also partly correspond to Jackson's 'hypersensitive students and intellectuals')

1917-1929

Author Bias	Year	Hero	Author	Work
(−)	1921	(hero)	F. Gladkov	*Trees Felled by the Storm* (p)
(+) (−)	1922	Martynov	J. Libedinskij	*The Week* (n)
(+)	1922	Surikov	J. Libedinskij	*The Week* (n)
(+)	1923	Leonid, Vera	V. Veresaev	*In a Blind Alley* (n)
(+) (−)	1924	Andrej Starcov	K. Fedin	*Cities and Years* (n)
(+)	1924	Griša	M. Slonimskij	*The Emery Machine* (s)
(+)	1925	Sergej	F. Gladkov	*Cement* (n)
(+) (−)	1926	Boris Lavrov	M. Slonimskij	*The Lavrovs* (s)
(−)	1927	Mečik	A. Fadeev	*The Rout* (n)
(+) (−)	1927-29	(teacher)	N. Ognev	*Diary of Kostja Rjabcev* (n)
(+)	1928	(hero)	I. Kataev	*The Heart* (s)

1929-1934

Author Bias	Year	Hero	Author	Work
(−)	1929	(girl)	G. Nikiforov	*The Woman* (n)
(+)	1929	(poet)	Ju. Oleša	*The Cherry Stone* (s)
(−)	1930	(engineer)	S. Budancev	*A House That Gives Access to the World* (s)
(+)	1930	Teločka	I. Kataev	*Milk* (s)
(+) (−)	1931	(professor)	A. Afinogenov	*Fear* (p)
(+) (−)	1931	(painter)	V. Kaverin	*Artist Unknown* (n)
(+)	1931	(actress)	Ju. Oleša	*A List of Blessings* (p)
(−)	1932	(young girl)	V. Gerasimova	*A Distant Relative* (s)
(−)	1932	(chief engineer)	V. Kataev	*Time, Advance!* (n)
(−)	1932	(engineer)	L. Leonov	*Skutarevskij* (n)
(−)	1933	(engineer)	S. Budancev	*The Engineer Vjazemskij* (s)
(+) (−)	1933	Volodja	I. Èrenburg	*The Second Day* (n)
(+) (−)	1933	(painter)	V. Levin	*The Young Man* (n)
(−)	1933	(engineers)	J. Rykačev	*The Engineers of the White Sea Canal* (s)
(+)	1933	Nina	V. Veresaev	*The Sisters* (n)
(−)	1934	(intellectual)	V. Gerasimova	*Pity* (s)

Author Bias	Year	Hero	Author	Work
	1934-1941			
(−)	1934-35	(journalist)	K. Fedin	*The Abduction of Europe* (n)
(+) (−)	1935	(intellectual, actress, painter)	I. Èrenburg	*Without Stopping to Draw Breath* (n)
(+)	1938	Kalabuč	A. Malyškin	*People from the Backwoods* (n)
(−)	1938	Sustin, Ol'ga	A. Malyškin	*People from the Backwoods* (n)
	1946-1953			
(−)	1947	(scholar)	B. Romašov	*A Great Power* (p)
(−)	1948	(railway director)	A. Surov	*The Green Street* (p)
(+) (−)	1949	Golovin	S. Mičalkov	*Il'ja Golovin* (p)
(−)	1949	(institute director)	K. Simonov	*Someone Else's Shadow* (p)
	C. *'Anarchists'* *1917-1929*			
(+) (−)	1922	Vas'ka Zapus	Vs. Ivanov	*Sky-blue Sands* (s)
(−)	1922	(hero)	A. Jakovlev	*Brigands* (s)
(+) (−)	1923	Čapaev	D. Furmanov	*Čapaev* (n)
(+) (−)	1924	(sailor)	B. Lavrenev	*The Wind* (s)
(+) (−)	1925	(Komsomol members)	A. Jakovlev	*Morass* (s)
(+) (−)	1925	(former soldiers)	Ju. Libedinskij	*Commissars* (n)
(+) (−)	1925	(revolutionaries)	B. Pil'njak	*Machines and Wolves* (n)
(+) (−)	1927	Morozka	A. Fadeev	*The Rout* (n)
(+) (−)	1927	(anarchists)	F. Gladkov	*Tipsy Sun* (n)
(−)	1927	(hero)	A. Karavaeva	*Shores* (n)
(+) (−)	1927	(attempted murderer)	V. Kiršon	*Rust* (p)
(+)	1927	Mit'ka Vekšin	L. Leonov	*The Thief* (n)
(+) (−)	1928	(student)	V. Lidin	*The Renegade* (n)
(+) (−)	1928-40	Grigorij Melexov	M. Šoloxov	*The Silent Don* (n)
	1929-1934			
(+) (−)	1930	(women workers)	B. Pil'njak	*The Volga Falls to the Caspian Sea* (n)
(+) (−)	1931	(workers)	V. Kaverin	*Prologue* (s)
(+) (−)	1931	(workers)	A. Platonov	*To Advantage* (s)
(+) (−)	1931	(peasant)	M. Šoloxov	*Virgin Soil Upturned* (n)
(+) (−)	1933	Avdeenko	F. Gladkov	*I Love*
(−)	1933	(peasants)	L. Leonov	*The River Sot'* (n)
(+)	1933	(workers)	V. Veresaev	*The Sisters* (n)
	1934-1941			
(+) (−)	1934	(criminal)	M. Čumandrin	*The Return* (s)
(+) (−)	1934	(drunkard)	I. Kataev	*The Encounter* (s)
(+) (−)	1934-37	(kulaks)	F. Panferov	*Bruski* (n)
(+) (−)	1934	(criminal)	M. Zoščenko	*The Story of a Life* (s)

Author Bias	Year	Hero	Author	Work
(+) (−)	1935	(criminal)	Ju. German	*Aleksej Žmakin* (s)
(+) (−)	1935	(criminal)	N. Pogodin	*The Aristocrats* (p)
(+) (−)	1938	(drunkard)	Ju. Krymov	*The Tanker Derbent* (n)

D. *'Bureaucratic Villains'*
1946-1953

(+) (−)	1947	Listopad, Lida	V. Panova	*Kružiliča* (n)
(+) (−)	1948-51	Sergej	S. Babaevskij	*Light over the Land* (n)
(−)	1949	Korostelev	V. Panova	*Bright Shore* (n)
(−)	1950	(false novator)	T. Tur-Pyr'ev	*The Family Lutonin* (p)
(−)	1951	(heroine)	V. Ovečkin	*Nastja Kolosova* (p)
(−)	1952	(young man)	V. Kočetov	*The Family Žurbin* (n)

II. LOVERS

A. *'Reluctant Lovers'*
1917-1929

(−)	1922	Arxip Arxipovič, Natal'ja	B. Pil'njak	*The Naked Year* (n)
(+)	1924	(two bolshevik leaders)	A. Malyškin	*Leaders* (s)
(+) (−)	1925	Mindlov	Ju. Libedinskij	*Commissars* (n)
(+) (−)	1926	(communist)	V. Lidin	*Ships are Sailing* (n)
(+) (−)	1927	(Party official)	F. Gladkov	*Tipsy Sun* (n)
(+)	1929	Bunčuk, Anna	M. Šoloxov	*The Silent Don* (n)

1929-1934

(−)	1931	Vetrov	F. Gladkov	*The New Earth* (n)
(+) (−)	1933	Vatagin, Ol'ga	F. Gladkov	*Energy* (n)
(+) (−)	1933	Uvad'ev	L. Leonov	*The River Sot'* (n)

1934-1941

(+)	1934	Pavel Korčagin	N. Ostrovskij	*That's How the Steel Was Tempered* (n)
(+)	1935	(scholar)	I. Èrenburg	*Without Stopping to Draw Breath* (n)
(+)	1935	Kurilov	L. Leonov	*Road to the Ocean* (n)
(+) (−)	1935	Klavdija	L. Leonov	*Road to the Ocean* (n)
(+)	1938	(police superintendent)	Ju. German	*Lapšin* (s)

1946-1953

(+)	1947	Nonna	V. Panova	*Kružiliča* (n)
(+)	1947	Voropaev	P. Pavlenko	*Happiness* (n)
(+)	1949	(old lovers)	K. Simonov	*Someone Else's Shadow* (p)
(+)	1950	(Party couple)	G. Nikolaeva	*Harvest* (n)
(+)	1953	(heroine)	E. Kazakevič	*The Heart of the Friend* (s)

B. *'Free Lovers'*
1917-1929

(−)	1922	(chekist heroine)	B. Pil'njak	*Cow-wheat* (s)

Author Bias	Year	Hero	Author	Work
(+)	1923	(heroine)	A. Kollontaj	The Love of Three Generations (s)
(+) (−)	1924	(women revolutionaries)	A. Jakovlev	Without Shores (s)
(+) (−)	1925	Daša	F. Gladkov	Cement (n)
(+) (−)	1926	(komsomols)	S. Malaškin	Moon on the Right Hand Side (n)
(+) (−)	1926	(free lovers)	P. Romanov	Without Cherry Blossoms (s)
(−)	1926	(deacon)	E. Zamjatin	Iks (s)
(+) (−)	1927	Tanja	I. Èrenburg	In Protočnyj Lane (n)
(−)	1927	(hero)	N. Nikandrov	The Road to Woman (n)
(+) (−)	1927	(free lovers)	P. Romanov	The New Table of Commandments
(+) (−)	1928	(free lovers)	G. Alekseev	Friends (n)
(−)	1929	(heroine's lover)	N. Čumandrin	A Former Hero (n)
(−)	1929	(young girl)	B. Pil'njak	Mahogany (s)

1929-1934

Author Bias	Year	Hero	Author	Work
(−)	1929	Inga, Dmitrij	A. Glebov	Inga (p)
(−)	1930	(heroine's lover)	N. Čumandrin	The Rable Works (n)
(−)	1930	Laslo	B. Pil'njak	The Volga Falls to the Caspian Sea (n)
(−)	1930	(revolutionaries)	G. Serebrjakova	Dew
(−)	1930	(old guard bolshevik)	A. Vojnova	Semi-precious Stones (n)
(−)	1933	(free lovers)	V. Švarkin	Another Man's Child (p)

1934-1941

Author Bias	Year	Hero	Author	Work
(−)	1934	(broadcaster)	V. Kataev	The Primrose Path (p)
(+) (−)	1935	(free lovers)	B. Levin	Blue Envelopes (s)

1946-1953

Author Bias	Year	Hero	Author	Work
(+)	1947	(peasant's wife)	V. Panova	Kružiliča (n)
(+) (−)	1949	Almazov	V. Panova	Bright Shore (n)
(−)	1950	(husband)	T. Tur-Pyr'ev	The Family Lutonin (p)

C. 'Victims of Forbidden Love'
1917-1929

Author Bias	Year	Hero	Author	Work
(+) (−)	1923	N. Kurbov	I. Èrenburg	The Life and Death of N. Kurbov (n)
(+)	1923	(revolutionary heroine)	A. Kollontaj	The Love of the Worker-bees (s)
(+) (−)	1924	(heroine)	B. Lavrenev	The Forty-first (s)
(+) (−)	1925	(lovers)	N. Ljaško	Blast Furnaces
(+) (−)	1925	(Cheka chief)	A. Sobol'	The Princess (s)
(−)	1926	(communist heroine)	K. Trenev	Ljubov' Jarovaja (p)
(+) (−)	1927	(communist heroes)	P. Romanov	The New Table of Commandments

Author Bias	Year	Hero	Author	Work
(+) (−)	1928	(communist heroes)	G. Alekseev	*Shadows of Tomorrow*
(+) (−)	1928	(proletarian hero, bourgeois wife)	V. Majakovskij	*The Bedbug* (p)
(+) (−)	1928	(rehabilitated bourgeois and ruined proletarian partners)	G. Nikiforov	*At the Lantern* (n)
(+) (−)	1929	(manager)	J. Libedinskij	*Heights* (p)
(+)	1929-30	(mixed couples)	S. Semenov	*Natal'ja Tarpova* (n)

1929-1934

(+)	1930	(old guard bolshevik)	J. Libedinskij	*The Birth of a Hero* (n)
(+) (−)	1931	(proletarian hero)	A. Afinogenov	*Fear* (p)
(+)	1933	Irina	I. Èrenburg	*The Second Day* (n)
(+) (−)	1933	(communist engineer)	V. Il'enkov	*Driving Axle* (n)
(+)	1933	(communist heroine)	B. Levin	*The Young Man* (n)

1934-1941

(+)	1934-37	Kirill	F. Panferov	*Bruski* (n)
(+)	1935	(husband, intellectual's girl friend)	I. Èrenburg	*Without Stopping to Draw Breath* (n)
(+)	1938	(husband)	L. Leonov	*The Wolf* (p)
(+)	1940-43	(lover)	L. Leonov	*An Average Man* (p)

1946-1953

(+) (−)	1947	(wife)	K. Simonov	*The Smoke of the Fatherland* (s)
(+)	1948	(mine director's wife)	A. Kornejčuk	*Makar Dubrava* (p)
(+)	1948	(manager's wife)	A. Sofronov	*The Moscow Character* (p)
(+)	1949	Ol'ga	A. Koptjaeva	*Ivan Ivanovič* (n)
(+)	1950	(komsomolka)	N. Asanov	*The Secretary of the Party Bureau* (n)
(+)	1950	Avdot'ja	G. Nikolaeva	*Harvest* (n)
(+)	1950	(Igor's beloved)	T. Tur-Pyr'ev	*The Family Lutonin* (p)
(+)	1952	(factory manager's wife)	V. Ketlinskaja	*The Days of Our Lives* (n)

While noting a progressive decline in tragic conflict in the course of the last three periods, Van der Eng-Liedmeier distinguishes, in all, the following sub-types:

Moral and Psychological Types

(1) The 'disillusioned idealist' who reacts critically, violently, or even with suicide. This is essentially a twentieth-century, more particularly a

Soviet type, quite unlike the nineteenth-century 'men of hope' who doggedly persist in their idealism or the 'men without hope' who, for the most part, have never been exposed to any serious illusions which might be subject to eventual deflation. First appearing during the NEP period, and protesting its abuses, he is usually the creation of a fellow-traveler and viewed sympathetically, though seldom rehabilitated. In the second period he is seen as 'anachronistic' and is negatively viewed. In the third period he is concerned only with superficial grievances, such as the incompetence or misconduct of individual bureaucrats, and receives satisfaction. In the fourth period he is an altogether infrequent phenomenon.

(2) The 'vacillating intellectual' who, while remaining idealistically loyal, develops sensitivity to frequent contradictions between theory and practice or becomes hesitant out of pity or due to moral reservations, hence disputing the principle that means are justified by their ends. He receives sympathetic treatment in the first period, where he prominently figures in the civil war setting; remains prominent in the second period, where he receives unfavorable depiction by communist writers, while becoming, as a minor character, the frequent advocate of artistic and scientific freedom in the works of sympathetic fellow travelers; is unfavorably regarded and subsequently reformed in the third period; and is mostly ridiculed in the fourth, again in the guise of a protesting artist or scholar.

(3) The 'anarchistic character' who is especially prominent in the first period as a so-called 'instinctive revolutionary', requiring reformation before he is useful to the Soviet cause. Exceptionally complex instances are Šoloxov's Grigorij in the Civil War period and Leonov's Mit'ka during the NEP. In the second period he is the tragic peasant who defies collectivization; in the third he is a completely negative individual without class stigma who is subsequently rehabilitated; he disappears in the fourth.

(4) The generations in conflict — again an occasional phenomenon in works appearing before the middle thirties. Here the older generation is seen as more humane, the younger as more opportunistic.

(5) The 'rare bureaucratic villain' who emerges principally in the fourth period as a social minority and is expertly 're-educated'.

Others have noted that a general 'romantic' approach characterizes the central tragic conflict in Soviet literature before 1934 — that between the individual and the collective — and have alluded to the following additional sub-types:

(a) The ineffectual intellectual (more reminiscent perhaps of the nine-teenth-century 'men of hope').

(b) The envious, narcissistic young man (suggesting Dobroljubov's analysis and bearing an affinity to the theoretician who envies the practical man of action, previously discussed).

(c) The conformist coward who, at a critical moment, fails the social cause.

(d) Leaders who, in devotedly performing their duty, lose rapport with their men or even their kin or who, as 'interim' types, sacrifice their unfulfilled lives for the collective future.

Lovers

(1) The self-denying reluctant lover, a fanatic communist, who in the first two periods either represses his amorous urges or utterly despairs at his lack of self-control; becomes more moderate in the third; then reverts to his former asceticism, though made less severe and more exemplary, in the fourth.

(2) The free lover, whose permissive standards create occasional distress for a jealous spouse in the first period; who becomes disparaged as the source of tragic consequences in the second, is satirized in the third and severely criticized in the fourth.

(3) The victim of 'forbidden love', whose outcome emerges throughout the four periods, increasingly less tragic and more easily redeemable as his partners successively change from counter-revolutionaries to class bourgeoise to bourgeoise by attitude.

OTHER CATEGORIES

In reviewing the themes in Soviet literature up to 1934, Slonim points to a certain 'romantic tendency'[4] in the approach of various fellow-travelers such as Vsevolod Ivanov, Leonov, Oleša, Babel', and, to some degree, Pil'njak, Fedin, Kaverin, and Tynjanov. He concludes that "the fun-damental theme common to these writers is the conflict between individual and collective which the Revolution has made 'tragic' ...".[5] He then adds the view that "Pasternak and Oleša are perhaps the only two Soviet writers who record their own strivings and doubts rather than describe

[4] Slonim, *Soviet Literature: An Anthology*, 36.
[5] *Ibid.*

the manifestations of the outer, actual world"[6] and suggests, in turn, that Leonov is preoccupied with irrationalism and the necessity even of suffering; that both he and Pil'njak tend to renounce 'machine-run civilization',[7] and that Pil'njak, in particular, opposes rural, peasant Russia to "organized Russia of the towns, symbolized by the determined and ruthless bolsheviks".[8]

Although the THEME OF FATHER-SON ALIENATION is relatively less frequent before 1953, Van der Eng-Liedmeier alludes to at least one such occurrence. In I. Kataev's *The Heart*, the hero father's humaneness is "contrasted with the callousness of the more bureaucratic Party members, to whom his son also belongs".[9] Mathewson, however, suggests two additional works which — in describing "the value conflict between an older generation whose humane questing radicalism is shown to be in direct collision with the schematic, shallow opportunism of the new generation"[10] — might loosely fit the same classification: Libedinskij's *The Birth of a Hero* and Èrenburg's *Out of Chaos*. (Such a father-son conflict is, of course, central to Andrej Belyj's remarkable pre-Revolution symbolist novel, *Petersburg* (1911-1913)). ADDITIONAL ALIENATED SUB-TYPES are suggested by the following. All but the first three, be it noted, are at the same time exemplary communists:

Oleša's Ivan Babičev (Envy), a sensitive, scruple-bound, impractical, often ineffectual intellectual.

Oleša's Kavalerov (Envy), a hyper-sensitive, cowardly, envious, self-pitying young man.

Fadeev's Metčika (Nineteen, 1927), who, though ostensibly loyal to communism, proves too cowardly to lose himself in the common cause and in a critical moment sacrifices an entire company of his comrades.

Fadeev's Levinson (Nineteen), a loyal, effective leader who, in the performance of his task, becomes nonetheless socially isolated from his men: "His authority came to depend more and more on the force of his will. ... As the company moves blindly toward annihilation, the final contest begins between Levinson's 'control' over himself and the weakness of his flesh, as his body disintegrates under the nervous and physical strain."[11] Hence Levinson's own revolutionary idealism becomes a deterent to rapport with others. Mathewson notes, incidentally, that

---

[6]   *Ibid.*, 36.
[7]   *Ibid.*, 40.
[8]   *Ibid.*, 41.
[9]   Van der Eng-Liedmeier, 59.
[10]   Mathewson, 280.
[11]   Mathewson, 247.

Levinson is saved from a tragic end by a 'verbal coda' that delivers him "from his lapse into the human" and returns him "to his political matrix".[12]

Šoloxov's Davidov (Virgin Soil Upturned), another dedicated leader who has been so ascetic and self-reliant that he is unaffected by sex and also unable to achieve "communion with the people he has been manipulating".[13]

Gladkov's Čumalov (Cement), whose marital estrangement may in part be attributed to the attention demanded by his public role. "But apparently it is an unimportant consideration", adds Mathewson, "since private matters are lost sight of in the triumphant resolution of the social problem".[14]

Leonov's Kurilov (Road to the Ocean), whose life is so uncompromisingly spent in behalf of the future that he becomes "a discarded means, not an end, whose personal claims on life are forcibly disconnected from the continuum of society's progress, since he is not already to die and his aspirations are not yet realized in society."[15] Mathewson points out that an effort is made to 'muffle'[16] the tragic comment on the life of this 'interim man'[17] by suggesting that his virtuous example will yet live in the noble deeds of another, younger character.

Mathewson restates his arresting argument[18] that, in general, positive heroes are, as such, 'incomplete men'[19] and therefore, even when oblivious to their deficiency, pathetic creatures:

The positive hero, unlike the estranged, 'superfluous', or alienated man of the nineteenth century, is not rejected by, or denied participation in, society. The Soviet hero is promised fulfillment only through his acceptance of the institutions and values of his status quo. In the very act of conformity significant losses are registered.

He is, first of all, entirely politicalized, with his needs and aspirations defined by his political allegiances. Although he is expected to respond with *inner* enthusiasm to grandiose public goals, the real locus of judgement in these matters is outside his own conscience. He makes decisions, so to speak, but no choices. He lives in a world of rationalized deprivations, subsisting on reduced rations of love, friendship, and family happiness because, he is always told, of the terrible urgencies besetting his community. Finally, he is

---

12   *Ibid.*, 252.
13   *Ibid.*, 287.
14   *Ibid.*, 263.
15   *Ibid.*, 304.
16   *Ibid.*
17   *Ibid.*, 305.
18   *Supra*, 32-33.
19   *Ibid.*, 323.

manipulated from above and in turn manipulates those beneath him: he lives in a hierarchy of these relationships.[20]

Boris Pasternak makes an interesting allusion to this same mentality as early as 1918 in his prose fragment, *Without Love,* as personified in the revolutionary, Kovalevskij (*Liberty of Labor*, November 20, 1918).

ASSESSMENT

In common with nineteenth-century alienated protagonists, Soviet heroes until after the period of the First Soviet Five-Year Plan may be said to voice a laudable minority protest against the status quo, yet to end as failures, often by taking their own lives or abandoning themselves to lust or despair — all obvious forms of escape. The continuation of such characters in the Soviet period is, in view of that era's concommitant totalitarian oppression, not surprising, while their disappearance from the thirties through the middle fifties is doubtless attributable, in the main, to the regime's stricter censorship and more thorough control of the arts under Stalin. Their contrast with foils — particularly in the case of 'underground' types — is not always especially favorable. 'Disillusioned idealists', however — a phenomenon peculiar to the earlier Soviet period — provide an especially poignant exception.

Heroes appearing in Soviet literature after the First Five-Year Plan and before 1953 tend to show an increasingly reverse tendency with respect to all of the foregoing features, *i.e.* as members of a minority voicing a laudable protest yet doomed to an unfortunate end. They therefore tend to be correspondingly less alienated, except perhaps in rather superficial ways that are easily corrected. Their writers' sympathies are, likewise, increasingly aligned with the status quo and, accordingly, for or against these same heroes.

The major themes occurring in the works of this period can be conveniently organized under the general heading INDIVIDUALITY AND FREEDOM VS. CONFORMITY AND CONSTRAINT (seen in terms of various conflicts: instinct *vs.* reason, anarchy and criminality *vs.* complicity and submission, rural abandon *vs.* urban constraint, *etc.*). Moreover, the themes of all such works appear to fit at least one of the following subheadings:

(1) UNIVERSAL APPLICATION: rebellion against a tyrannical, irrational, incomprehensible universe.

[0] *Ibid.,* 321.

(2) INTELLECTUAL APPLICATION: protest for artistic and sientific freedom.

(3) EMOTIONAL APPLICATION: alienation in love under various conditions — unrequited love, suppressed love, triangles, forbidden love, *etc.*

(4) REVERSE INTELLECTUAL AND EMOTIONAL APPLICATION: the 'incomplete' positive hero who is emotionally shallow and intellectually deluded or who lacks social rapport.

(5) ETHICAL APPLICATIONS:

(a) Idealistic disillusion.

(b) Integrity and social responsibility *vs.* duplicity and apathy (opposition to social injustice), egalitarianism (the people) *vs.* 'philistinism' (bureaucratic officialdom, *etc.*).

PART TWO

IDENTIFICATION OF THE ALIENATED HERO
IN SOVIET PROSE FICTION OF
THE FIRST 'THAW' DECADE

III

SURVEY AND SELECTION

SOURCES

Of pertinent critical reviews consulted — both articles and monographs treating Soviet literary prose of the decade, 1953-1963[1] — over 100 identify in well over 200 works of prose fictional characters who — by virtue of their critical or anti-social thoughts, victimized condition, or, rebellious action — can be considered socially and/or ideologically alienated. These reviews represent the opinion of some fifty-eight separate critics and are numbered and listed — first alphabetically by author, then by date of publication — in Appendix A.

Both the prestige and range of background of the critics in question are for the most part impressive and reassuring. Brown, Erlich, Friedberg, Gibian, Mathewson, Muchnic, Slonim, Simmons, Struve, Vickery, and Wilson are all recognized American scholar-critics. Alexandrova, Brown, Slonim, and Struve have each authored prominent book-length surveys on Soviet literature, and Muchnic and Simmons have written critical volumes on the same subject. Blake, Hayward, and Whitney have produced notable anthologies pertinent to the period under investigation. Blake and Johnson have covered the Soviet literary scene as correspondents in the USSR. Blum, Burg, Field, and Mihajlov have each studied the local scene as students at Moscow State University — Blum and Field as Americans, Burg as a Soviet citizen, Mihajlov as a native Yugoslavian who was in fact imprisoned[2] for publishing his observations.

---

[1] *I.e.*, those listed in the Library of Congress' Slavic Division's card file for the same decade and also for the following three years, 1963-1966. These works are almost exclusively Western in origin. In view however of the political and propagandistic intent which underlies most literary reportage in Socialist countries, the choice of Western critical materials likely provides a more objective picture with respect to both esthetic matters and 'social' content.

[2] An official if unwitting kind of authentication.

With typical German thoroughness, Bode has painstakingly followed post-War Soviet literary developments in the scholarly *Osteuropa*, printed in Stuttgart. Alexandrova has assiduously covered the Soviet literary scene in the anti-Soviet though liberally oriented Russian-speaking New York monthly, *Socialističeskij vestnik*, while Gaev and Mehnert have written knowledgeably and extensively for the equally slanted though conservative Radio Liberty Committee and Institute for the Study of the USSR, with offices in New York City and Munich. Other critics have comparable qualifications.

WORKS SURVEYED

In all, these critics cite some 213 works of prose fiction whose stories concern alienated protagonists. These works are listed in Appendix B, where the numbers which follow each title (except the number in parentheses) correspond with those assigned to the critical reviews enumerated in Appendix A and indicate which critical reviews treat which title. Where a given title is mentioned in more than one review by the same critic, only the first such review is indicated. The final number (in parentheses) indicates the total number of critics who refer to the title in question. Works are listed alphabetically by author, then by title. Dates and sources of publication are provided where mentioned in the corresponding reviews.

WORKS SELECTED

Since the forementioned 213 titles present too unwieldy a corpus for detailed analysis, the sample investigated restricts itself to those titles most frequently discussed in the critical reviews. Their recurrent mention insures that these titles (1) constitute, from a purely literary standpoint, the best works on the subject and (2) survey the most significant kinds of alienation appearing in the prose of the period in question.

In all, some thirty titles, representing the prose of twenty-four separate authors, are mentioned by FIVE OR MORE separate critics. Since thirty titles appear to constitute an adequately large yet sufficiently restricted number, mention by at least five critics has therefore been selected as criterion for the sample. Discussion by at least this many critics should also insure that all works in the sample display a more general and less exceptional appeal and significance. (Only an additional eight titles, be it noted, are mentioned by just four critics, and only an additional twenty-two by three.)

Despite the breadth and qualifications of the many critics consulted, a number of extraneous factors may well have influenced the greater attention which particular works are given: (1) the political sensation which accompanied the appearance of certain works, *e.g. The Thaw, Not by Bread Alone,* and for that matter all the works smuggled to the West and published abroad; (2) the co-occurrence of five of the works selected in a single volume, *Literaturnaja Moskva II,* which quickly became controversial and was subsequently banned; (3) the probability that more critics had greater opportunity to discuss those works which appeared first; (4) the caprice of Western journalism and the peculiar interests of its readership. Though these factors have doubtless tended to distort the final sample, it is difficult, if not impossible, to determine to what degree. In the absence of more certain criteria, therefore, those heretofore discussed are probably the best available.

The thirty works which constitute the consequent sample are listed below in order of publication, together with the following: (a) year of publication, (b) genre, and (c) number of critics surveyed who discussed each title:

TABLE 5

Sample Titles

Author	Title	Year	Genre	No. Critics
Panova, V.	*Seasons of the Year* (*Vremena goda*)	1953	novel	9
Zorin, L.	*Guests* (*Gosti*)	1954	play	12
Èrenburg, I.	*The Thaw* (*Ottepel'*)	1954	novelette	14
Kornejčuk, A.	*Wings* (*Kryl'ja*)	1954	play	6
Granin, D.	*One's Own Opinion* (*Sobstvennoe mnenie*)	1956	story	11
Dudincev, V.	*Not by Bread Alone* (*Ne xlebom edinym*)	1956	novel	20
Nilin, P.	*Cruelty* (*Žestokost'*)	1956	novelette	5
Jašin, A.	*Levers* (*Ryčagi*)	1956	story	11

Author	Title	Year	Genre	No. Critics
Kaverin, V.	Quests and Hopes (Poiski i nadeždy)	1956	novel	9
Nagibin, Ju.	Light in the Window (Svet v okne)	1956	story	5
Pogodin, N.	Petrarch's Sonnet (Sonet Petrarki)	1956	play	6
Ždanov, N.	Journey Home (Poezdka na rodinu)	1956	story	7
Pasternak, B.	Doctor Živago (Doktor Živago)	1957	novel	10
Kuznecov, A.	Continuation of a Legend (Prodolženie legendy)	1957	novelette	5
Kazakov, Ju.	The Renegade (Otščepenec)	1959	story	9
Terc, A.	The Trial Begins (Sud idet)	1959	story	9
Tendrjakov, V.	Three, Seven, Ace (Trojka, semerka, tuz)	1960	novelette	8
Aksenov, V.	Colleagues (Kollegi)	1960	novelette	6
Tendrjakov, V.	The Trial (Sud)	1961	novelette	6
Aksenov, V.	Ticket to the Stars (Zvezdnyj bilet)	1961	novel	13
Nekrasov, V.	Kira Georgievna (Kira Georgievna)	1961	novelette	10
Rozov, V.	ABCDE (ABVGD)	1961	'lit. film scenario'	5
Bondarev, Ju.	Silence (Tišina)	1962	novel	10
Tendrjakov, V.	Short Circuit (Korotkoe zamykanie)	1962	novelette	5
Kazakov, Ju.	Adam and Eve (Adam i Eva)	1962	story	5
Solženicyn, A.	One Day in the Life of Ivan Denisovič (Odin den' Ivana Denisoviča)	1962	novelette	21
Tarsis, V.	Tale of a Bluebottle Fly (Povest' o sinej muxe)	1962	novelette	6
Aržak, N.	This is Moscow Speaking (Govorit Moskva)	1962	novelette	5
Solženicyn, A.	Matrena's Home (Matrenin dvor)	1963	story	10
Solženicyn, A.	For the Good of the Cause (Dlja pol'zy dela)	1963	story	9

The foregoing thirty works include six novels, eleven novelettes or tales (*povesti*), nine short stories, three plays, and one 'literary film scenario'. Works by Aržak, Pasternak, Tarsis, and Terc have been published and distributed abroad but are as yet generally unavailable in the Soviet Union. The sample thus takes into account both officially recognized works and so-called 'underground' literature.

PLOT SUMMATIONS

The alienated protagonist (protagonists) in each of the foregoing will next be identified in terms of his (their) respective plot function(s). All plot actions occurring in these works which in turn reveal character alienation are synopsized in Appendix C and listed in the following table. In each listing, the alienated character(s) in question is (are) named in connection with the particular object of his (their) alienation. Numbers in parentheses accompanying each listing, and reappearing with the synopsis headings in Appendix C, correspond to those assigned to various thematic categories in Chapter IV. (See Table 8, p. 109.)

TABLE 6

Conflicts Showing Character Alienation

Character	Object of alienation
V. Panova, *Seasons of the Year*	
Gennadij Kuprijanov:	Sense of fulfillment through work (2).
Gennadij Kuprijanov:	Trust and approval of society and employers, trustworthy friends and associates (4, 10).
Gennadij Kuprijanov:	Members of Gennadij's family (4, 5).
Dorofea Kuprijanova:	Her son, Gennadij (5).
Larisa Kuprijanova:	Her husband, Gennadij (4).
Zinaida Ljubimova:	Her lover, Gennadij (4).
Saša Ljubimov:	His mother, Zinaida (5).
Bortaševič:	Integrity, conscience, social responsibility, self-respect (10).
Bortaševič:	Support of friends (4).
Bortaševič:	His wife, Nadežda (4).
Sergej Bortaševič:	Respect for his father (5).
Nadežda Bortaševič:	Her children (5).
Čurkin:	Integrity, responsibility to society and friends (10).
Sergej Bortaševič:	Success in love (4).
Saša Ljubimov:	Katja Bortaševič (4).
L. Zorin, *Guests*	
Pokrovskij:	Petr Kirpičev, the bureaucracy (8).
Petr Kirpičev:	Social justice (10).

Character	Object of alienation
Elder Kirpičevs and their daughter, Varvara:	Their son and brother, Petr (4, 5).
Nina Kirpičeva:	Her husband, Petr (4).
Sergej Kirpičev:	His father, Petr (5).
Petr Kirpičev:	His father, Aleksej (5).
Tema Kirpičev:	His girlfriend, Nika (4).

I. Èrenburg, *The Thaw*

Dmitrij Koroteev:	Truth, integrity (10).
Dmitrij Koroteev:	Emotional self-confidence, trust in others (4).
Lena Žuravleva:	Her husband, Ivan (4).
Lena Žuravleva:	Emotional integrity (4, 10).
Lena Žuravleva:	Mother, Antonina Pavlovna Kalašnikova (5).
Lena Žuravleva:	Ekaterina Alekseeva Dmitrieva (8).
Ivan Žuravlev:	Unpleasant reality, genuine emotional values (6).
Andrej Puxov:	His son, Volodja, and daughter, Sonja (5).
Volodja Puxov:	Artistic integrity (3, 10).
Tanečka:	Self-confidence, sense of purpose, artistic success (3, 4).
Sonja Puxova:	Emotional integrity (4, 10).
Grigorij Savčenko:	Sonja Puxova (4).
Vera Grigor'evna Šerer:	Others' 'good will' (4).
Vera Grigor'evna Šerer:	Emotional integrity (4, 10).
Evgenij Sokolovskij:	Vera (4).
Evgenij Sokolovskij:	Žuravlev, the bureaucracy (8).
Evgenij Sokolovskij:	His daughter, Maša; Western culture (2, 5).
Trifonov:	Free thought, toleration (6).

A. Kornejčuk, *Wings*

Petr Aleksandrovič Romodan:	Dremljuga, the bureaucracy (8).
Dremljuga and other bureaucrats:	Social justice, service, confidence in others, the people (8,9).
Dremljuga and other bureaucrats:	Unpleasant reality (6).
People:	The bureaucracy (9).
People:	Truth, integrity, self-respect (10).
Petr Aleksandrovič Romodan:	His wife, Anna, and daughter, Lida (4, 5).
Anna Andreevna Romodan:	Her husband, Romodan (4).
Lida Romodan:	Love (4).
Katerina Stepanovna Remez:	Love (4).

D. Granin, *One's Own Opinion*

Ol'xovskij:	His supervisor, Minaev (3).
Minaev:	His subordinate, Engineer Ol'xovskij (4).
Minaev:	Ethical responsibility (10).
Minaev and assistant:	Intellectual integrity, courage, self-respect (6, 10).

Character	Object of alienation

V. Dudincev, *Not by Bread Alone*

Lopatkin:	Drozdov, the bureaucracy (8).
Lopatkin:	Intellectual conformity (3).
People:	Affluent bureaucrats (9).
Leonid Ivanovič Drozdov:	Other people (6).
Scientists:	Truth, integrity (6).
Lopatkin:	Nadja's love (4).
Lopatkin:	Žanna (4).
Nadežda (Nadja) Sergeevna Drozdova:	Her husband, Drozdov (4).
Nadežda (Nadja) Sergeevna Drozdova:	Love for Lopatkin (4).
Žanna Ganičeva:	Lopatkin (4).
Valentina Pavlovna:	Love for Lopatkin (4).

P. Nilin, *Cruelty*

Venjamin (Ven'ka) Mališev:	Others' inhumanity, injustice, utilitarian morality (7, 10).
Venjamin (Ven'ka) Mališev:	Love of Julja Mal'ceva (4).
Uzelkov and communist officials:	Others' private lives, loyalty to truth (6).

A. Jašin, *Levers*

People:	Bureaucracy, voice in government, social justice (8, 9).
Citizens:	Integrity, social responsibility (10).
Citizens:	Mutual trust, freedom of thought (3, 4).
Bureaucrats:	Unpleasant reality, sense of dedication to and rapport with others (6).

V. Kaverin, *Quests and Hopes*

Tat'jana Petrovna Vlasenkova:	Kramov, the bureaucracy (8).
Andrej Vlasenkov:	Social justice, the bureaucracy, others' good will (4, 8).
Tat'jana Petrovna Vlasenkova:	Her husband, Andrej (4).
Tat'jana Petrovna Vlasenkova:	Integrity toward her son, Pavlik (5, 10).
Elizaveta Gordeeva:	Mitja Vlasenkov (4).
Glafira Kramova:	Her second husband, Kramov; free existence; acknowledgment of truth (4, 10).
Kramov and scientific bureaucrats:	Integrity (6, 10).

Ju. Nagibin, *Light in the Window*

Vasilij Petrovič:	Fellow citizens (10, 9).
Vasilij Petrovič:	Nastja, idolatry of leaders (4, 7).
Nastja and Stepan:	Idolatry of leaders (7).

Character	Object of alienation

N. Pogodin, *Petrarch's Sonnet*

Dmitrij Alekseevič Suxodolov:	Conventional impersonality, insensitivity, conformity (1).
Dmitrij Alekseevič Suxodolov:	His wife, Ksenija Petrovna (4).
Dmitrij Alekseevič Suxodolov:	Loyalty of friend, Armando and colleague, Dononov (4).
Ksenija Petrovna:	Her husband, Suxodolov (4).
Armando:	Personal ethics, Suxodolov's friendship, achievement (4, 10).
Maja:	Loyalty of friend, Klara (4).
Klara and Dononov:	Personal ethics, free thought, humanitarian values (6).

N. Ždanov, *Journey Home*

Pavel Alekseevič Varygin:	Unpleasant reality, the people (6, 9).
Pavel Alekseevič Varygin:	Devotion to his mother (10, 5).

B. Pasternak, *Doctor Živago*

Jurij Andreevič Živago:	Sense of purpose and self-determination, political power, the regime, political in- humanity, regimentation (1, 2, 8).
Jurij Andreevič Živago:	Ties of friendship (4).
Jurij Andreevič Živago:	Family ties (4).
Tonja Živago:	Her husband Jurij's love (4).
Paša Antipov:	Social injustice (8, 9).
Paša Antipov:	Human values, human life (6).
Lara Gišar (later Antipova):	Komarovskij (4).
Paša Antipov:	Lara's love (4).

A. Kuznecov, *Continuation of a Legend*

Tolja:	Sense of purpose, self-understanding (2).
Tolja:	Injustice (8).
Tolja:	Self-sacrifice (10).
Tolja:	His mother (5).

Ju. Kasakov, *The Renegade*

Egor:	Reality, the external world (1).
Egor:	Responsibility, conscientiousness, ambition, sense of duty (10).
Egor and Alen'ka:	Traditional mundane, sensible, unfeeling existence (1).

Character	Object of alienation

A. Terc, *The Trial Begins*

Karlinskij:
Regimentation, impersonality, de-humanization, extinction, insignificance, personal satisfactions (1, 2, 4).

Vladimir Petrovič Globov and colleagues:
Truth; humanitarian values; concern for son, Sereža (6, 5).

Vladimir Petrovič Globov:
His wife, Marina; progeny (4).

Marina Globova:
Everything and everybody but herself, non-carnal values (6).

Sereža Globov and Katja:
Soviet ideology, the regime, the older generation (7, 5).

People:
Established values, freedom (7).

Rabinovič:
Christianity (6).

V. Tendrjakov, *Three, Seven, Ace*

Nikolaj Petrovič Bušuev:
Scruples, fellow men (4, 6).

Aleksandr (Saša) Dubinin:
His men's loyalty, justice (4, 8).

Lumberjacks:
Courage (10).

Leška Malinkin:
Courage, conscience, integrity, illusions, loyalty (7, 10).

V. Aksenov, *Colleagues*

Aleksej (Leksej) Maksimov:
Mundane life, the uneventful future, socialist self-sacrifice (2, 7, 10).

Aleksej (Leksej) Maksimov:
Swindlers, hypocritical self-seekers (8).

Aleksandr (Saša) Dmitrevič:
Fedor Bugrov (4).

Aleksandr (Saša) Dmitrevič:
His eventual wife, Ina (4).

Daša Gurianova:
Saša's love (4).

Fedor Bugrov:
Sense of purpose and accomplishment (2).

Vladislav (Vladka) Karpov:
Vera Velesina (4).

Vera Velesina:
Leksej's love (4).

The generations:
One another (5).

V. Tendrjakov, *The Trial*

Semen Teterin:
Truth, integrity, courage, loyalty, conscience, self-respect (10).

Semen Teterin:
Encroaching civilization, Dudyrev (9).

Vasilij Maksimovič Mitjagin:
Teterin's loyalty (4).

Konstantin Sergeevič Dudyrev:
Privilege, personal advantage, pragmatic officials (8,10).

Konstantin Sergeevič Dudyrev:
Faith in Teterin and the people (7).

V. Aksenov, *Ticket to the Stars*

Dimka Denisov:
Tradition, conformity, responsibility, vocation (1, 10).

Character	Object of alienation
Parents and Viktor Denisov:	Dimka, the younger generation (5).
Galja Bodorova:	Realistic life role (10).
Dimka Denisov:	Galja Bodorova (4).
Viktor Denisov:	Compromise, materialism, self-seeking (3, 10).

V. Nekrasov, *Kira Georgievna*

Vadim (Dimka) Kudrjavcev:	His wife, Kira Georgievna (4).
Vadim (Dimka) Kudrjavcev:	Artistic conformity (3).
Kira Georgievna:	Her first husband, Dimka (4).
Nikolaj Ivanovič Obolenskij:	His wife, Kira Georgievna (4).
Kira Georgievna:	Ethical values, conscience (10).
Juročka:	Kira Georgievna, Nikolaj Ivanovič (4, 5).
Nikolaj Ivanovič and Kira Georgievna:	Truth, artistic excellence, personal satisfaction (3, 6, 10).

V. Rozov, *ABCDE*

Volodja:	Parents; his uncle, Vasilij (5).
Volodja:	Society; his cousin, Sima (8, 4).
Volodja:	Sense of purpose, vocation (2, 10).
Volodja:	Conformity, compromise, dogmatism, world conditions (7, 2, 10).
Sima:	Her cousin, Volodja (4).

Ju. Bondarev, *Silence*

Sergej and Nikolaj Voxmincev:	Social injustice, Uvarov, Bykov, slanderers (8).
Sergej Voxmincev:	Aftermath of World War II and Stalinism, sense of purpose, vocation (2).
Sergej Voxmincev:	Nina's love (4).
Nikolaj Grigor'evič Voxmincev:	His son, Sergej (5).
Konstantin Korobel'nikov:	Integrity, industry (10).
Konstantin Korobel'nikov:	Assja's love (4).
Painter, Fedor Mukomolov and poet, Xomin:	Critical toleration, artistic freedom (3).
Uvarov:	Principles, integrity (6).

V. Tendrjakov, *Short Circuit*

Vasilij Vasil'evič Stoljarskij and other subordinates (Boris Evgen'evič Šackix):	Ivan Sokovin, confidence, initiative, self-fulfillment (4),
Vadim Sokovin:	His father, Ivan; impersonality, pragmatism (5, 10).
Ivan Kapitonovič Sokovin:	Human values (6).
Automobile-owning couple:	People (6, 10).

Character	Object of alienation

Ju. Kazakov, *Adam and Eve*

Ageev:	Vika, other people (4).
Ageev:	Criticism, artistic freedom (3).
Ageev:	Mediocrity, compromise, mundane existence (10).

A. Solženicyn, *One Day in the Life of Ivan Denisovič*

Prisoners:	Inhumanity, injustice (8).
Ivan Denisovič Šuxov and fellow prisoners:	Loyalty to the system, absolute integrity (7, 10).
Ivan Denisovič Šuxov and fellow prisoners:	Spontaneous self-gratification, contemplation of the future.
Fetjukov and others:	Caution, fellow-feeling, restraint (10).

V. Tarsis, *Tale of a Bluebottle Fly*

Ioann Sinemuxov and Rozalija Zags:	Rational self-discipline, socialist discipline, theories, collectivist idealism (3).
Ioann Sinemuxov:	Orthodox colleagues, conformity, officials, bureaucracy, wife and son (4, 5, 8).
Ioann Sinemuxov:	Satisfaction in love (4).
Afanasij Zags:	Truth, his wife Rozalija's fidelity, involvement (4, 6).

N. Aržak, *This Is Moscow Speaking*

Anatolij (Tolja) Nikolaevič Karcev:	Official ideology (7).
Anatolij (Tolja) Nikolaevič Karcev:	People's duplicity, mutual fear, mistrust (10).
People:	Duplicity, mutual fear, mistrust (4).
Anatolij (Tolja) Nikolaevič Karcev:	Peoples' gullibility, inhumanity, lack of values (10).
People:	Gullibility, inhumanity, lack of values (6).
Artist, Saša Čuprov, and poet, Arbatov:	Conventional Soviet art, absence of genuine realism or artistic freedom (3).

A. Solženicyn, *Matrena's Home*

Matrena Vasil'evna Grigor'eva:	Bureaucratic indifference, social injustice (8).
Matrena Vasil'evna Grigor'eva:	Compassion of relatives and neighbors (2, 4).
Matrena Vasil'evna Grigor'eva and Narrator:	Materialism, personal satisfaction (10).
Matrena's neighbors:	Fellow-feeling (6).

Character	Object of alienation

A. Solženicyn, *For the Good of the Cause*

Teachers and students, Fedor Mixeevič, Ivan Gračikov:	The bureaucracy (8).
Bureaucrats:	Integrity (6).
Students:	Contemporary Soviet literature (3).

AFTERMATH

Analyses follow in the ensuing chapters with respect to:

(1) recurring themes pertaining to alienation;

(2) authors' biases;

(3) political and historical events affecting literary developments during the 'Thaw';
and

(4) comparison with similar types in earlier Russian literature (as discussed in Chapters I and II).

IV

SOURCES OF THE HERO'S ALIENATION: RECURRING
ARENAS OF CONFLICT AND UNDERLYING THEMES

CRITICAL ESTIMATES

The themes listed in Table 6, Chapter III, can generally be classified according to a number of broad categories. It was seen in Chapter II that the heading, INDIVIDUALITY VS. COLLECTIVITY, aptly defines the principal tragic conflict in works of the early Soviet period. Its obvious applicability to the predominant social protest of nineteenth-century alienated figures further recommends a similar labeling, where appropriate, of themes appearing in 'Thaw' works. The extent, in fact, to which various critics cited in Appendix A discuss 'Thaw' themes in terms of the subheadings listed in Chapter II[1] is evidenced in the following. Numbers in parentheses are those assigned to the various critical reviews in Appendix A:

INDIVIDUALITY AND FREEDOM VS. CONFORMITY AND CONSTRAINT. — Although all the works analyzed subscribe, technically, to the foregoing general heading — critics make particular reference to the following eight works, said overtly to espouse individuality and personal freedom:

Thaw (24)
Bread (39, 48, 70, 71)
Živago (55, 83, 107)
Renegade (9, 35)
Colleagues (4)
ABCDE (48)
Adam (35)
Bluebottle (50)

In addition, various critics make general reference to the same thematic tendency in the literature of the period, as such:

---

[1] *Supra*, 75-76.

Individualistic impulses, a rediscovery of such private, long forbidden themes as love and even death and uncertainty characterized this new literature.[2]

Several authors are now active who concentrate on the simple events of emotional life, paying no attention to politics, social questions, or the macrocosm of industry and agriculture. Private life has reclaimed part of the ground it lost under Stalin.[3]

One day it will perhaps be shown that not only Russia, but the whole world, is indebted to Soviet literature for keeping alive, in unimaginable conditions, that indefinable sense of freedom which is common to all men.[4]

Corollary to this theme is that which protests totalitarianism, particularly under Stalin. Some twelve works are mentioned in this context, as follows:

> *Thaw* (61, 73, 105)
> *Wings* (61, 73, 105)
> *Bread* (93)
> *Levers* (42)
> *Quests* (71)
> *Light* (106)
> *Trial Begins* (91, 94)
> *Colleagues* (26)
> *Kira* (5, 27, 77, 78, 93)
> *Silence* (77, 81, 93, 98)
> *One Day* (5, 17, 64, 77, 78, 87)
> *Bluebottle* (35, 93).

Both Friedberg (42) and Slavinsky (92) have observed that the earlier works treating this theme deal only with the pre-World War II Stalinist purges and emphasize those victims who are either intellectuals or Party members.

Rubin even notes the rise of an idealized anti-Stalin genre in which "the virtues of Stalin's victims are portrayed with a disconcerting extravagance", which amounts to "not a martyrology of Stalin's victims ... but a hagiography".[5] He makes particular reference to Georgij Šelest's *The Nugget* (*Izvestija*, November 6, 1962) and V. Gerasimova's *Pleasant Memory* (*Pravda*, November 11, 1962). Later and continuing manifesta-

---

[2] Heinz Kersten, "Die Sowjetische 'Tauwetter-Literatur'", *Politische Meinung*, IV (January, 1959), 84.
[3] George Gibian, "New Trends in the Novel: Kazakov, Nagabin, Voronin", *Soviet Survey*, No. 36 (April-June, 1961), 49.
[4] Max Hayward, "Introduction", *Dissonant Voices in Soviet Literature* (ed.) Patricia Blake and Max Hayward (New York, Pantheon Books, 1962), vii-xlii.
[5] Burton Rubin, "The Shock of Recognition", *Survey*, No. 47 (April, 1963), 163.

tions of Stalinism are treated, however, by works such as Bondarev's *Silence* and those which appear subsequent to it. Bode observes, further-more, that the anti-Stalinist polemic yet persists in works occurring after the period under investigation, as, for instance, in the sequel to *Silence*, *The Couple* (*Novyj mir*, December, 1964).[6]

UNIVERSAL REBELLION. — Certain writers indeed view Stalinism as less extraordinary and episodic than symptomatic of a general and continuing state of affairs. Their heroes are alienated from and tend to rebel against what is, for them, a kind of tyrannical universe. Friedberg therefore describes "the collective picture of Soviet Russia emerging from these works" as "a frightening one, not too different from that described by the poet Lermontov more than a century earlier — 'the land of slaves and the land of masters, the land of blue uniforms and the obedient people'".[7] Gibian speaks of the concern of writers such as Dudincev and Granin about "what is happening to the individual man while the ostensibly humanitarian projects are going on",[8] and Whitney in turn alludes to the "depths of murk, hopelessness, and evil"[9] which are encountered by the characters, for instance, of Kazakov.

A further cause of universal dissatisfaction is the state of world affairs and the ever present possibility of nuclear annihilation. The need for better understanding between twentieth-century peoples — so eloquently stated in the September, 1960, installment of Èrenburg's autobiography (*People, Year's, Life*) and A. Kron's essay, *On Land and Sea*, which appeared in the same issue of *Novyj mir* — finds particularly poignant expression in the sentiments of Rozov's young hero, Volodja (*ABCDE*).

In all, the depiction of universal distress and/or rebellion is said to occur in the following fourteen works:

> *Bread* (71)
> *Levers* (66, 97, 105)
> *Quests* (26)
> *Živago* (55, 58, 75, 78, 105, 107)
> *Trial Begins* (25, 35)
> *Three, Seven, Ace* (53)

[6]   Barbara Bode, "Sowjetliteratur 1964", *Osteuropa*, XVI (January, 1966), 30.
[7]   Maurice Friedberg, "The Background of the Third Congress of the Union of Soviet Writers", *Bulletin of the Institute for the Study of the USSR*, V (December, 1958), 38.
[8]   George Gibian, *Interval of Freedom: Soviet Literature during the Thaw 1954-1957* (Mineapolis, University of Minnesota Press, 1960), 72.
[9]   Thomas P. Whitney, *The New Writing in Russia* (Ann Arbor, University of Michigan Press, 1964), 98.

ABCDE (16)
Short Circuit (16, 93)
Adam (77)
One Day (35, 63, 103)
Bluebottle (99)
Moscow (34)
Matrena (48)
For the Good (23, 29, 109).

PROTEST FOR ARTISTIC AND SCIENTIFIC FREEDOM, FREEDOM OF THOUGHT.
— Gibian observes that Soviet writers, such as Dudincev, use 'the creative
scientist' to voice 'the return to inner values':[10]

Scientists are regarded in Russian novels as men apart from others only so
far as they are more creative and capable of contributing more. ... The higher
officials ... in an almost Dostoevskian sense ... may now be said to be working
for the other side, as if they were former servants of Christ now serving the
Antichrist. But the scientist, while regarded as a benefactor of mankind, is
not viewed as if he were garbed in the vestments of a priesthood; he is a ration-
alist humanitarian and humanist.[11]

Others, such as Kazakov, are seen to use the figure of a creative artist
— a painter or musician — to assert a similar demand for creative freedom.[12]

In whatever guise, says Pipes, such heroes are asserting

the right to surrender to one's impressions without being compelled for some
extraneous reason to interpret and distort them. ... Just as the concept of
'truth' ... signifies the assertion of the individual's right to unhindered perception of reality, so 'personalism' signifies a right to react to this reality in complete emotional freedom. Together, the two concepts represent a natural
reaction to the fantastic presumptions of totalitarianism toward the individual.[13]

Works which receive critical mention in the foregoing contexts include
the following four which register scientists' protests:

Opinion (55, 71)
Bread (5, 24, 55, 61, 71, 81, 100)
Quests (54, 66)
Ticket (16)

[10]   Gibian, *Interval of Freedom*, 72.
[11]   *Ibid.*, 69-70.
[12]   Rufus Mathewson, "The Novel in Russia and the West", *Soviet Literature in the
Sixties* (ed.) Max Hayward and Edward L. Crowley (New York, Frederick A. Praeger,
1964), 14.
[13]   Richard Pipes, "Russia's Exigent Intellectuals. A Eulogy and Warning", *Encounter*,
XXII (January, 1964), 84.

and the following six the rebellion of artists:

Thaw (24, 26, 42, 55, 58, 93, 96, 97)
Živago (24, 55, 75)
Kira (15, 17, 26)
Silence (81)
Adam (106)
One Day (18, 86)

Reference is also made to the discussion in the last-mentioned work of Ėjzenštejn's film, *Ivan the Terrible*, and its ensuing esthetic controversy — a discussion, says Bode, which touches upon "the chief problems of contemporary Russian art".[14] Zekulin adds that *For the Good of the Cause* — like still another of Solženicyn's works, mentioned less frequently by critics, hence not included in the sample, *Incident at Krečetovka Station* (*Novyj mir*, January, 1963) — deals with a corollary theme: "the role of members of the Russian intelligentsia in changing the conditions of life".[15] In a sense, the striving of youth for truthful answers and personal authenticity in turn relates to the intellectual protest of scientists, artists, and members of the educated class. Works observed to treat the theme of "young people in search of meaning"[16] include:

Colleagues (8)
Ticket (8, 24)
ABCDE (26).

ALIENATION IN LOVE AND FRIENDSHIP. — Gibian alludes to an equally significant sphere of personal disaffection when he says that "love is a frequent subject of those Soviet writers who have turned their attention to the private life of individuals".[17] As Slonim observes, "Family life marriage and divorce, the deceptions and joys of love ceased to hover ashamedly in the background of Soviet fiction; they came boldly to the fore and were treated as extensively as ... professional activities. ... Personal problems, emotional conflicts, erotic troubles now took priority in numerous works."[18] The following ten works are noted as treating such love-related conflicts or difficulties as well as striking instances of

[14] Barbara Bode, "Über Ästhetik, Ethik und ähnliche Nutzlosigkeiten", *Osteuropa*, XII (September, 1963), 637.
[15] Gleb Zekulin, "Solzhenicyn's Four Stories", *Soviet Studies*, XVI (July, 1964), 58.
[16] Ralph Blum, "A Reporter at Large. Freeze and Thaw: The Artist in Russia", *The New Yorker*, XLI (September 4, 1965), 76.
[17] Gibian, *Soviet Survey*, 51.
[18] Marc Slonim, *Soviet Russian Literature: Writers and Problems* (New York, Oxford University Press, 1964), 306.

abnormally strained rapport and emotional disaffection between otherwise amiable friends and acquaintances:

> *Thaw* (5, 24, 39, 93, 105)
> *Bread* (39, 55)
> *Levers* (66, 71, 97)
> *Sonnet* (26, 55, 66)
> *Živago* (55, 107)
> *Renegade* (5, 58, 72)
> *Kira* (24)
> *Short Circuit* (16)
> *Adam* (58, 72)
> *For the Good* (68, 109).

CONFLICT BETWEEN GENERATIONS. — As the synopses in Appendix III
reveal, alienation in love is often the consequence of an ideological or
ethical conflict belonging to one or another broad category such as those
yet to be discussed. Folejewski argues, for instance, that "Drozdov is
not a villain; he has his ideals, he fights for them, he works hard, he
seems, in the past at least, to have cherished values higher than mere
wealth and position. Indirectly one can surmise that what went wrong
with him in Nadja's eyes may have been the working of the entire
machinery of which he is a part."[19] Similarly, conflicts between representatives of the older and younger generations are often indicative of
other varieties of alienation.

As a theme of its own, however, the conflict between 'fathers' and 'sons'
is frequently alluded to by the critics. Bode calls it "the principal theme
of the literature treating social events (*publizistische Belletristik*)",
noting that "more than half of the more significant works of the year
1959 are dedicated to it",[20] while in 1962 Alexandrova lists "the traditional problem of 'fathers and sons'" together with "the problem of
private lives" as "the predominating themes in Soviet literature of the
past few years".[21]

Generally, it is a more idealistic youth who rebels against the apathy
or compromise of elders who capitulated under Stalinism. As Marin
explains, "It has become impossible to control or satisfy youth with the
old stereotyped formulae of Communist theory, for youth has turned

[19]   Zbigniew Folejewski, "Notes on the Problem of Individual vs. Collective in
Russian and Polish Literature, 1954-1957", *Indiana Slavic Studies*, III (1963), 31.
[20]   Barbara Bode, "Sowjetliteratur 1959", *Osteuropa*, IX (December, 1959), 813.
[21]   Vera Alexandrova, "Youth and Life in New Soviet Literature", *Studies on the
Soviet Union*, new series, II (March, 1961), 157.

from an 'object' of indoctrination by Party and Komsomol into a thinking 'subject' insisting on the right to determine its own fate, to think freely, and to influence life and politics in its country."[22]

Dramatically illustrative of the consequent incommunicability between the generations is the often mentioned Soviet film, *The Gates of Il'ič*, in which a youth encounters the ghost of his fallen soldier father. The latter can give him no satisfactory answers because, having remained at the age at which he died, he is now in fact younger than his son.

Of the works analyzed, the following nine are observed to involve such an impasse between the generations — mostly, though not invariably, between parents and their own children:

> *Seasons* (5, 73, 93, 100)
> *Guests* (5, 24, 70, 73, 100, 105)
> *Thaw* (73, 100)
> *Quests* (42, 66)
> *Colleagues* (3)
> *Ticket* (26, 93)
> *Kira* (27)
> *ABCDE* (16, 41)
> *Short Circuit* (16).

'INCOMPLETE' POSITIVE HEROES. — Unlike those who assert the self, protest inequity, champion intellectual inquiry, or at least consciously suffer from personal estrangement are those who — often themselves aggravating if not causing alienation in others — are nonetheless content with the injustice or compromise they help perpetuate. These are the 'Drozdovs' — the often "ordinary, decent people who have come to terms with Soviet society by suppressing the promptings of conscience and common sense".[23] "They have no pity for others or for themselves", says Gibian, with particular reference to Zhuravlev (*Thaw*), Drozdov (*Bread*), and Valgan (G. Nikolaeva's "Battle on the Way", *Oktjabr'*, March, May, July, 1957): "Their hearts are as calloused as their hands. From their singleminded eagerness to succeed as industrial tycoons follows a string of vices and abuses, culminating in serious crimes. The energy of these men makes bullies out of them. ... All three are inhuman, robot-like, monstrous."[24]

[22] Yury V. Marin, "A Reassessment of Values in Soviet Society", *Analysis of Current Developments in the Soviet Union*, No. 259 (February 5, 1963), 6.
[23] Tom Scriven, "The 'Literary Opposition'", *Problems of Communism*, VII (January-February, 1958), 29.
[24] Gibian, *Interval of Freedom*, 127.

Such a protagonist, Scriven continues, though "alien to the people and unresponsive to their needs ... is himself a victim of the system, and unable to change his ways".[25] His alienation is due, in a sense, to his own self-imposed limitations. His disavowal of truth, his callous indifference to others, his ethical insensitivity truly estrange him from other people as well as from the intellectual and emotional values for which other alienated types even forfeit their status and well-being. That he is often complacent, self-satisfied, and oblivious to his loss cannot change the fact that he is estranged, nonetheless. Gibian paraphrases Nikolaeva's own astute analysis of this type, as follows: "They ascribe to others their own thirst for power; paranoically, they see rivals and enemies in everybody. ... They detest cordiality, openness, human closeness. Thus they are afraid of others and react by trying to manipulate them through terror."[26]

Such characters have been noted in the following eleven works:

Thaw (55)
Wings (55)
Opinion (24, 55, 77, 93)
Bread (5, 55, 58, 89, 105)
Levers (24, 55, 66, 93, 105)
Quests (89)
Journey (24, 55, 90)
Živago (55, 61)
Kira (27)
Short Circuit (78)
For the Good (68).

IDEALISTIC DISILLUSION. — The foregoing character type, who is essentially negative and becomes alienated by personal default, in turn suggests several additional categories of themes whose orientation is less private and more social, hence also ethical. In relation to these themes and by contrast with the unscrupulous 'Drozdovs', other protagonists display a moral uneasiness with respect to inhumanitarian dogma, social injustice, their own inaction, *etc.* Of works whose heroes have become conscious of a disparity between political and private morality, reality and doctrine, and hence are idealistically disillusioned, critics mention the following seven:

Thaw (60)

[25] Scriven, *Problems of Communism*, 31.
[26] Gibian, *Interval of Freedom*, 129.

Bread (48)
Cruelty (1, 24)
Colleagues (16)
Ticket (26, 35, 48, 78, 93, 106)
ABCDE (16)
One Day (24, 98)

The frequent correspondence between this theme and that of genera-tions in conflict becomes immediately apparent and is discussed by Gaev as follows:

It is evident from literary works devoted to the conflict between the generations that these aspirations [to independence] are founded on a protest against the strict standardization of life, a feature of Soviet society which extends to world outlook, thoughts, and, indeed, to Man's entire mental and spiritual world. Youth's attitude is not merely romantic escapism. Life itself has forced the young to protest, and the more so because the form of life represented by the 'fathers' is riddled with lies, insincerity, sychophancy, and soullessness. The father-son problem could not have arisen earlier. The first Soviet generation did not have dogmatic predecessors.[27]

Blum, in turn, discusses the causes of disillusion among young writers as such, particularly the poets:

A great deal has been accomplished in Soviet Russia over the past decade in the name of truth, and still the poet's truth and the Party's truth fail to coincide. The Party's myth of its own past does not make sense to poets of the new generation whose fathers were sacrificed to that myth. The Party's myth of the present doesn't jibe with what the poets see around them. Finally, the Party's myth of a bright future must seem to Russian poets like the biggest Potemkin Village of them all.[28]

CRITICISM OF THE BUREAUCRACY AND SOCIAL INJUSTICE. — Laber suggests a consequent theme, which logically follows that of ideological disillusion — the protest of certain protagonists against "the evils of bureaucracy" and "the development of bourgeois values in Soviet society".[29] The villain of such works is again the so-called 'incomplete' positive type heretofore discussed — "a bureaucrat ... who abuses a position of authority by setting his own interests above those of the col-lective".[30] Here, however, it is not the villain's own internal predicament,

[27]   Arkadii Gaev, "The Father-and-son-Problem Becomes More Acute in the USSR", *Analysis of Current Developments in the Soviet Union*, No. 257 (January 22, 1963), 3.
[28]   Ralph Blum, "A Reporter at Large. Freeze and Thaw: The Artist in Russia", *The New Yorker*, XLI (September 11, 1965), 217.
[29]   Jeri Laber, "The Soviet Writer's Search for New Values", *Problems of Communism*, V (January-February, 1956), 16.
[30]   *Ibid.*

his own alienation, which receives attention so much as that which he fosters in others and in society at large. Such villains are now viewed as

representative of an influential class in Soviet society; more important, they [their authors] see them not as 'bourgeois remnants' but as products of the Soviet social system itself. It is the institutions, values, and ways of life developed after thirty-seven years of Soviet rule that Ehrenburg, Panova, and Zorin are probing. ... Theirs is not the idealized Soviet society found in so much of Soviet literature, a society of happy working people united in the common cause of building communism and scornful of a few 'negative' characters who represent 'vestiges of the past.' Theirs is a realistic society with real problems, a society with lost and unhappy people, with class distinctions and snobbery, with cynicism and careerism, crime and juvenile delinquency ... where people, despite the Communist credo, still ask themselves the question: What meaning can I find for my life?[31]

Vickery, in turn, discusses the essentially moral implications of such social criticism:

It amounts, in essence, to the attack of the intellectual, the uncompromising seeker, on the stuffed shirt of Soviet society, with all his 'bourgeois' characteristics — his apathy, his indifference to things of the spirit, his worldly wisdom, his egotism, his ability to compromise. This moral protest has been shown to be directed against falsehood, half-truth, insincerity, compromise, spiritual apathy, materialism — all the 'bourgeois' qualities.[32]

Gibian points, finally, to the frequent correlation between the foregoing type of social protest and that by the lone scientist in behalf of his own freedom of inquiry: "Science instead of being a tool under the control of the Party and the political bureaucracy has become an independent value, a rival — more important than the Party which is its antithesis. The scientific work of the lonely, individual inventor is celebrated; the Party, or at least the governmental bureaucracy, is the obstacle."[33]

Works which the critics discuss as involving protagonists at odds with and often beset by the bureaucracy as well as various consequent manifestations of social injustice include a striking majority, twenty in all:

> *Seasons* (70, 73, 97)
> *Guests* (24, 38, 42, 55, 61, 70, 93, 100, 105)
> *Thaw* (24, 55, 73, 93, 102)
> *Wings* (48, 55, 73, 102)
> *Opinion* (26, 55, 100)
> *Bread* (5, 7, 28, 35, 39, 42, 55, 61, 71, 97)

[31]   *Ibid.*, 17.
[32]   Vickery, 150.
[33]   Gibian, *Interval of Freedom*, 71.

Levers (28, 35, 55)
Quests (54, 55, 70, 71)
Light (54, 100)
Sonnet (26, 66, 70, 93, 100)
Journey (28, 54, 66)
Trial Begins (64, 84)
Trial (50)
Kira (27, 28)
ABCDE (16)
Silence (28, 48, 79, 81, 86)
One Day (7, 8, 64, 87)
Bluebottle (91, 93)
Matrena (24)
For the Good (44, 87, 93).

Interestingly, as many as eight of the foregoing works[34] make allusions to or actually depict the arrest or imprisonment of innocent people. Similarly, at least three[35] describe the unjust reprimand or expulsion of loyal Party members or the dismissal from employment of an otherwise dutiful and deserving worker.

PEOPLE VS. OFFICIALDOM. — Although closely related to the preceding category, the notion of the simple people, as a class, and their frequent exploitation by the regime and by those in power receives sufficient attention by writers of the period to be considered a theme of its own. It is this same theme, furthermore, which, according to Gibian, most distinguishes Soviet writers from those in the West: "Even the most critical anti-Stalinist writers share this earnest, dedicated sense of the linking of people together in a communal effort (except for Pasternak, the most individualistic of them all, who retains a feeling for the sharing of a common humanity but repudiates social, organized undertakings)."[36] Gibian elsewhere observes that "in Soviet literature, from Majakovsky and Fadeev onward the question of the individual's sense of being alone — or of belonging to some group — was crucial. ... First, the writers seem to feel an urge to clear away the false community, the pseudo community, foisted upon them by the official Soviet image of the *condition humaine*. Then, having disposed of that, they suggest where man may find at least a vestigial, true community."[37] Consequently, a whole

---

[34] *Thaw, Wings, Bread, Quests, Trial, Kira, Silence,* and *One Day.*
[35] *Thaw, Opinion, Sonnet.*
[36] Gibian, *Interval of Freedom,* 165
[37] Gibian, *Slavic Review,* 422.

school of Soviet writers has arisen since Stalin, whose members devote themselves primarily to the problems of the agricultural population. Slonim lists as such E. Doroš, D. Granin, F. Panferov, V. Solouxin, and N. Virta,[38] and Alexandrova and Bode respectively add the names of I. Antonov, G. Baklanov, V. Ovečkin, V. Tendrjakov, G. Troepolskij, S. Voronin, S. Zalygin, T. Žuravlev, on the one hand,[39] and F. Abramov, A. Jašin, and A. Solženicyn, on the other.[40] Hayward indicates that "the way in which the creative energy of the people has been squandered and continues to be squandered 'for the good of the cause'" constitutes the 'dominant' theme in the works of Solženicyn.[41] In addition, Kazakov, Nagibin, and Tendrjakov are observed to place their stories very often in a forest setting or hunting milieu,[42] which then frequently symbolizes the contrast between the natural countryside and restricted, highly organized city life.

Works from the sample which, according to the critics, treat some such theme include twelve in number:

Wings (55, 120)
Bread (24, 35, 58, 71, 89, 100, 105)
Levers (66, 100, 106)
Light (66, 100, 106)
Sonnet (55)
Journey (71, 106)
Trial (53, 77, 94)
Kira (15)
Silence (79)
One Day (58, 63, 68, 86, 90, 109)
Matrena (19, 48, 87, 109)
For the Good (68, 109).

INTEGRITY AND RESPONSIBILITY VS. APATHY, DUPLICITY, ETC. — Perhaps the most ethically demanding of alienating quandries are those which require not only a character's dissent but some difficult or unpopular action, some display of personal courage as well. The appeal to conscience is attributed by Bode to the situations which confront char-

[38] Slonim, *Soviet Russian Literature: Writers and Problems*, 314.
[39] Vera Alexandrova, *A History of Soviet Literature* (Garden City, Doubleday & Co., 1963), 297.
[40] Bode, *Osteuropa*, XII (September, 1963), 641; "Sowjetliteratur 1962/1963", *Osteuropa*, XIII (October, 1963), 703.
[41] Hayward, *Slavic Review*, 434.
[42] Gibian, *Soviet Survey*, 52, Whitney, 297.

acters in the works of Nagibin, Kazakov, Kuznecov, and Tendrjakov, among others.[43] Tendrjakov, who is mentioned most frequently in this connection, is elsewhere characterized as treating "problems of personal morality, giving much attention to individual differences of character and personality"[44] and as being "the most explicit of all contemporary Russian writers in his forthright expression of the new humanism in Russian literature ...".[45] Kazakov is, in turn, said to explore "the conflict between the necessity for escape and a sense of social and moral obligation which sometimes ought to take precedence over the need for isolation. ... Another area of potential conflict is the possibility that the escape may equally involve the rejection of those things most precious to a person. He comes closest to analyzing a character racked by such a conflict in 'Adam and Eve'."[46] Erlich observes that "as soon as the Soviet writer was granted a measure of self-expression, 'old-fashioned' human values came to the fore. The ethical leitmotiv of the 'thaw' was a hankering for moral absolutes...".[47] Gibian adds that, in this same respect, Soviet writers perhaps most resemble those in the West: "The most encouraging similarity to our values lies in what some Soviet authors appeal to as the highest moral sanction of the individual's behavior. This turns out to be not the Party, not the community, as we might expect, but ultimately one's own moral convictions."[48] Gibian particularly associates with such values the forthright scientist, heretofore discussed: "The scientist is regarded by Soviet authors of Dudintsev's persuasion as being at the peak of his moral heroism when he accepts loneliness, social disgrace, and material penalties for the sake of his innermost convictions — we should say, when he is a martyr to his own integrity."[49] Finally, characters confronted by conflicts of conscience, even those who betray their own sense of morality or justice, can most often be clearly distinguished from those previously discussed under the heading, 'Incomplete' Positive Heroes, who are generally conditioned to rationalize or even ignore the ethical implications of their behavior.

Works mentioned as dealing with the conflict between conscience, on

[43]   Barbara Bode, "1960: The Literary Harvest", *Soviet Survey*, No. 36 (April-June, 1961), 35.
[44]   Edward J. Brown, *Russian Literature since the Revolution* (New York, Collier Books, 1963), 284.
[45]   Whitney, 299.
[46]   Karl D. Kramer, "Jurij Kazakov:The Pleasures of Isolation", *The Slavic and East European Journal*, X (Spring, 1966), 30.
[47]   Erlich, *Slavic Review*, 416.
[48]   Gibian, *Interval of Freedom*, 73.
[49]   *Ibid.*

the one hand, and moral lassitude, on the other, include some twenty-one, again a majority of those sampled:

Seasons (93)
Opinion (1, 55, 70, 97, 100)
Bread (5, 100)
Cruelty (24, 70, 71, 93)
Quests (66)
Journey (54, 93)
Živago (24, 75, 107)
Legend (48)
Renegade (72)
Three, Seven, Ace (24, 61, 93)
Colleagues (5, 106)
Trial (24, 48)
Ticket (16, 35)
Kira (5, 15, 27)
ABCDE (16)
Silence (15, 81)
Short Circuit (16, 48, 78)
Adam (72)
One Day (19, 64, 68, 109)
Moscow (34, 35)
Matrena (35, 93).

CRITICAL SUMMATION OF THEMES. — Both Bode[50] and Gibian[51] refer to an additional theme — one "in regard to which Soviet literature since its beginning differs from most Western literatures ... the frequency with which most Soviet authors grapple with time — time as a long vista ... as an important factor in any situation."[52] Tendrjakov's *Short Circuit* and Dudincev's *New Year's Tale* are immediately brought to mind. As for the broad categories of themes heretofore discussed, most are, according to the critics, treated by an approximate third of all the works sampled, themes pertaining to universal rebellion by an approximate half, and those pertaining to criticism of the bureaucracy and social injustice as well as to integrity and responsibility *vs.* apathy, duplicity, *etc.* by approximately two-thirds.

[50] Barbara Bode, "Sowjetliteratur im Winterhalbjahr, 1959-1960", *Osteuropa*, X (September, 1960),
[51] Gibian, *Slavic Review*.
[52] *Ibid.*, 424.

Otherwise, the critics show a certain variance in their assessment of the period's predominant themes. Gibian, writing in 1960, deftly sums them up with the labels "science, love, and villainy".[53] Three years later, he offers another triple, though quite different breakdown: a "Problems of Youth Group", a "Personal Issues Group: Works dealing problematically with Marriage, Love, Divorce", and a "Central 'Thaw' Group" which "raises typical issues and vigorously opposes the various abuses and rigidities understood under the name 'cult of personality and its consequences'".[54] In the first of his later classifications, Gibian lists the works of such writers as Aksenov, Kuznecov, and Rozov; in the second of such as Pogodin and Tendrjakov; and in the third of such as Èrenburg, Kornejčuk, Zorin, and, again, Tendrjakov.

Mehnert, reviewing in 1964 the Soviet theatre and film circuit of that and preceding seasons, lists as his three choices issues related "to the problem of the War, second, to the question of the generations, third to Stalinism".[55] Gaev suggests a succession of, again, three phases "of open collision between the Communist system and the intellectual avant-garde":[56]

The first phase was the period of thaw, when the right to personal freedom, creative freedom, and freedom of thought was asserted. The second phase was the period of opposition from the younger generation, when the authority of the Party fathers was rejected in favor of a critical attitude toward life. The third phase is a period of renaissance in which universal truths are being resurrected and the role of the Party as dictator of ideology challenged.[57]

Whatever the classification, there is doubtless no other work of fiction which better "provided a concise guide to the themes and theses of post-Stalin literature"[58] than the novel by Èrenburg which gave the period its most popular label. Its implicit analysis of themes, early as this occurred, may well be as astute as the generalizations of subsequent critics.

TABULATION OF PLOT SITUATIONS SHOWING CHARACTER ALIENATION

ADDITIONAL PLOT SITUATIONS. — The extensive critical commentaries heretofore mentioned are often of a general nature, failing to specify in

[53] Gibian, *Interval of Freedom*, ix.
[54] Gibian, *Literature and Revolution in Soviet Russia 1917-1962*, 132-134.
[55] Klaus Mehnert, "Moskauer Theater und Kino, Frujahr 1964", *Osteuropa*, XIV (June, 1964), 422.
[56] Arkadii Gaev, "Intellectual Opposition to Party Takes New Turn", *Analysis of Current Developments in the Soviet Union*, No. 26, 7-8.
[57] *Ibid.*, 8.
[58] Brown, 247.

all instances even the protagonists to which they have reference. Furthermore, a large number of additional plot situations, nowhere mentioned by the critics consulted though fitting the same general thematic categories, can be extracted from the plot synopses in Appendix III. Among these are the following seventy-one:

TABLE 7

Plot Situations not Mentioned by Critics

Individuality and Freedom vs. Conformity and Control	
Suxodolov (*Sonnet*)	Impersonality and insensitivity, conformity
Dimka Denisov (*Ticket*)	Tradition, conformity

Universal Rebellion	
Gennadij Kuprijanov (*Seasons*)	Sense of fulfillment
Tolja (*Legend*)	Sense of purpose, self-understanding
Leksej Maksimov (*Colleagues*)	Mundane life, the uneventful future
Fedor Bugrov (*Colleagues*)	Sense of purpose and accomplishment
Sergej Voxmincev (*Silence*)	Aftermath of World War II and Stalinism

Protest for Artistic and Scientific Freedom, Freedom of Thought	
Artist, Saša Čuprov, and poet, Arbatov (*Moscow*)	Conventional Soviet art, absence of genuine realism or artistic freedom
Students (*For the Good*)	Contemporary Soviet literature

Alienation in Love and Friendship	
Gennadij Kuprijanov (*Seasons*)	Members of Gennadij's family
Gennadij Kuprijanov (*Seasons*)	Trustworthy friends and associates
Larisa Kuprijanova (*Seasons*)	Her husband, Gennadij
Zinaida Ljubimova (*Seasons*)	Her lover, Gennadij
Bortaševič (*Seasons*)	His wife, Nadezhda
Bortaševič (*Seasons*)	Support of friends
Sergej Bortaševič (*Seasons*)	Success in love
Saša Ljubimov (*Seasons*)	Katja Bortaševič
Nina Kirpičeva (*Guests*)	Her husband, Petr
Tema Kirpičev (*Guests*)	His girlfriend, Nika
Petr Romodan (*Wings*)	His wife, Anna
Anna Romodan (*Wings*)	Her husband, Romodan
Lida Romodan (*Wings*)	Love
Katerina Remez (*Wings*)	Love
Minaev (*Opinion*)	His subordinate, Engineer Ol'jxovskij
Ven'ka Malyšev (*Cruelty*)	Love of Julja Mal'ceva
Vasilij Petrovič (*Light*)	Nastja
Karlinskij (*Trial Begins*)	Personal satisfactions (pleasure in love)
Vladimir Globov (*Trial Begins*)	His wife, Marina; progeny
Saša Dubinin (*Three, Seven, Ace*)	Men's loyalty
Saša Dmitrievič (*Colleagues*)	His eventual wife, Ina

Daša (*Colleagues*)	Saša's love
Vladka Karpov (*Colleagues*)	Vera Velesina
Vera Velesina (*Colleagues*)	Leksej's love
Saša Dmitrievič (*Colleagues*)	Fedor Bugrov
Dimka Denisov (*Ticket*)	Galja Bodorova
Volodja (*ABCDE*)	His cousin, Sima
Sima (*ABCDE*)	Her cousin, Volodja
Sergej Voxmincev (*Silence*)	His mistress Nina's love
Konstantin Korobel'nikov (*Silence*)	Assja Voxminceva's love
Ioann Sinemuxov (*Bluebottle*)	His wife, satisfaction in love
Afanasij Zags (*Bluebottle*)	His wife Rozalija's fidelity
People (*Moscow*)	Mutual fear, mistrust
Matrena Vasil'evna (*Matrena*)	Compassion of relatives and neighbors

Conflict between Generations

Petr Romodan (*Wings*)	His daughter, Lida
Varygin (*Journey*)	Devotion to his mother
Tolja (*Legend*)	His mother
Sereža Globov and Katja (*Trial Begins*)	The older generation
Vladimir Globov (*Trial Begins*)	Concern for son, Sereža
Nikolaj Voxmincev (*Silence*)	His son, Sergej
Ioann Sinemuxov (*Bluebottle*)	His son

'Incomplete' Positive Heroes

Uzelkov and communist officials (*Cruelty*)	Others' private lives, loyalty to truth
Klara and Dononov (*Sonnet*)	Personal ethics, free thought, humanitarian values
Globov and colleagues (*Trial Begins*)	Truth, humanitarian values
Marina (*Trial Begins*)	Everything and everybody but herself, non-carnal values
Bušuev (*Three, Seven, Ace*)	Scruples, fellow men
Uvarov (*Silence*)	Principles, integrity
Fetjukov and others (*One Day*)	Caution, fellow-feeling, restraint
Afanasij Zags (*Bluebottle*)	Truth, involvement
People (*Moscow*)	Gullibility, inhumanity, lack of values
Matrena's relatives (*Matrena*)	Fellow-feeling

Idealistic Disillusion

Nastja and Stepan (*Light*)	Idolatry of leaders
Jurij Živago (*Živago*)	The regime
Rabinovič (*Trial Begins*)	Christianity
Leška Malinkin (*Three, Seven, Ace*)	Illusions
Dudyrev (*Trial*)	Faith in Teterin and the people
Ioann Sinemuxov and Rozalija Zags (*Bluebottle*)	Rational self-discipline, socialist discipline, theories, collectivist idealism
Tolja Karcev (*Moscow*)	Official ideology

Criticism of the Bureaucracy and Social Injustice

Tolja (*Legend*)	Injustice
Saša Dubinin (*Three, Seven Ace*)	Justice
Leksej Maksimov (*Colleagues*)	Swindlers, hypocritical self-seekers

People *vs.* Officialdom	
Paša Antipov (*Živago*)	Social injustice (pre-Revolutionary)

Integrity and Responsibility *vs.* Apathy, Duplicity, *etc.*	
Dmitrij Koroteev (*Thaw*)	Truth, integrity
People (*Wings*)	Truth, integrity in their relationship to the bureaucracy

TOTAL PLOT SITUATIONS. — A tabulation derived from the synopses of plot actions in Appendix C indicates that a total of 235 plot situations in the thirty works sampled reveal one or another variety of character alienation. The total number of such situations is broken down both by work and by thematic category in the subsequent table (Table 8) and correlates with the total of numbers in parentheses which accompany the listing in Table 6, Chapter III, and of synopsis headings in Appendix C. These numbers in parentheses in turn stand for the following previously discussed thematic categories and are represented by the correspondingly numbered ten columns in the subsequent table:

1: Individuality and Freedom *vs.* Conformity and Constraint.
2: Universal Rebellion.
3: Protest for Artistic and Scientific Freedom, Freedom of Thought.
4: Alienation in Love and Friendship.
5: Conflict between Generations.
6: 'Incomplete' Positive Heroes.
7: Idealistic Disillusion.
8: Criticism of the Bureaucracy and Social Injustice.
9: People *vs.* Officialdom.
10: Integrity and Responsibility *vs.* Apathy, Duplicity, *etc.*

TABLE 8

*Tabulation by Work and Thematic Classification
of Plot Situations in the Sample*

Work	Thematic Categories										Total
	1	2	3	4	5	6	7	8	9	10	
Seasons	0	1	0	8	5	0	0	0	0	4	18
Guests	0	0	0	3	3	0	0	1	0	1	8
Thaw	0	1	2	9	3	2	0	2	0	5	24
Wings	0	0	0	4	1	1	0	1	2	1	10
Opinion	0	0	1	1	0	1	0	0	0	2	5
Bread	0	0	1	6	0	2	0	1	1	0	11
Cruelty	0	0	0	1	0	1	1	0	0	1	4
Levers	0	0	1	1	0	1	0	1	1	1	6
Quests	0	0	0	4	1	1	0	2	0	3	11
Light	0	0	0	1	0	0	2	0	1	1	5
Sonnet	1	0	0	5	0	1	0	0	0	1	8
Journey	0	0	0	0	1	1	0	0	1	1	4
Živago	1	1	0	5	0	1	0	2	1	0	11
Legend	0	1	0	0	1	0	0	0	1	1	4
Renegade	2	0	0	0	0	0	0	0	0	1	3
Trial Begins	1	1	0	2	2	3	2	0	0	0	11
Three, Seven, Ace	0	0	0	2	0	1	1	1	0	2	7
Colleagues	0	2	0	5	1	1	0	1	0	1	11
Trial	0	0	0	1	0	0	1	0	1	2	5
Ticket	1	0	1	1	1	0	0	0	0	3	7
Kira	0	0	2	4	1	1	0	0	0	2	10
ABCDE	0	2	0	2	1	1	0	1	0	2	9
Silence	0	1	1	2	1	1	0	1	0	1	8
Short Circuit	0	0	0	1	1	2	0	0	0	2	6
Adam	0	0	1	1	0	0	0	0	0	1	3
One Day	0	0	0	0	0	0	1	1	0	3	5
Bluebottle	0	0	0	3	1	1	1	1	0	0	7
Moscow	0	0	1	1	0	1	1	0	0	2	6
Matrena	0	1	0	1	0	1	0	1	0	1	5
For the Good	0	0	1	0	0	1	0	1	0	0	3
Total:	6	11	12	74	24	26	10	19	8	45	235
# Works per Theme:	5	9	10	25	15	21	8	16	7	25	

CONCLUSIONS

The absence in Table 8 of any plot situations under the heading, Protest against Totalitarianism, and the relative sparsity of those which occur under the heading, Individual Freedom *vs.* Conformity and Control (column 1), are explainable in terms of the less abstract descriptions given the various plot situations involved. The two aforementioned headings are nonetheless implicit in many of the plot situations otherwise classified. The high incidence of situations relating to alienation in love and friendship and to ethical conflicts involving individual conscience (columns 4 and 10) is immediately apparent. The former category comprises nearly one-third of all plot situations tabulated and points to a prevalence of such themes not indicated by the previously discussed critical assessments. The latter category comprises nearly one fifth of all plot situations. The approximate ratio of incidence for all ten thematic categories is indicated in the following table, both in terms of total plot situations and the total of works surveyed (thirty). Each category is represented by the same number as in Table 8. The incidence of thematic categories for the total number of plot situations (middle column) is particularly revealing when contrasted to the critics' findings:

TABLE 9

Approximate Ratio of Incidence of Thematic Categories per Total of Situations and per Total of Works Sampled

Thematic Category	% of Thematic Categories per Total of Situations	% of Thematic Categories per Total of Works Sampled
1	3	17
2	5	30
3	6	33
4	32	83
5	10	50
6	11	70
7	4	27
8	8	53
9	4	23
10	19	83

The present investigation's more detailed analysis of the relevant plot synopses (Appendix C) reveals a number of discrepancies in the estimate of prevalencies and trends which was earlier derived from critical assessments alone (pages 104-105). These discrepancies are clearly evident in the table which follows. Thematic categories are again represented by the same numbers as in Tables 8 and 9:

TABLE 10

Incidence of Thematic Categories in Works Sampled according to
(a) Composite Assessment by Critics and
(b) Analysis of Plot Synopses in Appendix C

Thematic Category	Incidence of Thematic Categories	
	(a) per Composite Critical Assessment	(b) per Analysis of Plot Synopses (Appendix C)
1	1/3	1/5
2	1/2	1/3
3	1/3	1/3
4	1/3	4/5
5	1/3	1/2
6	1/3	2/3
7	1/3	1/4
8	2/3	1/2
9	1/3	1/4
10	2/3	4/5

As themes clearly distinctive to some but not to all the works sampled,[59] the following are, according to the analysis of synopses in Appendix C, substantially more frequent in the prose fiction of the first post-Stalin decade:

Alienation in Love and Friendship.
Conflict between Generations.
'Incomplete' Positive Heroes.
Integrity and Responsibility *vs.* Apathy, Duplicity, *etc.*

Of these, the first and third are markedly more frequent, occurring respectively in four-fifths rather than one-third and in two-thirds rather than one-third of the works cited. By contrast and, again, despite the considerably larger number of relevant plot situations identified and classified in the present investigation — all remaining thematic categories, except that pertaining to artistic and scientific protest, appear to occur somewhat less frequently in the prose fiction of this same period. Of

[59] Note explanation for the relative sparsity of plot situations described under the first category. *Supra*, 110.

these, only that pertaining to criticism of the bureaucracy, *etc.* occurs in half the works sampled.

On the basis of the foregoing findings, it is possible to conclude, therefore, that of the ten thematic categories which were originally formulated and used to classify all relevant plot situations, while all are significant, only five appear in as many as half of the works sampled —

> Alienation in Love and Friendship.
> Conflict between Generations.
> 'Incomplete' Positive Heroes.
> Criticism of the Bureaucracy and Social Injustice.
> Integrity and Responsibility *vs.* Apathy, Duplicity, *etc.*

— and only three —

> Alienation in Love and Friendship.
> 'Incomplete' Positive Heroes.
> Integrity and Responsibility *vs.* Apathy, Duplicity, *etc.*

— truly predominate. Thus, Gibian's analysis of 1960[60] appears most nearly substantiated by the preceding statistical count, two of whose three predominating themes — Alienation in Love and Friendship and 'Incomplete' Positive Heroes — coincide with two of the three major themes which Gibian himself posits.

---

[60] *Supra*, 105.

PART THREE

THE 'THAW' HERO AS AN OBJECT OF PRAISE AND / OR DERISION

V

POSITIVE VS. NEGATIVE ASPECTS OF CHARACTERIZATION

As significant as the themes which recur in a body of writings (and their distribution) is the ultimate intent behind them, the viewpoint authors take toward their subject matter.[1] Are they approving or pejorative?[2] Seldom, if ever, is this question thoroughly explored with respect to a whole school or period of writers and in terms of the only truly reliable criterion — the internal evidence of their writing, as such. The period in question is, in this respect, no exception. One of the subjects of the present study has since his defection, however, made his own interesting pronouncement, prejudiced though it may be:

Russian writers divide themselves into rather definite groups:
  1) The completely subordinate. Long live Soviet power! All that transpires is laudable. Such are: *Šoloxov, Mixalkov, Kočetov.*

---

[1]   Admittedly such an investigation runs counter to the expectations of some: "... the design or intention of the author is neither available nor desirable as a standard for judging the success of a work of literary art ..." W. K. Wimsatt, Jr. and Monroe C. Beardsley, "The Intentional Fallacy", *The Verbal Icon: Studies in the Meaning of Poetry* (Lexington, University of Kentucky Press, 1954), 3. It is noteworthy, however, that in taking this stance Wimsatt and Beardsley restrict themselves to discussing verse. Their essentially New Critical approach is doubtless less inviolate with respect to certain kinds of prose.

[2]   The significance of such investigation is attested by both Gibian and Vickery, on the other hand, in connection with their own studies of similar material: "The great interest of the books ... lies mainly in their subject matter and the authors' attitudes toward it, rather than in their artistic merits." Gibian, *Interval of Freedom*, vii. "'It is obvious that it is not the character of the main hero which determines the essence of a work, but the idea which the work affirms, where the author's sympathy lies, with what force and depth the work expresses the social and esthetic ideal, in whose name the offensive is being waged against the old world, in whose name the new and conquering is glorified.'" From "For a Profound Elaboration of the History of Soviet Literature", *Kommunist* (December, 1956), quoted in Vickery, 119-120. "As Soviet society grows older and older, it becomes increasingly difficult to represent negative characters and characteristics as survivals of capitalism. It becomes increasingly difficult to avoid the impression — without doing violence to artistic truth — that many failings are either inherent in human nature or spring from the background on which the author depicts them." Vickery, 120.

2) The moderately liberal. Long live Soviet power! But not all that transpires is laudable. If we have to write Stalin's praises — we'll write them, but if we can avoid them — we'll gladly do so. Such are: *Kataev, Simonov, Roždestvenskij.*

3) The militantly liberal. Long live Soviet power and communism with a humane countenance! But don't put us on trial! Such are: *Evtušenko, Voznesenskij, Tvardovskij.*

4) The opposition. Favor Soviet power, but not the kind that's been around the last fifty years. Prepared to be tried for the truth, and are: *Sinjavskij, Danièl', Solženicyn, Ginzburg.*

5) The hostile. Oppose Soviet power. Consider "communism with a humane countenance" a fiction, a myth. What is Soviet Russia? A world gendarme, a fascist nation. *? ... ? ... ? ...* Have you heard of them? I have. But their works are never mentioned. That is impossible. ...[3]

The following should to some extent confirm or disavow the foregoing categories.

CORPUS. — The subsequent analysis is again based on the thirty works heretofore cited and summarized in Appendix C. The number of plot situations is henceforth restricted, however, to those most central to each work. The situations selected total an even fifty and are listed in the following table. For greater comprehensiveness, certain themes represent a combination of two or more which involve the same protagonist but are listed separately in Table 6, Chapter III, and as headings to the synopses of plots in Appendix C:

TABLE 11

Plot Situations Most Central to Each Work in the Sample

Situation	Work
1) Gennadij Kuprijanov: Trust and approval of family, employers, society.	*Seasons*
2) Bortaševič: Integrity, conscience, social responsibility, self-respect.	*Seasons*
3) Pokrovskij: Petr Kirpičev, the bureaucracy.	*Guests*
4) Dmitrij Koroteev, Lena Žuravleva, Sonja Puxova, Vera Šerer: Emotional self-confidence, integrity, loved ones.	*Thaw*
5) Volodja Puxov: Artistic integrity.	*Thaw*
6) Evgenij Sokolovskij: Žuravlev, the bureaucracy.	*Thaw*
7) Petr Romodan: Dremljuga, the bureaucracy.	*Wings*
8) People: Truth, integrity, self-respect.	*Wings*
9) Romodan: His wife, Anna, and daughter, Lida.	*Wings*
10) Minaev: Ethical responsibility, intellectual integrity, courage, self-respect.	*Opinion*

[3] A. Anatol' (Kuznecov), cited from "Russkaja mysl'" (September 6, 1969), "Obraščenie A. Kuznecova k PÈN", *Novoe russkoe slovo* (October 5, 1969), 2.

11) Lopatkin: Drozdov, the bureaucracy, intellectual conformity. *Bread*
12) Ven'ka Malyšev: Others' inhumanity, injustice, utilitarian *Cruelty* morality.
13) Citizens: Mutual trust, freedom of thought. *Levers*
14) Tat'jana Vlasenkova: Kramov, the bureaucracy. *Quests*
15) Tat'jana Vlasenkova: Her husband, Andrej. *Quests*
16) Vasilij Petrovič: Fellow citizens. *Light*
17) Suxodolov: Conventional impersonality, insensitivity, con- *Sonnet* formity.
18) Pavel Varygin: Unpleasant reality, the people. *Journey*
19) Jurij Živago: Sense of purpose and self-determination, politi- *Živago* cal power, the regime, political inhumanity, regimentation.
20) Paša Antipov: Human values, human life. *Živago*
21) Tolja: Sense of purpose, self-understanding, self-sacrifice. *Legend*
22) Egor: Traditional mundane, sensible, unfeeling existence. *Renegade*
23) Egor: Responsibility, conscientiousness, ambition, sense of *Renegade* duty.
24) Karlinskij: Regimentation, impersonality, de-humanization, *Trial Begins* extinction, insignificance, personal satisfactions.
25) Vladimir Globov, colleagues, people: Truth, humanitarian *Trial Begins* values, freedom.
26) Saša Dubinin: His men's loyalty, justice. *Three, Seven, Ace*
27) Leška Malinkin: Courage, conscience, integrity, illusions, *Three, Seven, Ace* loyalty.
28) Leksej Maksimov: Mundane life, the uneventful future, so- *Colleagues* cialist self-sacrifice.
29) Saša Dmitrievič: Fedor Bugrov. *Colleagues*
30) Semen Teterin: Truth, integrity, courage, loyalty, conscience, *Trial* self-respect.
31) Konstantin Dudyrev: Faith in Teterin and the people. *Trial*
32) Dimka Denisov: Responsibility, vocation. *Ticket*
33) Viktor Denisov: Compromise, materialism, self-seeking. *Ticket*
34) Kira Georgievna: Ethical values, conscience, truth, artistic *Kira* excellence, personal satisfaction.
35) Volodja: Sense of purpose, vocation, conformity, compromise, *ABCDE* dogmatism, world conditions.
36) Sergej and Nikolaj Voxmincev: Social justice, Uvarov, Bykov, *Silence* slanderers.
37) Nikolaj Voxmincev: His son, Sergej. *Silence*
38) Painter, Fedor Mukomolov, and poet, Xolmin: Critical tolera- *Silence* tion, artistic freedom.
39) Vasilij Stoljarskij and other subordinates: Ivan Sokovin, con- *Short Circuit* fidence, initiative, self-fulfillment.
40) Ivan Sokovin: Human values. *Short Circuit*
41) Vadim Sokovin: His father, Ivan. *Short Circuit*
42) Ageev: Vika, other people. *Adam*
43) Ageev: Criticism, artistic freedom. *Adam*
44) Prisoners: Inhumanity, injustice. *One Day*
45) Ioann Sinemuxov: Rational self-discipline, socialist discipline, *Bluebottle* theories, collectivist idealism.
46) People: Duplicity, mutual fear, mistrust. *Moscow*
47) Artist, Saša Čuprov, and poet, Arbatov: Conventional Soviet *Moscow* art, absence of genuine realism, lack of artistic freedom.

48) Matrena Vasil'evna: Compassion of relatives and neighbors.	*Matrena*
49) Matrena's neighbors: Fellow-feeling.	*Matrena*
50) Teachers and students, Fedor Mixeevič, Ivan Gračikov: The bureaucracy.	*For the Good*

˙NARRATIVE AND VERBAL STRUCTURES SEEN AS EXTRINSIC AND INTRINSIC INDICES OF AUTHOR INTENT˙

René Wellek has soundly argued that the truly legitimate modes of literary interpretation "should, first and foremost, concentrate on the actual works of art themselves".[4] Wellek and Warren distinguish such an approach, which they call 'intrinsic',[5] from that of the more traditional, though less reliable 'extrinsic'[6] modes, which view literature, for instance, in relation to an author's biography, psychological theory, the author's social milieu, his philosophy, or parallels in the other arts. Wellek further rejects the conventional distinction "between form as the factor aesthetically active and a content aesthetically indifferent", arguing that both form and content can be esthetically relevant and, when so organized, may be thought of as esthetic 'structures'.[7]

The following analysis is strictly limited to what Wellek would consider 'intrinsic' esthetic structures — eight types in all. Without intentionally reasserting the disputed content-form dichotomy, the following investigation nonetheless presumes a fundamental distinction among these eight kinds of structures. There are narrative structures — those integral to the story-line and which are therefore explicit in effect. There are also verbal structures — those which concern the author's manner of verbal expression and whose effect is therefore more indirect, hence implicit.[8] In a sense, therefore, the distinction 'extrinsic'—'intrinsic' is

[4] René Wellek and Austin Warren, *Theory of Literature* (New York, Harcourt, Brace and World, Inc., 1956), 128.

[5] *Ibid.*, 125.

[6] *Ibid.*, 59.

[7] *Ibid.*, 128-129.

[8] In his analysis of Hemingway's style, for instance, E. M. Halliday speaks of the "implicit rather than the explicit mode" and adds that "both symbolism and irony truly serve this artistic purpose". E. M. Halliday, "Hemingway's Ambiguity: Symbolism and Irony", *American Literature*, XXVIII (March, 1956), 21. Warren makes this same distinction in fact when he says that "... complexities may be on one or more levels. In Hopkins, they are primarily dictional, syntactical, prosodic; but there may also, or instead, be complexities on the level of imagery or thematics or tone or plot: the works of highest value are complex also in those upper structures." Wellek and Warren, 233. Elsewhere Warren discusses "structures 'above' metrics and diction", arguing that "we have to ask about the appropriateness of the 'organ harmonies' to plot, character, theme". *Ibid.*, 236. One is reminded, by analogy, of the distinction

equally applicable in differentiating these two sub-categories and will hereafter be used with that meaning rather than Wellek's and Warren's.

Narrative structures, a number of which have already been examined with respect to nineteenth-century protagonists, include:

(a) The overt liability or stigma of the hero's function in the plot, *per se*.

(b) Circumstantial rationale for the hero's non-conformity and/or critical views.

(c) The hero's comparison with foils.

(d) The hero's denouement.

The credibility of such structures, as criteria, may, however, be seriously qualified by 'intrinsic' or essentially verbal structures, such as:

(e) Moralizing by the author or the narrator's over-all attitude, where evident.

(f) Understatement and irony (this, of course, can also be situational, *i.e.* narrative).

(g) Connotations of imagery and symbolism.

(h) Other stylistic features: parallelism, language texture, *etc.*

According to whether or not these eight indices betray an approving or a disdainful judgment of the protagonist, an author's ultimate bias toward the same and, contrarily, toward the object of the hero's aliena-tion, can be rather safely deduced. It is, of course, conceivable that, for a particular author, one structure may outweigh, with its slant, the im-pact of several, even all the others. This is especially likely where the author's intent is highly symbolic or ironic.[9] The ultimate determination is therefore to some extent subjective, though founded upon a number of discreet criteria.

The importance of such criteria is nevertheless attested by a number of the critics consulted — particularly George Gibian, who argues that "a little more difficult to define than topics and themes, but perhaps more important ultimately, are such literary qualities as tone, point of view, and technique of narration and characterization".[10] Gibian elsewhere expands this view with what might serve as a fitting preface to the present chapter:

---

in linguistics between, say syntactic and morphological structures and their immediate phonemic constituents — all essential to the analysis of a given language.

[9]   As with Pasternak and his 'underground' successors.

[10]   George Gibian, "Themes in Recent Soviet Russian Literature", *Slavic Review*, XXIII (September, 1964), 421.

In the Soviet Union of the 1950's we can distinguish two groups of relationships. The first is that between a writer's view of the reality of Soviet life and the official interpretation of that reality. This includes: literary representations of individual characters and the official versions of what Soviet people are; the writer's attitude towards their being such as he represents (approval, condemnation, neutral acceptance); his interpretation of the causes which produced them, their typicality or exceptionality, their projected future; and the relationship between such a judgement and the official views of where they 'belong' historically, morally and socially.

Secondly, there is the relationship between the official ideology, with its partially Utopian view of present day Russia and its totally Utopian projection of its future development, and whatever in a work of literature, openly or by implication, may be read as a comment upon these views. There is very little open contradiction of official ideology by writers, except in literature 'for the drawer' and in *Doctor Zhivago*. ... But there are books in which elements of plot, character, or attitude seem tacitly to contradict parts of official Soviet ideology. Here it is essential to pay attention to the nuances of views expressed by what character, under what circumstances; to the extent to which his opinions are refuted or left suspended; to whether other elements of the book (themes, mood, outcome) reinforce or nullify those views.) ...[11]

Gibian makes a similar reference to authors, among them Leonov (*The Russian Forest*, 1953), who utilize the same techniques to endorse rather than protest the circumstances which underlie their heroes' alienation. These authors "are very outspoken in their representation of adverse conditions in Russian scholarship ... [but] are careful to supply a counterbalance to the critical and denunciatory portrayals — a positive character, a hero, a refutation, a sign pointing to a way out, to a method of remedying the unsavory circumstances, and most important of all, an optimistic, happy ending".[12]

The special significance of more verbal or more strictly stylistic (intrinsic) features is discussed by several other critics, as follows. Bode: "Both under the autocratic regimes of Nicholas I and Alexander III as well as under Soviet rule, those views of human society and the state which could not be expressed in any other way have been and will yet be voiced in an indirect manner in imaginative literature."[13] Gaev:

Soviet literature today falls into two fairly distinct categories. The first category, which is the larger of the two, is a kind of gauge registering pressure from above, since it consists of poetry and prose written by authors who adhere strictly to Party directives in their work. The second category is more like a seismograph,

---

[11]   Gibian, *Literature and Revolution in Soviet Russia 1917-1962*, 127-128.
[12]   Gibian, *Interval of Freedom*, 47-48.
[13]   Barbara Bode, "Die Auseinandersetzungen in der Sowjetliteratur als Spiegel der politischen Strömungen", *Osteuropa* (January-February, 1965), 55.

sensitive to the undercurrents and trends of thought under the surface of Soviet society. This does not, however, imply that the writers of the second type reject the Party altogether — if they did, they would have no hope of seeing their work published. The difference between the two schools is more a matter of contrast in emphasis and nuances in the treatment of often identical themes.[14]

Gavrilov: "The writer must figure out how to deceive a fool, yet he can succeed at this only by showing himself also a fool. Thus, to say a word, he writes a phrase, to express a phrase he writes a page, and a page of his own thought requires a whole book."[15] Aleksandrov: "The Soviet reader has long since learned to read between the lines to find out what the author really means. He finds anti-Soviet statements and criticism of the system in statements which, from a Western standpoint, may appear extremely naive and innocent."[16]

In addition, critics have variously alluded to each of the eight fore-mentioned criteria (page 119), as follows:

(a) Overt Laudability or Stigma of Hero's Function in the Plot. — Aleksandrov observes that "every member of the Soviet state is faced at an early age with the problem of either becoming an opportunist or declining to participate in state and social life".[17] Exaggerated as this statement may be, it does suggest a preliminary basis for judging the favorability of certain protagonists. Aspects of overt behavior which can be seen as either laudable or reprehensible involve, for instance, the hero's inclination to resist, escape, or acquiesce to a formidable opposition and whether or not he defends and assists others or is indifferent to or, even worse, exploits them.

(b) Circumstantial Justifications for the Hero's Nonconformity and/or Critical Views. — As Gibian suggests, again with reference to the 'thaw' and its official sanctions: "The dark side of Soviet life was to be admitted here and there into literature, but only if the over-all effect was rosy."[18] Besides the hero's overt function in the plot, extenuating circumstances may well qualify the immediate impression produced by his explicit behavior. Is the hero more than a mere stereotype? Is his protest realistic, hence laudable, or illusory, hence unjustifiable? Does

[14] Arkadii Gaev, "Soviet Literature at the Beginning of the Second Stage of De-Stalinization", *Studies on the Soviet Union*, No. 4 (1965), 225.
[15] Nikolai Gavrilov ("a Russian writer known in the West by another name"), "Letter from a Soviet Writer", *The New Leader*, XLVI (December 9, 1963), 17.
[16] K. Aleksandrov, "Revisionism as Reflected in Soviet Literature", *Bulletin of the Institute for the Study of the USSR*, V (April, 1958), 55.
[17] *Ibid.*, 53.
[18] Gibian, *Interval of Freedom*, 24.

he understand the nature of his alienation or is he self-deluded? Is he the
passive, unwitting victim or the overt agent of his own predicament? Has
he alternatives or is his predicament tragically inevitable?

(c) HERO'S COMPARISON WITH FOILS. — As Gibian, again, observes:

The nature of villains in Soviet literature between 1954 and 1957 is important
for several reasons. They show us clearly what the writers consider dangerous
and harmful; they give us an insight into the author's ethics, negative as well
as positive ... in Soviet Russia, as in all countries with a closely supervised
literature, a villain has two other advantages. First, he may be a means of
saying what otherwise would expose the author to the charge of hostility
toward the government; the author can disassociate himself by claiming that
anything put into the mouth of a villain is meant not to be accepted but refuted.
Secondly, the thoughts, deeds, and words of a villain may cause the writer to
divulge views of which he may not be entirely aware. ... Villains, more than
heroes, have the strange magnetic property of attracting to themselves not
fully acknowledged thoughts, feelings, and facts.[19]

Particularly important considerations in this respect include the following: Is the protagonist morally superior or inferior to his foil (foils)?
Which, if either, is portrayed as a villain? What is the relationship of
each to the powers that be, *i.e.* to the Party? According to Aleksandrov:
"In the much talked of recent Soviet novels and verse, the hero has
usually not been a Party member. Furthermore, Communists have
frequently been portrayed as bureaucrats, persons retarding general
development, occupying high positions out of all proportion to their
knowledge and capabilities, and opposing the forces of progress."[20]
Where the total context is within the Party itself, characters can often
be contrasted, says Vickery, in terms of "the opposition between meaningful and meaningless Party activity. ... In prose, this contrast is commonly achieved by depicting two types of worker — the one dogmatic,
unimaginative, who plays it safe by obeying and imposing instructions to
the letter or who cynically uses Party work for his personal advancement;
the other sensitive, flexible, consistently placing the common good above
private interest, ever conscious of the human aspects of Party work,
willing to forget the letter of the law in order the better to interpret the
spirit."[21] Yet another distinction: the degree to which the protagonist is,
by contrast with his foil (foils), one of a minority or majority. If the
former, his protest is likely more courageous. On the other hand, his
very exclusiveness may indicate that his protest is insignificant or that,

[19] *Ibid.*, 109-110.
[20] Aleksandrov, 51.
[21] Vickery, 138-139.

in being atypical, he is alien if not foe to the people, as such. Further circumstances, again, can do much to qualify such an impression.

(d) HERO'S DENOUEMENT. — In its purest sense, this criterion simply assesses whether the protagonist is destined, either within the story or in the projected future, for ultimate victory or eventual defeat. There are works, for instance, in which "the obstacles are never formidable" and "one never doubts his [the protagonist's] ultimate success".[22] Such works, for all their posturing of problems, tend to give the lie to any serious kind of alienation. It is also true, of course, that "there are other ways in which the story justifies itself from the official point of view despite the absence of a cheerful ending".[23] Vickery argues to what extent in fact other criteria must also be considered:

As long as 'the struggle between the two systems persists, as long as Communism retains its crusading dynamism, pessimism can always be regarded as tantamount to a washing of dirty linen in public, or to the putting of weapons into the enemy's hands ... unhappy endings and personal tragedies are, in literature, not normally produced by having the hero and heroine run over by an automobile in the last chapter; they are forged link by inevitable link in obedience to the author's outlook on life and to the personalities of the characters whom he has elected to portray. And it is this outlook on life — be it genuinely pessimistic, outspokenly critical, or merely nonconformist — which is most likely to conflict with official Soviet thought.[24]

(e) AUTHOR'S MORALIZING AND NARRATOR PERSONALITY. — The 'journalistic digressions' which, says Alexandrova, abound in Soviet 'production base' novels[25] are obviously a ready indication of an author's true feelings. Whether in the form of outright commentary or in more subtle guise, the intrusion of the author's or narrator's personalities, where this occurs, can be most decisive. Critics have noted that the works of particularly fourth-generation Soviet prose writers "are either written in the first person or deal with events in which the author participates. The heroes are young and most of them are travelers and seekers who aim to dispel their doubts and disappointments engendered by Soviet stereotypes."[26] Bode, in turn, mentions the 'personal note'[27] in the writing of Tendrjakov and Kazakov, while Gibian speaks of "the

---

[22] Gibian, *Interval of Freedom*, 35.
[23] *Ibid.*
[24] Vickery, 165.
[25] Alexandrova, *Studies on the Soviet Union*, 157.
[26] "Soviet Youth Breathes Life into the Arts", *Soviet Affairs Analysis Service*, No. 14 (1961-1962), 4.
[27] Barbara Bode, "Sowjetliteratur 1961-1962 (II)", *Osteuropa*, XIII (January, 1963), 22.

exceptionally fresh angle of vision of the narrator" in works by Nekrasov, Nagibin, and Kazakov: "... we feel the narrator is an imaginative, living mind — sometimes confused, tentative, provoked, changeable — in short, a unique, imperfect centre of consciousness, rather than the generalized, scientifically impersonal, common denominator of a mind who is at work in most of the other novels and stories of the period".[28] Such a violation of objectivity can render the narrator more plausible and more persuasive, simply because his account appears less premeditated. The author has himself calculated this illusion, however, and his narrator doubtless functions as a kind of mouthpiece.

(f) UNDERSTATEMENT, IRONY. — It can be expected that, in their effort to make a point while they are nevertheless constrained to avoid its expression in certain words, Soviet authors frequently resort to those literary devices which gain effect by being either indirect or ostensibly untrue, which drop subtle hints, or which even assert one meaning in order to convey its opposite. "At the turn of the century", says Gibian, "Oscar Wilde and George Bernard Shaw produced paradoxes by reversing the established maxims. The technique which amused and shocked respectable London in 1896 produced consternation in official Moscow in 1956."[29] The right irony can obviously impose a completely opposite significance upon a number of other stylistic structures, both extrinsic and intrinsic.

(g) CONNOTATIONS OF IMAGERY, SYMBOLISM. — Imagery and symbols often serve to convey an author's ironic intent.[30] Commenting particularly on contemporary Soviet poets, Steininger observes that "behind realistic portraits and situations which ought to be entirely acceptable to a Soviet critic are hidden profound allegories. ... Symbol and allegory have become the principal means of expression for these young people."[31] Kersten refers to the same phenomenon with respect to the period's fiction in general: "One only begins to understand the deeper meaning

---

[28]   Gibian, *Literature and Revolution in Soviet Russia 1917-1962*, 146.

[29]   Gibian, *Soviet Survey*, 49. Northrop Frye's definition is especially noteworthy: "The term irony, then, indicates a technique of appearing to be less than one is, which in literature becomes most commonly a technique of saying as little and meaning as much as possible, or, in a more general way, a pattern of words that turns away from direct statement or its own obvious meaning." Northrop Frye, *Anatomy of Criticism* (Princeton, Princeton University Press, 1957), 40.

[30]   Elsewhere, E. M. Halliday implies an essential difference between the function of symbolism and that of irony: "Symbolism signifies through a harmony, irony through a discord; ... symbolism synthesizes, irony analyzes." Halliday, 22.

[31]   Alexander Steininger, "Die Junge Sowjetische Dichtergeneration", *Osteuropa*, VIII (July-August, 1958), 463.

of many works which appear at this time when one considers their symbolic character, so typical of Russian literature of the past."[32]

(h) OTHER STYLISTIC FEATURES, PARALLELISM, LANGUAGE TEXTURE, ETC. — Mathewson argues that

> the narratives of a Tendrjakov or a Nekrassov or a Solzhenitsyn are deployed in an orderly manner through time, do not 'distort' experience in order to see it freshly, do not shift point of view in any radical manner or divert the steady gaze of the observer-narrator. Language does not attempt to reproduce the actual flutterings and oscillations of consciousness but is 'logical' in the sense that it is a rational, ordered description of event, scene or feeling. ... It is ... low-tension, plain-spoken, photographic, confined on the whole to surfaces.[33]

There are nevertheless obvious instances where choice of or play with words connotes the definite attitude of an author toward his subject matter. Additional literary devices, such as repetition (or its narrative equivalent — plot parallelism), may be equally telling. One of the authors sampled has implied as much, albeit ironically, in remarks made in his own defense while standing trial:

> "It is an artistic device to keep on repeating the same phrases over and over again, and it is a powerful one. It creates a kind of shroud, a peculiar kind of electrified atmosphere in which the boundary between the real and the grotesque becomes blurred — rather as in the works of Arzhak and Tertz.
>
> "It really is very strange that literary images suddenly lose their make-believe character and are interpreted by the prosecution literally — so literally that these court proceedings merge into a literary text as a natural sequel to it. ..."[34]

APPLICATION. — Unavoidably, various critics have already commented on most of the works sampled in terms of one or another of the foregoing criteria. In the subsequent analysis, the observations of such critics are properly acknowledged. Again, however, but few of the works sampled have been comprehensively analyzed in terms of all or most of these eight criteria — either by a single critic or even in the composite assessment of all the critics reviewing a given work. No critics, either individually or compositely, have compared these works with each other in terms of even a majority of the same criteria.

Furthermore, many critical observations, while nonetheless valid, are often directed to the general style of a particular author without any specific reference even to the work or works which the reviewer has in

---

[32]   Kersten, 86.
[33]   Mathewson, *Soviet Literature in the Sixties*, 12.
[34]   A. Sinjavskij, "The Trial of Sinyavsky and Daniel" (trans.-ed.) Max Hayward, *The New York Times Magazine* (April 17, 1966), 122.

mind. The following table shows the paucity of any reference whatever
to a number of the works sampled in terms of the eight aforementioned
criteria. It will be noted that only one-third are in any way dealt with
by the critics surveyed in terms of as many as five of the eight criteria.[35]
In the table, small case letters represent each of the established criteria:
(a) overt laudability or stigma of hero's function in the plot; (b) circumstantial rationale for the hero's non-conformity and/or critical views;
(c) hero's comparison with foils; (d) hero's denouement; (e) author's
moralizing and narrator personality; (f) understatement, irony; (g) connotations of imagery, symbolism; (h) language texture, *etc.*

In the subsequent discussion, each of the fifty central plot situations
(Table 11) is analyzed in terms of the eight foregoing criteria, wherever
these criteria prove relevant and applicable. Each discussion of or statement about a given work in terms of a particular criterion is preceded by
the lower case letter assigned to that criterion in the list on page 119. The
plus or minus signs which follow each such analysis indicate a concluding assessment of the author's bias, in terms of the particular criterion, toward his protagonist and hence also toward the object of the protagonist's
alienation. A plus sign (+) indicates an author's inclination to sympathize with his protagonist rather than with that which alienates him
or from which he finds himself estranged, while a minus sign (−) indicates
either the reverse *or an Inclination to Resolve or Minimize the Protagonist's Alienated Quandry* — hence to neutralize his pathos.

The numbers (in parentheses) which follow each major heading indicate a composite assessment of the author's ultimate bias toward his
hero, based on the analyses which follow and according to the following
scale of gradations:[36]

---

[35] It is, of course, conceivable that all implicitly apply the first criterion without
alluding to it as such. Many make a kind of judgment when stating the basic conflict
involved in a given work or in one of its situations.

[36] Van der Eng-Liedmeier frequently assesses the attitude of a Soviet writer to his
alienated subject in terms of 'favorable' or 'unfavorable', while Mathewson proposes
at least four gradations. These he discusses, however, in the context of 'positive'
heroes, in terms of an author's "attitudes toward the dominant political power" in a
descending order from most to least approving:

(1) "The writer's identification with his protagonist and with his cause" (as in
Furmanov's *Čapaev* (1923) and Fadeev's *Nineteen*).

(2) The attitude of "the detached but sympathetic observer" (as in Fedin's *Cities
and Years* and Šoloxov's *The Silent Don*).

(3) The attitude of "the regretful agnostic" (as in Babel'´s *Red Cavalry*).

(4) "Open hostility", which, says Mathewson, "was proscribed" from the very
beginning.

Mathewson, 254.

TABLE 12

Critical Reference to Works in the Sample in Terms of
Eight Selected Criteria

Work	Criteria							
	a	b	c	d	e	f	g	h
Seasons		×	×			×		
Guests								
Thaw		×	×	×	×	×	×	
Wings								
Opinion			×	×		×		
Bread		×	×	×	×	×	×	×
Cruelty								
Levers				×				
Quests			×	×	×			
Light								
Sonnet			×	×			×	
Journey						×		
Živago	×	×	×	×	×	×	×	×
Legend								
Renegade				×	×		×	
Trial Begins			×	×		×	×	×
Three, Seven, Ace		×	×	×	×		×	×
Colleagues				×	×	×		×
Trial		×	×					
Ticket			×		×	×	×	×
Kira		×		×		×		
ABCDE		×	×	×		×	×	
Silence		×	×	×			×	
Short Circuit		×	×	×			×	×
Adam		×		×	×		×	×
One Day		×	×	×	×	×		×
Bluebottle						×		
Moscow				×				×
Matrena		×	×	×			×	×
For the Good		×		×		×		×

(1) Identification with the protagonist (presupposing a critical view
of the causes of his alienation).

(2) Detached sympathy.

(3) Pure detachment.

(4) Regretful disdain.

(5) Open hostility.

(6) Superficial optimism.

These composite assessments are to some extent unavoidably subjective, since the various criteria do not necessarily carry equal weight as indices of an author's attitude and may in fact vary in significance from one work to the next. (For more general plot summaries, refer to Appendix C.)

ANALYSIS OF SELECTED PLOT SITUATIONS IN TERMS OF AUTHOR BIAS

(1) Panova, *Seasons of the Year* — Gennadij Kuprijanov: Trust and approval of family, employers, society. (2)

(a) Gennadij is extremely irresponsible and self-seeking, entirely oblivious to the needs or feelings of others, particularly those of his wife and parents and, later, those of his landlady-mistress and her son, Saša Ljubimov. He is careless about his associates, obligates himself, and becomes implicated in their crimes. (−)

(b) In many respects, Gennadij is "the victim of bad environment and bad education",[37] "a product of Soviet society. He comes of good proletarian stock; both his parents are Party members."[38] Despite her good intentions, however, his mother, Dorofea, has always been unduly solicitous in his behalf. She interceded for him when he was liable for dismissal from the *Komsomol*; she has provided him with money on a number of occasions; and she even admires him on the New Year's eve he comes to see her, while she grieves about his unproductive life. In the depiction of her early career as a bureaucrat, Dorofea is said to have emulated a certain regional director, Zaletnaja, but to have lacked the latter's forcefulness. She has also indulged Gennadij more than his sister because of his physical attractiveness and tried to justify his failure to request his father's consent before marrying Larisa. His sister, Jul'ka, even remarks to her fiance that

"... mama literally ruined Gen'ka with her two hands!"
"But it wasn't your mother," said Andrej. "He is simply that kind ... a failure."
"There are no simple failures. It all depends on one's upbringing. ..."[39]

Gennadij's charm totally captivates others, such as Zinaida Ljubimova,

---

[37]   Brown, 245.

[38]   Vickery, 43.

[39]   Vera Panova, *Vremena goda, Novyj mir*, XXIX (December, 1953), 92.

who sacrifices for him her means and even her loyalty to her son, Saša. Accustomed as he is to being indulged by others, Gennadij therefore obligates himself to Cycarkin, who plies him with good wine and foreign records, even though he suspects Cycarkin's underhandedness. Furthermore, Gennadij is not intentionally unkind and is, until the end, seemingly blind to the consequences of his actions. (+)

(c) Gennadij is unfavorably contrasted to all the members of his family. His idealistic, hard working mother holds a prominent position in the local government. Her positive nature is reflected in the fact that she shows no sign of age and appears eternally young. By contrast, Gennadij's face is described as mirroring ugliness, lack of expression, indifference, *etc.* His unspoiled sister, Jul'ka, surprises even Dorofea by growing up a sociable and popular young woman, active in social causes. Gennadij's male peers are also more favorably depicted. Saša Ljubimov learned to be brave and thoughtful in his youth: he restrained his tears, though in pain, when in his father's presence; he was distressed when during the War they were short of money and his mother suggested selling his father's suit in anticipation that the latter would not return from battle. After the War, he becomes a conscientious student, then sustains himself and assists his mother as a construction worker, quickly rising to the position of a foreman. As soon as Gennadij and Cycarkin trick him into selling his father's government bonds, Saša unhesitatingly takes their money to the police, although he may stand to lose it in doing so. When the money is finally returned, with his share he dutifully buys clothes instead of a coveted radio. The Bortaševič children, Sereža and Katja, provide a further positive contrast: "Their mother is of non-proletarian origin. Their father is a high-placed official who is exposed in the course of the book as an embezzler. Everything is therefore wrong with these parents. Yet the children grow up straight and honest, a credit to Soviet society."[40] Finally, Larisa's new lover, Pavel, shows all the earmarks of an attentive, satisfying potential spouse. The latter gives lessons in poetry to a group of women workers, which suggests that he can also give Larisa the 'poetry' Dorofea senses she needs. As Dorofea observes: "'What a difference from Genja, altogether different manners and thoughts. It's not at all surprising that Larisa has fallen in love with him, even if he isn't very handsome.'"[41] For his own part, Pavel has resolved not to marry before he is totally committed to the other party: "'I have concluded that one should marry when one feels a need for the

[40] Vickery, 43-44.
[41] Panova, *Novyj mir* (November, 1953), 60.

other person. ... If you can exist without somebody and marry them just the same, that is deception, self-deception, needless to say.' "[42] With equal seriousness, Pavel completes his dissertation, then, discovering that Larisa is desperately in love with him, becomes convinced that they need each other. By contrast with all the foregoing, Gennadij is one of a decidedly anti-social minority, whose self-seeking character is in no way redeemed by a sense of righteous outrage, common cause, or idealism. (−)

(d) Although Gennadij nearly dies after being shot by Cycarkin's accomplice, he recovers in the hospital, where he becomes pensive and undergoes a change of character. He is attentive to his mother, confides in her, even cries in her embrace. He vows to testify against Cycarkin, *etc.*, even at the risk of being imprisoned should his testimony fail. He resolves to change and wishes to become reconciled to Saša Ljubimov. Gennadij and Saša's mother plan to live with Gennadij's parents after his recovery. (−)

(e) Panova concludes her novel with an extremely optimistic editorial note, which bears general implications for all the characters in her novel: "Let us toast to the happiness of Saša and Jul'ka and their friends, to the realization of their hopes and the flowering of the city, Ensk. Let us wish Dorofea courage in her future trials and much success to comrade Kozyx and the whole machine tool factory and to all honest working people an endless eternally youthful, eternally renewed life."[43] (−)

(f) Unlike the essentially well-intended Sergej and Katja, the profligate Gennadij comes from an exemplary socialist home. This irony, however, tends to cast more shadow on the effectiveness of Gennadij's upbringing than on Gennadij himself and, in view of his mother's unwise permissiveness, to lend Gennadij, if anything, additional sympathy. (+)

(2) Panova, *Seasons of the Year* — Bortaševič: Integrity, conscience, social responsibility, self-respect. (4)

(a) Like Gennadij, Bortaševič has allowed himself to become implicated in a network of graft and corruption. He has found it convenient to ignore the deception of subordinates and tolerated others' intrigues for their assistance in promoting his image and advancing his status. (−)

(b) Like Gennadij, Bortaševič is essentially blind to the effects of his behavior: "He's a good fellow who has fallen into crime because of the effect of environment: specifically the environment of upper-class Communist society. His criminal activity had begun very gradually, almost

---

[42] Panova, *Novyj mir* (December, 1953), 74.
[43] *Ibid.*, 158.

imperceptibly. ... He was the victim of social evil ...".[44] He is the victim particularly of his scheming, ambitious wife, Nadežda, who destroyed his earlier marriage and first steered him into a compromising position by urging him to become indebted to various opportunists, like the accountant who later dictates his decisions. He is neither a willful nor any too willing wrong-doer, nor does he particularly stand to benefit from the abuses he condones. (+)

(c) Though Bortaševič is contrasted to administrators like the scrupulous Dorofea Kuprijanova, he is more frequently distinguished from the large number of villainous individuals who practice conscious deception — Nadežda; the accountant; Red'kovskij; the former *rajkom* secretary, Golovanov; the newspaper editor, Bučko; Cycarkin; *etc.* Bortaševič therefore, like the local city administrator, Čurkin, who allots new apartments to his important friends, seems, though weak and dishonest, exceptional and especially pathetic in his wrong-doing. (+)

(d) Unlike Gennadij, Bortaševič perishes from a self-inflicted gun wound. He is also more seriously implicated in the crimes of others, whom for a time he was in a position to oppose. His apprehension, furthermore, serves as pretext for the desertion of his wife and of friends like Čurkin and also gives his children cause for deep disillusion. Had he not taken his life, his future would have been, in any event, tragic. (+)

(e) Panova reinforces the pathos of Bortaševič's position by declaring, before the resolution of his fate, that "his life had ended on the day that he reached out his hand for money. He had cut short his own life."[45] (+)

(f) Bortaševič is introduced to the reader long before the revelation of his criminal involvement. His original image is that of a model father and conscientious citizen. In fact, at the meeting in which Red'kovskij is expelled from the Party, Bortaševič volunteers an eloquent denunciation of Red'kovskij's crimes, which, as it turns out, closely resemble his own. Bortaševič seems most concerned about the corrupting influence of Red'kovskij's immoral example: "'And therefore we must condemn him the more severely for his moral plundering of the Party and of society than for his theft of material.'"[46] Later Panova tells us that Bortaševič's 'mirage' first disappeared as he finished his harangue against Red'kovskij: "He sat down — and everything collapsed: he saw that in talking about Red'kovskij, he was speaking about himself."[47] His denunciation is,

---

[44] Brown, 243.
[45] Panova, *Novyj mir* (December, 1953), 109.
[46] Panova, *Novyj mir* (November, 1953), 88.
[47] Panova, *Novyj mir* (December, 1953), 108.

therefore, not consciously hypocritical, yet further points up the pathos of his own tragic situation. Like Oedipus, he mercilessly hunts down the evil-doer who, it turns out, was himself all along. (+)

(3) Zorin, *Guests* — Pokrovskij: Petr Kirpičev, the bureaucracy. (1)

(a) Pokrovskij is the innocent victim of important bureaucrats who, in order to conceal their own guilt when certain court proceedings threatened to disclose them, sought to divert public attention by accusing one of the lawyers involved, Pokrovskij, of falsifying evidence. (+)

(c) Pokrovskij's arch opponent, Petr Kirpičev, is made to appear ruthless, unfeeling, and in every way unadmirable. Since he is feared by his wife and rejected on moral grounds by his own likeable father and son, and since the latter, instead, befriend the maligned stranger, Pokrovskij — Kirpičev is made to seem unworthy of the slightest sympathy. By contrast with his elder son, Sergej; his parents; and his sister, Varvara — all of whom are industrious, thoughtful, and just — Petr's wife and younger son, Tema, are in various ways as callous and self-centered as he. He is overheard on the telephone, moreover, viciously plotting Pokrovskij's downfall — which immediately wins for Pokrovskij all the sympathy the audience or the reader was unable to muster for Kirpičev. (+)

(d) Kirpičev's machinations and the whole plot against Pokrovskij are intercepted just in time by the fearless journalist, Trubin, who adroitly marshalls evidence against the plotters and sends an exposé to the papers. The plot mechanics which lead to this victorious finale are nonetheless rather crude and obvious and, therefore, unconvincing: an excessive number of quick entrances and exits which thus allow the right combination of characters to be brought together to speak about those not present; a number of contrived overhearings, particularly that whereby practically all the others manage to listen in on Kirpičev's denunciatory phone call (from an outdoor phone extension — Kirpičev seems especially gullible not to take more precautions, under the circumstances!); *etc.* (−)

(f, g) When, during their final confrontation, Kirpičev boasts that 'tomorrow' Pokrovskij's case will be finished, Trubin replies that it is already 'tomorrow'[48] and that an editorial is even now being circulated in *Pravda* disclosing the plot against Pokrovskij. Both the irony and its symbolism tend to imply that new times have dawned in which the injustice done to such as Pokrovskij will no longer be tolerated. (−)

(h) The attitudes of Kirpičev's father and elder son are sharply con-

[48]   Leonid Zorin, "Gosti", *Teatr*, XV (February, 1954), 45.

trasted to his own by the reaction of each to a revolutionary episode concerning a *chekist* subordinate who failed to absolve an unjustifiably accused general in order not to undermine the *Cheka*'s prestige. (+)

(4) Èrenburg, *The Thaw* — Dmitrij Koroteev, Lena Žuravleva, Sonja Puxova, Vera Šerer: Emotional self-confidence, integrity, loved ones. (1)

(a) Throughout most of the plot, the foregoing characters restrain their love impulses, mistrust their feelings and aspirations, and are consequently frustrated as well as evasive toward others. They are essentially likeable, which makes their situation all the more pathetic. (+)

(b) Though there is little explicit explanation for these characters' predicament, the very atmosphere of fear and inhibition points to some general and overwhelming cause. Moreover, none of these characters appears to have provoked his misfortune. Instead, it has descended upon him like an inevitable social inheritance. That Lena compromises her marriage, on the other hand, does not render her less sympathetic nor, for that matter, tragic, *à la* Anna Karenina. In this she is like Dudincev's Nadja (*Bread*). Their authors (and, doubtless, their twentieth-century Soviet readers) readily excuse them. (+)

(c) Contrasted to Koroteev, Žuravleva, and Šerer is Žuravleva's husband, Ivan, who poses a threat to each of them. Shockingly insensitive, Ivan is ostensibly impervious to others' disapproval, even to his wife's waning affection. While his ruthless disregard of other people keeps him from being disturbed like the rest, it nevertheless contributes to the others' general anxiety. (+)

(d) At the end of the first part, Žuravlev is summoned to Moscow to account to the Central Committee for the destruction of his workers' housing. He is subsequently transferred to another position and, hence, does not return. Meanwhile, Koroteev and Žuravleva achieve an unspoken understanding, which leads to his kissing her. As Sonja leaves Savčenko for her first work assignment, the tone of their long-drawn farewell is still ambigious, yet reassuring:

"Why didn't you come before?"
"I thought you didn't want me to. Would you have really liked me to?"
"I didn't say that. But it wouldn't have been very nice, in general, if you hadn't."
"You've talked like this before. ... So I figured you didn't want to see me."
"But did you want to yourself?"
"Why do you ask? That time at the gates. ..."
"Let's not quarrel at the last minute. ... Do you think I always say what I think?"

"Sonja, when will you return on vacation?"

"Don't be crazy! What vacation, when I'm just beginning my job?"

"Listen — I didn't take a vacation last year. I'll come to Penza."

"Not on your life! ... When will you take your vacation?"

"Soon. But will you forbid it?"

"What will you do in Penza? It will bore you if you don't have work there. It isn't the Caucasus."

"I'll be coming to see you, not the city. ... Sonja, you won't forget me?"

"I'll forget what's not important. You always remember what's important."

"But do you consider me important?"

"How do I know? I haven't tested it. Perhaps I will forget it."

"But how do you feel about it now?"

Sonja looks at him; her eyes darken. It is well that they are in a crowd or she might kiss him. ...[49]

Šerer likewise bestows an endearing expression upon the ailing Sokolov-skij, whom she has heretofore avoided. She is also visibly concerned about his physical condition. As Brown observes, "Each character seems to warm up a little toward the others, each becoming less hard and 'rational', more sympathetic and understanding. Each feels the need of giving and receiving love."[50] In the second part, the same couples continue to experience setbacks in rapport but arrive at reconciliations and become physically intimate. At the end, all barriers to further discord appear to be permanently removed: Koroteev overcomes his depression, convinced that he cannot solve everyone else's problems, and is more affable; Žuravlev has remarried, which frees his wife and puts an end to his interference; disillusioned by the encounter with his Belgian daughter, Sokolovskij turns to Šerer with renewed appreciation; and, after finally making love to Savčenko, Sonja determines to resign from her job and join him at the first opportunity. "Having once said the important things", says Brown, "Ehrenburg seems to have been willing to appease his critics by the relatively optimistic tone of Part II."[51] (—)

(e) Èrenburg's narrative technique is, though obviously contrived, unusually effective in conveying the inner thoughts and feelings of his various characters: "The story is told in a succession of episodes, each presented from the viewpoint of a particular character, whose personal idiosyncracies and unspoken thoughts are basic to the narrative pattern."[52] The author's presence is thereby artfully concealed, while the private logic of his characters' inner lives is revealed with sympathy and directness. (+)

---

[49]   Il'ja Èrenburg, "Ottepel'", *Znamja*, XXIV (May, 1954), 78-79.

[50]   Brown, 254.

[51]   *Ibid.*

[52]   *Ibid.*, 253.

(f) Koroteev is the focal point of an irony which lends additional sympathy both to Koroteev and to those who, like him, are unusually confused and repressed, yet crave freer self-expression and mutual communion. Says Koroteev at the readers' meeting:

"I will tell you frankly that I am not only displeased with the way the author portrays Zubcov's personal life. Above all, the incident he describes is far from authentic. Why, it is not at all typical. No reader can believe that an extremely confident but honest agronomist would fall in love with the wife of his colleague, a coquettish and fickle woman with whom he has nothing intellectual in common. In my opinion, the author is striving for a cheap effect."[53]

As Vickery observes, however: "The irony of this situation lies in the fact that Koroteev is himself secretly in love with Lena, the plant director's wife."[54] Koroteev's initial reservation about such emotional attachments is thus contradicted by his own experience. (+)

(g) The emotional 'breakthrough' which is eventually experienced by each of the foregoing protagonists is anticipated in the first part by numerous references to the freezing winter weather and to the eagerly awaited spring and finally by a number of allusions to the presence of a literal thaw. "Throughout the book", says Gibian, "runs a contrast between deep freeze (literally, in a sense of climate, and figuratively, in the sense of Stalinist attitudes) and the thaw ...".[55] The weather at any given moment serves in fact as a kind of barometer to a particular character's state of mind. As Koroteev leaves the readers' meeting, after delivering his tirade against the free love situation in a certain book, he encounters a fierce snowstorm: "He stepped onto the street. 'Look at the snowstorm! And when I entered the club, it was so still. ...'"[56] Likewise, when Savčenko earlier invites Sonja to go for a walk and she refuses, there is freezing weather. Toward the end of the second part, however, as Lena and Koroteev finally admit to each other their mutual affection, it is a warm day, the trees are beginning to show some green, and "from the street are heard the voices of children, car horns, and the din of a spring day".[57] The romantic potential between Sokolovskij and Šerer is similarly supported by Sokolovskij's pointed analogy about a century plant which, though accustomed to the desert, grew especially large when given special care. The eventual impression of all the fore-

[53] Èrenburg, *Znamja*, 15.
[54] Vickery, 42.
[55] Gibian, *Interval of Freedom*, 9.
[56] Èrenburg, *Znamja*, 16.
[57] *Ibid.*, 87.

going symbolism is that the characters' quandary is only temporary and that their situation will soon improve. Savčenko's letter to Sonja from Paris at the end of the second part — with its suggestion that life in the West is merely a review of past accomplishments, while Soviet society, with all its problems, has a significant future — displays the same facile optimism. (−)

(h) Èrenburg's effective use of parallelism on several occasions reinforces the impression of his subject's earnestness and universality. All three — Lena (Žuravleva), Vera (Šerer), and Sonja — crave affection and consolation but, at least in the beginning, purposely avoid that which is offered them. Lena will neither encourage Koroteev nor confide her domestic ills to Vera; Vera in turn refuses to discuss with Sokolovskij her depression over the recent deaths of several patients. Lena and Sonja both lie to their mothers in order to conceal their true feelings. Lena also long avoids revealing to Žuravlev the true state of her affections, while all three women are generally reluctant to recognize that they are in love and with whom. (+)

(5) Èrenburg, *The Thaw* — Volodja Puxov: Artistic integrity. (2)

(a) Volodja's opportunistic capitulation to Soviet utilitarian art is the more insidious because he possesses real talent and knows better. He even views his own paintings with cynicism and contempt. (−)

(b) Volodja's cynicism and, in the second part, his jealous denunciation of Saburov are nonetheless tempered by personal dissatisfaction and a bad conscience. Volodja suffers the most for his lack of integrity and his opportunism. (+)

(c) Sharply contrasted to Volodja is Volodja's guileless fellow-artist, Saburov, who remains content painting pictures which have no propagandistic value and are therefore unsellable. Meanwhile, Saburov remains kindly disposed toward Volodja and expresses genuine admiration for his talent, even after Volodja has maligned him. (−)

(d) Toward the end of Part One, Volodja becomes increasingly dissatisfied with his own kind of art. Meanwhile, the Artists' Union has asked Saburov to exhibit two of his paintings, while the portrait Žuravlev commissioned from Volodja is now of no account. On the pleasant day which concludes Part One, moreover, Volodja becomes cheerful again and friskily kicks at the ice, *etc.* This mood receives a prolonged setback in the second part, however, until, at story's end, a much less impulsive, more sober and considerate Volodja expresses his intention to reform. He has indicated to Sokolovskij that he will abandon art, try to live like ordinary people, and be useful to others. He has since remained aloof from his family, however, and kept the company of the accountant, Bušagin, who has a perhaps undeserved reputation as a drunkard. Volodja's ultimate outcome therefore remains obscure and ambiguous. The issue of his artistic integrity is not satisfactorily concluded either: it is unclear whether he intends to forsake painting because of the lack of opportunity for a genuine artist, whether he is disenchanted with art in general, or whether he is in fact committed to the pursuit of serious art despite the absence of further recognition or future reward. Meanwhile, "the true artist Saburov at last gains public recognition".[58] The optimistic tone of Èrenburg's conclusion tends generally to suggest that he wishes at this point to minimize the notion of conflict, in whatever form. (−)

(e) Èrenburg employs the same narrative technique as in the preceding plot situation. (+)

(f) Volodja's essential irony is based on the failure of public recognition and material compensation to substitute for the satisfaction of truly creative work. This tends to heighten the pathos of his personal conflict. (+)

(g) As Sokolovskij chastises Volodja for the latter's cultivated cynicism, Sokolovskij's dog turns on Volodja and tears a hole in his trousers — the implication being that Volodja's attitude is so false as to be repugnant to all natural creatures. In the main, however, Volodja's spiritual conflict and ultimate rehabilitation are anticipated by the novel's extensive snow-thaw symbolism. When, at one point, Volodja becomes particularly distressed about his second-rate art, we are told that "Volodja went to the window: snow, nothing but snow. ... It was warm in the room, but he felt so cold somewhere inside himself that he took his coat from the hall and threw it over his shoulders. But he couldn't warm himself."[59] Earlier, as he calculates the profit from Žuravlev's portrait, he incidentally asks himself: "But why is there so much snow? It is so mournful that I don't even care to live."[60] At the end of the first part, on the other hand, as he walks outdoors with Tanečka, they discover life in a pussy willow, the grass, and a blooming snowdrop. They also observe a pair of lovers, and all are warmed by the sun. Symbolism again dissipates the conflict. (−)

(h) Again, Èrenburg parallels Koroteev's discussion of a particular novel at the readers' club with a similar discussion of the same book by

---

[58]   Brown, 254.
[59]   Èrenburg, *Znamja*, 56.
[60]   *Ibid.*, 32.

the younger generation at the home of Volodja and Sonja. The latter
reacts to the work much as did Koroteev: "'I completely agree with
Koroteev. A Soviet citizen should master not only nature but also his
own feelings. But Zubcov loves so blindly. A book should instruct, not
perplex.'"[61] Again, like Lena, Volodja resorts to lies when discussing
Žuravlev: "'Your husband has very delicate features. He is hard to
paint. But I have tried to convey his inner substance. ...' Lena silently
walked out. 'What did he say about "inner" substance'? With a smile. ...
It's strange that Andrej Ivanovič has such a son. ... Are there really
many people on the earth who constantly lie? Like me. ... Wherever you
look, snow. And it's so long, so terribly long before spring. Yes, and
what will happen to me when spring comes?'"[62]

Further parallels thus reinforce the intensity and pathos of both
Volodja's and the others' predicament. (+)

(6) Èrenburg, *The Thaw* — Evgenij Sokolovskij: Žuravlev, the bureaucracy. (1)

(a) Sokolovskij's reputation is first attacked by Žuravlev, who resents
his constructive criticism. He is next reprimanded by members of the
local Party bureau, some of whom envy his professional success, others
who misunderstand his motives. This tends to make him feel persecuted
and to mistrust others. (+)

(b) Žuravlev's innuendoes about Sokolovskij's loyalty concern his
wife's long past defection. As such, they are vicious and obviously unfounded. Sokolovskij's illness has also been mistakenly interpreted as a
defiant refusal to return to work. His ideas are made to appear helpful
and sound, furthermore, despite the criticism of his several colleagues.
He is, in other words, a mostly innocent and unwitting victim. (+)

(c) Like Koroteev, Lena, and Vera — Sokolovskij is favorably contrasted to the cold, authoritarian Žuravlev and still later to Žuravlev's
cronies who remain at the factory after Žuravlev's transfer. (+)

(d) Koroteev has second thoughts about Sokolovskij's reprimand and,
together with others, succeeds in having it retracted. Those now in control are, presumably, more capable and also fair-minded. (−)

(7) Kornejčuk, *Wings* — Petr Romodan: Dremljuga, the bureaucracy.
(6)

---

[61] *Ibid.*, 28.
[62] *Ibid.*, 33.

(a) Although not himself the victim of any particular conspiracy, Romodan strongly identifies with the common cause and thus opposes other bureaucrats who serve themselves first and consequently neglect their responsibilities toward the peasants and the task of food production. Romodan's omniscience together with his impeccably selfless, courageous manner make him a most admirable, if somewhat implausible, figure. (+)

(b) As the new district committee secretary, Romodan is extended the usual privileges — including a sumptuous *dacha*. Everyone expects him to exploit his position like the other officials, but instead he lives, in exemplary fashion, for the social cause. His Herculean qualities may indeed strain credibility, but his behavior is unimpeachable. (+)

(c) The other officials, particularly Dremljuga, president of the local executive committee, are, by contrast to Romodan, oafs and opportunists. Dremljuga seems most concerned about his authoritarian image. He cows his subordinates, censors their speeches, mistrusts them, *etc.* He even makes one of them dig worms for his fishing. Tereščenko spends much of his time flirting with women. Whereas Romodan is modest, forthright, and candid — the others gloss over unpleasant facts and fawn on one another, while nevertheless taking personal credit for any local accomplishments. (+)

(d) Romodan instigates immediate reforms, despite the apathy and resistance of other officials. He arranges for the construction of a long delayed hospital wing, investigates the possibility of a new local museum, and inspires the sudden transformation of character in various workers and lesser officials. He argues that neither appeals nor pressure but only a sense of the glory of their work will impell agronomists and engineers to work on the *kolkhozes* and encourages a number of them to do so. Although Dremljuga contests Romodan's ultimate success, the latter's superior knowledge and dynamic leadership leave little doubt that he will be triumphant. He in fact warns Dremljuga to accept a pension before he is discharged. No serious obstacles interfere with Romodan's enactment of various reforms. Hayward, for instance, alludes to the play's "highly artifical 'optimistic' ending".[63] (—)

(g) Romodan's use of 'wing' imagery further reinforces the optimistic tone of the play's conclusion. He speaks, for instance, of the 'winged' inspiration which attended a recent Party plenum in Moscow: "The plenum revealed such vital truth, such power in us that it was as if we were winged. I felt then a number of times that I could fly above the

[63] Hayward, *Dissonant Voices in Soviet Literature*, xxx.

whole earth".[64] The same image occurs in the play of words as Romodan finally warns Dremljuga:

"The real specialists are perched right under your wing."
DREMLJUGA. "I'm no eagle. I haven't the kind of wings that can. ..."
ROMODAN. (interrupting) "I was thinking of a brood hen."[65]

Again, with reference to Vernigora, one of Dremljuga's underlings: "I see where he is heading and who gives him wings."[66] Even Romodan's sister, after speaking with her brother and resolving to return to the *kolkhoz* uses a similar expression: "I have regained ... my faith and the wings about which you spoke so beautifully."[67] Finally, at play's end, wild geese are heard flying overhead. Meanwhile, Dremljuga and Tereščenko have been unsuccessful at fishing. Nature itself has symbolically confirmed the victory of justice, social progress, Romodan, *etc.* In addition, Dremljuga's very name — Sleepyhead — has all along connoted a deluded and anything but formidable adversary. There is no foreseeable future conflict. (−)

(h) The foregoing 'wing' symbolism and the sounds of wild geese are made the more effective by the repetition of both during the play's conclusion. (−)

(8) Kornejčuk, *Wings* — People: Truth, integrity, self-respect. (2)

(a) Both Dremljuga's subordinates and the farm workers respond to their superiors with agreeable, obsequious words and gloss over the truth in their reports, speeches, *etc.* They consequently show little courage or initiative and reveal suppressed, frustrated personalities. (−)

(b) The workers' apathy and duplicity are a kind of learned reaction which enables them to avoid friction with their leaders, since the latter are less interested in real accomplishments than in being obeyed and in creating a favorable over-all impression, however inaccurate or distorted. The workers themselves are dissatisfied with their own behavior and are eager enough to reform when officially encouraged to do so. (+)

(c) The workers are characterized less as individuals than as a class which is maligned and has lost its vital spirit. As such, they are all equally demoralized by their unscrupulous and ineffective leaders. Romodan, though superior, belongs to another, the leader class, most of

---

[64] Aleksandr Kornejčuk, "Kryl'ja", *Novyj mir*, XXX (November, 1954), 43.
[65] *Ibid.*, 47.
[66] *Ibid.*
[67] *Ibid.*, 45.

whose members are however, like Dremljuga, decidedly inferior to the people, *per se.* (+)

(d) Romodan's victory is equally a victory for the workers, whom he both reforms and champions. He teaches them to speak forthrightly about practical matters, entrusts them with responsibility, and persuades a number who have abandoned *kolkhoz* work to return to agriculture. All seem overjoyed at the prospect of self-fulfillment through hard work. They have regained their self-respect and appear to have no more conflicts. (—)

(g) The 'wing' symbolism, heretofore discussed, is equally applicable to the peoples' optimistic outcome. (—)

(h) Repetition of the same symbolism further enhances its effectiveness with respect to this group of protagonists. (—)

(9) Kornejčuk, *Wings* — Petr Romodan: His wife, Anna, and daughter, Lida. (1)

(a) Romodan is ostracized by his wife, Anna, and daughter, Lida, because of his failure to intercede for Anna after her unwarranted arrest at the end of the War. (—)

(b) Anna and Lida do not know that Romodan was summoned away by the Central Committee before learning of Anna's arrest and was later prevented from recontacting or in any way assisting her. (+)

(d) The three are finally reconciled. Learning about the extenuating particulars, Anna forgives Romodan but remains emotionally aloof. However, through the intercession of her sympathetic colleague, Katerina, there is at play's end every indication that Romodan and Anna will soon renew their prior rapport and affection, and he has meanwhile achieved a complete understanding with Lida. There are no forseeable difficulties like those which originally provoked their estrangement. As Hayward notes, "the victim of the outrage renders impassioned thanks to the Central Committee ... for its timely intercession and its determination never to permit such things to happen again":[68] " 'Thank you, thank you so very much, Central Committee! This terrifying nightmare will never again return.' "[69] (—)

(g) 'Wing' symbolism again strengthens an optimistic conclusion. (—)

(h) ... as does its reiteration. (—)

[68] Hayward, *Dissonant Voices in Soviet Literature*, xxx.
[69] Kornejčuk, *Novyj mir*, 40.

(10) Granin, *One's Own Opinion* — Minaev: Ethical responsibility, intellectual integrity, courage, self-respect. (4)

(a) Minaev undermines the future career of his young subordinate, Ol'xovskij, first because Ol'xovskij's reforming zeal annoys him, then later because Minaev can no longer protect Ol'xovskij without endangering his own rapport with other colleagues. (−)

(b) The affair with Ol'xovskij forces Minaev to recognize his own habitual surrender to social pressure and that he has long been conditioned to sacrifice principle for convenience. Minaev deeply suffers from an accumulating sense of guilt — which renders him nonetheless pathetic. In a manner he had not anticipated, his hand is also forced by Ol'xovskij's vengefully malicious teacher, Loktev. (+)

(c) Ol'xovskij is perhaps the clearest foil to Minaev's compromising nature. Though naive and vulnerable, the former courageously asserts himself whenever he encounters error or senses the need for constructive criticism. Gibian contends that Minaev and his kind are "*typical, native, Soviet characters*"[70] and that in both this work and in Dudincev's *Not by Bread Alone* there are "passages in which a character expresses objectionable ideas not later adequately cancelled through being contradicted by some other positive character or refuted by ensuing action".[71] Though in the majority and decidedly pathetic, Minaev is, by contrast with Ol'xovskij, nevertheless unjustified in not risking disapproval to redeem his fellow creature. Uncomfortable as his choice may be, he has, like Ol'xovskij, a choice nonetheless. He is neither powerless to act nor constrained to avoid his moral obligation. (−)

(d) "Granin represents a complete victory of the men in power and defeat of the rebellious innovator."[72] The defeat is also Minaev's, however — morally and emotionally — and it is this which receives the greater emphasis at story's end. The conflict remains unresolved. In order not to appear ridiculous himself in view of what he has already said in Loktev's presence, Minaev can conceive of no alternative to denouncing Ol'xovskij. For all his own weakness and cowardice, and for all the permanent injury this will bring to Ol'xovskij, Minaev suffers the more severely and thus emerges especially pathetic. (+)

(f) Gibian recognizes a certain subtle understatement in the depiction of both Minaev and the hero of Ždanov's *Journey Home*, whose stories

[70]   Gibian, *Interval of Freedom*, 37.
[71]   Gibian, *Literature and Revolution in Soviet Russia 1917-1962*, 135.
[72]   Gibian, *Interval of Freedom*, 54.

"give the impression of approaching tragedies because on the one hand they concentrate on a moment of perception by the character into what had happened to him in the past (sometimes over a long period of time), and on the other hand there is irony in the reversal of good intentions".[73] The portrayal of Minaev's guilt as he leaves the crucial meeting at the city council is itself a masterful stroke of understatement. Although it is beginning to rain, he tells his chauffeur to drive on without him. He then walks, as in a daze, interested only in moving ahead physically, though in no particular direction: "He moved forward. Wherever he walked, it was at least forward. He could go to the square or turn toward the embankment. The one thing he could not do was return to the city council. Whatever he told himself, however much he tried to convince himself ...".[74] The net effect is greater sympathy for the pathetic Minaev. (+)

(g) Brief as is the account of Minaev's conflict, it is rich in physical details reflecting his various moods. During their first discussion, Ol'xovskij handles Minaev's glass ink well lid, the scraping of which produces an irritating sound that coincides with the effect of Ol'xovskij's conversation. When Minaev condescendingly warns Ol'xovskij not to tip over the ink well, an additional meaning also suggests itself. As, later, Minaev signs a denunciatory reply to Loktev, his pen makes another unpleasant scratching noise: "As he was signing the paper, he awkwardly scraped his pen and winced at its grating sound."[75] While crossing a bridge after the meeting at the city council, Minaev notices flowing chunks of ice through the bridge's rungs: "It seemed as if the ice stood still while the bridge was moving."[76] This illusion leads to the realization that he has aged and to recollections of his innocent, uncompromised youth. Later, while on vacation, he blames his depression on the rain. Through the smoke and the rain-spattered window in his train compartment emerges the figure of his youth, which reprimands him for delaying the time he will act with integrity. As he defends himself, a third figure, also a projection of his youth, stands to the side and sees through his self-delusion. As he leaves the train and glances back at the same window, the view is appropriately bleak: "The smoky pains reflected nothing; beyond them, in the gloomy interior, were visible a rumpled bed and an ash tray filled with butts."[77] The total effect: increased pathos for Minaev. (+)

[73] *Ibid.*, 142.
[74] Daniil Granin, "Sobstvennoe mnenie", *Novyj mir*, XXXII (August, 1956), 134.
[75] *Ibid.*, 130.
[76] *Ibid.*, 134.
[77] *Ibid.*, 136.

(11) Dudincev, *Not by Bread Alone* — Lopatkin: Drozdov, the bureaucracy, intellectual conformity. (1)

(a) With his ingenious invention, Lopatkin poses a threat to bureaucrats and other scientists whose ideas are current or who, in collusion, are advancing their own schemes. They therefore consistently sabotage Lopatkin's efforts to have his invention tested and fairly considered. (+)

(b) Lopatkin's invention proves far superior to anything in present use or as yet designed by anyone else. This alone strongly favors his cause, even according to the fundamental socialist criterion "of greatest usefulness to the 'collective' and 'future generations'".[78] This consideration therefore justifies Lopatkin's endeavor, despite Brown's reservations that "it is difficult to sympathize with his fanatic devotion to the centrifugal casting and mass production of large-diameter iron drainpipes" and that "the plot has a kind of textbook simplicity; suspense is not maintained; accident or coincidence plays a vital part in the development of the story".[79]

(c) As with Minaev (*Opinion*), Gibian again argues that Drozdov is a typical bureaucratic type rather than an "isolated case".[80] Slonim adds that "unlike other negative characters in Soviet fiction, Drozdov and the whole clique he represents are neither villains nor paid agents of American imperialism. They are Party members, solid citizens, and first-class business men."[81] Brown concurs that, despite Kruščev's later reservations on the matter,[82] "careerists and opportunists appear in this novel as an indigenous Soviet growth and as creatures of the Soviet power system".[83] Brown hastens to add, however, that, except for Drozdov, the novel's other characters are felt to be schematic and unconvincing.[84] Says Ruge, with respect particularly to the novel's more positive types: "Their author created them in good faith. He created them as embodiments of his ideals, and perhaps for this reason therefore they impress one as so much paler than Drozdov and his friends, who are drawn according to nature."[85] Ruge cites a similar judgment by Èrenburg.[86] According to Swayze, on the other hand, "Dudintsev indicates that

[78] Gibian, *Soviet Survey*, 49.
[79] Brown, 261.
[80] Gibian, *Interval of Freedom*, 17.
[81] Slonim, *Soviet Russian Literature: Writers and Problems*, 305.
[82] Brown, 263.
[83] *Ibid.*, 262.
[84] *Ibid.*, 260.
[85] Gerd Ruge, "Zu Besuch bei sowjetischen Schriftstellern", *Der Monat*, X (September, 1958), 40.
[86] *Ibid.*, 33.

Lopatkin's predicament is not unique by depicting two other figures who have already been defeated in similar struggles."[87] Still, Lopatkin, unlike Drozdov, is decidedly in the minority: "A single minded lonely man, obsessed by his project, he does not belong to the gang, lacks the 'right connections', and seems a dull nuisance to pedantic experts and ministry employees."[88] Lopatkin's little circle — Nadja; the inventor, Busko; the S'janov family; his only official benefactor, Galickij — are nonetheless characterized by Gibian as "mavericks, loners ... [with] another sense of community, with another set of people".[89] It is indeed Lopatkin's consistent identification with the exploited, impoverished little people which, in the long run, actually places him with the broad, powerless majority and wins for him, by contrast with Drozdov, etc., still further sympathy. This contrast is intensified by the lack of scruples and the ruthless, power-hungry mentality of Drozdov and his cronies. Even in his personal relations, Drozdov is a despot. He treats his mother like a servant, insists that Nadja receive special treatment at the hospital, and enjoys his reputation as a Napoleon at the factory. None of the bureaucratic villains, including the academician, Avdiev, is above tampering with standards or otherwise falsifying the facts in their favor. (+)

(d) The general consensus reiterates Gibian's finding that the "villains" are "still in power at the end of the book".[90] Others who support this view include Brown,[91] Erlich,[92] and Ruge:[93] Lopatkin's "case is reviewed; he returns, his machine is built and accepted; yet the novel concludes with a testimonial meeting in honor of his opponent, who, together with his henchmen, is still very much in the saddle — in spite of the isolated breakthrough of Lopatkin's machine."[94] It is also true that, as in *One's Own Opinion*, there are again a number of "passages in which a character expresses objectionable ideas" which are "not later adequately cancelled by some other, positive character or refuted by ensuing action".[95] The conflict remains, and this in turn accounts for Lopatkin's inclination to engage in politics in the future. Mathewson's contention therefore that

[87]   Harold Swayze, *Political Control of Literature in the USSR, 1946-1959* (Cambridge, Harvard University Press, 1962), 165.
[88]   Slonim, *Soviet Russian Literature: Writers and Problems*, 304.
[89]   Gibian, *Slavic Review*, 406.
[90]   Gibian, *Interval of Freedom*, 14.
[91]   Brown, 263.
[92]   Erlich, *Slavic Review*, 406.
[93]   Ruge, *Der Monat*, 28.
[94]   *Ibid.*, 54.
[95]   Gibian, *Literature and Revolution in Soviet Russia 1917-1962*, 135.

in this work, as in *Ticket to the Stars*, "the final solutions all coincide with a broader definition of conformist expectations and there is no very strenuous moral inquiry"[96] needs qualifying. (+)

(e) *Not by Bread Alone* truly suffers from the excessive opinionizing of its author: "Things happen in the novel as the result of the inner needs and purposes not of the characters but of the novelist himself, who has very much to say ...".[97] The following is typical of Dudincev's obtrusive editorializing:

One rarely has the opportunity to recognize a genuine hero. Not because there are few heroes, but for quite another reason. A hero ascends to the heights of his noble life without yet displaying on his chest an attractive gold medal. Then suddenly he is a hero! Sometimes the ascent takes years, decades, during which he remains unnoticed to the very end. Heroes can be right with us, and we don't see them — it sometimes happens that way! For this reason there are invariably people who say that there are no heroes whatever, while prudent sowers plant the field in order later to reap ten fold.[98]

In addition, Dudincev almost caricatures with his physical descriptions, thus early prejudicing the reader for or against a given hero. His first description of Drozdov, for instance — "thin, with pointed yellowish ears"[99] — strikingly contrasts with his original picture of Lopatkin on the occasion of his and Drozdov's first depicted encounter: "The inventor held himself straight, inclining his head slightly, and Leonid Ivanovič immediately noticed a special grace about his whole figure, a carriage which is so pleasant in lean soldiers. ... his soft stare slightly unsettled Leonid Ivanovič, who lowered his own eyes."[100] Lopatkin's visage unavoidably captivates Drozdov's wife in turn: "The collar of his night shirt was unbuttoned, revealing his powerful neck. ... Nadja became irresistably infatuated with the sharp angled strength of his arms and shoulders, his masculine beauty ...".[101] Dudincev's commentary and his sharply pointed descriptions thus strongly intrude where the story might itself more convincingly demonstrate the proper conclusions. These crude devices at least leave no question as to their author's approval of Lopatkin and his dislike for those who oppose him. (+)

(f) There is an essential irony in the fact that Dudincev "took one of the party's favorite subjects, the technological novel about an inventor's

---

[96]   Mathewson, *Soviet Literature in the Sixties*, 13.
[97]   Brown, 261.
[98]   Vladimir Dudincev, "Ne xlebom edinym", *Novyj mir*, XXXII (October, 1956), 84.
[99]   Vladimir Dudincev, "Ne xlebom edinym", *Novyj mir*, XXXII (August, 1956), 33.
[100]   *Ibid.*, 36.
[101]   *Ibid.*, 51.

struggles, and perverted it, breaking many of the canons of socialist realism"[102] and in the fact that "nationalistic motivation ... is rechanneled by Dudintsev from an attack against foreign enemies into an onslaught on domestic ones ...".[103] (+)

(g) Both Alexandrova[104] and Kobetz[105] have commented on *Not by Bread Alone*'s 'complex subtext'[106] and the implications of its title, obviously "taken from the reply of Jesus to the devil's threat to turn bread into stone if Jesus persisted in fighting him".[107] These implications appropriately extend to the novel's central conflict, which opposes economic planners with idealists, like Lopatkin. Gibian further observes that "to express his conceptions he [Dudincev] resorts to images drawn from Greek mythology, Christianity (there are many biblical echoes and images in the novel), art, and Russian history (when a reference is made to what might happen if a Russian genius like Lomonosov appeared before a twentieth-century, Soviet Drozdov). He defends the great individual's uniqueness and his need to differ."[108] There are also literary allusions such as: "'You remember that Brjusov said: "We will remove the lighted torches to the catacombs, the deserts, the caves" — he was wrong! When they are lit, we will no longer be able to carry them off!'"[109] — as well as occasional 'thaw' symbolism: "It was still January, but the asphalt was bare, as in the summer: occasional drops fell from the roofs; somewhere sparrows were chirping. ... He already sensed the subtle and distant fragrance of nature reviving in January and was joyously alert: isn't this an illusion? And his spirit greeted each gust of vibrant wind."[110] On at least two occasions reference is made to the biblical words in the novel's title, first by Busko — "'I like mystics, who do not live by bread alone'"[111] — then, at story's end, as Lopatkin confronts his long-term adversaries: "In the silence echoed the voice of Dmitrij

[102] Gibian, *Interval of Freedom*, 14.
[103] *Ibid.*, 57.
[104] Vera Alexandrova, *A History of Soviet Literature* (Garden City, Doubleday & Co., 1963), 14.
[105] Johann Kobetz, "Die Sowjetrussische Literatur in Kraftfeld der Wandlungen und Spannungen zwischen dem XX. und XXI. Parteitag der KPdSU", *Sowjet-Studien*, No. 7 (July, 1959), 50.
[106] Alexandrova, 323.
[107] *Ibid.*
[108] Gibian, *Interval of Freedom*, 59.
[109] Dudincev, "Ne xlebom edinym", *Novyj mir* (August, 1956), 88.
[110] *Ibid.*, 94.
[111] Vladimir Dudincev, "Ne xlebom edinym", *Novyj mir*, XXXII (September, 1956), 46.

Alekseevič: 'A man does not live by bread alone, if he is genuine.'"[112]
The general import obviously favors Lopatkin at the expense of Drozdov,
etc. (+)

(h) Although "official euphemisms which cover the abuse of power
[e.g. "'cult of the individual'"] are resolutely abandoned in this novel",[113]
its heavy verbosity and its multitude of plot machinations impede rather
than assist the author's efforts to create a compelling illusion. Truly, as
Brown observes, "Dudintsev has less verbal power than a number of his
contemporaries."[114] It is therefore ironic that particularly Dudincev
should show such a keen appreciation for transparent prose:

"When a writer tries to understand a human being and to help him, then his
hand grows so strong that form becomes subservient in order to serve the high
goal with love. This fusion of content and form transforms a book into a
miracle. One sits and forgets the paper, seeing people whom the writer has so
arranged that one can view their inner life. One no longer notices the form.
That is the peculiarity of Russian literature."[115]

Unfortunately, one is all too conscious of certain features of form in
Dudincev's prose whose unfortunate effect is to destroy plausibility.
These features do not so much reflect the author's strategy in depicting
his hero as Dudincev's own mediocrity as a stylist. The assessment of
this aspect of the novel, as an indication of Dudincev's ultimate bias, is
therefore neutral. (+)

(12) Nilin, *Cruelty* — Venjamin (Ven'ka) Malyšev: Others' inhumanity,
injustice, utilitarian morality. (1)

(a) Ven'ka equates his faith in socialism with a sense of justice and the
notion of an absolute ethic. This faith is subsequently betrayed by those
of his comrades who, like Ven'ka, espouse socialist idealism but deal
with others in a pragmatic manner. In his disillusion, Ven'ka kills
himself, for which he is reproached, even in death. (+)

(b) Ven'ka's disillusion is made plausible and earnest by intervening
events that are beyond his control and not of his choosing: "the two
climaxes of the outer action — the visits to Klan'ka Zvyagina's hut, one
in winter, one in summer — are in each case immediately followed by a
climax of the internal action — the *komsomol* meeting and Ven'ka's
suicide."[116] (+)

[112]   Dudincev, "Ne xlebom edinym", *Novyj mir* (October, 1956), 97.
[113]   Brown, 262.
[114]   *Ibid.*, 260.
[115]   V. Dudincev, quoted in M. J., "Literaturnaja Moskva, Sbornik II, 1956", *Soviet Studies*, IX (January, 1958), 37.
[116]   T. J. Binyon, "Introduction", *Žestokost'* (Oxford, Pergamon Press, 1963), xxvi.

(c) Binyon points out that "opposed to Malyshev is the figure of Uzelkov, the young journalist. It is significant that the story begins with his description: he is the representative of the forces that are to lead to Malyshev's downfall and is, in fact, unwittingly one of the causes of the latter's suicide."[117] Uzelkov is Ven'ka's opposite in every undesirable respect — a pretentious braggard and opportunist who distorts truth, cultivates influential persons, and lives by few if any scruples. He consults encyclopedias, then shows off his knowledge of esoteric facts; exaggerates the detectives' exploits for good copy and to please their chief; purposely misleads Ven'ka regarding Julja's affections; and evades any stigma in connection with Ven'ka's death by arguing that Ven'ka's suicide was, as such, a political offense: "'Irresponsibility — that, if you will permit, is the most serious sin. ... And so at the bottom of this sad fact lies a crude political error, even, I would say, a lack of political tact. And this we cannot forgive Malyšev. We are obligated to look at the truth head on. Don't you agree?'"[118] In addition, each of the other detectives is also to some degree culpable of either dishonest behavior or preferring convenience to principle. Ven'ka's chief readily deceives Lazar', for instance — perhaps Ven'ka's most serious disappointment. This action is later justified by one of the detectives as a means of raising their prestige in the eyes of the local populace: the collaborator, Lazar', must not share their credit, though without it he remains a condemned man: "'You see, right now he [the chief] is trying to strengthen the authority of the Soviet government.'"[119] Besides this ends-justify-means rationale, however, the chief is also motivated by personal vengeance against Lazar''s previous insults. Finally, even the narrator — Ven'ka's most loyal and sympathetic friend — expresses regret that Ven'ka's death has cast a shadow on their collective honor: "Vas'ka Caricyn silently touched my sleeve and said, nodding toward the coffin: 'It would have been better if the bandits had killed him.' He must have guessed my thoughts. And that reconciled him to me. ... I remembered that Ven'ka liked to say that we are responsible for everything about us. But, most likely, we must also answer for that which comes after us if we want to be genuine communists."[120] No one, except the reader, fully comprehends the moral protest behind Ven'ka's suicide — the unwillingness of a loyal and sensitive idealist to support or condone the disparity between good

---

[117]   *Ibid.*, xxvii.
[118]   Pavel Nilin, "Žestokost'", *Znamja*, XXVI (December, 1956), 75.
[119]   *Ibid.*, 71.
[120]   *Ibid.*, 74.

intentions and noble aspirations, on the theoretical level, and their betrayal, in practice. (+)

(d) Ven'ka's conflict ends perhaps more tragically than that of any other protagonist in the present survey. Even his death does not subdue his adversaries and actually causes his very best friend, the narrator, to misunderstand him. During the burial all present seem to regret his action because of its effect upon their group image. As Binjon remarks, "When he finally perishes the ideals seem to perish with him too. This change of approach hides a change of attack: in the other stories the individual is at fault; here it is society."[121] Ven'ka's conflict is still in force, even without him. (+)

(e) Nilin's ingenious use of a third person narrator (never identified by name) enables him to characterize Ven'ka in a convincingly intimate and sympathetic fashion. The narrator is made to speak of and relate to Ven'ka in a consistently deferent manner so that the reservations he expresses at story's end do not seriously alter Ven'ka's long established positive image: "It seems to me that I exist the way grass grows. All around me people achieve something they have planned in advance, attain something with all their strength. But what do I attain? ... I only follow Ven'ka about, like an observer or some sort of body guard."[122] On a still later occasion, as they are underway to capture Voroncov and detect the presence of nearby bears, the narrator enviously comments about Ven'ka's ability to restrain his fear, *etc.* Ven'ka comes alive and wins the reader to his viewpoint in great measure because of the innocent, unwitting commentary by this additional character. (+)

(f) Binyon mentions an obvious yet striking irony which all the more supports the maligned Ven'ka: "He is in fact a perfect positive hero, but instead of recording his triumph, the story ends with his death."[123]

(g) At least two symbolic touches occur in this otherwise straight-forward narrative. Just before the detectives embark on Voroncov's capture, Ven'ka encounters a fortune-telling organ grinder who leaves the narrator, at least, with an ominous foreboding. Then, both before and after the capture, the roaring of bears tends to suggest a kind of jungle attitude on the part of those hunting down the bandit: "Perhaps only I imagined how the males were now standing on their hind legs, how they were clawing each other with their fierce paws, how clumps of moulting fur were flying from their bodies. And standing nearby, staring

---

[121]   Binyon, xvii.
[122]   Nilin, *Znamja*, 7.
[123]   Binyon, xxiv.

at them, was a breathless female, waiting for the victor, the one to love —he who would prove the strongest and most aggressive."[124] This imagery anticipates and reinforces the tragic atmosphere of Ven'ka's ensuing disillusion and death. (+)

(13) Jašin, *Levers* — Citizens: Mutual trust, freedom of thought. (4)

(a) As officials of a *kolkhoz* community, the story's several male characters express conformist views which contradict their casual private opinions: during a Party meeting they react to each other and to the wishes of their regional secretary with extreme deference. Their duplicity and inhibition seem motivated by long conditioned, even subconscious fear. It is their own discomfort, rather than that of the people they supervise, which receives the story's chief attention. (+)

(b) Although themselves officials who at their own level perpetuate the same autocratic approach they so resent in their superiors, these characters are nonetheless expected, as middlemen, to exact unreasonable demands from their own people. They therefore appear compelled to resort to the same kind of pressure that is in turn applied to them. Their position is far from enviable — laboring as they must under such total duress. (+)

(c) To these characters' credit, no one else appears to demonstrate a more courageous or independent mode of behavior. The impression remains, in fact, that theirs is not an atypical situation but one imposed from above and generally manifest throughout the social hierarchy. (+)

(d) When the same characters are allowed to be themselves at the end of the meeting, they become once more likable and humane. Akulina removes her kerchief and behaves more naturally upon the arrival of people her own age. Ščukin turns his attention to the young girls. Kuzmič reassures Akulina about firewood for the school. Then, as he and Konoplev walk out to the street, "they renewed the conversation about life, customs, and work which had engaged them before the meeting."[125] (+)

(e) With his final and only subjective sentence, Jašin evidences true sympathy for his characters: "And again they were honest, sincere, straightforward people, people and not levers."[126] Unlike Dudincev's ubiquitous commentary, this single dogmatic statement (coming as it

[124] Nilin, *Znamja*, 56-57.
[125] Aleksandr Jašin, "Ryčagi", *Literaturnaja Moskva II* (Moscow, Gosudarstvennoe izdatel'stvo xudožestvennoj literatury, 1956), 513.
[126] *Ibid.*

does at the end of Jašin's consistently terse, detached narrative) has the force of a final, irrefutable verdict. It is also well demonstrated in the immediately preceding action. (+)

(f) As much as any other work in the sample, this story and its central situation are fraught with merciless irony: as the local warehouseman and a Party member, Ščukin takes advantage of his position to acquire scarce sugar, *etc.* for his own use; this he openly alludes to, while the others, including the local *kolkhoz* and Party chairmen, remain unaffected and indifferent; all fear the lowly cleaning woman who might have overheard their earlier exchange of opinion; Konoplev, who before the meeting coughed and freely expressed himself, now smothers his cough and restrains a derisive smile; during the meeting Kudrjavcev overlooks the most pressing and only practical item of business — the matter of firewood for the school; *etc.* The central irony is, of course, the complete transformation which affects each character throughout the Party meeting and which contradicts all they had said previously. The general effect is to condemn the characters' hypocrisy, as such. (—)

(g) The single word title, which derives from the speech of the regional secretary — " 'The people have to be persuaded. Lenin showed that one must actively persuade. And he tells me: "You persuade too! We persuaded you earlier, when the *kolkhozes* were organized, and now it's for you to persuade the others, to enforce the Party line. You", he says, "**are** now our levers in the country." ' "[127] — is invoked in turn by the local officials and finally by the author. As applied to the characters in the plot, it suggests the mechanical, impersonal force they in turn exert upon their fellow workers and makes them seem heartless and repugnant. (—)

(h) The use of colloquial dialogue in the first part markedly contrasts with the characters' 'bureaucratese' during the Party meeting —

"Comrades!" said the president of the *kolkhoz*, "neither the regional committee nor the regional executive committee has endorsed our production plan. I consider that we have overlooked something and allowed it to evade us. This does not become us. We have not fulfilled our explanatory task with the masses and have not convinced them. But the people have to be persuaded, comrades. You and I are the Party's levers in *kolkhoz* territory ...' It looked as if Ščukin was just about to laugh again. But he did not laugh and only poked Konoplev in the side and whispered: "Do you see what's happening? Do you recognize him now?"[128]

The return to more natural and colloquial dialogue at story's end shifts the reader's sympathy to the characters depicted. (+)

[127]   *Ibid.*, 504.
[128]   *Ibid.*, 511.

(14) Kaverin, *Quests and Hopes* — Tat'jana Petrovna Vlasenkova: Kramov, the bureaucracy. (1)

(a) Like Dudincev's Lopatkin, Tat'jana is maligned by other scientists and bureaucrats whose projects and whose consequent status her research threatens to jeopardize. They eventually frame her husband, Andrej, who is subsequently sentenced to a labor camp; their intent is, first, to impede the acceptance of Tat'jana's discovery by tarnishing her personal reputation, then to exact her complicity by offering to arrange for Andrej's release. Tat'jana is clearly the innocent victim of vengeful, unscrupulous men of influence. (+)

(b) Tat'jana's situation is rendered the more pathetic by at least two circumstances — first, the fact that she is a woman while her opponents are invariably men; second, the fact that her discovery, penicillin, is obviously so vital and beneficial. (+)

(c) Critics have noted that the villains who oppose Tat'jana "are many. There is nothing of the lonely or isolated evildoer about them",[129] and that "Kramov ... is the almost exact counterpart in medical science of Dudintsev's Avdiyev in engineering. The Deputy Minister Maximov is the same type as Dudintsev's Deputy Minister Shutikov".[130] The critic, M. J., hastens to add that "Kaverin's heroine, however, is such a wonderful woman in every respect that she is quite incredible, and the bad bureaucrats are too wicked for credibility."[131] In any event, there is no question of their wickedness or of Tat'jana's relative virtue. (+)

(d) Although Gibian contends that the novel concludes "with a question — will the Kramovites remain in or return to power, or will a better future come despite the grim past?"[132] — there are equally positive omens. Already toward the end of the War, Tat'jana observes that "all of this is only an instant which seems like an endless night, but night does not continue into night because night ends and morning does finally arrive."[133] If only death can unseat Kramov, at least his chief disciple and principal adversary, Skrypačenko, has been expelled from the Party and dismissed as an institute director. If, after the War, Tat'jana's diary

[129] Gibian, *Interval of Freedom*, 116.
[130] J., *Soviet Studies*, 324.
[131] *Ibid.*
[132] Gibian, *Interval of Freedom*, 116. "Only minor improvements take place at the end of the book", Gibian says elsewhere; "there is no obligatory happy end. The main villain happens to die, but he had been in power and generally honored up to his death and countless others remain in the saddle." George Gibian, "The Revolt of the Moscow Writers", *The New Leader*, XL (August 26, 1957), 19.
[133] Venjamin Kaverin, "Poiski i nadeždy", *Literaturnaja Moskva*, II (Moscow, Gosudarstvennoe izdatel'stvo xudožestvennoj literatury, 1956), 266.

notes that they must still contend with propagandists, artificers, and pseudo-scientists[134] and if Andrej is still ostracized, Tat'jana nonetheless senses that "no one speaks to me about Andrej. But I hear his voice in the rustling of young leaves on the future Promenade of Heroes. In the din of a carpenter's hammer, in the scraping of a brick layer's trowel. In the sirens of giant new factories. In the laughter of children playing in the Pioneer garden."[135] Andrej does finally return and finds another opportunity in research. Although Tat'jana anticipates that, as a scientist, her son will have difficulties and disappointments similar to their own, the general opinion seems now to be that "they still operate, these people [e.g., like Kramov], but they are already becoming anxious, constantly aware that they have stolen their influence and position from others who are a hundred times more worthy. They are still holding on to their plush chairs with their teeth, but one fine day they will simply dissolve in the air, like a mirage, like a bad dream."[136] Tat'jana even concedes that "by contrast with the future, the past has never before been so insignificant. ... I am quite convinced that what is most important will yet transpire in the forthcoming ... year."[137] (—)

(e) The entire novel is told from Tat'jana's point of view, in the form of journal-like notes. Thus Tat'jana's position always seems justifiable or pathetic. The author's concluding comment further enhances her sympathetic characterization: "Here breaks off Tat'jana Petrovna Vlasenkova's notes — on the early morning of January, 1956. ... it's time we were both resting — Tat'jana Petrovna from my demands, my ceaseless inquiries ... and I from this novel, which I have already been writing for ten years and in which you will find the true story of both a typical yet unusual life."[138] (+)

(f) Perhaps the novel's chief irony is that those who have the most to contribute are, for this very reason, suppressed and victimized. (+)

---

[134] "In the post-War years we were faced with a strange assignment — to prove that our medical science was developing at an exceptional pace or, at least, more quickly than the science of other countries or of the rest of the world. We and no one else had made all the greatest discoveries of the nineteenth and twentieth centuries — this was affirmed in books and articles, in films and in the theatre. ... How many clever people, having nothing in common with medical science, received high positions under the protection of secret connections, without which it appeared impossible to work or live ... this was Kramov's victory — a victory whose whole terrible significance even he perhaps could not foresee." Ibid., 275-276.

[135] Ibid., 279.

[136] Ibid., 288.

[137] Ibid., 289.

[138] Ibid., 291.

(g) Like Panova's *Seasons*, this work also ends on a New Year's Eve. The close circle of old friends and kin has survived the fight with Kramov, *etc.* Their anticipation of the new year itself conveys a kind of facile optimism which in turn dissipates any serious concern about further confrontations or future difficulty. (−)

(15) Kaverin, *Quests and Hopes* — Tat'jana Petrovna Vlasenkova: Her husband, Andrej. (2)

(a) In the absence of her husband, Andrej, Tat'jana becomes enamoured of her childhood acquaintance, Volodja Lukaševič, whom she first meets while on assignment in Stalingrad, then again in a Moscow hospital. Though conscience-struck, Tat'jana avoids discussing with Andrej her attraction to Volodja until the latter awkwardly arouses unfounded suspicions. Andrej then reproaches Tat'jana with never having loved him. (+)

(b) The long periods of separation and loneliness occasioned by the War have created an unusual opportunity for husbands and wives to be thrown together with other people equally hungry for solace and affection. Despite this, Tat'jana long discourages Volodja and is indeed never intimate with him. Her feelings for Andrej also remain fairly constant. She is hardly unfaithful in the conventional sense nor is her infatuation in any way willful or wanton. (+)

(d) Soon after Andrej reproaches her, Tat'jana confesses both her fleeting feelings for Volodja and her consequent mendacity, begging Andrej's forgiveness. Although she wonders if she is trying to convince herself as much as Andrej — "only once perhaps the bitter half conscious thought flashed in my mind that I was persuading not only him but also myself. But it occurred to me only momentarily"[139] — they talk through the night and are reconciled by morning. (−)

(e) Again, the first person point of view does much to reconcile the reader to Tat'jana. (+)

(16) Nagibin, *Light in the Window* — Vasilij Petrovič: Fellow citizens. (2)

(a) Vasilij Petrovič has long denied his special apartment to various deserving or needy fellow citizens. When, finally, Nastja and Stepan defiantly appropriate its facilities, he berates them, as beseems his official duty. They in turn snub him. (−)

[139]   *Ibid.*, 182.

(b) The prohibition on the apartment's use did not originate with Vasilij Petrovič. He has always felt guilty about denying it to others and doubtless suffers more than anyone else in having to enforce this regulation. (+)

(c) That Vasilij Petrovič is, basically, more thoughtful and fair-minded than even Nastja is revealed on an earlier occasion when Vasilij slaughters his own pig in order to keep a number of vacationers from going hungry and for which he incurs Nastja's disapproval. Nastja appears to enjoy pleasing those for whom she works because of the attendant personal satisfaction. When she appropriates the apartment she seems motivated by self-pity and spite more than, as with Vasilij Petrovič, from a sense of the injustice to others. (+)

(d) Vasilij Petrovič's self-disgust after evicting the trespassers, Nastja and Stepan, is described in the story's concluding sentence and further corroborates the view that he is repelled by the waste and deprivation which result from proscribing the apartment's use: "... Vasilij Petrovič suddenly cut himself short, fell silent, and with astonishment heeded the strange, new, unfamiliar feeling which arose, was engendered within him, penetrating to the tips of his toes, a feeling of unbearable disgust toward his very own person".[140] At this juncture, furthermore, no reconciliation has been effected. (+)

(g) As he slaughters his pig, Vasilij Petrovič becomes aware of the "despairing reproach in [its] dull, amber, narrow little eyes. ... None of the pigs he had ever slaughtered for his own use had looked at him in that way."[141] (+)

(17) Pogodin, *Petrarch's Sonnet* — Dmitrij Alekseevič Suxodolov: Conventional impersonality, insensitivity, conformity. (1)

(a) Suxodolov refuses to be restrained by public opinion or social pressure from pursuing his quite platonic and harmless interest in a young girl, Maja. (+)

(b) He opposes those who try to threaten or shame him on grounds that his interest in Maja is his own affair and in no way endangers his loyalty to the Party, his work, or the already long effete relationship with Ksenija Petrovna, his wife. Maja has in fact inspired a renewed interest in life and motivated him to be more effective in his work: "'Some kind of transformation took place in my being. I breathe more easily, I get

---

[140]   Jurij Nagibin, "Svet v okne", *Literaturnaja Moskva*, II (Moscow, Gosudarstvennoe izdatel'stvo xudožestvennoj literatury, 1956), p. 403.
[141]   *Ibid.*, 396.

along better with people ... I am inspired in my work ...'".[142] In addition, Suxodolov's attraction to Maja may well reflect his belief that "'truly there are no longer any dangerous classes — which raises the question, whom should one hate? There are still good-for-nothings, outcasts, thieves ... Perhaps they deserve our scorn, but sometimes also our sympathy. I am speaking here about hatred. Whom should I hate in my native country? Perhaps it is time I learned to love ...'".[143] (+)

(c) Those who oppose Suxodolov are, as Gibian notes, in turn attacked for "representing the opposite point of view" and "are uniformly described as *meshchane*, bourgeois, or petty middle-class people".[144] Both Armando and Suxodolov's wife have had their own far from platonic affair together. Armando becomes a professional failure and is a disloyal friend, moreover, while Ksenija is shrewish and unwarrantedly suspicious as well as vengeful. As Suxodolov's professional rival, the puritanical Dononov appears far too eager to denounce him to the Party, encouraging Ksenija, as he does, to file complaint. Suxodolov also opposes Dononov on philosophical grounds, as does their likeable superior, Pavel Mixajlovič, who remains in basic sympathy with Suxodolov:

PAVEL MIXAJLOVIC. "... According to your logic, the world consists of two opposite colors — black and white. Everything else is double dealing, deception, and so forth. Can you neither comprehend nor imagine any other kind of situation?"
DONONOV. "I try, but can't."
PAVEL MIXAJLOVIC. "But there is also a third position ... then a fifth, and a tenth. There are a myriad of situations which your and my hobbled dogmas simply reject. According to dogma Suxodolov is a dishonest person, according to life he is respectable, a saint."
· ·
DONONOV. "I don't know. ... I'm used to making absolute judgments."
PAVEL MIXAJLOVIC. "Because of this absoluteness people have frequently been imprisoned."[145]

Unlike Suxodolov, his adversaries display a malicious tendency: they presume error rather than see the good in others who are not like them. (+)

(d) The resolution of Suxodolov's woes is fairly optimistic. The charges brought against him by Ksenija and Dononov are dismissed by Party officials, and he retains his former position. And as, at story's end, he parts with Maja, who will presumably marry a more eligible suitor, she

[142] Nikolaj Pogodin, "Sonet Petrarki", *Literaturnaja Moskva*, II (Moscow, Gosudarstvennoe izdatel'stvo xudožestvennoj literatury, 1956), p. 306.
[143] *Ibid.*, 314.
[144] Gibian, *Interval of Freedom*, 89-90.
[145] Pogodin, *Literaturnaja Moskva*, 337.

nonetheless tells him: "'And remember that I ... if you call me, with just
a word, I'll abandon everything, fly to you.' (*She leaves.*)"[146] Dononov
is to be transferred; Armando, drunk and dissolute, is deeply disturbed
at having betrayed Suxodolov; and even Ksenija now realizes that she
and Dononov have "'pushed him into someone else's arms'"[147] and
admits that Suxodolov is "'not just some sort of average muddlehead ...
but a great man'".[148] The misunderstandings are ostensibly resolved. (—)

(g) *Petrarch's Sonnet* is, with its unrealistic images and nebulous
allusions, in some ways reminiscent of symbolist dramas *à la* Blok or
Maeterlinck. At the play's outset, Suxodolov encounters a drunken
beggar who sings a song in couplets, then indicates that he was himself
once a successful musician until he became the victim of women — thus
ominously anticipating Armando's own end after falling in with Ksenija
against her husband. In the same scene a portly couple twice cross the
stage, the woman rudely scolding the man. All of this doubtless implies
that a man is doomed to certain downfall by submitting to a domineering
woman, *e.g.* Ksenija. Musical imagery, on the other hand, is used in
support of love "as an emotion which is each person's own private
business".[149] Suxodolov indicates, for instance, that in his letters he has
addressed Maja as "'my song'".[150] This provokes Armando to liken the
pair to Petrarch and Lara and Suxodolov's letters, in turn, to Petrarch's
sonnets — hence the play's title. Later, during a concert intermission,
two girls cross the stage, one of them remarking that "'music has a
negative effect on me ... it demobilizes me'".[151] By contrast, Maja
declares that "'music is pure emotion'"[152] and that Suxodolov's letters
are "'pure poetry'".[153] At play's end a mysterious ferryman (Life? Time?)
intercepts first Maja, then Suxodolov, declaring their kind of relationship
"'forgiveable, if, of course, an affair of the heart'"[154] and admonishing
Suxodolov to look to the future — "'it's still too early for you to be
looking back at the past.'"[155] Meanwhile, allusions are made to Maja's
flying off like a quail, to falling stars, and to burning *tajga*. Finally,
Suxodolov addresses the ferryman: "'Hey, on the other shore, listen!

[146]   *Ibid.*, 350.
[147]   *Ibid.*, 347.
[148]   *Ibid.*
[149]   Gibian, *Interval of Freedom*, 88.
[150]   Pogodin, *Literaturnaja Moskva*, 306.
[151]   *Ibid.*, 307.
[152]   *Ibid.*, 309.
[153]   *Ibid.*, 312.
[154]   *Ibid.*, 348.
[155]   *Ibid.*, 351.

Summon the people to the wharf! The *tajga* is burning!'"[156] Unclear as is the import of this concluding imagery, that of the play's symbolism as a whole is an obvious endorsement of Suxodolov's courageous and independent life-affirming position. (+)

(h) Occasional parallelism helps reinforce the same imagery, favoring Suxodolov: the ice cream vendor at the play's beginning, who, like the ferryman at its end, sympathizes with Suxodolov's love; the quarrelsome wife, who resembles Ksenija scolding Suxodolov; the discussion of music by two anonymous young women, then by Maja and Klara — one of each pair indicating displeasure, the other satisfaction. (+)

(18) Ždanov, *Journey Home* — Pavel Varygin: Unpleasant reality, the people. (5)

(a) As a bureaucrat, Varygin has been shielded from the facts of common life. On the occasion of his mother's funeral, however, he experiences at first hand the impoverished conditions and the neglect to which his mother and others in her village have been subjected. His reaction is less one of sympathy than of mixed annoyance, displeasure, and guilt. (+)

(d) Varygin takes the first opportunity to return to the city, there to escape his unpleasant impression of rural existence. (−)

(e) Varygin becomes increasingly guilt-ridden and thus condemns himself in the reader's eyes. There is nonetheless a certain selection at work in the author's portrayal of Varygin's character: all of Varygin's reactions are self-centered and his personality so generalized (he is nowhere physically described and much less distinctly depicted than each of the secondary characters whom he briefly encounters) that one instinctively equates Varygin with the forces that have permitted the peasants' sorry situation. Even the question posed by one of them which, at story's end, he reviews in his mind — " 'Is it right, what they have done to us?'"[157] — can be construed as a kind of indictment. (−)

(f) Gibian similarly discusses the hidden irony in this work and Granin's *Own Opinion* (see pp. 142-143). In Varygin's case, however, the condemnation is greater, for he endeavors to escape his ordeal and, after he has boarded his train, we are told, "the feeling of some sort of guilt did not long remain".[158] (−)

---

[156] *Ibid.*
[157] Nikolaj Ždanov, "Poezdka na rodinu", *Literaturnaja Moskva*, II (Moscow, Gosudarstvennoe izdatel'stvo xudožestvennoj literatury, 1956), 414.
[158] *Ibid.*, 414.

(g) Varygin's guilt is effectively reinforced by what he imagines to be his mother's *samovar* and a knot in her table mocking him and by the vision of his mother, in her coffin, posing the question of justice. (−)

(h) The recurrence of the laughing *samovar* and the winking knot of wood in Varygin's thoughts while on the train reinforces the fact of his guilt and its awareness in his subconscious. (−)

(19) Pasternak, *Doctor Živago* — Jurij Andreevič Živago: Sense of purpose and self-determination, political power, the regime, political inhumanity, regimentation. (1)

(a) Of the conflicts heretofore discussed, Ven'ka Mályšev's rebellion against social inhumanity and Suxodolov's insistence on the primacy of the unrestricted private life both blend in the complex personality of Jurij Živago, whose own rebellion against any and all forms of human regimentation is, though perhaps less overt, clearly the most uncompromising. "A far-reaching individualism — more extreme than that of the West — is Pasternak's own philosophy. Zhivago even writes a pamphlet on the theory of individuality as the biological basis of the organism."[159] Živago's tragic aspect is most apparent, however, after he finally returns to Moscow from Varykino and finds himself so out of tune with the prevailing social order: "He arrived in Moscow at the beginning of NEP, the most ambiguous and dishonest of all Soviet periods."[160] As Neander explains, "an individualist can be liquidated, compelled, or allowed to fade away, like Dr. Zhivago fades away and as in the West, under considerably more pleasant outward circumstances, countless only-individuals fade away, which can occur in existentialist bars as well as in the upholstered interiors of luxury automobiles."[161] Judged by his overt actions, however, Živago is, if pathetic, far from admirable. He is extremely self-centered, something of a libertine, undedicated as a physician, and most unvaliant as a citizen of the dawning social order. If he later becomes so estranged from the new life, it is to some extent because he has himself preferred to stand apart rather than assimilate to it. As Komarovskij tells him:

"There is a certain communist style. Very few are equal to it. But no one else so openly contradicts this manner of living and thinking as you do, Jurij

[159] Gibian, *Interval of Freedom*, 149.
[160] Boris Pasternak, *Doktor Živago* (Ann Arbor, The University of Michigan Press, 1959), 477.
[161] Irene Neander, "Pasternaks Neuer Roman", *Osteuropa*, VII (December, 1958), 786.

Andreevič. I don't understand why you play with fire. You are a mockery, an insult to this way of life. It would be well if you were discreet about it. But there are influential people here from Moscow. They know your inner thoughts very well. The local priests of Themis are very displeased with you. Comrades Antipov and Tiverzin have bared their fangs in yours and Larisa Fedorovna's direction."[162]

Levitzky enumerates the 'specific weaknesses', which distinguish Živago from Dostoevskij's 'contemplator', Myškin — both of whom are "meek, naive, and spiritually profound. ... he is indecisive, not especially heroic, a far from exemplary father and husband, and he succumbs to the charms of women (if that is a weakness)".[163] Brown adds that "in every important crisis Zhivago temporizes, yields, retreats from action. His life in historical terms is a failure. Even his doctor's skill has not been put to use. He has had two families, but took care of neither, and the woman he loved he surrenders to a scoundrel ...".[164] (—)

(b) In Živago's defense, however, one can argue that his circumstances are unusual, even extreme, and that his very irresponsibility is, in its way, an act of courage, a plea for the badly threatened and fast extinguishing claim to individuality and personal freedom. To be fully appreciated, Živago must also be understood in terms of his (and Pasternak's) distinct system of values:

Although he is himself not too religious in the traditional sense of this word, he [Živago] remains true throughout his entire life to the legacy of the immortality of spiritual values. For just this reason, and despite his strongly emphasized apolitical concern, he sublimely, indeed emotionally expresses his protest against militant materialism, with its possessiveness, power madness, and spiritual blindness.[165]

Thinking about life, the perception of aesthetic experience, and the understanding of history are the highest activities of which man is capable, in his opinion. To him the great contribution of Christianity is that the Gospels teach that in the new way of living born of the heart, and in the new form of society, which is called the Kingdom of Heaven, there are no nations, there are only individuals.[166]

"The sense of relationship to the highest forces of earth and heaven" is also at the root of the hero's exceptional nature.[167]

[162] Pasternak, 431.
[163] Sergey Levitzky, "Svoboda i bessmertie. O romane Pasternaka 'Doktor Živago'", *Mosty*, II (1959), 230.
[164] Brown, 273.
[165] Levitzky, *Mosty*, 229.
[166] Gibian, *Interval of Freedom*, 149-150.
[167] Leonid D. Rzhevsky, "O tajnopisi v romane 'Doktor Živago'", *Grani*, XV (October-December, 1960), 159.

Thus, in terms of a more abstract, more philosophical frame of reference Živago is dynamic and noble. His vacillation and failure of nerve, his lack of commitment and devotion to temporal causes or other persons is explained by the implicit fatalism which ostensibly pervades his life — the uncontrollable forces of revolutionary devastation, the many chance encounters, the unforeseen recurrences, the uncanny coincidences of time and place which seem to dictate the passage of events and a given individual's successive choices, his relationships with others, his fortune or misfortune. Here the autobiographical echo is indeed undeniable. One recalls the essential metaphysical concern of Pasternak, the poet,[168] with the interaction, say, between natural phenomena and the emotional tone of a given mood or speculation. One recalls, further, the great significance which Pasternak attributes to the chance encounters in his own early life — the presence in his home of Rilke; his subsequent acquaintance with, first, Scriabin, then Hermann Cohen; and, later, his disillusion with the pursuit of music, then philosophy (his disappointment with philosophy in turn provoked by his rejection in love), both disciplines which nonetheless remained integral to his verse and helped to form in him his distinct and profound poetic gift. "'He never really abandoned music, he merely changed his instrument.'"[169] Finally, in his antagonism, as such, to the forces of contemporary history, Živago "opposes the Soviet system but does not struggle against it. His destruction is the tragedy of a passive victim."[170] (+)

(c) Živago contrasts not unfavorably with his rivals for Lara's affection — her seducer, Komarovskij, and her husband, Antipov-Strel'nikov. If Živago is self-centered, he is neither ruthless nor a cynical opportunist like Komarovskij, who unscrupulously manipulates others' lives to serve his own worldly ends. One need but recall Komarovskij's role in the death of Jurij's father and his conquest of Lara to question his motive in offering to escort both her and Živago to safety. Lara's subsequent account of her life with Komarovskij in the East, though nebulous and inconclusive, implies that she was forced to endure as yet unimagined abuse. Whether at Komarovskij's or another's hand is not altogether clear:

"No one is left. The one has died. The other took his own life. And only he has remained alive who should have been killed ... whose life I attempted to

---

[168]   Helen Muchnic, "Boris Pasternak and the Poems of Yurii Zhivago", *From Gorky to Pasternak: Six Writers in Soviet Russia* (New York, Random House, 1961), 370.

[169]   *Ibid.*, 387.

[170]   Gibian, *Interval of Freedom*, 150.

take but missed, that alien, insignificant nonentity who transformed my life into a chain of unheard of crimes."[171]

. . . .

"Do you remember, how I bade farewell to you there in the snow? How you deceived me! Would I really have left without you? Oh, I know, I know, you did it against your will, for the sake of my supposed welfare. But after that everything went wrong. Lord, what I went through there, what I endured! But you know nothing about it. Oh, what did I do, what did I do! I am such a criminal, you could never imagine! But I am not at fault. I lay for three months in the hospital, for one month I was unconscious. And ever since, Jura, my life has been a cross. I've had no peace from spiritual grief and suffering. But I haven't told you, haven't revealed the worst. I can't name it, I haven't the strength. When I recall that part of my life my hair stands on end out of horror. And, you know, I'm still not sure that I can answer for myself, that I'm completely normal. But, you see, I don't drink, like many, I haven't taken that path, because a drunken woman is irredeemable, unthinkable, don't you agree?"[172]

If, on the other hand, Živago is socially apathetic, he is no deluded zealot like Paša Antipov, whose 'other-directed' aspirations prove abortive and far more harmful than the evil they were intended to cure: "'But we viewed life like a military expedition, we dislodged boulders for the sake of those we loved. And, although we brought them nothing but sorrow, we didn't in the least offend them because, as it turned out, we suffered much more than they.'"[173] If Antipov contrasts with Živago "as 'a man of action' to a man of contemplation",[174] a Don Quixote to a Hamlet, the contrast largely favors Pasternak's Hamlet, for "Pasha has been wrecked as a human being", says Edmund Wilson, "by his attempt to play a Marxist role".[175] (+)

(d) Živago's end, like his life, is ostensibly a failure: "Zhivago and Larisa, who do not attempt roles, will outlive him [Pasha], but they, too, are to be destroyed."[176] "... at the book's close, Živago loses his family by exile, his Lara, his pride, and even his medical career".[177] Still, on quite another level, Živago's life has been both positive and purposeful. Hampshire vindicates Živago, for instance, in that "sources of renewal have been discovered, whenever a man achieves some heightened sense

---

[171] Pasternak, 511.
[172] *Ibid.*, 514.
[173] *Ibid.*, 471.
[174] Levitzky, *Mosty*, 231.
[175] Edmund Wilson, "Doctor Life and His Guardian Angel", *The New Yorker*, XXXIV (November 15, 1958), 213.
[176] *Ibid.*
[177] Levitzky, *Mosty*, 232.

of his own part in the processes of life that makes his own death seem
not a final waste. Men arrive at this deliverance and rest when they have
succeeded in communicating perfectly with one other person, giving the
testimony of their experience, either in love or in a work of art."[178]
"Nonetheless", says Levitzky,

> he has remained within himself a free spirit. He is not subject to the collectiviza-
> tion of souls and has preserved his own personality from the terror-imbued
> hypnosis of mass standardization. ... Especially noteworthy is the novel's
> epilogue, where the action shifts to the period of World War II where Živago's
> two former friends, Dudorov and Miša Gordon, reminisce about their war
> experiences and about the long deceased Živago. In order to understand the
> epilogue in its true perspective, it is necessary to remember the philosophy of
> immortality introduced at the novel's beginning. ... we see that this philosophy
> of freedom and immortality ... finds its application in the novel, particularly
> in the epilogue. We see how Doctor Živago's friends preserve his memory and
> how his legacy reinforces their hopes in the advent of a new era of a "free
> soul." ... despite the novel's tragic conclusion, it ends on a life affirming note.[179]

Part of Živago's 'legacy' is, of course, his cycle of poems, which are,
significantly, appended at the very end of the novel and of which Brown
says the following: "... Zhivago's testament, his thin volume of poetry,
is assembled and preserved as special revelation by his friends and follow-
ers. The life that he lived had little importance; the life that he created
in art was a priceless treasure bequested to all men. ... The poet insists
that creatures like himself who produce nothing of immediate value, do
have use."[180] (+)

(e) The novel's (and its hero's) strongly autobiographical implications
should be obvious to any reader at all acquainted with the circumstances
of Pasternak's first family and their eventual emigration: his sojourn in
the Urals as a tutor; his return to Moscow soon after the Revolution; his
profound, yet tenuous relationships with a number of women, one
actually named Larisa (Reisner),[181] another — the gifted and tragic

---

[178] Stuart Hampshire, "'Doctor Zhivago' As from a Lost Culture", *Encounter*, IX
(September, 1958), 5.
[179] Levitzky, *Mosty*, 232-234.
[180] Brown, 273.
[181] Edmund Wilson, "Legend and Symbol in 'Doctor Zhivago'", *Encounter*, XII
(June, 1959), 13-14. Gleb Struve, for one, disputes this particular association: "Nor
do I think ... that Lara Guichart is modeled after Larisa Reisner. I shall not go into
details, but I knew Larisa Reisner, and I see no resemblance between the two women."
Gleb Struve, "Sense and Nonsense about *Doctor Zhivago*", *Studies in Russian and
Polish Literature*, (ed.) Zbigniew Folejewski, *et al* (The Hague, Mouton & Co., 1962),
247.

Marina Cvetaeva. In addition to the parallel events in Pasternak's life and in his story as such, however, "there can be no doubt that ... the author's very thoughts ... are put in Zhivago's mouth".[182] Rzhevsky concurs that Pasternak's principal characters are "interpreters of the author's viewpoint"[183] and that the "cryptogram 'The Poems of Jurij Živago'" constitutes the 'form' of the "inner novel's culmination".[184] The novel's 'poetic part' is therefore the "entrenchment of the author's monologue where 'what is the author's and 'what is Živago's' already fuse beyond reckoning".[185] Levitzky adds that "the image of Živago is, above all, one of the emanations of the author himself. To this testify the general order of his thoughts and the partial analogies in the first poetical experiments of both the author and his hero."[186] To the extent that Pasternak invests his hero with his own person, the treatment is, as might be expected, sympathetic and understanding. (+)

(f) Perhaps the key irony of *Doctor Živago* is the discrepancy between its hero's ostensible life of indecisiveness and failure, on the one hand, and his rare, courageous life- and freedom-affirming nature, on the other. In view of the latter, Živago's image acquires both meaning and inspiration. (+)

(g) *Doctor Živago*'s barren narrative is well conpensated by the novel's abundant symbolism. According to Levitzky, "it is not a realistic novel. It contains not a little impressionism, bordering on symbolism. It contains not a few 'leaps' which distinctly remind one of Pasternak's poetic devices ...".[187] Wilson adds that "it is a modern poetic novel by a writer who has read Proust, Joyce, and Faulkner",[188] that it "is studded with symbols and significant puns. ... there is something in it of *Finnegan's Wake* and something of the cabbalistic *Zobar*, which discovers a whole system of hidden meanings in the text of the Hebrew Bible. ... poetic symbolism does really pervade *Zhivago*. ... from the moment one begins to get the sense of this, the story gains another dimension".[189] Finally, "the whole book is an enormous metaphor for the author's vision of life. ... it is not only the imagery of these metaphors, but their rhythms of recurrence, their alienations, their confluences and interfusions that

---

[182] Levitzky, *Mosty*, 230.
[183] Rzhevsky, *Grani*, 154.
[184] *Ibid.*, 164.
[185] *Ibid.*, 155.
[186] Levitzky, *Mosty*, 230.
[187] *Ibid.*, 226.
[188] Wilson, *Encounter*, 15.
[189] *Ibid.*, 5.

express the real sense of *Zhivago*".[190] Gibian, Muchnic, Rzhevsky,[191] Silbajoris, and Wilson each allude to Pasternak's symbolic use of nature:

Nature is the most striking setting of the book. Far from being mere background, it is a rich, poetically rendered presence ever before us, placed into a vital relationship with the characters' fates.[192]

Throughout the book, Pasternak notes the power of nature to communicate to human beings the impulse towards freedom, towards rebirth. (It is, for example, a sudden storm, sweeping the smell of rain into the school-room where she sits ... that rouses Lara to her decision to escape from Komarovskij.)[193]

In Pasternak's highly integrated world, a room forms a whole with that which is outside its windows, a man's soul is what he is "in others"; thoughts and emotions are part of the Nature in which they take place, "subject" and "object" are one, and the angel wings of Fate cast great shadows by the light of candles on the ceilings of small rooms.[194]

Silbajoris in turn makes special mention of such images as shadows, trains, a rowanberry tree, black horses, as well as of specific human beings and the very language of Lara and Živago — each of which, in its way, connotes "the mysterious force of life".[195] According to Rzhevsky, "the novel's central and 'transparent' image-symbol is that of a *burning candle*".[196] Both he and Muchnic trace this image's continuity of associations from its first appearance in Živago's words to Tonja's ailing mother — '"Consciousness is a poison for one who indulges it for his own sake. Consciousness is a light, shining outward, it lights the road before us so that we will not stumble. Consciousness is the lamps on an advancing train. Turn them inward and you will have a catastrophe.'"[197] — to its recurrence in Jurij's thoughts of Blok, the latter's evocation of the Christmas spirit, the vision of lighted yule trees, Jurij's observation from the street of a single candle lit by Lara in Paša Antipov's window, his simultaneous incantation of "'A candle burned on a table. A candle burned' ... Jurij whispered to himself the beginning of something unclear, unformed, in the hope that the rest would come by itself without con-

[190] *Ibid.*, 16.
[191] Rzhevsky, *Grani*, 158.
[192] Gibian, *Interval of Freedom*, 148.
[193] Wilson, *Encounter*, 11.
[194] Muchnic, *From Gorky to Pasternak: Six Writers in Soviet Russia*, 350.
[195] Rimvydas Silbajoris, "The Poetic Texture of *Doktor Zhivago*", *The Slavic and East European Journal*, IX (January, 1965), 21-22.
[196] Rzhevsky, *Grani*, 151.
[197] Pasternak, 68.

straint. But it did not come."[198] — to related allusions in Lara's and Živago's affectionate dialogue: "'Are you still burning and glimmering, my bright little candle?' she softly whispered, misty and heavy with sleep. 'Sit beside me for a minute. I'll tell you about my dream.'"[199] — to the author's speculation whether, as Lara views Živago's corpse, she could know that he once saw her candle burning in the very same room — to the recurrence of the identical line in Živago's own poem, "Winter Night":

The snow storm modelled on the window pane
Circles and shafts.
A candle burned on a table,
A candle burned.[200]

— to related allusions in his companion poem, "Star of the Nativity".[201] This latter, like the preceding reference to Blok and Christmas, immediately establishes a tie between candle light and the novel's Christian symbolism. Živago's identification, moreover, with one or another comparable individual from history, myth, or *belles lettres* suggests to Wilson that Pasternak was influenced by *Finnegan's Wake*:

Zhivago, the "living man," is simultaneously Hamlet, St. George, and Jesus, just as H. C. Earwicker, "Here Comes Everybody," is Adam, Tristam, Finnegan, etc., and he is, just as Earwicker is split in two as the brothers Shem and Shawn, divided into the two personalities of the half-brothers, Evgraf and Yury. Larisa — the feminine principle ... — is given, like Anna Livia, the essence of liquid element.[202]

Wilson explains that "the characters, all named — as was customary in Russia under the old regime — after saints of the Orthodox calendar, were partly to be understood in terms of the legends of those saints".[203] His exhaustive analysis emphasizes Živago's identification with St. George, who defended Christianity before the emperors, Diocletian and Maximian (and about whom Živago composes one of his poems, "Fairy

---

[198] *Ibid.*, 82.
[199] *Ibid.*, 450.
[200] *Ibid.*, 550.
[201] *Ibid.*, 554-556.
[202] Wilson, *Encounter*, 15. Struve, however, disagrees: "I am almost sure that before he wrote *Doctor Zhivago*, Pasternak knew little of Joyce." Struve, *Studies in Russian and Polish Literature*, 249. Matlaw's interview with Pasternak would appear to substantiate this view: "'It has nothing to do with Joyce. There is such a book (*knizhka*) Finnegan, isn't there?'" Ralph E. Matlaw, "A Visit with Pasternak", *The Nation*, CLXXXIX, No. 7 (September 12, 1959), 134.
[203] *Ibid.*, 5.

Tale"):[204] "St. George is supposed to have died three times, and three times to have been resurrected, as happens with Yury on the three occasions when he feels himself going under and is revived by his half-brother Evgraf."[205] Wilson also draws intricate parallels between three sets of triangular relationships: Strel'nikov — Lara — Živago; Emperor Maximian — his wife Queen Alexandra — St. George; and Stalin — his wife N. S. Allilueva — Boris Pasternak. Finally, the name George (which derives from the Greek for farmer or 'cultivator', *georgos*) is meant to suggest that Jurij is "the idealistic but still down-to-earth man"[206] with positive values. As for Lara's name, Wilson discovers mythical referents in a St. Larisa, in one of the names for the wife of Poseidon,[207] in the sea gull,[208] and in associations with the sea in general "because it is an image of the free, the spontaneous — the truly alive":[209] "'Lara is just like this. It is impossible to converse with them [life and existence], but she is their representative, their expression, their means of hearing and speaking ...'".[210] Wilson thereupon identifies a series of passages which associate Lara with marine elements:[211]

In the pantry a window had been broken out by the beating of a linden branch and on the floor were huge puddles, as well as in the room which had been Lara's, a sea, a regular sea, a whole ocean.[212]

. . . .

The promise of her proximity, restrained, cold like the bright northern night, unowned by anything or anybody, will rush to meet him, like the first wave of the sea which you run toward in the dark along the beach's sand.[213]

. . . .

"I'll depict you this way. I'll put your features on paper the way after a storm an explosive sea lays traces on the sand of the strongest, farthest lapping wave."[214]

"When Zhivago first visits her, in Yuryatin", Wilson adds, "he finds her

[204] Pasternak, 545-548.
[205] Wilson, *Encounter*, 6.
[206] *Ibid.*, 8.
[207] Wilson, *The New Yorker*, 222.
[208] Wilson, *Encounter*, 11.
[209] *Ibid.*, 9.
[210] Pasternak, 402.
[211] Wilson, *Encounter*, 10. Struve is nonetheless sceptical: "The images of flowing water, and of rain especially, have always played a great part in Pasternak's poetry: the latter is saturated with rain and thunderstorms, but this is not anything especially connected with *Doctor Zhivago* and its characters." Struve, *Studies in Russian and Polish Literature*, 245-246.
[212] Pasternak, 152.
[213] *Ibid.*, 314.
[214] *Ibid.*, 464.

drawing water from a well. It is again very windy."[215] Such imagery, he finds, is in turn related to poetic inspiration and, usually in conjunction with wind, to social upheavals like the Revolution.[216] Živago's recorded encounters with Lara — some six or seven in number — tend to coincide with threats to or with the taking of someone's life. In addition, "her appearances seem to coincide with political events".[217] Wilson concludes that "probably ... Larisa represents the spirit of freedom ... and ... once the new system has been got under way, she prefers to be free of that, too".[218] (Hence, Lara's quick departure from Moscow to Siberia shortly after the October Revolution.) Muchnic adds the following: "With Lara, minor, commonplace, day-to-day interests reflect the greatness of the orbit within which they take place. And in his [Jurij's] poems she figures as the Magdalene, the Virgin, the Maiden saved from the Dragon. She represents the lesson of Christianity that "the individual human tale has become the tale of God".[219] Still other critics, including Struve,[220] see Lara as the personification of Živago's native land. Indeed, for Mary and Paul Rowland, his three successive life companions together represent "his motherland in all her varied aspects".[221] The "three mother-daughter pairs" — Anna Ivanovna and Tonja Gromeko, Amalija and Larisa Gišar, Agafja and Marina Ščapova — respectively symbolize the pre-revolutionary aristocratic 'cultured milieu',[222] the milieu of the bourgeoise",[223] and "working class Mother Russia in her older and younger aspects".[224] This does much to explain Živago's inconstancy as a lover:

[215] Wilson, *Encounter*, 10.

[216] *Ibid.*, 10-11.

[217] *Ibid.*, 12. Komarovskij's seduction, for instance, is supposed to reflect the "vicious circle of revolutionary violence and reactionary reprisals that finally brought on the Moscow insurrection of December 22nd", while Lara's attempt upon Komarovskij's life and her consequent wounding of Moscow's attorney general relates to the assassination of the prime minister, Stolypin "in September, 1911. The revolutionary movement, which he succeeded in suppressing, did not emerge again until 1917." *Ibid.*, 12-13.

[218] *Ibid.*, 13.

[219] Muchnic, 402.

[220] "... if Lara does symbolize anything besides the life-giving power, it is *Russia*". Struve, *Studies in Russian and Polish Literature*, 247.

[221] Mary F. Rowland and Paul Rowland, *Pasternak's 'Doctor Zhivago'* (Carbondale, Southern Illinois University Press, 1967), 57.

[222] *Ibid.*, 45. Anna Ivanovna's names, for instance, and the names of her husband's family all reflect those of various Russian rulers. When she dies therefore it is very much like the putting away of "Imperial Mother Russia". *Ibid.*, 17.

[223] *Ibid.*, 46.

[224] *Ibid.*

Faithfulness to Tonya means clinging to the old order. The principle of the tsarist regime as the legal authority in Russia. In that case he must eventually go into exile or perish, for each day it grows plainer that Tonya and what she represents cannot survive in the new world. ... In short, he is not *spiritually wedded* to the doctrine of Russia as Tsar's daughter. What he does feel is that a true middle class, whose education, progressive spirit, and Christian ethics are potential in Larisa ... ought to lead Russia and shape her future.[225]

Lara's seduction by Komarovskij thus comes to symbolize "one aspect of a greater seduction".[226] Her predicament, as Mother Russia, is also made more comprehensible and more profound by the rich allusions to a variety of archetypes: "... Lara is no Roma/Babylon, complacently giving herself to her drag-on-consort. She is Persephone carried off by Hades. She is an ensnared and terrified Magdalene unwillingly forsaking the Christian way."[227] One also better understands why "the Doctor refuses to clarify the situation involving Tonya and Marina, despite the reproaches of Gordon and Dudorov; he will not repudiate or stigmatize *any* aspect of his motherland. Marina bears him two daughters, thus replacing his two children by Tonya, now lost to Russia. In the new Third Rome the girls' names seem quite fitting: Capitolina and Claudia."[228] The name Evgraf, on the other hand, not only derives from that of the martyr, St. Evgraphos,[229] but, meaning as it does in ancient Greek, 'good letterer', suggests in turn that Jurij's half-brother is also his "poetic inspiration",[230] "his poetic self", who "arrives unexpectedly, nobody knows from whence, but always from somewhere above, and when he has given his helping hand, he vanishes. Is it possible for an artist to understand whence or how his creative genius comes?"[231] "But more than that, he is whatever it may be that shakes the kaleidescope of human lives, and, standing apart, is alone capable of seeing their pattern, a manipulator like Pasternak, himself ...".[232] Thus, besides his miraculous intervention on a number of occasions in Jurij's behalf, besides being a symbol of fate, that is, Evgraf performs something of the function of Puškin's Tat'jana, who, in that poet's digressions, is also equated with his artistic muse. In addition, says Muchnic, Evgraf

[225] *Ibid.*, 135.
[226] *Ibid.*, 49.
[227] *Ibid.*, 170.
[228] *Ibid.*, 178.
[229] Wilson, *The New Yorker*, 222.
[230] Muchnic, 350.
[231] Wilson, *Encounter*, 8.
[232] Muchnic, 350.

represents Živago's 'death'[233]. Thus, at story's end, both Evgraf and Lara stand before Živago's coffin: "These two, though immortal, *were* Yury. One was his creative genius, the other the life-giving force which for a time he had made his own."[234] This affinity between art, death, and life is already advanced in Živago's meditation at the time of his wife's mother's funeral: "Now, as never before, it was clear to him that art is always, unceasingly, occupied with two questions. It undeviatingly contemplates death and thus undeviatingly creates life."[235] Pasternak's obsession with the interaction of life and death is further symbolized in the names, Živago and Strel'nikov.[236] Wilson elaborates, explaining that, in its very spelling, *Živago* derives from the Old Church genitive-accusative singular form of 'the living one', as found in the angel's celebrated "*Quem quaeritus?*" address — "Why seek ye the living among the dead?" (Luke 24:5) and as it similarly occurs in the novel's very second paragraph: "'Whom are they burying?' They answered them: 'Zhivago'."[237] Wilson further observes[238] that Jurij Živago, like Lara, is to some extent associated with water images, either alone or in conjunction with her:

In response to the desolation induced by death in the people slowly walking behind him, he wished, with the irresistability of water eddying in a funnel and rushing into its depths, to work out forms, to create beauty.[239]

. . . .

[233] *Ibid.*, 356.
[234] Wilson, *Encounter*, 9.
[235] Pasternak, 91.
[236] Gibian, *Interval of Freedom*, 149; Levickij, 232; Muchnic, 402.
[237] Pasternak, 91.
[238] Wilson, *Encounter*, 10. This is also mentioned by the Rowlands (Rowland and Rowland, 10), although debunked, apparently, by Pasternak himself: "'The article of Edmund Wilson is very good, he is very smart, but what he says about ... the name Zhivago is just nonsense. I am an enemy of this kind of symbolism. That Lara is a foreigner just happened that way, it has no specific meaning, and the remarks about her and history are just not so. The name Zhivago has no special significance. It is just a name.'" Matlaw, *The Nation*, 134. The validity of such symbolism must therefore be left to the reader's own discretion. In any event, Pasternak's statement — "'I am an enemy of this kind of symbolism'" (*Ibid.*) — tends to belie what all critics generally concede to be the very essence of his poetic style. Matlaw himself registers the following reservations: "I concluded that while a great deal of symbolism in the novel is conscious, there is also much that is equally valid if not conscious or intentional and that Pasternak's objections to Wilson's article may well be a negative application of the so-called intentional fallacy, the notion that a work of art necessarily means what its creator intended it to mean." As for *Zhivago* itself, "... its structural and symbolic ramifications, while consistent, far exceed Pasternak's conscious efforts". *Ibid.*, 135.
[239] Pasternak, 91.

"Farewell, my mighty and native one, farewell, my pride, my rapid blue dear river, how I loved your day-long splashing, how I loved to dive into your cold waves."[240]

(Lara addressing the deceased Jurij). Sandwiched between Uncle Nikolaj's discussion of history-Christianity-death-resurrection and the suicide of Jurij's father is this telling comment —

"Metaphysics, my little father. My doctor has forbade it, it doesn't settle on my stomach." "God forgive you. Let's forget it. How fortunate you are! What a view you have — but you don't appreciate it! You live but don't comprehend it."
  It was painful to look at the river. It flowed under the sun, shimmering like a sheet of metal. Suddenly it was full of folds. A large steamship loaded with horses, carriages, old women, and peasants was drifting from this to the opposite shore.[241]

— which early establishes the association of water with the themes of death and resurrection. "Hamlet", the first of Živago's twenty-five poems and "the truly key poem of the cycle",[242] further supports this association, as do the concluding poems, which treat the figure of Christ and the subject of his passion. (And in both the Hamlet and Christ allusions, Rzhevsky discovers further echoes of Blok.)[243] The foregoing literary-historical allusions do much to qualify and even vindicate Živago's essentially alienated and ostensibly anti-social, egoistic behavior: "Pasternak has chosen Christ's very words to describe Hamlet's dominant motive. And this is the key to an understanding of Pasternak's own hero. Instead of being a spineless figure (as Hamlet, too, is sometimes misrepresented), Yuri Zhivago is conceived as a resolute Hamlet who, in his self-renunciation for a great cause, is following Christ's example."[244] Struve affirms this view: "They [other critics] have thus wholly overlooked the main theme of Zhivago, the theme of self-abnegation, self-sacrifice, self-immolation."[245] The Rowlands in fact devote an entire chapter to Živago as an essentially 'kenotic' sufferer.[246] Not only is Christ the subject of some seven of the cycle's poems, but His story, "which unavoidably attends the self-discovery of the author's 'self' is in essence the 'transparent' theme of the novel's whole prose section":[247] "The star of

[240] *Ibid.*, 514.
[241] *Ibid.*, 10.
[242] Rzhevsky, *Grani*, 156.
[243] *Ibid.*, 152.
[244] Rowland and Rowland, 61.
[245] Struve, *Studies in Russian and Polish Literature*, 240.
[246] Rowland and Rowland, 173-194.
[247] Rzhevsky, *Grani*, 158.

the nativity, the Magi, Magdalena, Jesus, the tragic themes of Gethsemane and Golgotha shadow the figures of the novel's hero and heroine, the theme of their life, their fate, and their love."[248] According to Wilson, "one sequence" of Živago's poems "recapitulates certain incidents of Zhivago's life and grows darker with the parting from Larisa and the darkness of the oppression of Stalin", while, "sombre yet affirmative, ... the other of these sequences commemorates the holy days of the Church and the main events of the life of Jesus".[249] Equally profound is the adaptation of Christ's Gospel, again symbolically, to Pasternak's particular philosophy, which in some respects resembles "Hegel's account of the historical role of Christianity in creating the modern man, who need no longer be either master or slave"[250] as well as Bergson's *élan vital*.[251] This is related to the novel's revolutionary-collectivist context by allusion to the Book of Revelations and its own veiled reference to Rome in terms of Babylon. The Rowlands insist in fact that "the Bolshevik Revolution and its makers are constantly associated with motifs from the New Year festivals of ancient Near Eastern religions"[252] and view the entire novel as "a Russian apocalypse".[253] Lara's various suitors thus represent the four horsemen of the Apocalypse, the archangel Michael, *etc.*[254] Pasternak's approach is, in any event, distinctly literary and, at least in Živago's poems, strikingly unique in presenting "the Christian myth, not in the modern fashion, by reworking it in terms of contemporary incidents, but by re-creating it dramatically, so that its relevance to modern times appears not as parody but as symbol".[255] Its fullest elucidation in the prose section comes not from Jurij but from his uncle, Nikolaj,[256] and, later, from Lara's wierd female acquaintance (a fool-in-Christ?), Simuška.[257] Christianity is thus interpreted in the broadest possible fashion, as the symbol or "echo, or another expression, of that which lies at the heart of all aspects of life; of history, ethics, metaphysics, and aesthetics, as well as of theology".[258] This amounts, for Pasternak, to the interaction of birth, death, and rebirth (resurrection, immortality,

---

[248]   *Ibid.*, 160.
[249]   Wilson, *The New Yorker*, 225.
[250]   Hampshire, *Encounter*, 5.
[251]   Rowland and Rowland, 160-161.
[252]   *Ibid.*, 31.
[253]   *Ibid.*, 16.
[254]   *Ibid.*, 66.
[255]   Muchnic, 380.
[256]   Pasternak, 10.
[257]   *Ibid.*, 421-425.
[258]   Muchnic, 403.

human succession, legacies, memory, *etc.*). Hence the symbolism at-
tached to the birth of offspring to both Tonja and Lara — that of boats,
havens, and crossroads: "This timeless image of the boat at anchor,
bringing new souls from unknown shores, with its Platonic, Virgilian,
and Dantesque echoes, underscores the difference between the transient
and the eternal, and strikes once more upon the major theme of *Doctor
Zhivago*, which begins with death and ends with resurrection."[259] Even
the town of *Jurjatin*, an obvious play on the hero's name, suggests "the
spiritual harbor which, in future, she [Lara] is to find in him. Here, too,
is Lara's three-year-old Katenka, playing in the yard under an upturned
boat, finding her own child's shelter beneath its roof. Yuriatin is, moreover, both a shipping town and a station of the Ural Railway, on which
much momentous traveling is to take place; the symbol of the crossroads
is unmistakable...."[260]

A further instance of death-and-rebirth symbolism is the parallel
between the elder and younger Živago's deaths — in both cases as they
leave a train or train-like vehicle — and of which Wilson adds that

in the interval between these two deaths, the incidents that join them together
are now seen to compose a sequence of images ... of the cycle of extinction and
survival. The vodka and pancakes of Shrovetide — which in Russia is dedicated
both to the dead and to the renewal of life by marriage — are a ritual symbol
of the theme. ... The book begins with the burial of Yury's mother and the
night in the monastery, in which no special ray of light is seen; and we have
afterward the escape from the train of the prisoners condemned to forced
labor; the shooting, on the edge of a precipice, of the vodka distillers and other
offenders, of whom one, a backward boy, survives; the burial of the old woman
by her murderer in the pit in which she has been hoarding potatoes and the
escape, through taking refuge in an underground cave, in the raid that follows
the murder, of a boy who is suspected already of having committed it; and the
trapping in the cellar of the murderer of the husband of the peasant woman
with whom the daughter of Zhivago and Larisa has been living. In this last-
mentioned instance of burial, there is no resurrection for the brute. ... she
allows him to strangle her little boy, whom he has taken down with him as a
hostage. The abandoned daughter of Zhivago and Larisa flags a passing train ...
and the trainmen bring out the murderer, tie him to the tracks, and run over
him. The woman, as a result of all this, goes mad. Here it is the girl who
escapes from the household which has for her been a tomb.[261]

Such symbolism is carefully interwoven with and related to that of the

---

[259] *Ibid.*, 352.
[260] *Ibid.*, 353. Of these crossroads, the Rowlands add that "to picture the alternatives open to his main characters, he [Pasternak] introduces significant intersections
without number". Rowland and Rowland, 161.
[261] Wilson, *The New Yorker*, 223-225.

Christ story — "the 'Lara-Živago' theme is assimilated by that of 'Magdalena-Jesus'".[262] "From the almost symbolic burial of Živago's mother, through the suffering of souls, to the gates of Golgotha", says Levitzky, "the path is a religious-symbolic one."[263] Wilson observes, moreover, that "Pasternak's book is studded with the symbolism of the Orthodox Church. The five barless windows of the house in Siberia are the five wounds of Jesus. (The number five elsewhere appears, and always with sinister significance: the five-o'clock train from which the older Zhivago throws himself, the five conspirators in the forest who try to murder the partisan leader."[264] Numerous allusions tend to suggest, moreover, that Živago is, among other things, a Christ figure. His patronymic "identifies him as the spiritual son of St. Andrew the Apostle who, according to Russian tradition, first brought Christianity to the pagan Slavic tribes".[265] His mother, whose name is Marja (Mary), may also stand for 'the Mother Church' and her burial suggest "that when the twentieth century opened, the Russian Church was a body without spirit".[266] When Zhivago shoulders firewood this may symbolize "the most spiritualized example of the *transitus*: Christ's bearing of the cross to Golgotha".[267] Of his last days in Moscow, we are told that

the doctor empties himself — renouncing his profession, his social status, his one-time friends. He humbles himself — becoming poor, living with his former servants and marrying their daughter. He, too, is offering his body to be broken that his country may one day recover its lost spiritual food. When he enters Markel's kitchen in the heart of Flour Town, the evocation of broken bread is unmistakable. The large table in the center, we are told, is the same one on which, in the days of bread rationing, loaves of bread for the whole house were "cut and broken and crumbled." (Later this penumbrial image hovers around Yuri's table when his body lies upon it in death.)[268]

And, in his later poems, "the human figure of Yuri Zhivago blends into the legendary figure of St. George, and both of them merge with the human-divine figure of the Christ, all three united in acts of love and self-sacrifice".[269] In this same religious symbolic context, Evgraf, who "may even be intended to embody the old conception of 'Holy Russia'", is, in addition, "a guardian angel, but he is also, with his dark face, the

[262] Rzhevsky, *Grani*, 162.
[263] Levitzky, *Mosty*, 236.
[264] Wilson, *The New Yorker*, 221.
[265] Rowland and Rowland, 10.
[266] *Ibid.*, 19.
[267] *Ibid.*, 97.
[268] *Ibid.*, 179.
[269] *Ibid.*, 170.

angel of death. And yet death is always followed by resurrection. Three
times, like the fairy in the folk tale, he comes to Yury Andreyevich's
rescue. ... On his third intervention, he brings death in the flesh. ... but
Evgraf preserves his manuscripts, the poems in which Yury lives again".[270]
Even the sign which Živago reads on, again, FIVE separate occasions
— "Moro and Vetčinkin. Seeders. Threshers." — is related by Wilson
to the theme of birth, death, and resurrection in both a mundane and a
religious context. In the first instance, Wilson argues, Moro is in French
a compound "of *mort* and *eau*, death and water".[271] There are, beyond
this, applications of the Russian root, *mor*, in "the word *mor*, pestilence
(the typhus which Yury comes down with in the winter of the Bolshevik
Revolution?)" and in "'the verb *morit'*, to extenuate, starve, or exhaust,
as well as in the word *more*, sea".[272] In the second instance, the Russian
name, Vetčinkin, is formed from the root of *vetčina*, literally ham, which,
when punned with the diminutive suffix, -*ka*, becomes, quite literally, a
'hamlet'. "Yury, in his service with the partisans, will shoot, in a senseless
and compulsive way, a young officer of the whites", says Wilson, "just
as Hamlet kills Polonius and Laertes".[273] In the final instance, and in the
context of Živago's 'key' poem, "with these references on his left, and
on his right the seeders and threshers, Yury's Hamlet, in great embarrassment, finds himself — 'to be or not to be?' — solicited both by life and
death, which, however, like the buried seed, like the compact ambiguity
of the word *Moreau*, embody a single process: the indestructable continuity of life".[274] Leastways, this same Hamlet mouths the words of

---

[270] Wilson, *The New Yorker*, 221.
[271] Wilson, *Encounter*, 15.
[272] *Ibid.*
[273] *Ibid.*, 14.
[274] *Ibid.*, 15. The Rowlands suggest an altogether different version — equally mundane although consistent with their 'apocalyptic' interpretation of the novel itself:
"The names suggest a Franco-Russian business partnership. *Moreau* is a common
French surname derived from the archaic adjective *moreau* (jet-black), now found
chiefly in the phrase *cheval moreau* (jet-black horse). We immediately think of the
Black Horse of the Apocalypse, which bore the rider Famine. *Vetchinkin* apparently
comes from the adjective *vetkhy* (old, ancient, decrepit, worn-out). The full significance
of the ubiquitous signboard would seem to be, 'The same old famine despite new-
fangled machinery and mechanized agriculture'." Rowland and Rowland, 121.
Struve reacts with his usual caution: "I prefer not to discuss the 'Moreau and Vetchinkin' business. If a *pun* had been intended its symbolism escapes me completely. But
I don't think Pasternak intended here a pun, which as far as Hamlet was concerned
would have been in bad taste while the other half of it is poor from the linguistic point
of view and quite pointless. Although in his early days of excessive verbalism Pasternak
was given to poetic punning, this is not exactly his style." Struve, *Studies in Russian
and Polish Literature*, 247.

Christ in Mark 14:36 — "'if thou be willing, Abba, Father, Remove this cup from me'"[275] — implying perhaps that Živago's art, his very verse, is a means to immortality. This idea is at least reminiscent of Pasternak's view in a student paper written in 1910, entitled "Symbolism and Immortality". Adds Muchnic: "It is something like this that Yurii Zhivago says to the dying Anna Ivanovna, and something of this kind too that seems to him to be embodied in folk art, in the Russian folk song ...".[276] It is also worth remembering that, for Pasternak, "... immortality ... is another word for life, a somewhat intensified word. The resurrection of all humanity in another world is unthinkable and ridiculous. ... But life, which pervades the universe, does incessantly renew itself in its innumerable different forms. Our birth is a resurrection, and we shall rise again in our children as well as in our work."[277] As Muchnic puts it, "Time does not stop, but words and actions give immortality to all that dies. Herein ... lies the meaning of history and of Christianity as Pasternak understands them."[278] From such a truly transcendental frame of reference, therefore, "the modern idea of the individual's, and especially of the artist's 'alienation' is here curiously modified".[279] Not only in his art but in the story proper, in its symbolism, the idea of regeneration emerges as a major theme. This is already anticipated in the young Živago's reassuring discourse on death to the ailing Anna Ivanovna and prefigured, even earlier, in the separate ritual-like initiations of the three young boys — Jurij, Miša Gordon, and Nika Dudorov. The Rowlands, for example, liken Jurij's experience in the gully at Dupljanka to "a descent to the underworld",[280] Miša Gordon's train ride and witnessing Andrej Živago's death to an ancient 'scapegoat'[281] ritual, and Nika's struggle in the water with Nadja Kologrivova to the legendary Babylonian "battle between the god and the she-dragon".[282] There follow numerous incidents[283] and journeys, each a kind of death, burial, and return to life: as plotted by the Rowlands, the train trip to Siberia and Varykino "carries forward the implications of the hero's dream-descent to Hades, a part of his mystic initiation during typhus. His train journey externalizes

[275] Pasternak, 532.
[276] Muchnic, 357.
[277] Wilson, *The New Yorker*, 206.
[278] Muchnic, 377.
[279] *Ibid.*, 382.
[280] Rowland and Rowland, 34.
[281] *Ibid.*, 35.
[282] *Ibid.*, 41.
[283] *Supra*, 174.

the *descensus*."[284] The stay at Varykino and Jurjatin itself serves as "a period of incubation as the prelude to regeneration".[285] "Following Christ, Yuri Andreyevich sets out once again upon a symbolic descent into hell. The blasted land through which he walks toward Moscow teems with underworld imagery identifying his route. ... Such a death may be violent, like Christ's, or a long, slow death of voluntary suffering, like Dr. Zhivago's."[286] The ritual of Živago's death — "three steps before his final collapse, indicating that his three-day battle in hell (his poem 'Turmoil') is finished"[287] — the return of Lara — "on still another level, Lara is recognized as the Russian Mary Magdalene addressed by Serafima, and her arrival affirms Sima's implied prediction that Russia will one day come back to the faith she forsook and, with bitter tears, entreat forgiveness"[288] — and even the reunion of a more thoughtful Dudorov and Gordon fourteen years after Živago's death are construed as further extensions of this same symbolism:

Both these men have served long prison terms. ... Gordon's lot was much the more terrible — a twofold descent into hell: first the icy hell of a concentration camp in the far north, then the fiery hell of a death battalion at the front. How he regards his ordeals is revealed by a familiar symbol; he wants to wash his filthy clothes. Here we have St. John's imagery again: "Blessed are those who wash their robes." Gordon, who made the ardent defense of Christianity in Chapter 4 of the novel, apparently became an apostate to curry favor with the Communist regime. Now, to signify his penance and rebirth, he washes his clothes and bathes in the river.

Dudorov is no longer a pipe (*duda*) on which others play. He, too, has washed his robes — in his own blood. He has suffered wounds, imprisonment, and the loss by death of the girl he loved.[289]

Pasternak manages to invest the particulars of experience with a rewarding mystery to which fallible human judgments are entirely alien: "Consistently does Pasternak admire what he calls 'the modesty' of the particular, the given instance, the immediate perception."[290] "For him, history exists, not in abstractions and philosophical generalizations, but *only* in the immediately concrete."[291] The conclusions he draws are, if

---

[284] Rowland and Rowland, 115.
[285] *Ibid.*, 127.
[286] *Ibid.*, 175.
[287] *Ibid.*, 190.
[288] *Ibid.*, 191.
[289] *Ibid.*, 196.
[290] Muchnic, 393.
[291] David Burg, "Um Pasternaks Platz in der Sowjet-literatur", *Osteuropa*, IV (September, 1964), 645.

anything, metaphoric, hence truly poetic — the observable consequences of the interplay of experiential phenomena:

Thus in the depths of delirium, through the confused symbols of transformed memories and perceptions, the major theme is once more adumbrated. The Sadovaya crossroads are recalled because of the emotions they had stirred, the boy with Kirghiz eyes had actually been visiting Zhivago's sick room, while the idea of death and resurrection is naturally induced by illness and the hope of recovery. The concept of the stormy three days' entombment as an attempt of earth to engulf immortal love could be an imaginative transmutation of Tonya's three-day confinement, as well as of the Gospel story, and the dual nature of death as both destructive and creative is a ruling idea of the novel.[292]

If *Doctor Živago* also represents "a historical-political fable ... of the kind that since the time of Turgenev has been traditional in Russian fiction",[293] this is incidental to its other values. In such a context, the deaf-mute encountered by Jurij in the train may well represent "the insulation from reality of a certain type of *exalté* in the first phase of the Revolution",[294] and it is probably also true, as Gibian suggests, that, as symbols of social protest, "individuals reach each other ... through the ages, by the mediation of art" or, as with Živago and Lara, have recourse to 'extramarital love':[295] "... political life is replaced not by family life but by the life of the individual. The greatest love of the book is not married love. ... The love of Zhivago and Lara is a fulfillment through the communion of two individuals, not through the family unit. Lara and Zhivago later separate. Pasternak is careful to avoid Tolstoy's exaltation of the family."[296] Such protest and its accompanying tragic implications are far outweighed by the novel's overwhelming, life-affirming transcendental interest, albeit in symbolic guise. For all his reservations about its symbolic interpretation, for instance, a critic like Struve does not hesitate to endorse Wilson's ultimate thesis: "He understood at once that what mattered most was not the indictment of the Revolution but the affirmation of positive values, 'presented with such an overwhelming power.'"[297] As a poet-novelist, Pasternak would be at home on any planet and somehow marvel, whatever his predicament. (+)

(h) Gibian harshly characterizes the novel's story line, as follows:

[292] Muchnic, 357.
[293] Wilson, *The New Yorker*, 218.
[294] Wilson, *Encounter*, 15.
[295] Gibian, *Slavic Review*, 423.
[296] Gibian, *Interval of Freedom*, 150.
[297] Struve, *Studies in Russian and Polish Literature*, 245.

... it is clearly the author's first novel. Some transitions are clumsy and tenuous, the handling of dialogue slovenly. The reader occasionally loses track of who is talking to whom. The beginning of the book overwhelms one with too many underdeveloped characters, in too many brief scenes; the end is shadowy, schematic, perhaps even unfinished. It is clear that the author is contemptuous of what other novelists consider correctness, and is so impatient to speak about what to him are the important things that he jumps over all trivial matter. When he wants to move to a new dialogue or scene, he does so in a few bold, brief sentences, ignoring continuity, point of view, and probability.[298]

From a conventional standpoint, certainly, the book's myriad coincidences provide an equally devastating sense of implausibility. There is already the gathering, in Živago's childhood, at Ivan Ivanovič's, where those present witness the stopping of a distant train, caused by Živago's father's suicide and involving the participation, to some extent, of Komarovskij, Lara's future corrupter; the father of Miša Gordon, Živago's future friend; and an old woman, the future guardian of Paša Antipov. Then there are the strange coincidences: that — in all of expansive Russia — Lara and her mother should first come from Jurjatin, Lara and Paša return there, and Tonja's family have property at nearby Varykino, to which Živago and Tonja should in turn repair; that Živago's first two encounters with Lara should coincide with, first, her mother's attempted suicide, then, the death of Tonja's mother; that particularly Lara's candle should have once shone in the window of the very room where the deceased Živago had by chance acquired accommodations and is brought for viewing, and that for this reason Lara chances upon him; that the birth of Živago's and Tonja's son should coincide "with the acknowledgement of Živago's first, brilliant diagnosis and also with the news that he is to be called to the front";[299] that, at the front, Lara, Gordon, and Živago should unwittingly come together —

The wounded man who had just died was the reservist, Gimazetdin; the man shouting in the forest — his son, Sub-lieutenant Galiullin; the nurse was Lara; Gordon and Živago — witnesses; all were together, along side one another, but they either did not recognize or had never known each other; and some matters would remain forever uncertain, while others would have to wait for an explanation until a later occasion, a new encounter.[300]

— etc. Other critics have nonetheless stoutly defended both the novel's extensive coincidences and its other narrative idiosyncracies, as follows:

[298]   Gibian, Interval of Freedom, 150.
[299]   Muchnic, 351.
[300]   Pasternak, 121.

The apparent formlessness of *Doktor Zhivago*, which from the point of view of novelistic technique could be regarded as a handicap, turns out to be almost an artistic virtue. It is in effect a device for the author to show us the vicissitudes of individual human fate. ... the artistic impact and suggestiveness of the novel is far greater than in works where the author arranges and re-arranges, re-models, re-shapes human thoughts and emotions so that they form a constructive pattern.[301]

The presence of the realistic techniques of an objective narration and of subjective techniques ... is, as it were, an expression of the novel's fundamental conflict — the conflict between the inner world of a human soul of exceptional merit and the world surrounding it.[302]

Pasternak's crisscrossing lines of Fate are not the stock in trade of those eighteenth- and nineteenth-century novelists whose purpose was to astonish and amuse; they are exempla, rather, necessary demonstrations of an uncanny, but not unnatural world, a world of mystery, where man must wonder at how strange the evolution of events may be and at how illogically a moment may contain the past, how unpredictably the future.[303]

. . . .

Coincidence, which plays a major role, far from being a structural flaw, is a symbol of Pasternak's awe before the play of Fate.[304]

That Pasternak employs coincidence with some such intent is well indicated by a further stanza from Živago's "Winter Night":

On the lighted ceiling
Fell shadows,
Of crossed arms, of crossed legs,
Of crossed destinies.[305]

Critics have suggested other meaningful effects which can be attributed to the novel's ostensibly faulty narrative structure:

The whole truth about the experience of these years is to be built up gradually, and, partly for this reason, the first fifty pages of the novel are confused by the lack of a firm narrative. The reader is required to accept a series of impressions,

---

[301] Folejewski, *Indiana Slavic Studies*, 32-33.

[302] Rzhevsky, *Grani*, 153.

[303] Muchnic, 357.

[304] *Ibid.*, 348. Thanks to Matlaw, Pasternak has himself provided the definitive answer: "'Of course I made the coincidences on purpose, that *is* life, just as I purposely did not characterize the people in the book. For I wanted to get away from the idea of causality. The innovation of the book lies precisely in this conception of reality. ... For me reality lies ... in the multiplicity of the universe, in the large number of possibilities, in a kind of spirit of freedom, a coincidence of impulses and inspirations (not *religious* inspiration, just inspiration — *vdokhnovenie*). Even modern science and mathematics, about which I know little, or better, nothing, is moving in that direction, away from simple causality.'" Matlaw, 134.

[305] Pasternak, 550.

not yet intelligibly related to each other, and a set of unexplained characters who are not clearly identified in his mind until much later.[306]

As the complicated plot develops, the reader becomes more immersed in the hero's inner world. These immersions alternate with related narratives which appear to serve as background for the main action. Thus, when the main characters speak "from the soul," while unimpressive in the narration, they again come alive; in the dialogues and meditations they reveal their fundamental personality, and such sections are full of drama or saturated with poetic inspiration.[307]

Pasternak was deeply convinced that the nature of events and experiences does not reveal itself in clearly layed out causal chains, but in the most astonishing ... conjunctions, identifications, and associations. The hidden connecting lines, causes, and tendencies in chaos — these it was whose exposition Pasternak strove for throughout his life. He did not wish to deny chaos, but to clarify it. Chaos, however, is not amenable to direct analysis. For this reason, Pasternak's portraits are complicated — a by no means casual "complexity".[308]

Rzhevsky in turn discusses the novel's "repetition of images",[309] which perhaps suggests that, of Pasternak's literary progenitors, he whom Pasternak so lovingly translated and whose own complex and obstruse genius has so long mystified the world is after all among the foremost:

If any single literary influence is to be mentioned, it seems to me that the most prominent is Shakespeare. The use of the wild dialogue of the characters of the under-plot, the short scenes that somehow, as in *Antony and Cleopatra*, suggest the great distances, and, above all, in the suggestion of signs of the supernatural in the natural order. ... There is something Shakespearean ... in the sudden blending of the imagery and the philosophical reflections, in the affinities found between thought and natural appearances.[310]

In a more subtle, but equally fundamental respect, Pasternak shows a distinct affinity to Puškin:

His natural gift for feeling was accompanied by a well-cultivated habit of balanced and detached perception, which became second nature and made his work in essence, though not in its outward aspect, more like Pushkin's than any other poet's in the Russian language. It may lack Pushkin's chiseled quality and ebullience; it may be sober in tone, more cerebral, but what it shares with Pushkin's is a broad, calm, independent view of human destiny, through which the deeply experienced event stands out in all its individuality, because without being typical it is seen in relation to the general lot of men.[311]

---

[306] Hampshire, *Encounter*, 4.
[307] Levitzky, *Mosty*, 225.
[308] Burg, *Osteuropa*, 644.
[309] Rzhevsky, *Grani*, 161.
[310] Hampshire, *Encounter*, 4.
[311] Muchnic, 394-395.

The parallel between *Doctor Živago* and *Evgenij Onegin* as esthetic manifestoes is further brought to mind, particularly in terms of Živago's verse, which becomes "the conclusive, necessary resolution, the final chord in which a wandering melody has come to rest. It is a scheme which is, so far as I know, unique in fiction. Other novelists have been concerned with writers and their work, but none, with the possible exception of Pushkin, has taken his stand on so profoundly, so essentially aesthetic a position".[312] For a full appreciation of its narrative values, therefore, it is perhaps necessary to recognize that, ultimately, "*Doctor Živago* is not so much a novel as both an esthetic confession and sermon",[313] that it "is not about the Revolution; it is about how and why poetry is written":[314]

One is aware throughout that this is not only a philosopher's, but also a painter's and a poet's novel. A painter's, because it leaps from one visually conceived image to another. A poet's, because its logic and system of connections rely on symbolic rather than the conventional narrative continuities of prose fiction. An insistent symbolism is basic to the book.[315]

Again, Pasternak uniquely 'dramatizes'

what he conceives to be the function of art. And this function he sees as nothing less than the means whereby the experience of individuals is made permanent as well as comprehensible. ... The poems [Živago's] show how even slight and wholly personal incidents become significant, how a casual episode turns into a human value, and so endures beyond the life of any one man.[316]

. . . .

His [Pasternak's] conclusions are a sheaf of poems, and his answers — what answers there can be to the final *how* and *why* — are given in the structure of the story: the improbability of events and their summing up in poetry. ... The inclusive symbol is nothing less than the marvel of life itself in Pasternak's own, special view of it, as an endlessly reiterated challenge to death.[317]

. . . .

... what he does write is a definition of art in terms of his experience which, though entirely his own, is not at all exclusive. The end, like Zhivago's poems, gives meaning to all that precedes; and in the light of the goal toward which everything is pointed, chance meetings and casual occurrences take on magical significance. ...[318]

As Rzhevsky suggests with respect to Živago's poems, "the image-symbol

[312] *Ibid.*, 345.
[313] Levitzky, *Grani*, 225.
[314] Muchnic, 387.
[315] Gibian, *Interval of Freedom*, 150-151.
[316] Muchnic, 346.
[317] *Ibid.*, 358.
[318] *Ibid.*, 358-359.

becomes an *image-secret cipher*. The form of creative self-disclosure produces a *kind of mystery*."[319] So, too with the novel's prose, whose narrative structure — ingenious and skillful, in the view of most critics — but reinforces the sublime image of its central hero and all that, as a reflection of the author, he philosophically, esthetically, represents. Indirectly, too, the novel serves "to resurrect the language, to restore to words the burden of meaning which has been corrupted by what Pasternak called 'the power of the glittering phrase.' ... the language of life itself was extinguished; this is the most terrible of the indictments contained in *Doctor Zhivago*."[320] (+)

(20) Pasternak, *Doctor Živago* — Paša Antipov: Human values, human life. (4)

(a) After the Revolution, Paša becomes, as Strel'nikov, an inhuman terrorist who, in order to realize the system in which he believes, does not spare the innocent. (—)

(b) Though Paša-Strel'nikov's is a typically vicious ends-justify-means rationale, he nonetheless has good intentions. His zealousness is a reaction to the social injustice he had earlier experienced as a lower class youth:

You couldn't understand this. You grew up differently. Ours was a world of urban outskirts, railroads, and workers' slums. Filth, crowding, poverty, the degradation of workers and women. Then there was the amusing, unpunishable impudence of corrupt mamas' boys, the student sons of bureaucrats and merchants who put off the tears and entreaties of the cheated, humiliated, deluded people with a joke or a burst of scornful annoyance. It was an Olympus of parasites who were remarkable for never exerting themselves, never aspiring, never giving or bequeathing to the world anything at all.[321]

(+)

(c) In terms of the story's symbolic-philosophical intent, Paša emerges less favorably than his foil, Živago.[322] The Rowlands suggest that, even before the Revolution, "Antipov has taken an antipodal direction from Zhivago. ... [he] loses interest in his major field, the humanities, and turns with a passion to physics and mathematics ... [which] connotes the materialistic mechanistic philosophy of the Russian Marxists."[323] (—)

[319]   Rzhevsky, *Grani*, 156.
[320]   Patricia Blake, "New Voices in Russian Writing", *Encounter*, XX (April, 1963), 38.
[321]   Pasternak, 471.
[322]   *Supra*, 162-163.
[323]   Rowland and Rowland, 82.

(d) Paša's rationale ultimately collapses as means become their own ends and Pasha turns into his own victim:

The commissar, now under suspicion, has hoped to clear himself of the charges against him, but he knows from his own methods with others that he will not be given a chance to defend himself. The interesting point is made that he has elicited so many confessions of counter-revolutionary guilt that he is tempted by the guilt of his inhumane acts to make a 'self-unmasking' confession not of these but of political offenses he has not committed. He shoots himself in the morning, but not before, in the talk of the previous night, he has poured out ... the whole apologia for his generation.[324]

Paša ends as one of "the inconsolable people" who have never succeeded in "communicating perfectly with one other person"[325] — a truly tragic figure:

The very self-discipline, to some degree heroic, which has transformed the railroad worker's young son into an uncompromising commissar imposes a false mold which in the long run would prove fatal. The thing that redeems him as a human being is that he cannot quite submit to this mold. When Zhivago confronts him, the Doctor discovers that this young man is not quite what his formidable reputation has led Zhivago to expect to meet. ...[326]

In his symbolically self-appointed death, Paša shows a recognition of his faulty ways and truly vindicates himself as a human being. (+)

(f) Paša's whole purpose — to enforce principles — so undermines itself that force becomes a principle of its own, dominating all else. (−)

(g) Paša's transformation to something less than human is well characterized by Lara's description of him —

"... he had hardly changed. The same handsome, honest, determined face, the most honest of all the faces I have ever seen. ... But still I noticed one difference, which terrified me.

It was as if something abstract had entered his countenance and drained its color. A living human face had become the personification of a principle, the portrayal of an idea."[327]

— and earlier by the offhand remark of a secondary child character — "'We had an outstanding mathematician in Jurjatin. He taught at two high schools, the boys' and ours. How he could explain. ... He volunteered for the army and never returned, got killed. Some say that Antipov has come alive again as God's scourge and plague, Commissar

---

[324] Wilson, *The New Yorker*, 212.
[325] Hampshire, *Encounter*, 5.
[326] Wilson, *The New Yorker*, 210.
[327] Pasternak, 412.

Strel'nikov. But that's untrue, of course."[328] — with its suggestive death-rebirth imagery. The symbolic implications of the story's historical-revolutionary framework are also pejorative: "Lara and Pasha are strung up to an unbearable degree of misery and determined to blot out the painful past by marrying each other! Lara is here a counterpart of poor, bewitched Russia about to rid herself of one tyranny, at untold cost, only to throw herself into the arms of a worse."[329] The later transformation of Paša into Strel'nikov may in turn reflect that of the biblical Saul of Tarsus into "St. Paul, Pasha's namesake", but "*in reverse*, as his name, 'Paul Exact-opposite', indicates".[330] A redeeming note does suggest itself, however, in the symbolism of Strel'nikov's demise: "The whole amazing episode — the conversation, Strelnikov's apologia for his misguided life and his confession of failure, followed by his death — awakens an echo of the repentant thief at the Crucifixion. And the forgiveness extended to that malefactor seems to be implied for Strelnikov when the blood spurting from his head freezes into red beads and lies beside his body, like rowanberries in the snow. In his last hours, he too asked for and received the fruit of the Tree of Life."[331] In general, however, such imagery, while favoring Živago, is uncomplimentary to Antipov-Strel'nikov. (−)

(21) Kuznecov, *Continuation of a Legend* — Tolja: Sense of purpose, self-understanding, self-sacrifice. (2)

(a) Upon finishing school and leaving home, Tolja resents that his teachers have not better prepared him for 'life'. He becomes disenchanted with the drudgery and crude living conditions in connection with his first work assignment. He envies his Moscow acquaintances and is first tempted to save enough money to buy a car with which to impress his former girl friend, then impelled to borrow the return fare and leave his job at once. At one point he feels that his problem would be solved, were he only able to buy some fresh apples. His interests appear self-centered and extremely petty. (−)

(c) While traveling to Siberia, Tolja encounters beguiling gypsies, whose parasitical existence nonetheless repels him: "... I ... decided ... that to live on the earth as a parasite is disgusting swinishness and that, if there were no such lowly peddlers of post cards and fortunetellers, the

---

[328] *Ibid.*, 285.
[329] Rowland and Rowland, 77.
[330] *Ibid.*, 78.
[331] *Ibid.*, 171.

world would be a little cleaner and better ...".[332] He also evidences a superior character by contrast with a number of the young recruited laborers with whom he travels East: one is an inveterate thief, another unduly suspicious; others retrieve a companion's lost money, then spend it on drinks. Speaking of two of them, Tolja remarks:

If I were to become like Griška, I would hang myself, honestly! How can this be? How many generations must pass before the *kulak* dies in a man?
   And Leška? One of the kind who are "interested" in being a hooligan? They have their own world, own morality, own folklore, and detest anyone not like them. ...
   Of course, Leška detests Grigorij, but is horse-radish really sweeter than a radish?[333]

Tolja is no match however for Len'ka, the young brigade leader who induces him to apply for work at Irkutsk, looks after homeless waifs, and loves his work more than girls; nor for Tonja, who comes from a family of eight daughters, left home to make things easier for the rest, and sends them all her extra earnings; nor for a number of model workers like the selfless, hard working truck driver Zaxar Zaxaryvič, who gives his money to widows and zealously dies behind his steering wheel; Nikolaj, who cheerfully moves from one construction site to the next; and the well read *komsomol* secretary, the Burjat, Miška, who is stabbed defending a woman against three drunkards. All generally adhere to the philosophy expressed by Zaxar:

"Remember just one thing: what is important is to live life fully. So that everything is grand; love — but real love, friendship — but real friendship, happiness — but real happiness, and no silliness. Let there be grief, but grief like an ocean. That's how people live who don't seek the superficial, who don't just live for themselves. ...
   "Oh, how much stupidity there is in a human being! Is there really happiness in money, in a sated and well covered belly, in a city apartment? That's obviously just stupid window dressing, small stuff! Happiness is this: happiness is a storm, a battle, enough sun in your heart for yourself and others and then some besides for after you've died ...."[334]

This view is sharply contrasted to that of Tolja's Moscow friend, Vit'ka, who, having inherited an easy, lucrative job, advises Tolja that "'in life you have to play for big stakes — and without sentimentality. People are wolves, jackals.'"[335] When contrasted to various groups of characters

---

[332] Anatolij Kuznetsov, "Prodolženie legendy", *Junost'*, III (July, 1957), 8.
[333] *Ibid.*, 13.
[334] *Ibid.*, 52.
[335] *Ibid.*, 57.

representing opposite extremes, Tolja emerges a scrupulous, if not valiant citizen. As such, he appears still capable of greater devotion to the social cause, hence, redeemable. His image is, above all, that of a typical Soviet youth who could do better but still represents his society's hopes for a bright future. (+)

(d) Tolja manages, despite doubts and discouragement, to meet all the challenges at Irkutsk. Thanks to the advice and example of his fellow workers, he finally resolves to stay. Their solicitations while he is in the hospital and the collective effort required to build a new dam seem to work a change in him. He finally concludes, "How tedious life would be if everything were already built ...."[336] and, in his notes, challenges Vit'ka: "I see now that you and I are enemies. ... We will destroy you."[337] He feels adult now, one with the other workers. He has overcome his ego to the point that his search for identity and the demands of society are no longer a problem. His conflict is resolved. (−)

(e) The journal form again aids an author to present his hero's case in an essentially positive and sympathetic manner. The hero is only condoned, however, when he overcomes his alienation and behaves like a loyal, conformist citizen. Though other characters provide abundant moralizing, there is little question as to Kuznecov's own attitude toward Tolja — that of a condescending parent, teacher, or Party official. (−)

(g) One symbolic note, already suggested by the title, reinforces the tale's conformist ideology and its ensuing effect on the hero: he twice hears the legend of the 'disobedient' rivers, Angara and Enisej, which people later mollified (*i.e.* by building dams):

They began to provide people with light, warmth, and happiness because they had begun to labor. And only then did they understand that until then they had known little happiness and had experienced very little in life.

Because he who does not toil does not work, but only churns up sparkling waves and understands nothing about life. Because to work, to produce happiness, light, and warmth — that is the very, very greatest happiness in the world.[338]

Inspired by this legend, Tolja feels that he is helping to create a great sea by working on the dam. His conflict is, again, dissipated. (−)

(22) Kazakov, *The Renegade* — Egor: Traditional mundane, sensible, unfeeling existence. (3)

---

[336] *Ibid.*, 55.
[337] *Ibid.*, 56.
[338] *Ibid.*, 58.

(a) Egor's dissolute, anti-social manner has all the earmarks of a narrow, self-centered, unambitious mode of life. (—)

(b) The fact that his wife died so violently inclines the reader to commiserate with Egor and perhaps excuse his indifferent qualities. (+)

(d) The discovery that Egor has an exceptionally beautiful and captivating voice which he fully indulges only when, as at story's end, he and Alen'ka are alone adds a completely new dimension to his character, suggesting in fact that he is sensitive to certain private values which he will not compromise by displaying his talents to the public. Egor's behavior may therefore be a kind of purposeful social protest, a rebellious defense of his own unique individuality. As Mathewson puts it, Egor "is presented as thoroughly reprehensible by socialist and by human standards until we are told that he and his slatternly mistress possess the magic gift of song".[339] Kramer adds that "his [Kazakov's] real success lies in convincing the reader that the emotional fulfillment which Egor and Alen'ka find justifies or at least compensates for their escape".[340] (+)

(e) As with all of Kazakov's stories, *The Renegade* is written with detachment and restraint. "The criterion of his art is unsympathetic truth in the depiction of everyday life."[341] This very quality permits the story's conclusion to be all the more impressive and overpowering, however, in its disclosure of Egor's sensitivity and its conceivable justification for his idiosyncratic behavior. (+)

(f) The discovery of Egor's talent and social sophistication comes as a pleasing, rather paradoxical surprise. (+)

(g) Citing a Soviet critic, Whitney points out that

the content of the stories of Kazakov is not so much in the interplay of incident or direct statements of the writer and heroes as in the implication which seeps little by little through eloquent details. We hardly ever encounter in him heroes who disclose themselves in their thoughts and judgements, or arguments. He sculpts characters, fixing upon an expressive gesture, a particular manner of conduct and, particularly, external characteristics.[342]

Egor's erratic nonconformity is well suggested by the opening description of his meal of unfried, unsalted fish; his lodge, though new, bare, and incomplete; his habits — he awakens as the sun is setting. The implication of these seeming contradictions is, at this point, rather derisive. (—)

(h) "All Kazakov's stories are memorable for their compact plot, the

[339]   Mathewson, *Soviet Literature in the Sixties*, 12.
[340]   Kramer, *The Slavic and East European Journal*, 30-31.
[341]   Bode, *Osteuropa*, XIII (January, 1963), 29.
[342]   Whitney, 101.

precision and economy of the verbal pattern ... [and] attention to accurate detail."[343] In this regard, Bode mentions his careful and compelling selection of "odors, colors, sounds" and his lifelike "Russian landscapes".[344] Such details help individualize his Egor and encourage the reader's interest as well as his indulgence of Egor's nonconformity. (+)

(23) Kazakov, *The Renegade* — Egor: Responsibility, conscientiousness, ambition, sense of duty. (3)

(a) Besides his nonconformity, Egor displays a marked reluctance to perform his duties conscientiously. He haphazardly lights his beacon lamps; neglects the leak in his boat; fails to make more money ferrying; *etc.*: "The work of a buoy keeper, suitable for an old person, has decisively spoiled and corrupted him."[345] Occasional memories of his service in the navy or the sight of passing ships create in him a short-lived yearning to find more responsible and challenging work:

His native country is truly beautiful — the dusty roads he has traversed and tramped from his youth, the rural landscapes. ... Why then is he waking; who is calling to him in the night, like stars crying to him from down the river: 'Ego-o-or!? He is frightened and shivering, as the great distances, the din and lights of cities call to him. And the longing for work, for genuine labor — with its deathly weariness and its joy![346]

But he quickly sinks back into his accustomed lethargy. (−)

(d) The story's startling conclusion tends to redeem Egor in this respect. It tends to argue other values, other premises than those which always presuppose the private person's collective responsibility. (+)

(e) Factors discussed under 23 above are here equally applicable and have a similar favorable effect. (+)

(f) Factors discussed under 23 above are here equally applicable and have a similar favorable effect. (+)

(g) Factors discussed under 23 above are here equally applicable and have a similar favorable effect. (+)

(24) Terc, *The Trial Begins* — Karlinskij: Regimentation, impersonality, de-humanization, extinction, insignificance, personal satisfactions. (1)

[343]   Vera Alexandrova, "Voices of Youth", *Soviet Survey*, No. 36 (April-June, 1961), 29.

[344]   Bode, *Osteuropa*, XIII (January, 1963), 29.

[345]   Jurij Kazakov, "Otščepenec", *Oktjabr'*, XXXVI (July, 1959), 113.

[346]   *Ibid.*, 114.

(a) Karlinskij ridicules prevailing institutions and cynically stalks Marina, the wife of the city prosecutor Globov, whom he finally manages to seduce. (—)

(b) On another level, however, Karlinskij's behavior reflects the personal dissatisfaction of a deeply thoughtful and sensitive man. His frustration arises from the regime's suppression of the individual and its disparagement of eternal values — God, immortality — which leads him to despair for his existence:

Jurij could not sleep. Recently, at night, he would suddenly remember that he must some day die and would become afraid. ... The coffin and the grave did not frighten him. The chief worry was that there would be nothing after he died — nothing and forever, for an eternity of centuries. If he were consigned to hell, why, that would be better: let him fry in the skillet — at least his self-awareness would still remain. ... Why had they destroyed faith? Replaced personal immortality with communism? Can a thinking person really have any goal which excludes himself?[347]

He is cynical toward the regime and tries to achieve a semblance of personal power and permanent identity in sexual conquest:

There was only one way out — self-delusion. ... Some involved themselves in politics, like the bear, Globov. Some, like Marina ... Marina! Here he must find his salvation. In this, the most beautiful of all the women he had ever known.[348]

. . . .

He and his victory over her will be the goal. He will astonish her with the same means (deceitful praise of her beauty), use any means to prove his superiority.[349]

(+)

(c) Karlinskij's most direct foil is the ambitious, vengeful Globov, who staunchly supports the regime. He is unfavorably contrasted to Karlinskij in terms of his relationships with his own family. Marina prefers Karlinskij's company to his, while Saša, whom Globov eventually disowns, receives Karlinskij's understanding and sympathy. (+)

(d) Field maintains that "all of Tertz's stories and novels end with the central character (who is very often the narrator) in some form of grave 'leap' either anticipated or in progress".[350] Karlinskij also takes such a leap — that of sexual conquest — from which he nevertheless emerges even more shaken and disillusioned. His conflict remains, and if really

---

[347] Abram Terc, "Sud idet", *Kultura*, special number (May, 1960), 81.
[348] *Ibid.*
[349] *Ibid.*, 82.
[350] Andrew Field, "Abram Tertz's Ordeal by Mirror", *The New Leader*, XLVIII (July 19, 1965), 11.

the narrator, he ends up digging ditches in a forced labor camp — so uncannily prophetic of Terc-Sinjavskij's own consequent fate an exact ten years later.[351] In fact he is accused of similar crimes — "slander, pornography, and the disclosure of state secrets".[352] (+)

(e) Field's remarks (above) suggest what may well be the author's unstated identification with both his narrator and with Karlinskij. The narrator says, at one point, that he fears the prospect of a machine that would detect one's thoughts.[353] Judging by Terc's other writing — particularly his *Thought Unaware*[354] — both characters' thoughts and apprehensions come close to the author's own. Whatever the ultimate impression of Karlinskij as a man, his ideas are presented in a forceful and serious manner that invites the reader's reflection. (+)

(f) The comparison of Globov and Karlinskij (in the plot, *per se*) is ironically modified by their depiction as personalities. According to Field, "it is typical of Tertz's complexity that the repugnant Globov is presented with considerable (clinical) sympathy, while the 'liberal' who is having an affair with Globov's wife and who listens to Radio Free Europe turns out to be a spineless villain".[355] Karlinskij's actual 'villainy' is certainly disputable, however. It is also ironic that Karlinskij debases himself before Marina in order to appeal to her vanity so that, eventually, he can debase her all the more and that, in so doing, he himself becomes the 'fall guy' and is thoroughly disillusioned. Both Karlinskij's mode of perception and Terc's narrative are fraught with biting satire — rendering *The Trial Begins* the most ironic of all the works sampled. As Burg suggests, "the only answer to futile striving and inevitable defeat — if one is to avoid going insane — is all-embracing irony".[356] Further instances include: the two detectives who literally confiscate the type and punctuation marks in the narrator's manuscript, then tell him, "'You are being trusted'";[357] Karlinskij's pointed question: "'Marina Pavlovna, do you believe in communism? And another question please: do you love your husband?'";[358] Karlinskij's cynical comment that it may some day be desirable to sell human embryos in tin cans in order to supplement

---

[351] The narrator indicates that he arrived at prison in 1956. *Ibid.*, 126.

[352] *Ibid.*

[353] *Ibid.*, 115.

[354] See Abram Terc, *Mysli vrasplox* (New York, Rausen Publishers, 1966) or Abram Tertz, "Thought Unaware", *The New Leader*, XLVIII (July 19, 1965), 16-26.

[355] Field, *The New Leader*, 13.

[356] David Burg, "The 'Cold War' on the Literary Front", *Problems of Communism*, XI (July-August, 1962), 8.

[357] Terc, 65.

[358] *Ibid.*, 68.

the fish reserves: "'We will return to cannibalistic appetizers ... but, so to say, for a more sublime and delicate purpose'";[359] Marina's suppression of tears, which might create facial wrinkles; *etc.* Most of this irony, and its associated imagery, supports either Karlinskij's cynical observations or the pathos of his position. (+)

(g) The two detectives actually scoop characters and punctuation marks from off the pages of the narrator's manuscript and deposit them in their pockets. While visiting a planetarium with Marina, Karlinskij is amused by the analogy to their relationship of the earth revolving about the sun and by the possibility that the earth may be the real sun and the sun its satellite. For all her beauty, Marina makes an unsightly impression on Sereža, her stepson, while in a mudpack. She later decides upon an Argentine brand of lipstick for future use. Finally, there is Terc's symbolic use of sex, which is well characterized by Field:

There are frequent sexual scenes in Tertz's fiction and sometimes they can be as uproarious as Henry Miller. ... Tertz himself, oddly enough, seems to have a fierce aversion to the very sex act. This aversion is expressed not only in terms of repulsion, but also in demonic laughter. ... It is a matter of serious debate as to whether Tertz's portrayal of women is an "exorcism" of sex in general, or whether, on a lower plane, it is specifically an exploration of the latent homosexuality in all men ... the "positive" female characters in Tertz's fiction are all old mothers, nurses, and *babushki.* ... Latent homosexuality is certainly the subject of two of the stories, *Iced Over* and *You and I.*[360] ...

. . . .

As in *The Trial Begins,* Tertz deftly translates the external gestures whose sum is society and politics into their very personal psychological and sexual components.[361]

(+)

(h) Terc's ingenious use of episodic transitions forcefully contrasts Karlinskij to his chief rival, Globov. The latter lectures Sereža for asking too many unorthodox questions about history, while Sereža in turn indicates that "'Jurij Mixajlovič Karlinskij explained it to me this way. He said it all depends on the particular point of view.'"[362] With these same last words, Karlinskij begins his address to Marina in the scene which follows.[363] Similar links include Globov's argument that everything is subordinate to "'our great purpose'",[364] which idea is immediately

[359]   *Ibid.,* 78.
[360]   Field, *The New Leader,* 12.
[361]   *Ibid.,* 14-15.
[362]   Terc, 70.
[363]   *Ibid.*
[364]   *Ibid.,* 72.

picked up by Karlinskij in quite a different context: "'I fully agree with you, Marina Pavlovna. The end justifies the means. ... So let's drink to the end, to your face, to the inevitable conjunction of ends and means!'"[365] Sereža and Katja have a rendevouz at the zoo, while, at an art museum, Karlinskij and Marina discuss animal instincts; just after the children observe a tiger sleeping on its side, Globov, in his sleep, turns over on his side; he dreams he sees Marina as a sphinx; meanwhile she and Karlinskij are viewing an actual sphinx at the museum; *etc.* The whole technique is reminiscent of 'expressionistic fantasy'[366] or 'Gogolian grotesque', in which "a straightforward descriptive passage ... at the end, flicks its heels and takes a sudden leap into grotesque fantasy".[367] (+)

(25) Terc, *The Trial Begins* — Vladimir Petrovič Globov, colleagues, people: Truth, humanitarian values, freedom. (5)

(a) Faithful to his ends-means doctrine, Globov ruthlessly prosecutes all who in any way oppose the prevailing system — Jewish abortionists (an echo of the Stalinist 'doctors' plot'?), free thinkers, even his dissenting son, Sereža. When it is hinted that, by protecting his son, he too may fall under suspicion, Globov readily disowns him and remains impervious to pleas by the boy's grandmother. Globov appears nonetheless fairly typical of the other bureaucrats who banquet him. Their unquestioning, herd-like mentality is also characteristic of the people in general, who, we are told, react on the occasion of Stalin's death like dogs who have lost their master: "'I don't want freedom. I need a Master.'"[368] (−)

(c) As already contrasted with his chief rival, Karlinskij, (see 24, above), Globov's image is essentially unfavorable. (−)

(d) At story's end, Globov is caught in the mob which stampedes the streets to view the deceased Master (Stalin) and becomes, unwittingly, a weapon of destruction as the Master's giant hand uses his body to flay the crowd. Momentarily, and rather like Paša Antipov, Globov senses that the means have got out of hand and voices protest:

"Stop it! It's painful. ... These are your own people. They are completely innocent. Many are women, children, even war veterans who brought you fame."
But the hand did not release him from its tight grip. Indignant and cruel, it beat and beat with his body the screaming, suffering crowd as with a club.[369]

[365] *Ibid.*, 73.
[366] Howe, *The New Republic*, 21.
[367] Field, *The New Leader*, 11.
[368] Terc, 123.
[369] *Ibid.*, 125.

Even after he learns that a little girl has been crushed in the melee and imagines that she might have been his daughter, Globov again argues that victims are necessary for the general purpose, that the girl is "'herself at fault. ... We won't get anywhere without victims. And it's all in the name of our goal'".[370] (—)

(e) The author-narrator's identification with Karlinskij (see 24, above) also works in Globov's disfavor. At one point, as Globov orders Rabinovič to turn off his "thinking machine", the narrator interjects: "But it was too late".[371] (—)

(f) Globov feels assured of ultimate victory because God (Stalin) is with him. While at a concert, Sereža imagines the music to represent the drowning of the bourgeoise in a flood; what impresses Globov, however, is the conductor's domination of the orchestra. When Sereža is unable to make out the Master in a crowd of people, Globov insists that Sereža is blind. As, at one point, Globov boasts of the people he has sent to their deaths, his ears become flushed, whereupon the narrator remarks that "a good bloodletting is now in order".[372] The grandmother, who avidly follows the Korean campaign with a map and pins, has for some time been unable to move them forward. Globov's colleagues are described as kindly, innocent, home-loving people — one of them even knits and embroiders — who nonetheless "have terrified a whole hemisphere".[373] Their banquet table is likened to a 'battlefield'.[374] When Sereža insists he is only a defendant and not yet convicted, his interrogator, the embroiderer, replies, pointing to the people on the street, that "all of them are defendants. ... You, brother, are no longer a defendant. You are convicted."[375] Globov appears more upset by the puddles Sereža's grandmother leaves on his office floor than by her pleas in the boy's behalf. Finally, the narrator suggests that he has tried to assign each of his characters an appropriate punishment: Katja, therefore, having collaborated with Sereža in neo-Trotskyist speculations, is the little girl who was trampled to death by the mourning mob. Such irony, of course, strongly ridicules Globov and the values he represents. (—)

(g) As does the imagery which likens him to a tiger (a beast of prey) and shows him kneeling before the Master's giant clenched fist; the

[370] Ibid., 126.
[371] Ibid., 103.
[372] Ibid., 106-107.
[373] Ibid., 111.
[374] Ibid.
[375] Ibid., 118.

reference to the latter as 'God';[376] Globov's association of a soccer game with the sexual act; his inspection of pencilings in the booths of a women's restroom; the human brain which, in his dream, Rabinovič shows him and which guarantees, with its expedient thought, the impermanence of all systems as well as the possibility of universal annihilation; his symbolic hand-washing, à la Pontius Pilate; the embroidering interrogator; and, finally, the crucifix-shaped dagger which Rabinovič unearths and with which he invokes deity: "'God, look how they've corrupted it. Turned it into a deadly weapon. ... It was a goal, and they made it a means. ... Oj-oj-oj! Where is God now, where is the sword? Both are eternally frozen.'"[377] (—)

(h) And, to the extent that they support Karlinskij instead, the tale's transitional technique, its fantasy structure, and its very language, whose "freshness and complete correspondence to the subtlest nuances of contemporary Soviet speech, and its ability to turn them all (Russian bureaucratic speech has not been parodied so effectively since the days of Zoshchenko) into dazzling literary play — is the surest proof that he could be nothing else but a Soviet writer ...."[378] (—)

(26) Tendrjakov, *Three, Seven, Ace* — Aleksandr (Saša) Dubinin: His men's loyalty, justice. (1)

(a) Dubinin, a capable and kindly supervisor, is unwittingly betrayed by his men — first as they collaborate with the gambler, Bušuev; then as, after Bušuev has cheated them, they fail to subdue him; and finally when Leška Malinkin, fearing for both his safety and his reputation, avoids divulging Bušuev's winnings and thus exonerating Dubinin from suspicion of premeditated murder. (+)

(b) Dubinin's plight is made the more pathetic by the fact that, in part due to the lesson which he learned from the crippled Jaša Sorokin, he now subscribes to the view that happiness is not only

"to work in order to fill yourself, and be well provided for — to have a cozy roof over your head, a warm stove, a fond wife — be satisfied, yet take care that no one on the sidelines begins to envy you and noses in on your comfortable happiness. But, it seems, there's also another way to live. To raise up the fallen, comfort the distraught, protect the weak, and thus come to realize your ability to make others happy, your generosity and strength — that is real happiness!"[379]

[376] *Ibid.*, 67.
[377] *Ibid.*, 129.
[378] Field, p. 13. Written prior to Terc's official unmasking as the Soviet critic, Sinjavskij.
[379] Vladimir Tendrjakov, "Trojka, semerka, tuz", *Novyj mir*, XXXVI (March, 1960), 10.

It is this which causes him to take the former convict, Bušuev, under his wing and give him another chance. (+)

(c) Dubinin, who alone and unarmed dares to settle accounts with Bušuev, is morally superior to his cowardly men, of whom Hayward says "it would have been unthinkable a few years ago to suggest, however obliquely, that it would be possible for a whole collective of honest working men to be corrupted by one evil man".[380] (+)

(d) Garrard speaks of Tendrjakov's "Chekovian 'open ending'",[381] which, according to Hayward, "leaves the reader in doubt as to whether justice — even 'socialist justice' — will be done or not."[382] In terms, however, of the circumstantial evidence accumulated against him, the tenacity of the investigator — "he was already suspicious and mistrustful. Such a person could not be convinced either with shouts or soft words. One could only be patient",[383] and the money's irredeemable loss in the river — it would appear that Dubinin's future is indeed grim and that official justice will only aggravate his predicament. (+)

(e) As in Kazakov, the narrator's presence is carefully hidden. One senses, however, that, unlike Kazakov, Tendrjakov is strongly intent on pointing a moral, though in a manner unobtrusive and organically tied to his tale: "He is captivated by the short distance between an observed event and a conclusion. In Tendrjakov's eyes, only the possibility of an immediate deduction makes his observations significant."[384] Thus, the conclusions he arrives at are plausible and convincing and in this case sustain his sympathy for Dubinin as the victim of miscarried justice. (+)

(f) The irony that the best man in the tale must suffer on behalf of the others' weakness adds to the poignancy of his situation. (+)

(g) Solov'eva speaks of the tale's 'allegorism of details'.[385] Both Bode[386] and Garrard[387] point to the symbolism of its title, which echoes that of Puškin's tale and suggests, in Solov'eva's view, "the 'spirit of money', the 'spirit of chance'" which is a "substitute for spiritual life as is religiosity itself in 'The Miracle Worker' and 'An Extraordinary

[380] Hayward, *Dissonant Voices in Soviet Literature*, p. xxxv.
[381] J. G. Garrard, "Vladimir Tendrjakov", *The Slavic and East European Journal*, IX, No. 1 (Spring, 1965), 5.
[382] Hayward, *Dissonant Voices in Soviet Literature*, p. xxxv.
[383] Tendrjakov, 29.
[384] Inna Solov'eva, "Problemy i proza (zametki o tvorčestve Vladimira Tendrjakova)", *Novyj mir*, XXXVIII (July, 1962), 238.
[385] *Ibid.*, 239.
[386] Bode, *Osteuropa*, X (September, 1960), 623.
[387] Garrard, *The Slavic and East European Journal*, 4.

Event'".[388] There are, in addition, the tale's 'river symbolism'[389] — its description of the various logs which are floated down it, some which swell and sink to the bottom and are forgotten, others which continue to the mills, where they become useful and enjoy a 'new life';[390] Bušuev's sorrowful, pessimistic songs; and Ivan Stupin's frequent expression "'*perepeteia*'" — which, though he does not understand it, clearly underscores the tale's tragic conclusion.[391] (+)

(h) "Tendrjakov uses strong, rich, yet concise language without apparent need for external devices. His sentences are remembered — a rare achievement for most novelists."[392] And, again, "thought is here engendered, not by induction, not by a complicated network of associations — thought arises as an immediately demanded explanation of fact, an identification, or juxtaposition of contiguous facts".[393] (+)

(27) Tendrjakov, *Three, Seven, Ace* — Leška Malinkin: Courage, conscience, integrity, illusions, loyalty. (4)

(a) Leška, who deeply admires Dubinin, nonetheless betrays him after Bušuev implicates Leška in the extortion of the other workers' money. (−)

(b) Leška fails to disclose Bušuev's money, fearing that he will be misunderstood and ostracized by his own villagers, convicted by the authorities, or even murdered by the irate Egor. He thus typifies the same weakness that all the men displayed when confronted by Bušuev. (−)

(c) By contrast with Dubinin, Leška is cowardly and indecisive (see 26, above). Like Dubinin, he has befriended Bušuev, even saved his life, and known "some of the happiness"[394] which Dubinin experienced under similar circumstances. Unlike Dubinin, however, he fails to face the unpleasant consequences which sometimes reward good intentions. (−)

(d) At tale's end, Leška sobs unconsolably on his pillow as he realizes the consequences of his cowardice and disloyalty. Though the opportunity to prove Dubinin innocent is now irretrievable, Leška is at least genuinely remorseful. (+)

---

[388]   Solov'eva, *Novyj mir*, 241.
[389]   Garrard, *The Slavic and East European Journal*, 4.
[390]   Tendrjakov, *Novyj mir*, 3.
[391]   *Ibid.*, 32.
[392]   Mihajlo Mihajlov, "Moscow Summer, 1964", *The New Leader*, XLVIII (March 29, 1965), 28.
[393]   Solov'eva, *Novyj mir*, 235.
[394]   *Ibid.*, 241.

(e) To the extent that related factors favor Dubinin (see 26, above), they incriminate Leška. (—)

(f) To the extent that related factors favor Dubinin (see 26, above), they incriminate Leška. (—)

(g) To the extent that related factors favor Dubinin (see 26, above), they incriminate Leška. (—)

(h) To the extent that related factors favor Dubinin (see 26, above), they incriminate Leška. (—)

(28) Aksenov, *Colleagues* — Aleksej (Leksej) Maksimov: Mundane life, the uneventful future, socialist self-sacrifice. (2)

(a) Although Leksej is hard-working, he is suspicious of collective propaganda. He seeks challenges, but for their own sake, and dismisses the appeal to service and sacrifice for others. (—)

(b) One of Leksej's colleagues, Petr Stolbov, is especially calculating. Leksej criticizes his opportunism and eventually uncovers a network of graft, implicating Stolbov. By contrast, however, with Saša, another young doctor described as 'pensive' and 'impulsively honest', Leksej is 'thoroughly cynical'.[395] Saša readily volunteers for a hardship assignment, arguing that "we are responsible not only to our conscience but to all people, to the heroes of Senate Square and the Field of Mars, our contemporaries, and especially those in the future".[396] (—)

(d) On one occasion an older doctor, Dampfer, argues the importance of dedication to one's vocation and the respectability of all work, however menial. His words deeply affect Leksej, as do, eventually, Saša's. As he encounters various thieving opportunists and indifferent time-servers, Leksej becomes repulsed by their hypocrisy and all the more admires idealists like Saša: "Maksimov remembered how he had quarrelled with Saša about the value of high flown words. Now he viewed it differently than before. Lofty words retain their meaning when the old communist, Dampfer, or Saša Zelenin pronounce them or when they are sung and shouted by millions of honest people."[397] He decides that "he had never been completely happy. Something had always been missing. ... But a man can't be completely happy because he has to keep moving ahead."[398] As he assists in saving Saša's life he finally realizes, like Tolja (*Legend*), the importance of work and discovers his true self as a man of

[395]   Vasilij Aksenov, "Kollegi", *Junost'*, VI (June, 1960), 4.
[396]   *Ibid.*, 8.
[397]   Vasilij Aksenov, "Kollegi", *Junost'*, VI (July, 1960), 58.
[398]   *Ibid.*, 70.

medicine: "They were doctors! They would stand and move forward in different parts of the earth, wherever they were assigned, with the one and only purpose of fighting off attacks of disease and death amid other people. Amid happy, impatient, wise beings solidified in one grand family. Everything else was secondary."[399] He is no longer alienated: "... all the chief characters find their orientation in life in a positive sense".[400] (−)

(e) Burg suggests that, as exceptions, Aksenov and his peer, Gladilin, "avoid the technique so common in classical Russian and Soviet literature — the description by an author of background, of characters' physical appearance, of inner emotions. Only rarely do they introduce philosophical and lyrical digressions in their own voices. Their basic techniques are rather dialogue and action, or at most discourses by the characters themselves."[401] Aksenov's characters indeed resort to a kind of moralizing which thinly veils the author's own idealistic viewpoint. That such preachment seriously affects Leksej strains plausibility and weakens the tale's intrinsic action. (−)

(g) Early nature symbolism tends to substantiate Leška's confusion and insecurity: while swimming, he observes that the sunset on the horizon is dangerous because it makes one feel that life elsewhere is exciting, when it really isn't. Later, he avoids looking at the stars while trying to go to sleep, fearful of losing his identity. (+)

(29) Aksenov, *Colleagues* — Aleksandr (Saša) Dmitrievič: Fedor Bugrov. (1)

(a) Saša's only conflict is, like that of Romodan (*Wings*), with minority types who themselves oppose the collective order, particularly one Bugrov. Saša threatens Bugrov as a potential rival in love who has also called his bluff on a number of occasions, thus weakening his image as a tyrannical bully and daring nonconformist (*à la* Lermontov's Pečorin and Grušnickij). When Saša accosts Bugrov in the act of theft and persists in his pursuit, the latter retaliates with a near fatal knife blow. (+)

(c) As already noted (see 28, above), Saša is, from the beginning, more socially conscious and 'collectively' oriented than his colleagues. By contrast with the bully Bugrov, he is indisputably more admirable. (+)

(d) Despite a close call on his life, Saša's victory is assured. His life is

[399] *Ibid.*, 80.
[400] Whitney, 56.
[401] David Burg, "The 'Cold War' on the Literary Front, II", *Problems of Communism*, XI (September-October, 1962), 38.

saved by the medical skill of his colleagues, Leksej and Vladka, and the cooperation of his fellow-villagers, who keep the electric power going during his operation. The villagers also round up Bugrov, who will now be properly dealt with by the authorities. Leksej even beats him up for good measure. Saša will even have the chance to hear a taped rebroadcast of his young wife's piano playing, which he missed while in pursuit of Bugrov. All losses have been made good, and there is no further conflict. (−)

(e) The moralizing of various characters strongly supports Saša in contrast to Bugrov. (+)

(30) Tendrjakov, *The Trial* — Semen Teterin: Truth, integrity, courage, loyalty, conscience, self-respect. (4)

(a) Teterin has discovered evidence which, contrary to general expectations, would free his friend, Mitjagin, from suspicion of murder, yet incriminate an important bureaucrat, Dudyrev. After unintentionally destroying part of the evidence and fearing that his testimony will be discredited — Teterin, much like Leška Malinkin (*Three, Seven, Ace*), discards the remaining evidence and denies his former testimony. He thus forsakes Mitjagin and intentionally falsifies the facts. (−)

(b) Teterin mostly changes his story because, imagining Dudyrev will in any event use his influence to evade legal censure and fearing that he, Teterin, may become implicated by testifying against him, he begins to question the advantage of being so scrupulous and conscientious. His argument later proves unfounded, a pure rationalization. Teterin is thus made to seem both a coward and a liar. (−)

(c) Dudyrev appears to be another ruthless manager type. His aggressive development of the local forest industry threatens in fact to destroy Teterin's profession. However, Dudyrev proves to be admirably scrupulous and fair-minded. Despite strong pressure from the detectives, who fear the consequences that might befall them for interfering with so poular and successful an administrator, Dudyrev insists on sharing any punishment which might be meted to Mitjagin: "'Listen to me and don't be so apprehensive just because I am in a disadvantageous position. It will be easier for me to account for my own guilt than hide behind someone else's back.' ... They finally understood that he wasn't joking with them or just acting noble."[402] It is as inconvenient for Dudyrev to insist on being impartially tried as for Teterin to persist in espousing the truth:

[402] Vladimir Tendrjakov, "Sud", *Novyj mir*, XXXVII (March, 1961), 53.

He, who had given all his strength, his whole life in order that others might have a better life. ... he required very little for himself: a roof over his head, plain food, and, as his only luxury, one free day each month for a little recreational hunting. Everything for others — sleepless nights, tense days, and a constant fraying of nerves. And now he was supposed to confess to the most terrible of all human crimes — murder![403]

Like Dubinin (*Three, Seven, Ace*) and unlike Leška Malinkin and Teterin, Dudyrev faces up to an unpleasant obligation. Though Teterin at first disagrees with the pragmatism of the local *kolkhoz* manager, Borovikov — "besides Mitjagin's truth, which you dug out of the bear along with the bullet, there is another"[404] — he eventually follows Borovikov's suggestion. (—)

(d) At the trial Teterin perjures himself, while, together with Mitjagin, Dudyrev faces possible conviction. Both are finally exonerated. Meanwhile, Teterin realizes his error and, like Leška Malinkin, suffers deep remorse: "Semen held his head and almost howled along with [his dog] Kalinka. There is no more difficult trial than that of one's own conscience."[405] Teterin's ultimate self-recognition and accompanying anguish reconcile him to his former values. Unlike other such endings, however, his is not a happy one. Teterin is still miserable and despairs at his self-image: "'There is always the possibility of becoming scientific. Science? But after seventeen years, didn't his own science let him down? Besides, he is no longer a boy — but an old man, he'll be sixty in four more years. Isn't it too late still to be learning'".[406] Teterin remains a truly pathetic being. (+)

(e) Only once, early in the tale, does the author venture an opinion that might not also be in the mind of a given character: "A tragedy had occurred, and people had nothing better to do than find somebody to blame and reproach for the same."[407] Otherwise, his viewpoint is carefully concealed in the action itself. (See 26, above, on Tendrjakov's intrinsic moralizing.) The moral of this tale seems to be that dishonesty does not, after all, pay. Still, its application to Teterin is, because of its integration with the tale's action, less that of a condescending judgment than the statement of a natural law whose violation brings immediate and ill consequences to the unfortunate offender, however unwitting. The absence of ridicule suggests the presence of a genuine pity. (+)

---

[403]   *Ibid.*, 45.
[404]   *Ibid.*, 49.
[405]   *Ibid.*, 60.
[406]   *Ibid.*
[407]   *Ibid.*, 36.

(f) The plot's chief irony is, of course, that Teterin has underestimated Dudyrev and, in so doing, himself as well. While this makes him doubly wrong, it also strengthens his pathos: "He had possessed one consolation — slight, uncertain, shameful, but nonetheless a consolation. He had thought that all people are bad, that such as Dudyrev would save their skin and not suffer with conscience. Therefore, why look better than the rest, why kick against the pricks? He had that consolation, but no more."[408] Even the young victim's father, who has most cause for being petty, vindictive, and bitter, appears admirably forgiving and broad-minded: "'We can't bring back Paša now. ... There is no reason for ruining someone else's life as well. I won't be the warmer from someone else's misfortune.' 'That's true, you can't cure with ill will,' agreed his companion."[409] (+)

(g) The tale's very imagery suggests that Teterin's offense is due less to malice or egoism than to a basic shortsightedness, inexperience, or misunderstanding of certain human realities. This in turn provides one of the work's crowning ironies: that the man of nature, the primitive — traditionally so eulogized for his finer instincts and greater ethical awareness — is in fact less capable of coping with actual moral quandries than his shrewd, calculating, highly civilized counterpart, Dudyrev. Teterin's essential weakness — his fear and timidity, his unfounded apprehensiveness, his and others' inattention to unpleasant truth — is anticipated or implied by his dogs' early unwillingness to cross the bridge where later the bear is held at bay and killed; his inability, by contrast with Dudyrev, to shoot his wounded hunting dog, Malinka (ironically, he deals a blow which is nearly as fatal to his equally trusting friend, Mitjagin); Dudyrev's trucks and bulldozers, which ominously destroy, yet transform the primitive forest; Dudyrev's own anecdote about the drunkard who sought his missing purse under a street light, even though he had lost it on the other, darker side of the street; finally, his older dog Kalinka's mournful barking and the fact that, like her master, she has failed herself, *i.e.* has an unhealed paw, loses the trail, and fails in strength. (—)

(h) Tendrjakov's incisive narrative, his terse, compelling, unobtrusive language (discussed under 26, above), together with his frequent recourse to native idioms, lend his tale authenticity, thus underscoring Teterin's poignancy at its conclusion. (+)

[408]   *Ibid.*, 59.
[409]   *Ibid.*

(31) Tendrjakov, *The Trial* — Konstantin Sergeevič Dudyrev: Faith in Teterin and the people. (1)

(a) As heretofore suggested, Dudyrev becomes deeply disillusioned by Teterin's duplicity:

He had denied the bullet, but something kept Dudyrev from completely believing his denial. Whatever had happened, the hunter had either lied to him now at the trial or earlier, producing a false bullet. In either case it was deceptive.

Semen Teterin! The bear hunter! An obvious personification of the people. But from his early youth Dudyrev had been accustomed to venerate the people, unconsciously, almost with religious idolatry.

He, Dudyrev, expected more from Semen Teterin than from his own self. The stable bear hunter, undisturbed by reflection, a whole being, a pristine force — how could one not be impressed. ... he was amazed that Semen Teterin, finding himself outside the forest, with its stern but guileless laws, should lose himself, be confused, and behave in an unseemly way.[410]

Teterin's disappointment thus becomes a kind of disillusion in the people, as such. (+)

(c) Dudyrev has good cause to censure Teterin's behavior, whatever its ultimate explanation. As previously discussed (see 30, above), Dudyrev also proves to be morally superior. (+)

(d) His concluding thought: "'people change much slower than outward life. ... It is necessary to teach people how to live. Blind acquiescence is not love. Genuine love is active.'"[411] His disappointment remains, despite the hope that eventually something can be done about it. (+)

(e) The tale's implicit moralizing (see 30, above) clearly vindicates Dudyrev's position. (+)

(f) As does its irony (see 30, above). (+)

(h) And also its distinctive narrative and verbal power (see 30, above). (+)

(32) Aksenov, *Ticket to the Stars* — Dimka Denisov: Responsibility, vocation. (2)

(a) Dimka resembles both Tolja (*Legend*) and Leksej (*Colleagues*) in his confused, bewildered groping for a sense of purpose and a satisfying role in the adult world. Like the others, he at first escapes responsibility (encourages his friends to run away with him to the Baltic rather than pursue their education) and criticizes prevailing social conditions. His

---

[410]   *Ibid.*, 59-60.
[411]   *Ibid.*, 60.

criticism, however, is generally far too petty and capricious to be taken seriously. Like the poet, Evtušenko (*Prologue*), he has a penchant for the foreign and novel for their own sake.

(c) Dimka's principal foil — his older brother, Viktor — is wholly dedicated to his work as a doctoral candidate and scientific researcher. Viktor even prevails upon Dimka and his friends to accept work at his institute in lieu of their Bohemian existence. Their parents in turn try to impress Dimka with Viktor's earnest, hard-working example. Viktor nonetheless defends Dimka as representative of his age and even envies his fresh, impulsive, unpremeditated approach to life: "'... everything is already planned for us, our future is already decided! Damn it! Better to be a tramp and amount to nothing than be a little boy your whole life, complying with every one else's decisions.'"[412] By contrast Dimka tends to force his and others' decisions by a flip of the coin, yet maneuver the outcome as he would really most prefer it. This makes him, in comparison to Viktor, unduly irresponsible and self-indulgent. (—)

(d) Viktor's unexpected death works a crisis in Dimka which leads him to forsake his adolescent ways. Although, shortly before the tragic news, he is still unsure of himself — "'Everything is already clear to my pals. They have already solved everything for themselves. And, it's clear, they don't need to toss a coin either. But I? ... I still haven't planned my life.'"[413] — the subsequent vision of Viktor's 'starry ticket' suggests his determination to assume a fully challenging and responsible professional role in the near future: "'Now it is my starry ticket! Whether Viktor knew about it or not, he has willed it to me. A ticket, to where?'"[414] Erlich notes that Dimka's transformation occurs "without protest, though at the moment the boy's only credentials are a distrust of 'phonies' ... and a dogged insistence on personal honesty and authenticity".[415] In a sense, however, Dimka has already proved himself as the valuable helper on a ship's crew. In its depiction of a likeable and representative if somewhat rebellious Soviet youth who finally comes of age, the novel's impact is nonetheless ambiguous and diluted — as if its author wished to air existing problems without treading on anyone's toes. As Mathewson observes, Aksenov's young people, though "fresh, charming figures, ... risk very little and discover less in their flight from home". Again, "the final solutions all coincide with a broader definition of conformist

---

[412]   Vasilij Aksenov, "Zvezdnyj bilet", *Junost'*, VII (June, 1961), 12.
[413]   Vasilij Aksenov, "Zvezdnyj bilet", *Junost'*, VII (July, 1961), 65.
[414]   *Ibid.*, 66.
[415]   Erlich, *Slavic Review*, 412.

expectations and there is no very strenuous moral inquiry".[416] (−)

(e) A good portion of the narrative is told in the first person by Viktor and then Dimka — always with a sympathetic and indulgent view of both heroes. (+)

(g) Chief among the novel's symbols is the cluster of stars which, in its semblance to a punched railway ticket, motivates the ultimate aspirations of both brothers and finalizes the resolution of Dimka's conflict. Before his 'conversion', however, Dimka deflates Viktor's astral vision, referring to rockets as unmanned cosmic busses. Further imagery points up Dimka's adolescent rebellion and social protest: the train they take to Estonia is an elongated pencil case; men and women lie in the sleeping cars like anods in juxtaposition to cathods; the beach is strewn with bare flesh; waves are likened to spreading waffles; and the Tallin skyline is compared to a saw with broken teeth. Dimka's experience with a demolition crew is likened to breaking down ideological walls; when Galja jilts him, life becomes a poker game in which someone else holds the royal flush. The flipping of a coin also signifies his unwillingness to assume responsibility for his decisions. Finally the news of Viktor's death reminds Dimka of the home-made arrow he once shot in the air which fell back, hitting him in the forehead when it should have landed elsewhere. On the whole, however, such strained, exaggerated imagery tends to discredit Dimka more than the values he opposes. (−)

(h) Critics comment particularly on Aksenov's use of "humor through wordplay",[417] his frequent foreign borrowings (often Americanisms), and his younger peoples' jargon in general — their 'slanginess', viewed by Rzhevsky as "a protest against the drab jargon of the newspapers and officialdom"[418] and regarded by Gaev as "an expression of protest against everything stereotyped and dogmatic, just as Mayakovsky before them invented words for the same reason".[419] Illustrative is: "'horse — that means father. It's very pleasant when the horse leaves.'"[420] His humor, like the tale's imagery, makes Dimka, while basically harmless, seem sensational and superficial — a poseur. (−)

---

[416] Mathewson, *Soviet Literature in the Sixties*, 13.

[417] Ralph Blum, "A Reporter at Large. Freeze and Thaw: The Artist in Russia", *The New Yorker*, XLI (August 28, 1965), 72.

[418] Leonid D. Rzhevsky, "The New Idiom", *Soviet Literature in the Sixties* (ed.) Max Hayward and Edward L. Crowley (New York, Frederick A. Praeger, 1964), 77.

[419] Arkadii Gaev, "The New Party Campaign for Ideological Control over Literature", *Analysis of Current Developments in the Soviet Union*, No. 215 (February 27, 1962), 1.

[420] Aksenov, *Junost'*, VII (June, 1961), 5.

(33) Aksenov, *Ticket to the Stars* — Viktor Denisov: Compromise, materialism, self-seeking. (1)

(a) Viktor's alienation involves, like Dimka's, a protest against useless, hypocritical social values. Viktor's area of concern, however, is that of the scientist and academician. When his dissertation is contradicted by his own subsequent research, he refuses to postpone the latter until first credited for the dissertation — even though his superiors encourage him to do otherwise. (+)

(c) In Viktor's case Dimka's example is doubtless salutary. As Bode observes, "Viktor undertakes a risk for the first time in his scientific career and openly opposes his superior at the research institute ... asserting his own point of view."[421] Viktor's true foil, however, is his peer and colleague, Boris, who ingratiates himself with the bosses and is obviously not above prevaricating or defaming others to gain status. He also advises Viktor to desist from his research, not for Viktor's sake but because his own work will otherwise be discredited. Viktor, on the other hand, dares oppose the work of his chief superior, VV, before a learned council. VV — like Drozdov (*Bread*) and Kramov (*Quests*) — had once opposed a new development, cybernetics, which (now that it is generally accepted) he champions. Boris meanwhile attempts to aggravate VV's prejudice against Viktor. (+)

(d) Viktor prevails against VV. We later learn, however, that his dissertation defense was unsuccessful. Although the reason is not made clear, his basic honesty and the ill will of Boris and VV are likely factors. Viktor's conflict remains in force. He is fully appreciated only after his untimely, accidental death. (+)

(e) The first person narrative also favors Viktor's image. (+)

(g) The imagery in Viktor's lines strongly supports his idealism, *e.g.* reference to the 'starry ticket'; his impression of a ferris wheel —

"Jazz music sounds from the park's depths; the wheel turns like our whole little sphere, all started up in a mysterious combination. The park revolves and so do we, the people in it. Some of us laugh, some are silent. The correlation of all these motions — try to figure it out. Jazz and symphony. There it is, our heaven, ready made for fireworks and the upward flight of rockets."[422]

— his reply to his wife, Šura, that he would travel in circles, like motorcycle riders climbing vertical walls, in order to achieve; his play on VV's initials (in Latin) by analogy to W formations in soccer: "'Once the W

[421] Bode, *Osteuropa*, XIII (January, 1963), 16.
[422] Aksenov, *Junost'*, VII (June, 1961), 6.

formation was regarded as progressive, but now it is old fashioned.' "[423] (+)

(34) Nekrasov, *Kira Georgievna* — Kira Georgievna: Ethical values, conscience, truth, artistic excellence, personal satisfaction. (4)

(a) Kira is long accustomed to circumventing principle and taking the easy way. Years before she formed an alliance with Nikolaj, her mentor and second husband, after Dimka, her first husband, had been convicted and sent to Siberia. Now she rationalizes her subsequent affair with a young model, Juročka. Her mediocre, traditional sculpture further evidences her lack of genuine idealism. (—)

(c) Compared to her first husband, Dimka, Kira is made to seem petty and shallow. Dimka's superiority is well dramatized when, after meeting him, his rival, Juročka, immediately prefers his company to Kira's. Kira herself feels inferior to Dimka's common-law wife, Marija, and is quickly rebuffed by Dimka's young son, Vovka. Unlike Kira, Dimka has learned to see through artistic fads and cliches. He finally resolves to remain with Marija and his offspring, while Kira returns to Nikolaj only under duress (after she learns of his heart attack). Even then she is half tempted to renew intimacies with Juročka. (—)

(d) At story's end, Kira discovers that both her art and her old way of life no longer suffice. After leaving for another rendezvous with Juročka, she ashamedly reconsiders and returns home: "For the first time in her life Kira Georgievna acted contrary to her immediate desires. Did this signify anything? Even she could not yet be sure. She only knew that she would not soon return to the studio where that summer she had been so happy and that she would not be happy too soon again."[424] Burg incisively analyzes the tale's conclusion: "Kira is made aware that her complicated relationships with Nikolaj Ivanovich, Vadim and Jurochka are indeed essentially false and dishonest and based on one and the same thing: the suppression of her shame."[425] The conclusion's tragic overtones thus tend to redeem her without altogether dismissing her culpability. (+)

(e) As the foregoing passages indicate, Nekrasov interjects a steady judgment upon his characters and skillfully manipulates the reader's attitude toward them, for the most part in Kira's disfavor. (—)

[423] Aksenov, *Junost'*, VII (July, 1961), 45.
[424] Viktor Nekrasov, "Kira Georgievna", *Novyj mir*, XXXVII (June, 1961), 126.
[425] David Burg, "Der moralische Bankrott des Nachstalinismus (über Nekrassows Roman 'Kyra Georgijewna')", *Osteuropa*, XII (February-March, 1963), 133.

(f) This tale rivals *The Trial Begins* in its masterful irony, an irony which invariably discredits Kira Georgievna: The story begins, for instance, "almost like an idyll. Kira lacks nothing"[426] — yet ends in quite an opposite key. "Time and again Nekrasov describes situations whose development and solution seem quite obvious, yet every time things move in an unexpected direction."[427] Bode mentions the paradox that "a free man is created out of Vadim while in prison"[428] and Burg reiterates this point — " 'the man who has grown wise' brings with him the experience not of a builder of communism, as one would expect in orthodox Soviet fiction, but of twenty years innocently spent behind barbed wire"[429] — then adds: "The transgressions of the sculptress Kira are not of the officially fashionable kind, like parasitism or acquisitiveness; they are mindless conformity with officially prescribed values in life and art. Nekrasov, similarly to other 'critical realists', has sought to convey new ideas by investing a commonplace literary scheme with unexpected content."[430] Other instances include Kira's observation, immediately after Juročka has kissed her and just before she entices him to be her lover: "she thought how fine it was that Nikolaj Ivanovič was such a good, thoughtful, genuine person — her husband";[431] her original oblivion to the equally sharp contrast between her age and Juročka's:

"Surely you understand that my relationship with Nikolaj Ivanovič is founded on something quite different? I regard him, always have and always will, as the best person on earth ... but there's still a difference of twenty years between us — a detail with which it is difficult not to reckon." ... As she broached these twenty years, she could not but reflect that there was also a difference of twenty years between the two of them. It must have occurred to Kira also, because she suddenly said in a brusque and excited tone: "But you can do, in general, as you want, dear comrade. You have your own mind."[432]

Nikolaj's subsequent comment that he would like to have had a son from Kira like Juročka and her sudden realization that such a son could have been Juročka's same age; her failure, in view of Nikolaj's celebration of her birthday, to disclose to him her newly revived interest in Vadim; *etc.* As Burg again observes:

[426]   *Ibid.*, 129.
[427]   *Ibid.*
[428]   Barbara Bode, "Sowjetliteratur 1961-1962", *Osteuropa*, XII (November-December, 1962), 807.
[429]   Burg, *Problems of Communism*, XI (September-October, 1962), 37.
[430]   *Ibid.*
[431]   Nekrasov, *Novyj mir*, 72.
[432]   *Ibid.*, 79.

The positive heroine in a positive milieu has, unfortunately, one weakness ... and the reader awaits from the author that he will, as befits his duty, show how she overcomes this weakness. The irony of Nekrasov's novel lies in the fact that this actually happens. Only the means of "recovery", the approach and the consequences are so unusual that the "weakness" itself lies somewhere far in the background.[433]

(—)

(g) A few pointed images further suggest Kira's superficial, escapist mentality: her view of Moscow's skyline from a high apartment balcony coupled with her unwillingness to look at what lies directly below suggests her shallow optimism and anticipates hers and Nikolaj's eventual dissatisfaction with their own pat artistic endeavors. It is also perhaps symbolic that Kira and Nikolaj, unlike Vadim, have had no children and that Nikolaj's son by his previous marriage was killed in the war: "... nothing ties them to the future. ... Thus one tragedy compounds another, that of the War being equated, so to speak, with that of Stalinism."[434] (—)

(h) The repetition of a particular phrase — "'Everything is clear, everything is clear, everything is clear'"[435] — tends, again ironically, to belie what is in fact being said. (—)

(35) Rozov, *ABCDE* — Volodja: Sense of purpose, vocation, conformity, compromise, dogmatism, world conditions. (2)

(a) Volodja's problem is reminiscent of Tolja's (*Legend*), Leksej's (*Colleagues*), and Dimka's (*Ticket*) — uncertainty of a life's role and resentment toward a number of prevailing practices and institutions. Volodja's alienation is compounded, however, by his apprehension about the possibility of nuclear annihilation. He leaves his new job as a railroad flagman; refuses to accompany his parents on vacation or remain with his provincial kin; avoids his adopted cousin, Sima; and is for some time generally antagonistic to everyone he encounters. (—)

(b) In its forthright earnestness, Volodja's rejection of his elders' hypocrisy has a definite appeal and imparts a certain conviction:

"I love everything that is good. But you are satisfied with both the good and bad. You've compromised yourselves."[436]

. . . .

---

[433]   *Ibid.*, 34.
[434]   *Ibid.*
[435]   Nekrasov, *Novyj mir*, 87.
[436]   Viktor Rozov, "ABCDE", *Junost'*, VII (September, 1961), 14.

MOTHER. "... Remember, Vova: there is only one road to the truth, while there are countless paths which lead to deception."
VOLODJA. "And maybe that isn't true either, Mama."[437]

The fact that "he is helpless against those with whom he clashes, and extremely direct in the expression of his opinions"[438] favors him. (+)

(c) Volodja's most direct foil is Vladimir Palčikov, a jovial, optimistic, industrious young steeplejack. The two are in fact namesakes, as Sima points out.[439] Palčikov is, as it were, Volodja come of age. He too had left home to travel — inspired by 'false romanticism'.[440] Now his work is extolled on the local radio, but he is oblivious to its dangers: "The main thing is not to think about it."[441] Palčikov favorably contrasts with the irritable, neurotic Volodja and suggests that the latter's pessimism is perhaps not so inevitable. (−)

(d) In common with Kuznecov's and Aksenov's comparable heroes, Volodja is eventually reformed. He is carefully exposed to a succession of characters and situations, whose cumulative influence persuades him to a more optimistic and conformist turn of mind: he and Sima witness the ecstatic affection between a young farmer and his bride; after Palčikov's death, the latter's example seems to impress itself upon his conscience; he becomes anxious for Palčikov's mother, whom he meets at a train station and who is as yet unaware of her son's fate; he is forced to sing with a group of young people in order to pass as one of them and avoid paying for train fare; an old conductor, mistaking Volodja for a volunteer laborer, extolls him, then gives him the benefit of his own folksy wisdom:

"... everyone has his own virgin land from the day he is born, and he plows it his whole life long. ... And at the end he sees what sort of harvest he has gathered. ..."
VOLODJA. "Why does a man plow this Universal, Eternal Virgin Land?"
OLD MAN. "He must."
VOLODJA (shuddering). "Must? Why?"
OLD MAN. "For perfection, my dear."[442]

Volodja is challenged to test his endurance as a steel worker. Meanwhile Sima becomes seriously ill — which provokes Volodja to exhibit unusual tenderness. Though his words remain defensive, he becomes thoughtful

[437]   *Ibid.*, 15.
[438]   Bode, *Osteuropa*, XIII (January, 1963), 18.
[439]   Rozov, *Junost'*, 24.
[440]   *Ibid.*
[441]   *Ibid.*, 25.
[442]   *Ibid.*, 29.

toward other people, notably Sima and her father, and appears at last prepared to participate in society. He has also been exposed in the meanwhile to a number of unattractive cheats and opportunists whose example he is now especially inclined to avoid. His conflict is totally resolved: "... as a general rule, while Rozov has gone further than almost any other writer in the outspoken expression of the attitudes and moods of Russian young people he has also managed with great skill to combine this with a handling of his plots in such a way that in the end the erstwhile perhaps errant young people are brought back effectively into the communist fold."[443] Burg concurs that the depiction of "Volodja's 'positive' reformation"[444] is most unconvincing. (−)

(f) The scenario's principal irony involves the complete reversal which Volodja undergoes by story's end: Whereas his uncle had carried Volodja's suitcase as the latter came to visit him and Volodja had mocked his discussion of local affairs, now Volodja carries his uncle's suitcase and enthusiastically describes the steel mill, simultaneously greeting passers-by. As Volodja and Sima leave the steel mill, it is he who now chases her. The scenario's ironic reversal thus underscores its placid ending. (−)

(g) The following are symbolic of Volodja's earlier misanthropy and cynicism: his failure to wave back to people as, in the capacity of flagman, he stands on a train's rear platform; the title, *ABCDE*, suggesting life's fundamentals, which, in a discussion with his uncle, Volodja arrogantly purports to have mastered; Volodja's pleasure upon discovering that Sima is an orphan — "a human being for whom there are no registration papers .... The usual life, which is explored layer after layer, has no secrets, is crudely classified, entered in documents — this life angers and embitters Volodja":[445] "'You are nobody! Do you understand? You are just you! You are a secret, a riddle! ... How charming! ... You have no name, no patronymic, no nationality! ... You're simply a human being!'"[446] Such symbolism is gradually overshadowed, however, by more positive images like the ostriches Palčikov hopes to see some day in Africa and which Volodja later adopts as emblematic of his new philosophy espousing adjustment and normalcy. It is less important what one does, he concludes, than that one "'have his own ostriches in his head. ... And even if he lives for a hundred years and dies without ever having

[443] Whitney, 152.
[444] Burg, *Problems of Communism*, XI (September-October, 1962), 41.
[445] Bode, *Osteuropa*, XIII (January, 1963), 19.
[446] Rozov, *Junost'*, 24.

seen them.'"[447] The story's harmonious conclusion is further under-scored. (−)

(h) The reversals discussed in connection with the story's resolution involve various parallelisms which contrast with like events in the first part and further underscore Volodja's transformation. (−)

(36) Bondarev, *Silence* — Sergej and Nikolaj Voxmincev: Social justice, Uvarov, Bykov, slanderers. (1)

(a) Both Voxmincevs have incurred the enmity of unscrupulous but influential persons. Nikolaj is consequently imprisoned on false charges, while his son, Sergej, is unjustly expelled from the Party and, in effect, forced to abandon his education for menial work. (+)

(b) Despite the Voxmincevs' lack of restraint (they needn't have criticized their adversaries), their indignation is just. Both are men of principle and innocent victims. Thus, despite Struve's reservations —

There is no reason to doubt Bondarev's sincerity, though in his attempt to "devarnish" the reality he seems to lay it on rather thick. When one reads of his hero's brave and uncompromising stand in the face of his "judges," and of the unspoken but clearly felt sympathy of his fellow students and even some of his judges, one suspects him of reading post-Stalin attitudes into the 1949-50 situation. Vivid though some of the scenes and episodes in the novel are, it is unconvincing overall.[448]

— both father and son are pitiable. (+)

(c) Although Uvarov, the novel's "would-be Communist villain ... remains a shadow",[449] villain he nonetheless is. His chief crime is the cowardly betrayal of his men as an officer in the War. When Sergej threatens him with exposure, Uvarov plots to have Sergej charged for failing to report his father's arrest to their local Party committee. He also attempts to transfer to Sergej the blame for his own dereliction during the War. Uvarov's zeal as an informer is motivated by vengeance and personal ambition. Nikolaj's foil, Bykov, has exploited his position as a factory director and become involved in smuggling. Presumably because of Nikolaj's suspicion and his failure to give Bykov a reference, Nikolaj is eventually arrested. (+)

(d) Struve's view of the novel's ending — that it is 'inconclusive and lame'[450] — is again unfavorable. Although Sergej's mentor, Morozov, is

[447]   *Ibid.*, 37.
[448]   Gleb Struve, "After the Coffee-Break", *The New Republic*, CXLVIII (February 2, 1963), 16.
[449]   *Ibid.*
[450]   *Ibid.*

among the majority who fail to oppose Sergej's expulsion from the Party, he later excuses his silence on tactical grounds that are presumably in Sergej's best interest. What this means is never explained, although Morozov does offer to write Sergej a reference for mining work in Kazakhstan. Sergej is consequently accepted at the mine despite his bad record and belligerent attitude. The implication is that the new position will be a real professional opportunity in disguise. Although his father, doubtless broken, remains in prison, Sergej, as a member of the younger generation, faces his own future 'undefeated'.[451] The remaining conflict and its future implications are essentially avoided. (—)

(f) The novel's principal irony is that those most deserving are least rewarded and must even suffer. (+)

(g) The novel's overriding symbol is the single word which constitutes its title and, like a *leitmotif*, frequently reappears at crucial moments in its narrative. According to Gaev, "the title of the novel has three meanings: first *Tishina* is the name of the *Zamoskvorechye* market where the heroes of yesterday acquire the means for subsistence; second *tishina* means the peace of the postwar period; third and most important, it means the silence resulting from fear and solitude, when a man is abandoned and left defenseless".[452] Silence also ensues on the following occasions — after Sergej's and Uvarov's first confrontation in a restaurant; during Sergej's first evening with his future mistress, Nina (incommunicability); after she reveals to him that she is already married; after Bykov threatens Nikolaj; as Sergej vainly waits in the offices of the MGB after his father's arrest; after Sergej's expulsion from the Party; after he is reprimanded for speaking out during his trial. Sergej even invokes the same word when he accuses Morozov of supporting, by his silence, such as Uvarov. According to its use in the plot, therefore, 'silence' predominately connotes the fear which oppresses the novel's heroes and renders them pathetic, if not tragic. On the evening of Sergej's and Nina's first encounter, furthermore, the mutual estrangement created by divided telephone booths and their physical awkwardness further convey an atmosphere of mistrust and apprehension. (+)

---

[451]   Jurij Bondarev, "Tišina", *Novyj mir*, XXXVIII (May, 1962), 92.

[452]   Arkadii Gaev, "The Decade since Stalin", *Soviet Literature in the Sixties* (ed.) Max Hayward and Edward L. Crowley (New York, Frederick A. Praeger, 1964), p. 45. Bode also cites the second of these meanings: "... everyone in the country wants peace after the War — hence the novel's title — no one desires quarreling, contention, or the regulation of accounts that were unsettled during the War". Bode, *Osteuropa*, XII (November-December, 1962), 799.

(h) The same symbolism achieves its effectiveness by frequent reiteration. (+)

(37) Bondarev, *Silence* — Nikolaj Grigor'evič Voxmincev: His son, Sergej. (1)

(a) While in the service Sergej disowned his father. After his return from the army he rarely speaks to him and, when he does so, usually in a derisive, disrespectful manner. His attitude seems, on the surface, most unkind and unjustly severe. (+)

(b) Sergej's prejudice is founded on the impression that Nikolaj had deserted his wife for another woman and is overly timid in the presence of Bykov. Although Nikolaj does not deny that he had an affair during the War, he has long brooded over his wife's letters since her death and his return home. His timidity is explained by the fact that, despite his heroism in the War, he was reprimanded for the loss by a subordinate of a regimental safe containing Party documents. His reputation was consequently blemished, and he fears that he is still under constant suspicion. His behavior is, under these circumstances, understandable. (+)

(d) After his father's arrest, Sergej discovers that Nikolaj has been seriously ill and acquires additional insight into the latter's position: "... he understood that he had been unable to forgive his weariness after the War, after his mother's death, his reticence, bordering on indifference, his premature grayness. He had been unable to forgive his having aged."[453] Later, Sergej receives a letter from Nikolaj, reaffirming his love, presuming his own blame for their estrangement, *etc.* Though physically separated, father and son have achieved an understanding and are reconciled. (−)

(g) The same symbolism — that of silence — earlier underscores Sergej's and Nikolaj's mutual alienation, thus reinforcing Nikolaj's pathetic position. (+)

(38) Bondarev, *Silence* — Painter, Fedor Mukomolov, and poet, Xolmin: Critical toleration, artistic freedom. (1)

(a) Independent artists, like Mukomolov and the poet, Xolmin, are either slandered or physically persecuted. Mukomolov is eventually censured by the Painters' Union, while Xolmin is denounced by Uvarov as a counterrevolutionary. (+)

---

[453] Bondarev, *Novyj mir*, 46.

(b) Neither evidences actual political disloyalty. Mukomolov's paintings are merely avant-garde and Xolmin's poetry non-political in content. (+)

(d) Their predicament does not improve. Although Mukomolov still vows to fight his critics and avoid being expelled from the Union, his bravado seems illusory: "Mukomolov's animation seemed unnatural; he had obviously aged very suddenly; patches of silver glistened in his beard, and his spine seemed to have curved and weakened."[454] Their conflict remains. (+)

(39) Tendrjakov, *Short Circuit* — Vasilij Vasil'evič Stoljarskij and other subordinates (Boris Evgen'evič Šackix): Ivan Sokovin, confidence, initiative, self-fulfillment. (1)

(a) During an emergency Ivan Stoljarskij blindly adheres to Sokovin's written orders. By failing to exercise his independent judgment, he nearly jeopardizes a whole regional power system. (−)

(b) Both Stoljarskij and his colleague, Šackix, are always ill at ease in the presence of Ivan, their tyrannical superior. Stoljarskij has been drained of all self-confidence and initiative as, over the years, he has deferred both the responsibility for decisions and the credit for ideas to Ivan. He is doubly affronted therefore when, after following Ivan's prescribed orders, he is severely reprimanded. (+)

(d) A belated reconciliation brings both Stoljarskij and Sokovin to a kind of understanding. Ivan first approaches Stoljarskij after a mis-understanding leads him to believe his own son, Vadim, has been acci-dentally killed. The shock causes him to empathize, as never before, with others' suffering. Ivan and Stoljarskij walk together, each dissatisfied with his past. The conclusion's general tone is nonetheless optimistic, implying, with Vadim's thoughts, that such " 'experiences never transpire without leaving their trace. They force one to think, they make one less hard, more responsive, deeper.' "[455] To some extent, the two men's differences, hence the sources of Stoljarskij's distress have been removed. (−)

(e) Tendrjakov's intrinsic moralizing (see 26 and 30, above) is equally applicable to *Short Circuit*. The foregoing quotation, though expressed as a character's thoughts, is illustrative. In *Short Circuit*, moreover, "each chapter has a philosophical colophon which 'twists out' the

---

[454]   *Ibid.*, 67.
[455]   Vladimir Tendrjakov, "Korotkoe zamykanie", *Znamja*, XXXII (March, 1962), 51.

meaning of the depicted events to the last aphorism".[456] The general tenor of such philosophical remarks is, again, optimistic. They deal, for the most part, with time, *per se*. As the elder Stoljarskijs and Sokovins await the birth of their grandchild, for instance, the narrator suggests that the New Year will bring a new life and, with it, an unknown future. Time is elsewhere spoken of as both an enemy and an ally: "When Vasilij Vasil'evič got up from his chair, time was an enemy. From second to second it was leading to a catastrophe. Now time was an ally. With every second the station was gaining strength."[457] At tale's end, time is again invoked in a positive manner: "Within five minutes it would be New Year's Day — 365 days. How should one spend them? It would pay to ponder."[458] (—)

(g) The tale's optimistic time and New Year symbolism[459] (in turn reminiscent of that in *Seasons* and *Quests*) accompanies the dissipation of Stoljarskij's alienated quandry. A further image which points in a similar direction likens the darkened city to a night in the Middle Ages: "Suddenly, without warning, like God's plague, like a hurricane or an earthquake, medieval darkness fell upon the people of the twentieth century, spoiled by technology."[460] Significantly, the lights come on again. (—)

(h) Repetition strengthens the impact of the tale's symbols, as such. (—)

(40) Tendrjakov, *Short Circuit* — Ivan Kapitonovič Sokovin: Human values. (4)

(a) In correcting the local power failure, Sokovin unwittingly brings about the death of a young industrial worker. His action, though it countermands his prior orders to Stoljarskij, is nonetheless effective and proper, under the circumstances. (+)

(b) Although, as Solov'eva explains,

at the moment the father gave the order, he was not guilty. ... however, he not only then but always put problems first ....

Ivan Kapitonovič is ... guilty of San'ka's death because he is too decisive, too accustomed to thinking according to "scales", fails to recognize real people and take them into account. Ivan Kapitonovič is also guilty that his assistant,

---

[456] Solov'eva, *Novyj mir*, 246.
[457] Tendrjakov, *Znamja*, 29.
[458] *Ibid.*, 54.
[459] In its concern with time, as such, the tale is said to be "an echo of Dudintsev's 'New Year's Tale'". Bode, *Osteuropa*, XIII (January, 1963), 29.
[460] Tendrjakov, "Korotkoe zamykanie", *Znamja*, XXXII (March, 1962), 23.

Vasilij Vasil'evič, is indecisive, is unaccustomed to thinking by scales, and takes too much into account.[461]

Indeed, San'ka's death might have been avoided, had Ivan approved his son's original recommendation that the chemical factory be equipped with its own turbine. Ivan dismissed this suggestion, favoring economy to the safety of individual lives. Instead of human values, Ivan worships impersonal forces such as Time and Energy: "'If the mighty god, Time, serves me, there is another god whom I faithfully serve. This is god Energy! Without him we are all moles rooting in the dark. He is the chandelier in the ceiling, the loom which weaves our trousers! He is many-faced and omnipresent, this god. And I am both his servant and master!'"[462] (—)

(c) Ivan's 'essential foil' is "his son, a young engineer, Vadim",[463] whose humane philosophy runs directly counter to his father's: "The young Vadim's spiritual development began during the War .... This feeling became stronger with the years, increased with his conscience. It demanded of him that he take others' burdens upon him, share their misfortune and sorrow, completely become the brother of his fellow men."[464] As such, he is indisputably more admirable than Ivan. (—)

(d) The forementioned misunderstanding and its consequent moral shock induce Ivan to commiserate with San'ka's young widow, who must undergo the same trauma he has just experienced at the morgue. He is also impelled to visit and be reconciled with Stoljarskij. Like a number of heroes previously analyzed, he converts to another, more humane value system and is no longer estranged. (—)

(e) The author's moralizing (see 39, above) also supports the foregoing positive resolution. (—)

(f) As does the tale's symbolism (see 39, above). (—)

(g) And its iteration (see 39, above). (—)

(41) Tendrjakov, *Short Circuit* — Vadim Sokovin: His father, Ivan. **(1)**

(a) Vadim's disagreement with his father (see 40, above) leaves them mutually estranged. Vadim appears to suffer most, however, and also to be least culpable. (+)

461   Solov'eva, *Novyj mir*, 248-249.
462   Tendrjakov, *Znamja*, 6.
463   Mehnert, *Humanismus in der jüngsten Sowjetliteratur?*, 10.
464   Bode, *Osteuropa*, XIII (January, 1963), 28.

(c) The comparison of father and son (see 40, above) unquestionably favors Vadim. (+)

(d) Ivan's recognition of human values leads to his reconciliation with Vadim, whom he regards with intense nostalgia after he believes that Vadim was his victim. Thus he remembers Vadim's childhood and reflects that Vadim will never see his own child, which tends to counteract his previous notion (so reminiscent of Globov (*Trial Begins*)) that "'of course, it is better not to have victims, but even if I had known in advance that there would be a victim, I would still just the same have given the order to turn off the power! One victim redeems many misfortunes. One victim can save a situation ....'"[465] In turn, his solicitations toward San'ka's widow and Stoljarskij further substantiate Ivan's reconciliation to Vadim's point of view. (−)

(e) Again (see 39, above), Tendrjakov's moralizing upholds the positive resolution. (−)

(g) As does the tale's symbolism (see 39, above). (−)

(h) And its iteration (see 39, above). (−)

(42) Kazakov, *Adam and Eve* — Ageev: Vika, other people. (3)

(a) Ageev, like Volodja (*ABCDE*), is extremely misanthropic. He is critical of crowds — their music, noise, levity — the smells that emanate from public kitchens, *etc.* He even rejects Vika after, upon his invitation, she travels to be with him. As Kramer observes,

One important dimension of Kazakov's theme is the conflict between the necessity for escape and a sense of social and moral obligation which sometimes ought to take precedence over the need for isolation .... Another area of potential conflict is the possibility that the escape may equally involve the rejection of those things most precious to a person. He comes closest to analyzing a character racked by such a conflict in "Adam and Eve."[466]

(−)

(b) Although there seems to be a tie between the artist Ageev's sensitivity and lack of compromise, on the one hand, and his misanthropism, on the other, its inevitability is never fully demonstrated. (−)

(c) Vika's good-natured manner — her pleasure at the appearance of the provincial town which so oppresses Ageev and her exceptional accommodation to Ageev's needs and whims — favorably contrasts with his moodiness and egocentrism. (−)

---

[465] Tendrjakov, *Znamja*, 47.
[466] Kramer, *The Slavic and East European Journal*, 30.

(d) The conflict ends with Ageev's complete rejection of Vika. Though tempted a time or two to declare his love and prevail upon her to remain, he in fact does nothing to prevent her leaving on the next boat. Even if he had detained her, one has the impression, he would have ostracized and abused her as before. Thus, though the ending sustains his conflict, it does not render Ageev any the more sympathetic — this despite Kramer's insistence that "the central movement in the story is the artist's growing awareness of his own effort to 'hide' by means of Vika" and that "Ageev is ultimately faced with the impossibility of escape".[467] (−)

(e) Kazakov's typical narrative detachment (see 22 and 23, above) renders Ageev all the less sympathetic in relation to Vika. (−)

(f) Ageev's craving for a woman and his essential fondness for the attractive, kindly disposed Vika strikingly contrast with his inability to tolerate her presence or become intimate. If anything, this poignant paradox makes Ageev a pathetically frustrated being. (+)

(g) According to Kramer, the story's very title "becomes a symbol for the ambivalence in Ageev's attitude toward Vika. Identifying his protagonists as Adam and Eve, Kazakov forces the reader to accept their antagonisms and attractions as a basic human relationship. Ageev himself tries to use the identification as an escape route. 'The two of them, like Adam and Eve, on a dark, uninhabited island alone with the stars and the water.'"[468] Perhaps the story's images, invariably reflected in Ageev's thoughts and essentially personal, best explain his morbid state of mind and thus reinforce his pathos in spite of his gauche social behavior. After reaching their island retreat, Ageev feels as if at the end of the world. He recalls the countess' solo from *The Queen of Spades*, whose reminder of death frightens him. At one point, "bitter alienation, renunciation by the world descended upon him, and he did not wish to know anything or anybody. He remembered that sick beasts hide themselves in inaccessible solitary places and are there cured by mysterious herbs or die."[469] An airplane approaches, then recedes in the distance, further intensifying his sense of isolation. The northern lights make him feel as if the earth is turning under him and remind him again of Adam and Eve — "Eve left Adam"[470] — which in turn suggests impending death. Finally, the combination of the ship's beam, the old woman's lantern, and northern lights seems to work a kind of metaphysical

[467]   *Ibid.*, 28.
[468]   *Ibid.*
[469]   Jurij Kazakov, "Adam i Eva", *Moskva*, VI (August, 1962), 150.
[470]   *Ibid.*, 156.

transformation and to provide Ageev with an epiphany and a personal justification. (+)

(h) Kazakov's skillful employment of details as such — metaphoric or other (see 22, above) — helps individualize Ageev and in this sense again vindicates his peculiar personality and behavior. (+)

(43) Kazakov, *Adam and Eve* — Ageev: Criticism, artistic freedom. (1)

(a) As vehemently as any of the alienated artists so far analyzed, Ageev berates the critics who have snubbed him. He accuses them of hypocritically advancing for their own personal gain views about which they themselves have no convictions. He also opposes the dominant, officially sanctioned school of painting. His professional attitude thus bespeaks an admirable fearlessness and integrity. (+)

(d) His decision to stay on the island without Vika and there undertake further serious painting all the more favors him as an artist. (+)

(e) The story's narrative detachment further supports him in this regard. (+)

(g) As does its imagery (see 42, above), including his ecstatic view of a neighboring church and that of the sunset from its bell tower. (+)

(h) And Kazakov's use of individualizing detail (see 42, above). (+)

(44) Solženicyn, *One Day in the Life of Ivan Denisovič* — Prisoners: Inhumanity, injustice. (1)

(a) Ivan Šuxov and his fellow prisoners are daily subjected to various humiliations and deprivations by the prison authorities. Perhaps the most insidious aspect of all they undergo is that, by strictly observing regulations, they could not survive, so must themselves resort to deceit and subterfuge. If caught, however, they are subjected to still worse punishment. (+)

(b) Despite their severe maltreatment, the prisoners are mostly innocent people who were unjustly sentenced. Their sentences are also often extended without cause. (+)

(d) The tale's prisoners are depicted during a typical day's routine. There is no resolution to their predicament. They will obviously undergo the same or worse treatment on the next day and again on the next. If some critics berate Ivan for acquiescing to his intolerable predicament,[471]

---

[471] *E.g.*, V. Buščin in *Neva* (March, 1963), according to Bode (*Osteuropa*, XIII (October, 1963), 707) and a number of others, according to Lakšin: "Ivan Denisovič is reproached for becoming reconciled with the camp, 'accommodating' to it. But

others extoll him for remaining, despite his inhuman situation, "a decent, gentle human being whose ordeal has only added to his stature and dignity".[472] The tale's final exposition provides a distinctive coda which cites Ivan's patience and strength at day's end, while recounting the trials and difficulties he must regularly face, now and in the future:

... he had lots of luck today: he was not sent to the guard house; his brigade had not been assigned to work at the Socialist City construction site; at dinner he'd had an extra share of cereal; their brigade leader had managed to have them credited for a full day's work; Šuxov had done a good job laying a wall; he was not caught bringing back a broken hack-saw blade; he earned some favors from Cezar that evening; and he had bought tobacco. He had not become ill and had subdued his fever.

The day had passed without incident — almost a happy day.[473]

(+)

(e) Although critics, like Zekulin, readily recognize the tale's noteworthy objectivity, its depiction of life as seen by a "'normal' person", they also refer to its author's identity with his characters and the "sincere and impassioned moral and intellectual engagement" which give it a mood "of universality and authenticity".[474] Slonim mentions the "unity of its 'point of view', in the Jamesian sense",[475] while Rzhevsky speaks of its "strange and productive, that is, striking, amalgam" of "ordinary first-person narrative with a peculiar form of indirect speech in which the personality of the narrator intrudes, speaking of himself as if in the third person (and sometimes in the first person as well)".[476] Though the tale is "clean of the usual 'ideological content' of Soviet literature",[477] a number of critics are quick to recognize in its hero the "traditional representative of the 'simple people'",[478] "a 'simple heart', ... another version of Platon Karatayev"[479] — "idealized as he was by Grigorovich, Turgenev, Nekrassov, Lev Tolstoy, et al."[480] and exemplifying "two in-

---

isn't that the same thing as reproaching a sick person for his illness, a sad person for his misfortune?" (V. Lakšin, "Ivan Denisovič, ego druz'ja i nedrugi", *Novyj mir*, XL (January, 1964), 231).

[472] Alexandrova, *A History of Soviet Literature*, 354.
[473] Aleksandr Solženicyn, *Odin den' Ivana Denisoviča, Novyj mir*, XXXVIII (November, 1962), 74.
[474] Zekulin, *Soviet Studies*, 50.
[475] Slonim, *Soviet Russian Literature: Writers and Problems*, 333.
[476] Rzhevsky, *Soviet Literature in the Sixties*, 76.
[477] Rubin, *Survey*, 164.
[478] Hayward, *Slavic Review*, 435.
[479] Slonim, *Soviet Russian Literature: Writers and Problems*, 333.
[480] Zekulin, *Soviet Studies*, 50.

tangibles ... patience and love of work", which constitute the "corner-
stone of a myth known the world over under the name of 'The Russian
soul' ".[481] While Howe contends that "the control Solzhenitsyn exerts
over his narrative seems to me excessive and self-denying, an inhibition
revealing the extent to which even a writer of complete integrity finds
himself anticipating — or 'introjecting' — the totalitarian censorship"
and hence that "tautness of realistic notation becomes a means of limiting
imaginative power, and the need for a faithful recollection, a cause for
repressing the dangers of meaning. The book is emotionally parched",[482]
— Hayward directly refutes him —

To my mind it is precisely the deliberate restrictions of the hero's mental
horizon, indeed the "constrictedness" of which Irving Howe complains, that
give the work its power and thus distinguish it from the common run of present-
day Soviet writing. The limitations that the writer imposes on himself are a
consciously chosen device. It was very important for Solzhenitsyn to try to
make us see the whole experience ... not through the eyes of an intellectual
like himself but through the eyes of a semiliterate person like the hero Shukhov.[483]

— and both Gaev and Lakšin support Hayward's point of view:

It is a virtue of this story that it does not descend into melodrama.[484]

That about Solženicyn's tale which is particularly amazing, in our view, is
not that he "did not reflect" or "did not generalize" anything, but, on the
contrary, how broadly he grasped life, how much he was able to elucidate in
such narrow bounds as those of a single day in the life of a prisoner. Indeed,
we not only learned about daily habits of the inmates, their forced labor, and
their joyless way of life. We learned that these are people, in each of whom
there emerged something typical and something substantial for the understanding of the times.[485]

A clue to Solženicyn's achievement resides, as others note, in the tale's
"businesslike narrative manner that comes from the concentration of its
energy in the most meticulously minute description of the details of
getting through the single day of prison life":[486] "The grim routine of
'l'univers concentrationnaire', the unspeakable squalor and misery, the
back-breaking labor, and the animal scrounging for scraps of food, is
authenticated here by a wealth of detail and made more credible by the

[481] *Ibid.*, 51.
[482] Howe, *The New Republic*, 19.
[483] Hayward, *Slavic Review*, 435.
[484] Gaev, *Soviet Literature in the Sixties*, 46.
[485] Lakšin, *Novyj mir*, 227.
[486] Rubin, *Survey*, 165.

author's quiet, undramatic manner."[487]   The universality of Ivan's
predicament is further corroborated by various subtle allusions to other
characters: "From Šuxov's brigade leader we learn of the latter's trials
as the 'son of a *kulak*' in 1930, from Šuxov himself about the War,
from the letters sent by Šuxov's wife about the peasants' situation on
the *kolkhoz*."[488]   Thus, as Erlich suggests, "Solzhenitsyn's central
narrative strategy obviates the need for, indeed eliminates the possibility
of, an explicit verdict",[489] for, as Howe validly contends, "it is *he*, Solzhenitsyn, the man remembering with sobriety ... who emerges most vividly
from the book".[490]   *One Day in the Life of Ivan Denisovič* is, after all, like
Dostoevskij's *Notes from the House of the Dead*, written by a former
Siberian prison inmate about people and a way of life that were for a
time essentially his own. That he sympathizes with them is beyond
question. (+)

(f) The author's very restraint achieves a most effective ironic impact
that is totally in sympathy with the hapless prisoners:

... not a cry of pain; it does not pile on horrors. The shattering impact ... is
produced precisely by its restrained, objective manner; the suppressed force
of that matter-of-fact appraisal of a bread crust's superiority over a spoon is
sprung by the reader's imagination, and how slight a movement of it is needed
to understand how hungry a man can be.[491]

It is strange to admit, but our first impression, as we began to read the tale
was that here there are also living people, who work, sleep, eat, fight and make
up, who take pleasure in small joys, hope, quarrel, and even make fun of each
other.

As if on purpose (I do not doubt it was on purpose), the author chose for his
story a relatively felicitous time in his hero's career as a concentration camp
inmate. While in the North, at Ust'-Ižme, where Ivan Denisovič had gone
originally, he spent the winter with no felt boots, had nothing to eat, and
almost "died" from severe dysentery. And the regimen there was incomparably
more severe. ...

What is most paradoxical and bold, in this relatively easy period of his prison
term, the author chooses from the long sequence of the days Ivan Denisovič
spends behind barbed wire not only an average but also a successful day for
Ivan, an "almost happy" one.[492]

---

[487]   Erlich, *Slavic Review*, 409-410.
[488]   Bode, *Osteuropa*, XIII (October, 1963), 707.
[489]   Erlich, *Slavic Review*, 410.
[490]   Howe, *The New Republic*, 19.
[491]   Burtin Rubin, "Highlights of the 1962-1963 Thaw", *Soviet Literature in the Sixties*,
(ed.) Max Hayward and Edward L. Crowley (New York, Frederick A. Praeger, 1964),
90.
[492]   Lakšin, *Novyj mir*, 224.

(+)

(g) The tale's imagery is sparing, perhaps more so than in any other work sampled. The whole concentration camp setting, on the other hand, can perhaps be thought of as a microcosm of the general peasant situation in the Soviet Union today. (+)

(h) The critics are unanimous in their admiration of Solženicyn's verbal gift. Rzhevsky[493] and Zekulin[494] both mention his neologisms. Howe,[495] Rzhevsky,[496] and Slonim[497] also discuss his extremely colloquial dialogue, which individualizes and lends sympathy to his inmate-heroes:

In keeping with Shukhov's village speech, it is frequently ungrammatical, composed in rich variety of the colloquialisms of the uneducated folk and the semi-obscene, harsh argot of the camp. It has a jagged texture. Frequent ellipsis and the staccato brevity of thoughts and observations reported on the run, broken down into the most simple primitive statements. It is a coarse style, completely adequate to the unbeautiful material it governs, capable of striking with a kinetic immediacy at the reader's perception.[498]

Lakšin and Zekulin comment on Solženicyn's style and its effectiveness, as follows:

Solženicyn's artistic daring is indicated in his first tale by the fact that he did not spoil it with our usual notions about the adornment of art. He did not in essence construct any sort of external plot, did not try to conclude the action more tautly or develop it with more effect, did not engage the reader's interest in his narrative with the artifice of a literary intrigue.[499]
Probably the most striking feature ... is the calm and detachment of presentation. The emotional stress which the subject-matter itself created must have been tremendous, but it never appears on the surface.[500]

This is in turn achieved, first, 'internally' by Solženicyn's concern "with more than the immediate subject-matter" and also

externally ... firstly, by careful selection of facts, secondly, by strict control over his vocabulary and use of language.
The facts selected for representation are in both stories ordinary-life, external, commonplace facts. ... Never is there resort to emotional coloring, hyperbole or cheap sensationalism. ... The impact on the reader is achieved through his realization of how and why these commonplace facts of life are different from anything we know in our own life.

[493] Rzhevsky, *Soviet Literature in the Sixties*, 76.
[494] Zekulin, *Soviet Studies*, 52.
[495] Howe, *The New Republic*, 21.
[496] Rzhevsky, *Soviet Literature in the Sixties*, 76.
[497] Slonim, *Soviet Russian Literature: Writers and Problems*, 333.
[498] Rubin, *Soviet Literature in the Sixties*, 90.
[499] Lakšin, *Novyj mir*, 224.
[500] Zekulin, *Soviet Studies*, 52.

The description and narrative are conducted in a language which is cool and placid, simple and matter-of-fact. ... There is no intentional play with words.[501]

(+)

(45) Tarsis, *Tale of a Bluebottle Fly* — Ioann Sinemuxov: Rational self-discipline, socialist discipline, theories, collectivist idealism. (1)

(a) Ioann becomes disenchanted with the theory of man's personal infallibility or collective virtue when, while contemplating the advantages of socialist discipline, he proves incapable of restraining his own anger in the presence of a bothersome fly. The net effect discredits such idealism and lends credence to Ioann's protest. (+)

(b) The malicious, irrational behavior of Ioann's socialist colleagues further confirms his convictions about the disparity between ideals and their application. (+)

(c) Ioann's direct foils are, obviously, his three colleagues — Akaciev, Dubov, and Osinovaty — who merely collect quotations. In their camp are the sycophant, Arxangelov, and the leader, Il'ja Apostolov (an unmistakable parody of Xruščev), who rose to power by never crossing any one else; confuses his own propaganda with the voice of the people; justifies the state's economic progress by comparing it *in percentages* with that of the U.S.; and is in effect only knowledgeable about potatoes. (+)

(d) Ioann is dismissed from his institute for holding critical, non-conformist views, then offered the position of a housing inspector in order to become reconciled to Soviet life. The outcome, however, is quite the opposite: Ioann's observations of the bureaucracy in action only support his previous suspicions. He resorts to profound cynicism, and his idol, in a sense, becomes the blatantly selfish and promiscuous, yet refreshingly honest Rozalija Zags. (+)

(e) The tale appears to be strongly autobiographical in philosophy and point of view. Although begun in the third person, its long concluding section is told in the guise of Ioann's memories, then as a journal extract — much in the vein of Dostoevskij's *Notes from the Underground*. The work is studded, furthermore, with a variety of epigraphs from Western authors as diverse as Pascal, Goethe, Thomas Sterne, and the contemporary, Graham Greene — each selected to underscore the narrator's satiric viewpoint. Its narrator also interjects himself when he

---

[501] *Ibid.*

suggests that he has no plot in mind but that his tale should have meaning for everyone, since if the reader is not a philosopher he cannot "prove that you are not a fly".[502] He also coyly denies any intent to cast aspersions at socialist society: "Some have thoughtlessly contended that the author maliciously contrived this conflict, then used it to slander both the philosopher and the bluebottle fly in order, indirectly, to undermine the theory of rational discipline and prove that there is a debauchery of things in our socialist reality."[503] He protests, instead, that the narrative will itself vindicate his objectivity and adds that the title should suggest where his sympathies lie — with flies, particularly those with unusual temperaments, but which, like other dumb animals, do not deceive. Defending his notes, Ioann insists that, if they are an exaggeration, still the finest things in life — Paradise, Prometheus, Juliet — have all been imagined. He then advances the notion that only chaos is real, order a lie; that some day his words will be revered like communion. He is then warned that he might be declared insane (Tarsis' own fate prior to his exile). At tale's end he invokes the soul's most courageous explorer, Dostoevskij, and charges that the soul itself is now being suppressed, adding that "I hope the bluebottle fly will teach you how to live."[504] Despite his pose, the narrator's sympathy for and identification with his hero are fairly obvious. (+)

(f) The narrator's foregoing remarks are themselves filled with devious intent, as is in fact the tale's ostensibly trivial and mundane, yet chief event — the affair with the fly: "The pangs of conscience and tormented soul of a Soviet philosopher who, in meditating upon the death of a fly that had annoyed him during his work on a book about the perfect state, lead to a debunking of Soviet ideology."[505] As in *The Trial Begins*, in fact, the subtext of almost every statement and situation is itself ironic: Ioann smashes the fly with the twelfth volume of his work on rational discipline; he is led to speculate that his inability to resist killing a meddlesome insect may well cause him to dispatch his wife and department head, both of whom have been far more aggravating; the fact that his foes must suppress his writing, when all he desires is to help others, seems to him to vindicate his own cause and shed all the more doubt on their own; *etc.* Such irony further debunks the prevailing idealism. (+)

[502]   Valerij Tarsis, "Skazanie o sinej muxe", *Grani*, XVII (December, 1962), 7.
[503]   *Ibid.*, 11.
[504]   *Ibid.*, 85.
[505]   László Tikos, "Die andere 'unbewältigte Vergangenheit'", *Osteuropa*, XV (January-February, 1965), 72.

(g) The work's symbolism is also invariably ironic in the same satirical vein: people are equated with flies (Ioann later changes his name, in deference to his victim, from Bluebelly to Bluefly); his colleagues' names suggest the wooden qualities of the trees they resemble; the names, Arxangelov and Apostolov, bear hierarchical but otherwise inappropriate connotations; after he is denounced by his colleagues, Ioann likens himself to Adam expelled from Paradise; the rain is likened to flies, as are the memories he has vainly tried to 'tame'; life, like his first mistress, had seduced him until the moment of his affair with the fly; as a bureaucrat, he sees himself like one of the fangs in a monster's jaw which, in Dantesque fashion, rends his department's petitioners; *etc.* (+)

(h) The work's rambling style and stream of associations, which are rather Gogolian, lend weight to Tarsis' satire. The tale's self-conscious, semi-fictional polemic further intensifies his didactic intent. (+)

(46) Aržak, *This is Moscow Speaking* — People: Duplicity, mutual fear, mistrust. (5)

(a) As a reaction to the announcement of an officially endorsed Public Murder Day, the people become fearful and devious, resorting meanwhile to a false bravado and endeavoring to ingratiate themselves with and appease one another so as not to incur vengeance on the day in question. What strikes one as pathetic is less their predicament than the hypocrisy and cowardice with which they prepare to meet it. (−)

(c) Contrasted to the people as such and to most of his friends and acquaintances is the narrator, Tolja, who resolves to walk the streets on Murder Day rather than hide from others: "I'll go onto the street and shout, 'Citizens, don't kill one another! Love your fellowman!' And what will come of it? Whom can I help? Whom save? I don't know, I know nothing. ... Perhaps I will only save myself. If it isn't too late."[506] By contrast, his friend Volodja indicates he will fight in the event of another Jewish pogrom — but Tolja cannot be sure with or against whom; his mistress, Zoja, urges him to assist her in doing away with her husband on the fatal day; a terrified acquaintance becomes hysterical and collapses in his presence on the morning of the same day; and various others, like his hen-pecked neighbor, cynically approve of the prospective blood-letting. (−)

(d) According to Dalton, "Arzhak's stories all concentrate upon one major character, and they have a clearly anticipated climax which results

---

[506]   Nikolaj Aržak, *Govorit Moskva* (Washington, B. Filippov, 1962), 45.

in an anti-climactic ending."[507] It is determined, in the tale's aftermath, that less than 1000 people were murdered in the Russian Republic and that the occasion met with varying success in other areas. The consequent reaction on the part of Tolja's acquaintances, however, suggests to his new girl friend that they were all victims of terror. The implication would seem to be that, under repeated circumstances, they would again behave in a similar fashion. (−)

(e) The first person narrator, who is in fact Tolja, is openly critical of others' reactions to Murder Day. Like Tarsis, he prefaces the sections of his tale with the statements of other writers — in this instance with quotations of verse written ostensibly by unfamiliar Russian poets whose thought conveys the same criticism as is implied in the tale itself. At tale's end, furthermore, the narrator plainly avows that any man who loves his country as he does would write the same thing, for he has judged both it and himself without being intimidated. He has answered for himself and for the others, and he senses that "with a quiet rumble of subconscious approval, the endless streets and squares, shores and trees, sleeping ship-like buildings, which float in a gigantic caravan into anonymity, all answer me with overwhelming encouragement."[508] (−)

(f) Like the tales of Terc and Tarsis, this one is packed with double meanings whose general tenor is, again, to belittle that which would deprive the people of their identity, scruples and/or self-respect: the license to kill on Murder Day is qualified by a prohibition on murders committed for private gain or consequent to sexual abuse; the event's announcement is followed by a program of light music; the author, who modestly disclaims his talent, continues to write because nobody will read him; in like manner, he says that "I can afford the luxury of being a communist when I am alone";[509] after people are no longer shocked by the official announcement, they begin to celebrate it, while *Literatura i zhizn'* even publishes poetry dedicated to the forthcoming event; after a young man defends the decree, an older man, who has all along protested it, threatens to bash his head in; as Tolja is himself attacked on Murder Day at the very feet of the sentries before Lenin's tomb, the latter remain impassive, one of them seriously studying the dust mark on his boot; in Central Asia on the day in question the ethnic groups, instead of fighting each other, only kill Russians; the leadership in the Ukraine have to be

---

[507] Margaret Dalton, "Nikolai Arzhak", *The New Leader*, CXLVIII (November 8, 1965), 17.

[508] Aržak, 61.

[509] *Ibid.*, 17.

reprimanded for taking the decree too seriously and formalizing it; the fact that no one is killed in the Baltic states is viewed, on the other hand, as a provocation; the event is heralded in *Izvestija* as a glorious educational experience for the youth, akin to the technical revolution in the virgin lands; the resulting statistics are felt to be accurate because reported on foreign radio broadcasts; *etc.* (−)

(g) Occasional symbolism reinforces the author's consistent disapproval of the people's psychology: on the day of the announcement, Tolja and his friends, who, as an exception, have met together in swimming attire, are already shocked and amused by the sight of their true selves; older buildings designed by Stalin stand menacingly between new apartment houses; Tolja conjectures about the mathematical theorem which authorities have drawn upon their backs (shades of Kafka?) to the point that the pencil is broken, the paper is torn, and their skin is being scourged; *etc.* (−)

(h) According to Dalton, "… Arzhak shows most clearly Soviet life … which connects him with Zoshchenko and Ilf and Petrov, the famous Soviet satirists of the '20' s".[510] His essentially simple, direct, unostentatious style — despite the obvious exaggeration of the situation, proper — helps make Tolja's associates seem typical enough, hence all the more frightening in their failure of moral nerve and their lack of human dignity. (−)

(47) Aržak, *This is Moscow Speaking* — Artist, Saša Čuprov, and poet, Arbatov: Conventional Soviet art, absence of genuine realism or artistic freedom. (2)

(a) Like Saburov (*Thaw*) and Ageev (*Adam*), Čuprov is unable to sell his nonconformist art. Even the propaganda poster he draws for Public Murder Day is found unacceptable. Arbatov writes poetry of so liberal a hue that he will read it only to the most sympathetic listener. (+)

(b) That Čuprov's poster is anything but inadequate realism is demonstrated when, on Murder Day, Tolja encounters a corpse which exactly resembles that of the poster. (+)

(d) Neither reformation nor good fortune intervene for the two esthetes, nor any indication that their circumstances will improve in the future. (+)

(e) Arbatov shares with Tolja his most candid views and reveals to him his collection of 'dangerous' philosophical literature. Tolja, *i.e.*

---

[510] Dalton, *The New Leader*, 17-18.

the narrator (*i.e.* Aržak?) must therefore be sympathetically disposed to him. (+)

(f) The resemblance between Čuprov's poster and real events is perhaps a crowning irony, as is the fact that, in general, artists are penalized for being original. (+)

(48) Solženicyn, *Matrena's Home* — Matrena Vasil'evna Grigor'eva: Compassion of relatives and neighbors. (1)

(a) Matrena's sisters vie for her estate, while her brother-in-law persuades her to break up her top room for his newly married daughter even before her death. After her death, the same relatives blame Matrena for their dissension over her property, and one of the sisters-in-law even ridicules her for being so guileless. (+)

(b) Matrena's whole life was one of service. Instead of appreciating her, however, her friends and relatives have exploited her generosity and abused her instead. Without receiving the least remuneration she has willingly helped the other women with their gardens and agreed to assist the *kolkhoz* during harvests, even after it would no longer employ her and had arbitrarily decreased her allotment of land. (+)

(c) Matrena suggests "the simple hearted one, ... a descendant of Turgenev's Lukeria in 'The Living Relic', ... a true Christian model of self-sacrifice and love of one's neighbor".[511] By contrast, "'the setting in which Matryona passes her life has become completely dismal, but she herself shines the more brightly, shines with a kind of unearthly, supernatural light'".[512] Everyone avoids repaying Matrena for her services, even when she is in need. Her sisters also stay away when they suspect that she might require their help. (+)

(d) As indicated, Matrena is no more revered after her death than before, and her death is itself "brought about by the greed and dishonesty of certain villagers".[513] (+)

(e) The first person narrator, her tenant, is a lone exception.[514] Even he scolds Matrena on the day of her death for wearing his jacket, which she might dirty while lifting lumber. He has learned to appreciate her personality, however: he would like to capture her smile with a camera, which would please him more than if she were to cook better food. At

---

[511] Slonim, *Soviet Russian Literature: Writers and Problems*, 334.
[512] V. Čalmajev, quoted in Priscilla Johnson, *Khrushchev and the Arts: The Politics of Soviet Culture, 1962-1964* (Cambridge, The MIT Press, 1965), 272.
[513] Slonim, *Soviet Russian Literature: Writers and Problems*, 334.
[514] Matrena's niece, Kira, and one sister-in-law (Faddej's wife, also named Matrena) are the only others who truly mourn her demise.

story's end, he eulogizes her in a manner technically reminiscent of the concluding enumeration in *One Day in the Life of Ivan Denisovič*: "The ending ... inwardly corresponds — in the rhythm of its speech as well — to the beatitudes in the new testament. From the negative, disdainful remarks of the relatives about the dead Matrena rises a hymn to the saving righteousness of this simple peasant woman":[515]

She did not gather possessions .... Did not spend her efforts in buying things and then cherishing them more than her own life.

She was indifferent to her dress, did not seek the attire which adorns both monsters and villains.

She was unappreciated and deserted by even her husband; buried six children but did not lose her sociable character; was regarded as strange by her sisters and sisters-in-law, comical, stupid for working for others without pay — she did not acquire possessions for her later years. A dirty white goat, a lame cat. ...

We all lived right next to her but did not understand that she was that same righteous person without whom, according to the saying, no village can stand.

Nor a city.

Nor our whole earth.[516]

(+)

(f) The story's overwhelming irony concerns the fact that such a righteous person would, in both life and death, go unrecognized and unrewarded. (+)

(g) Matrena's hard lot is bitterly underscored and her fate ominously foreshadowed by the theft of her water pot at the church during Epiphany and by the desertion of her cat. Her character is also imbued with a strongly suggestive religious or hagiographic quality. Resembling, as she does, his young baptist, Aleša (*One Day*), "this Russian woman ... is characterized by Solzhenitsyn with the expression 'righteous' or 'blessed' (*pravednitsa*), with an expression, that is, which antireligious propaganda had attempted to abolish".[517] In a broader sense, and like *One Day in the Life of Ivan Denisovič*, this story may also be construed to imply that the 'fate' of the peasant "was not changed by the 1917 revolution, thus implying that the revolution was, in a very important aspect, a failure".[518] (+)

(h) The analysis of Solženicyn's style in *One Day in the Life of Ivan Denisovič* (see 44, above) is equally applicable to *Matrena's Home*. With respect to the author's selection of "ordinary-life, external, commonplace

[515] Bode, *Osteuropa*, XIII (October, 1963), 710.
[516] Aleksandr Solženicyn, "Matrenin dvor", *Novyj mir*, XXXIX (January, 1963), 63.
[517] Bode, *Osteuropa*, XIII (October, 1963), 709.
[518] Zekulin, *Soviet Studies*, 62.

facts", Zekulin adds that "in the case of Matryona, their range is deepened (but not extended) by her hopes, dreams, and memories".[519] He also remarks that, "in its formal aspect", this story "appears to be almost an imitation of Turgenev. The method of construction, exposition and narration, and also the use of the language and even of expressive and descriptive vocabulary (*e.g.*, compound adjectives) is more than reminiscent of Turgenev's method."[520] The story's stylistic effectiveness is entirely directed at enhancing Matrena's martyr image in the reader's eyes. (+)

(49) Solženicyn, *Matrena's Home* — Matrena's neighbors: Fellow-feeling. (5)

(a) Matrena's neighbors mistreat her, as previously indicated (see 48, above). (−)

(c) Their comparison with her is, as already suggested, highly unfavorable (see 48, above). (−)

(d) They still show no particular compassion after Matrena's death, but make her a scapegoat for their own difficulties and continue to revile her instead. (−)

(e) The first person narrator, a former Siberian prisoner (like Solženicyn himself), is not a long-term or truly established member of the community. His criticism of the others' misconduct is apparent in the very manner of his narrative and in what he discloses about them. (−)

(f) Again, their general lack of regard for one who has done so much in their behalf is, in its blindness and unfairness, highly ironic. (−)

(h) To the extent that the story's style enforces its author's sympathetic view of Matrena (see 48, above), it creates an opposite and equally powerful pejorative image of her neighbors. (−)

(50) Solženicyn, *For the Good of the Cause* — Teachers and students, Fedor Mixeevič, Ivan Gračikov: The bureaucracy. (1)

(a) This story's protagonists, who are, as it were, representatives of the Soviet mass or 'consumer' public, are, in their way, as much victimized by the bureaucracy as are Ivan Denisovič by the prison authorities (*One Day*) or Matrena by her fellow peasants (*Matrena*). Both the young students of an electronics institute and their faculty are shrewdly deceived by a clique of bureaucrats, who ruthlessly deprive them of a new building the students are badly in need of and have themselves constructed. (+)

[519]   *Ibid.*, 52.
[520]   *Ibid.*, 52-53.

(b) The bureaucrats' motives become the more suspect as it is learned that, by furnishing the building to a research institute, they will enlarge their community, hence their own prestige, and also advance (at least Xabalygin) to better positions. "For the good of the cause" thus comes to mean "for the cause of a few powerful opportunists and no more". The students are required to make an irredeemable sacrifice not for society as such but for the private gain of a few. The prospect that when they learn the truth the students may become cynical and even corrupt also seems likely. Gaev indicates what makes their predicament so insidious: "Although in some respects the story resembles Dudintsev's novel, *Not by Bread Alone*, there are important differences: in Solzhenitsyn's story a fairly large number of individuals, not just one, are the victims of injustice. Moreover, in the collision between the two officials, the one with the lower rank is the champion of justice, while the more responsible official in the Party apparatus upholds the unjust decision."[521]

(+)

(c) The likeable, conscientious, well intended school principal, Fedor Mixeevič, and town Party committee secretary, Gračikov, are, like most of the less well characterized but equally sympathetic students and teachers, positively contrasted to such as the unscrupulous, self-seeking plant manager, Xabalygin, and Party committee first secretary, Knorozov. Zekulin adds that

... evil is represented by a high party official and his protege, and good by a man whose party affiliation is uncertain. ... the 'true' party and party spirit (represented by only one man, the secretary of the town organization) are on the side of the school principal, that is of the good; but they are powerless against the little tyrant on the oblast committee. This peculiar constellation of forces is, probably, a reminder by the author that Stalinist practices have not disappeared. Here, again, one tends to think at first that, anti-Stalinism being today rather commonplace, Solzhenitsyn is only following a vogue. But this would be underrating the forcefulness and bitterness of his diagnosis of 'Stalinism.' ...[522]

(+)

(d) Gaev observes that "there is no happy ending; the decision is postponed indefinitely"[523] and Zekulin that "the ending of the story is not a happy one, evil having won, apparently, the battle against the

[521] Arkadii Gaev, "Soviet Literature after the Last Attacks", *Analysis of Current Developments in the Soviet Union*. No. 3 (1963-1964), 4.
[522] Zekulin, *Soviet Studies*, 57.
[523] Gaev, *Analysis of Current Developments in the Soviet Union*, No. 3 (1963-1964), 4.

good".[524] There is no reason to expect that Fedor Mixeevič and Gračikov will ever prevail against their more powerful adversaries. The story's graphic conclusion suggests, in fact, that ruthless might will prevail. Content not alone with the newly transferred building, Xabalygin instructs his surveyors to claim as much of the school's adjacent ground as they can measure off. Ignoring Fedor Mixeevič's protests, he first completes the survey, then turns to the latter: "'It has to be this way, dear comrade.' 'Why does it have to be?' Fedor Mixeevič raged, shaking his head. 'For the good of the cause, is it? Is it? Well, we shall see!' he said, clenching his fists. But he could no longer speak; he turned around and quickly moved to the street ...."[525] (+)

(e) The story's narrative approach is especially novel. Its first four and a half pages are devoted to the purely random conversation of a group of students, and this same impressionistic technique is frequently employed throughout the rest of the story. Solženicyn's presence is therefore perhaps even more effectively concealed than in his previous writings — which creates an even more vivid, life-like impression of his pathetically abused students and educators. Only once does the author intrude with his own omniscient judgment — at the end of Gračikov's unsuccessful appeal to Knorozov and upon Gračikov's discovery that Knorozov has himself approved the building's transfer: "Looking, not at Gračikov but in front of himself at those distant places which only he could see, he opened his lips, only as much as was necessary, and sharply answered: 'Yes'. And, in truth, the conversation was concluded."[526] (+)

(f) The fact that the deserving should be so discriminated against, and *vice versa*, is Solženicyn's central irony. (+)

(g) The use of a cliche expression in the story's title — "for the good of the cause"[527] — symbolically conveys that same irony: "All the injustice of the [story's] manipulations are covered over with the trite expression that all this has happened 'for the good of the cause.'"[528] In the broader social sense, Solženicyn's students and educators can be construed as typical of their particular class and of its general fate in the society he depicts: "His *intelligent* is the bearer of good and valuable ideals who is not able to transform his ideas into actions (*e.g.* Turgenev's Rudin)."[529] Zekulin yet contends (also discussing *Incident at Krečetovka Station* as

---

[524]   Zekulin, *Soviet Studies*, 57.
[525]   Aleksandr Solženicyn, "*Dlja pol'zy dela*", *Novyj mir*, XXXIX (January, 1963), 90.
[526]   *Ibid.*, 86.
[527]   *Ibid.*, 74.
[528]   Bode, *Osteuropa*, XVI (January, 1966), 40.
[529]   Zekulin, *Soviet Studies*, 58.

the second of Solženicyn's stories whose central hero is a representative of the intelligentsia) that "both pairs [of stories] ... show that, fundamentally, the fate of these two important groups of Russian people was not changed by the 1917 revolution. ..."[530] (+)

(h) Solženicyn's lifelike impressionism, already mentioned, makes the plight of his hapless students and teachers seem immediate and convincing. (+)

ASSESSMENT OF AUTHORS' BIASES

The table which follows indicates the criteria according to which the heroes heretofore discussed are positively or negatively viewed by their respective authors. Plot situations are assigned the same numbers (listed vertically in the left column) and criteria the same lower case letters (listed under the heading "Criteria") as above. (The corresponding pluses and minuses are underscored where the criterion in question has not been explicitly applied by previous critics. See Table 12, page 127.) Also indicated are the year of publication, the thematic categories relevant to each plot situation (as previously numbered — see page 108), each hero's position in relation to the status quo (reconciled or opposed), and a concluding assessment of each author's relative overall bias. This assessment (found under the heading "Author Bias") is designated by numbers according, again, to the following scale: (1) identification with the protagonist (presupposing a critical view of the causes of his alienation), (2) detached sympathy, (3) pure detachment, (4) regretful disdain, (5) open hostility, and (6) superficial optimism:

TABLE 13

Author Bias in Fifty Selected Plot Situations

#	Work and Year	Thematic Categories	Hero and Status Quo Pro	Con	a	b	c	d	e	f	g	h	Author Bias
1	*Seasons* '53	4 5 10		×	=	+	−	=	=	+	−		2
2	*Seasons* '53	10	×		=	+	+	±	±	+			4
3	*Guests* '54	8		×	±		±	=		=	±		1
4	*Thaw* '54/56	4 10		×	±	+	+	−	+	+	−	+	1
5	*Thaw* '54/56	3 10		×	=	+	−	−	+	+	−	±	2
6	*Thaw* '54/56	8		×	±	+	+	−					1
7	*Wings* '54	8		×	±	±	±	=			=	=	6
8	*Wings* '54	10		×	=	±	±	=			=	=	2

[530] *Ibid.*, 62.

#	Work and Year	Thematic Categories	Hero and Status Quo Pro	Con	a	b	c	d	e	f	g	h	Author Bias
9	*Wings* '54	4		×	=	±		=			=	=	1
10	*Opinion* '56	6 10	×		=	±	−	+		±	±		4
11	*Bread* '56	3 8		×	±	+	+	+	+	+	+		1
12	*Cruelty* '56	7 10		×	±	±	±	±	±	±	±		1
13	*Levers* '56	3 4	×		±	±	±	+	±	=	=	±	4
14	*Quests* '56	8		×	±	±	+	−	+	±	=		1
15	*Quests* '56	4		×	=	±				−	+		2
16	*Light* '56	9 10	×		=	±	±	±			±		2
17	*Sonnet* '56	1		×	±	±	+	−			±	±	1
18	*Journey* '56	6	×		±		=	=	−	=	=		5
19	*Živago* '57	1 2 8		×	−	+	+	+	+	+	+	+	1
20	*Živago* '57	6	×		−	+	−	+	+	−	−	−	4
21	*Legend* '57	2 10		×	=		±	=	=		=		2
22	*Renegade* '59	1		×	−	±		+	+	±	−	±	3
23	*Renegade* '59	10		×	=			+	+	±	+		3
24	*Trial Begins* '60	1 2 4		×	=	±		+	±	+	+	+	1
25	*Trial Begins* '60	6	×		=		−	−	=		−	−	5
26	*Three, Seven, Ace* '60	4 8		×	+	+	+	+	+	±	+	+	1
27	*Three, Seven, Ace* '60	7 10	×		−	−	−	+	−	=	−	−	4
28	*Colleagues* '60	2 7 10		×	=		=	−	−		±		2
29	*Colleagues* '60	4	×		±		±	−	+				1
30	*Trial* '61	10	×		=	−	−	±	±	±	=	±	4
31	*Trial* '61	7		×	±		+	±	±	±	±	±	1
32	*Ticket* '61	1 10		×	=		−	=	+		−	−	2
33	*Ticket* '61	3 10		×	±		+	±	+		+		1
34	*Kira* '61	3 6 10	×		=		=	+	−	−	=	=	4
35	*ABCDE* '61	2 7 10		×	=	+	−	−		−	=	=	2
36	*Silence* '62	8		×	±	+	+	−		±	+	±	1
37	*Silence* '62	5		×	±	+		−		+			1
38	*Silence* '62	3		×	±	+		+					1
39	*Short Circuit* '62	4		×	=	+		−	=		−	−	1
40	*Short Circuit* '62	6	×		±	−		−	=		−	−	4
41	*Short Circuit* '62	5		×	±		+	−	=		−	−	1
42	*Adam* '62	4		×	=	−	=	−	−	±	+	+	3
43	*Adam* '62	3		×	±			+	+		+	+	1
44	*One Day* '62	8		×	+	+		+	+	+	±	+	1
45	*Bluebottle* '62	7		×	±	±	±	±	±	+	±	±	1
46	*Moscow* '62	10	×		=		=	−	=	=	=	−	5
47	*Moscow* '62	3		×	±	±		+	±	±			2
48	*Matrena* '63	2 4		×	±	±	+	+	+	±	+	+	1
49	*Matrena* '63	6	×		−		−	−	−	=		−	5
50	*For the Good* '63	8		×	±	+	±	+	±	+	±	+	1

Of the fifty central plot situations analyzed, twenty-four (almost half) manifest the author's personal identification with his alienated protagonist; ten (one fifth) show the author's detached sympathy; only three elicit his regretful disdain and four his open hostility; while but one evidences superficial optimism throughout its narration. Furthermore, although the sum of positive *vs.* negative biases is not always directly equatable with the concluding assessment (final column), the following correlations do occur:

(1) Of the twenty-five protagonists whose overt plot function appears laudable from the story's very beginning, twenty (four fifths) receive the author's personal identification; of the rest, two (the citizens, *Levers*; and Ivan Sokovin, *Short Circuit*) receive the author's regretful disdain and one (Varygin, *Journey*) his open hostility. Of the twenty-five protagonists whose overt plot function appears from the story's outset to be unfavorable, fourteen (three fifths) are later redeemed by extenuating circumstances; of these fourteen, four manifest the author's personal identification, six his detached sympathy, three his regretful disdain, but none his open hostility.

(2) Of the twenty-three protagonists who are favorably contrasted to foils, sixteen (two thirds) receive their author's identification, three his sympathy, three his disdain, none his hostility. Of the fifteen who are unfavorably contrasted to foils, none are identified with, five (one third) receive the author's sympathy, five (one third) his disdain, and three (one fifth) his open hostility.

(3) Of the twenty-four heroes whose denouement either vindicates them or prolongs their alienation, thirteen (over half) are identified with, while only half again that number, seven (under a third), receive the author's disapproval. Of the twenty-six heroes the conclusion of whose story in some way dispels their alienation, eleven (two fifths) receive the author's identification, eight (almost one third) his sympathy, only one his disdain, but four (over a seventh and all who are so classified[531]) his hostility, and (as one would expect) Romodan (*Wings*, situation 7) his superficial optimism.

(4) Where moralizing or narrator personality is a consideration, the twenty-four heroes of whom the author has something good to say include fifteen (three fifths) with whom he identifies, four with whom he sympathizes, and three only whom he regretfully disdains. The fourteen, on the other hand, whom he in some way didactically reproaches

---

[531] Varygin, *Journey*; Globov, *Trial Begins*; People, *Moscow*; Matrena's neighbors, *Matrena*.

include three (one fifth) with whom he sympathizes, four (nearly one fourth) of whom he disapproves, and all four again (another fourth) to whom he is openly hostile.

(5) Of the twenty-three heroes whose alienation is underscored by irony (plot or verbal), thirteen (well over half) are identified with, three sympathized with, four discredited. Of the eight whom irony ridicules or deflates, only one receives the author's overall sympathy, but three his disapproval, and three more his hostility.

(6) Imagery and symbolism support at least twenty-one protagonists, the large majority of whom (sixteen, or over two thirds) are identified with by their author, two more who receive his sympathy, only one of whom he disapproves, and none toward whom he is hostile. Negative symbolism, however, either reinforces an optimistic conclusion, as in the case of five protagonists with whom the author identifies and six with whom he sympathizes, as well as Romodan, *Wings*, situation 7 (superficial optimism again), or tends to debunk and disparage the hero, as with some six protagonists whom the author disdains and three to whom he is hostile (nine in all, or almost half of the twenty-two so affected).

(7) Other stylistic considerations, including choice of language, tend to support some seventeen protagonists — twelve (almost three fourths) who are identified with, one who is sympathized with, and only two who are discredited. In fourteen instances, like considerations either enhance a positive ending or again debunk a protagonist — three wherein the hero is identified with, three sympathized with, three disdained, all four (again) in which opposed, and also in the case of Romodan, *Wings*, plot situation 7 (superficial optimism).

It will be noted that ALL plot situations which show either an author's regretful disdain or his open hostility involve a protagonist who supports rather than opposes the status quo. In terms, therefore, of THE AUTHOR'S OWN VIEW toward his hero's status quo, all but six of the fifty central plot situations indicate that the authors concerned either (a) identify or sympathize with those who oppose it or (b) evidence disdain or open hostility toward those who support it. The six exceptions include three by Kazakov (situations 22, 23, 42), which reflect their author's detachment; situation 7 (*Wings*), which, throughout the plot, displays a superficial optimism toward the hero's difficulties; situation 16 (*Light*), where, though he both enforces the status quo and receives the author's sympathy, the hero acts under a sense of compulsion and duress for which (not for his action, as such) the author pities him; and situation 29 (*Colleagues*), in which the hero's opponent is a criminal type who, as such, opposes in the most abstract context such generally indisputable values as work, service to others, *etc.*

The correlation of authors' biases with thematic categories is indicated in the following table, in whose headings the horizontal row of numbers corresponds to the ten previously employed thematic categories and the vertical column of numbers to the six gradations of ultimate bias (concluding assessment, Table 13, last column). (All such numbers are as heretofore assigned.) The numbers within the table indicate the frequency of occurrence of a given thematic category in conjunction with a particular bias for the total of fifty plot situations.

TABLE 14

*Correlation of Author Biases and Thematic Categories in
the Fifty Selected Plot Situations*

Scale of Biases	Thematic Categories										Total
	1	2	3	4	5	6	7	8	9	10	
1	3	3	4	7	2		3	9		3	34
2	1	3	2	2	1		2		1	8	20
3	1			1						1	3
4			2	1		4	1			5	13
5						3				1	4
6								1			1
Total	5	6	8	10	4	7	6	10	1	18	75

As the table indicates, authors tend to identify most completely with protagonists alienated by the bureaucracy and by social injustice. They also strongly identify with those whose alienation involves love and friendship and, to a lesser degree, where protagonists stand for artistic or scientific freedom or freedom in general. They equally as much sympathize and also identify with protagonists whose rebellion is of a more universal character and, to a significant degree, sympathize where, again, freedom of thought, love and friendship, and idealistic disillusion are at issue. They most sympathize, however, in terms of moral conflicts (category 10). They also strongly disapprove in terms of this same category and also as concerns 'incomplete' positive heroes (category 6) and, to a lesser degree, free thinkers (category 3). 'Incomplete' positive heroes receive their most complete rejection, as do also one other group of heroes — certain moral cowards (category 10). In only one instance (whose theme concerns the bureaucracy and social injustice) does an author resort to superficial optimism. Pure detachment, which is again typical of but one author, is evenly distributed over three categories — those pertaining to individuality and freedom in general, to alienation in love, and to moral issues, as such.

SUMMARY. — The authors of the central plot situations heretofore analyzed show, in general, an overwhelming tendency either to identify (50%) or at least sympathize (20%) with their alienated heroes and an even greater tendency (88%) to be critical of the depicted status quo, be this the object of the hero's protest or that which he defends. When broken down in terms of specific relevant criteria, the fifty protagonists are fairly evenly approved or disapproved of by their authors in terms of their overt plot situation (25 to 25), their story's conclusion (24 to 26), symbolism (21 to 22), and other stylistic considerations (17 to 14); show slightly more approval in their comparison with foils (23 to 15) and in terms of the narrator's outright interjection of a personal judgment (24 to 14); and show overwhelming approval in terms of irony (23 to 8). In correlation, finally, with their respective thematic categories, the fifty plot situations reveal overwhelming bias in favor of those heroes who oppose the bureaucracy, who are alienated in terms of love and friendship, who wage universal protest, or who assert their individuality, in general, as well as, somewhat less consistently, with those challenged to think for themselves or confronted with a difficult ethical dilemma. In the last two categories are those — like Kira Georgievna, the citizens in *Levers*, and other weak-willed conformist types — who reject the author's preferred choice and therefore receive his condemnation. 'Incomplete' positive heroes — like Minaev (*Opinion*), Varygin (*Journey*), Antipov (*Živago*), Globov (*Trial Begins*), Ivan Sokovin (*Short Circuit*), and Matrena's neighbors (*Matrena*) — either merit their author's disapproval or his outright invective. These are the least favored protagonists. Otherwise, in only one instance — that of a bureaucratic reformer (*Wings*) — is the approach superficially optimistic and in only three, involving three separate thematic categories (and each by Kazakov), is the hero viewed with pure detachment.

PART FOUR

THE 'THAW' HERO AS BOTH THE OUTGROWTH OF A PRIOR LITERARY TRADITION AND A DISTINCTLY NEW CHARACTER CREATION

VI

LITERARY POLITICS AND THE SOVIET 'THAW'

In a 1966 article appropriately subtitled "Why Many Youths Today are Alienated Heroes", Ernest J. Simmons suggests that the current generation of Soviet youth are concerned with problems which "had no existence in the mythology of the positive hero of the past".[1] Symptomatic, he says, is their mounting resentment at prohibitions imposed by the regime and their cynical reaction to those who would imbue them with a sturdier idealism. As specific causes, A. Karavaev cites "the economic difficulties inherent in the Soviet system and, what is more important, the lack of individual freedom, which has engendered a skeptical, enquiring mood in the Soviet Union".[2] Others have made similar observations about the total mid-century Soviet scene. "Alienation", says Mihajlo Mihajlov, writing the year before, is "no less pronounced in a totalitarian society where mankind is made into a collective force than it is in the capitalist world",[3] while in 1959 Barbara Bode maintained that "'superfluous men' are now ever more frequently encountered in the Soviet literature of optimism — men who find no proper place in the construction of Communism".[4]

PERTINENT EVENTS

A chronological enumeration of significant political-literary events both before and during this same mid-century period helps explain why such types so prominently appear in the literature of the time and why at

---

[1] Ernest J. Simmons, "Russia's Different Generation", *The National Observer*, V (February 28, 1966), 22.
[2] A. Karavaev, "Between Thaw and Freeze in Soviet Literature", *Bulletin, Institute for the Study of the USSR*, XI (March, 1964), 37.
[3] Mihajlo Mihajlov, "Moscow Summer 1964", *The New Leader*, XLVIII (June 7, 1965), 13.
[4] Bode, *Osteuropa*, IX (December, 1959), 817.

particular intervals. In the listing which follows, events prefixed with a plus sign (+) generally indicate a liberal tendency with respect to creative freedom, while events prefixed with a minus sign (−) suggest a reactionary tendency and further literary restrictions. Events set off by solid lines are of a purely political nature but precede or accompany other events more directly related to literary conditions or policy:

TABLE 15

Pattern of Political-Literary Events in the First Soviet Half-Century

Date	Event
October 25, 1917	Bolshevik Revolution.
1918	(−) Proletcult.
1921-1927	New Economic Policy (NÈP).
1921	(+) Serapion Brotherhood.
1922	(−) Glavlit: institution of literary censorship.
January 21, 1924	Death of Lenin: Stalin's subsequent consolidation of power.
1924	(+) The Pass (*Pereval*).
January, 1925	(+) Trotskyist-dominated Writers' Congress.
December 27, 1925	(−) S. Esenin's suicide.
1925	(+) Resolution of Central Committee recognizing diversity in literature.
1928-1932	First Five-Year Plan.
1929	(−) Defamation of B. Pil'njak and E. Zamjatin.
1930's	(−) Revision of earlier works: A. Fadeev's *The Young Guard*, F. Gladkov's *Cement*, M. Šoloxov's *The Silent Don*, A. Tolstoj's *The Road to Calvary*, etc.
April 4, 1930	(−) V. Majakovskij's suicide.
1932	(−) Union of Soviet Writers: dissolution of all previous writers' organizations.
1934	(−) First Writers' Congress: Proclamation of 'socialist realism': "'Socialist realism being the basic method of Soviet literature and literary criticism, requires from the artist a truthful, historically concrete representation of reality in its revolutionary development. Moreover, truth and historical completeness of artistic representation must be combined with the task of ideological transformation and education of the working man in the spirit of Socialism'."[5]
1936-1940	Stalinist Purges.
1937	(−) Purge of numerous nonconformist writers. (+) Centennial commemoration of Puškin's death: reprintings in tens of millions of copies.
1941-1945	World War II.

[5] Slonim, *Soviet Russian Literature: Writers and Problems*, 160-161.

Date	Event
1946-1949	Stalinist Purges: 'Ždanovščina'.
August 14, 1946	(−) Ždanov's purge of the arts: – new literary policy: enforcement of socialist realism. – expulsion of A. Axmatova and M. Zoščenko from Writers' Union. – attack upon Leningrad journals *Zvezda* and *Leningrad*.
1946	(−) Discontinuance of publication of works by Dostoevskij.
1948	(−) Fadeev's campaign as First Secretary of Writers Union against cosmopolitanism in literature.
1949	(−) K. Simonov's attack upon liberal critics.
October, 1950	(+) A. Belik's statement in *Oktjabr'* hinting at forthcoming literary 'thaw'.
July 2, 1951	(+) *Pravda* editorial against bourgeois nationalism in literature.
March, 1952	(+) Simonov's statement in *Pravda* hinting at forthcoming literary 'thaw'.
October, 1952	(+) Malenkov's statement at Nineteenth Party Congress hinting at forthcoming literary 'thaw'.
1952	(+) Leadership's general recognition of dearth of appeal in contemporary literature and "need for satire".[6]
March 5, 1953	Death of Stalin.
April 16, 1953	(+) Poetess O. Berggol'c' article in *Lit. gazeta*, "Conversation about Lyric Poetry", criticizing impersonality in contemporary verse.
May, 1953	(+) Student of cinematography O. Šmarova's article which "deplored the absence of 'love' from Soviet films".[7]
June, 1953	(+) Publication in *Novyj mir* of A. Tvardovskij's poem "Horizon beyond Horizon", stressing function of the writer's own 'inner editor'[8] and deploring literary regimentation.
June 17, 1953	East German Uprising
October, 1953	(+) I. Èrenburg's article in *Znamja*, "On the Work of a Writer", pleading for "'truthfulness'" and "'passion'" rather than "'literature by order'"[9] and referring to Western writers in a "tolerant and objective manner".[10]

[6] Vickery, 25.

[7] Brown, 239. Source of article not given.

[8] Vera Alexandrova, "Soviet Literature since Stalin", Problems of Communism, III (July-August, 1954), 11.

[9] *Ibid.*, 12.

[10] Gleb Struve, "Russia Five Years after Stalin", *The New Leader*, XLI (April 7, 1958), 16.

Date	Event
November, 1953	(+) Composer Abram Xačaturjan's "plea for the rights of the individual composer"[11] in *Soviet Music*.
November, 1953	(+) V. Panova's *Seasons* (*Novyj mir*).
December, 1953	(+) Critic V. Pomerancev's article in *Novyj mir*, "On Sincerity in Literature", attacking 'positive' heroes, particularly in S. Babaevskij's *Cavalier of the Golden Star*, and calling for broader themes and approaches, while displaying a new 'impressionistic' critical style, "moving gently from one idea to another without apparent ulterior purpose, and giving the effect of immediate contact with thought in process. ... the approach of the author and his style, rather than the actual idea content of the article, were most likely what really disturbed the pontiffs".[12]
1953	(+) Simonov's criticism of 'positive' and 'negative' hero stereotypes and request for republication of works of twenties and thirties at plenum of Writers' Union.
April, 1954	(+) F. Abramov's article in *Novyj mir*, "Collective Farm People in Postwar Literature", attacking heroes of Stalin Prize-winning novels of forties by Babaevskij and G. Nikolaeva.
	(+) Publication of ten poems by B. Pasternak (from *Dr. Živago*) in *Znamja* — his "first original work to appear since 1945".[13]
	(+) F. Abramov's article in *Novyj mir* criticizing prior Soviet literary standards.
May, 1954	(+) Èrenburg's *The Thaw* (*Znamja*).
August, 1954	(−) Meeting of presidium of Writers' Union to discuss errors of *Novy mir*.
September, 1954	(−) Simonov's replacement of Tvardovskij as editor of *Novyj mir* due to latter's publication of liberal criticism and reviews by Pomerancev, Abramov, and Ščeglov.
December 15-26, 1954	(+) Second Writers' Conference (originally scheduled for 1937):
	(+) – revision of official definition of socialist realism: "'Socialist realism being the basic method of Soviet literature and literary criticism, requires from the artist a truthful ... representation of reality in its revolutionary development'".[14]
	(+) – recognition of affinity between "Soviet socialist realism and bourgeois critical realism".[15]
	(+) – speeches by Èrenburg, Čuxovskij, Šoloxov, Berggol'c, Kaverin,

---

[11] Brown, 239.
[12] *Ibid.*, 241.
[13] Struve, *The New Leader*, XLI (April 7, 1958), 17.
[14] Vickery, 70.
[15] Gleb Struve, "The Second Congress of Writers", *Problems of Communism*, IV (March-April, 1955), 11.

Date	Event
	and Ovečkin criticizing current literary situation.
	(−) – rebuttal by F. Gladkov and subsequent passage of reactionary resolutions.
	(−) – Surkov's condemnation of Èrenburg's *The Thaw* and of liberal criticism by Pomerancev, Lifšic, and Ščeglov in issues of *Novyj mir* appearing in late 1953 and early 1954.
1955	(+) Commemoration of 75th anniversary of Dostoevskij's death and reissuance of his works.
	(+) Rehabilitation of writers purged or denounced in the thirties: Babel', Pil'njak, Bunin, Cvetaeva, *etc.*
	(+) General agitation for objective scholarship.
	(+) Inception of annual Poetry Day.[16]
February, 1956	Twentieth Party Congress: Xruščev's denunciation of Stalin's 'personality cult' in secret speech on 2/24/56.
February, 1956	(+) Šoloxov's liberal protest against Fadeev.
May, 1956	Bulganin's and Xruščev's visit to England — a gesture toward peaceful co-existence.
May, 1956	(+) Article in *Voprosy filosofii*, "On the Question of the Lag in Drama and the Theatre", by B. A. Nazarov and O. V. Gridneva.
May, 13, 1956	(+) Fadeev's suicide: rumors suggesting his implication in denunciations of Babel, Kiršon, *etc.* as secret archives are unearthed.
July, 1956	(+) Review of V. A. Razumnyj's *The Problem of the Typical in Esthetics* in *Kommunist*, criticizing notions of socialist realism.
August, 1956	(+) V. Dudincev's "Not by Bread Alone" and D. Granin's "One's Own Opinion" (*Novyj mir*).
October, 1956	Political dissention in Poland.
October, 1956	(+) Arrival of copy of 796 page *Literary Moscow, II* at printers in time for publication in same year. – Editorial board: Aliger, Kaverin, Paustovskij, Tendrjakov, *etc.* – Contents: Èrenburg's favorable critique of Marina Cvetaeva, A. Kron's and M. Ščeglov's unfavorable reviews of conflictless Soviet plays, and numerous works of fiction criticizing status quo.
November, 1956	Revolt in Hungary.
1956	(+) *Day of Poetry* and appearance of "excellent lyric poetry".[17] (+) Simonov's criticism in *Novyj mir* of Stalin's forced revision of Fadeev's *The Young Guard, etc.*[18]

[16] Whitney, 10.
[17] *Ibid.*, 9.
[18] Struve, *The New Leader*, 18.

Date	Event
	(+) Revolt of satellite nations, especially Poland and Hungary, against socialist realism.
	(+) Èrenburg's *Essay on Stendhal*, justifying "such critical novelists as Vladimir Dudincev".[19]
	(−) Simonov's removal from editorship of *Novyj mir* for publication of *Not by Bread Alone*.
	(−) Rejection of Pasternak's manuscript, *Dr. Živago*, by editorial board of *Novyj mir* and accompanying critical letter.
	(−) Xruščev's 'Garden Party': denunciation of 'revisionist' writers.
March, 1957	(−) Meeting of executive body of Moscow branch of Writers' Union to criticize *Literary Moscow, II* and *Not by Bread Alone*.
May, 1957	(−) Attack upon editors of *Literary Moscow, II* by Writers' Union and attempt by same to exact recantations from erring members.
October, 1957	Launching of first Sputnik.
1957	Publication abroad of *Dr. Živago*.
	(−) Formation of Union of Writers of the Russian Republic "to assist the Party in reasserting its authority".[20]
	(−) Declarations of loyalty by poetess Aliger and others after launching of first *sputnik*.
	(−) Xruščev's advocacy of contemporaneousness (*sovremennost'*) in literature.
Oct., Nov., 1958	(−) Pasternak Affair: aftermath of Nobel Prize — Pasternak's expulsion from Writers' Union and denial to him of further rights of publication "until his death".[21] — Intent: "to create an atmosphere of fear among the writers".[22]
1958	(+) Tvardovskij's reappointment as editor of *Novyj mir*. (−) V. Kočetov's *The Brothers Eršov*, satirizing liberal tendencies in the arts and parodying *Not by Bread Alone*. (−) First failure to award Lenin Prizes for literature in a given year.
May, 1959	Third Writers' Conference: (+) — Xruščev's defense of Dudincev and plea for literary tolerance; his recognition of younger writers (only three of 497 delegates then under thirty): "'In order to learn to swim you have to jump into the water and try your own strength. ... Let young writers develop their talents in their own way.'"[23] (+) — K. Paustovskij's plea for liberalization and improved quality in literature; his praise of new young writers, including Bondarev, Kazakov, and Tendrjakov.

---

[19]   Gene Sosin, "Talks with Soviet Writers", *Survey*, No. 36 (April-June, 1961), 11.

[20]   Whitney, 10.

[21]   Slonim, *Soviet Russian Literature: Writers and Problems*, 318.

[22]   David Burg, "The Cold War on the Literary Front: III", *Problems of Communism*, XII (January-February, 1963), 49.

[23]   Max Hayward, "Conflict and Change in Literature", *Survey*, No. 46 (January, 1963), 14.

Date	Event

(+) – General confusion and reservations as to *sovremennost'*, assigned themes, *etc.*

(−) – Surkov's condemnation of Pasternak and *Dr. Živago*.

(−) – Reinsertion of words "'historically concrete'" in official definition of socialist realism.[24]

(+) Fedin's replacement of Surkov as First Secretary and Tvardovskij's and Panferov's appointment to board of Writers' Union.

(+) Kočetov's removal as editor of *Literaturnaja gazeta*.

(+) Èrenburg's *Rereading Čexov* (*Novyj mir*) with implicit criticism of *partijnost'* in socialist realism.

1959

(+) Appearance of numerous young writers.

(+) Liberally slanted *Short Literary Encyclopedia*.

(+) V. Nekrasov's critique of film *Poem of the Sea*.

September 19, 1961

(+) E. Evtušenko's "Babi Jar" (*Lit. gazeta*).

October, 1961

Twenty-Second Party Congress:

(+) – Tvardovskij's speech asserting duty of writer to describe reality and not to propagandize.

(−) – Speeches by Šoloxov, Kornejčuk, Tvardovskij, Kočetov, and Il'ičev berating V. Aksenov's *Ticket to the Stars*; V. Rozov's *A, B, C, D, E*; and other works treating young Soviet 'beatnik' generation.

November 22, 1961

(+) Critique of Soviet authoritarian higher education by Aleksandr Aleksandrov, Rector of Leningrad University: "'A student is not a vessel to be filled but a lamp to be lighted.'"[25]

1961

(+) Publication of collected verse by Axmatova and Cvetaeva in editions of 50,000 and 25,000 copies respectively (promised in 1956).

(−) Appointment of Kočetov as editor of *Oktjabr'*, replacing the late Panferov.

(−) B. Polevoj's replacement of V. Kataev as editor of *Junost'*.

(−) Withdrawal of *Pages of Tarusa* from circulation, after publication of 75,000 copy edition.

(−) Kočetov's reactionary *The Provincial Party Secretary*.

March, 1962

(+) A. Lebedev's unfavorable critique of socialist realism's historical antecedents in article "Černiševskij or Antonovič?" (*Novyj mir*).

(+) Ju. Bondarev's *Silence* with first description, in subsequent installment, of house arrest on false denunciation during post-World War II purges. (*Novyj mir*).

April, 1962

(+) Replacement of conservatives by Evtušenko and A. Voznesenskij on board of Moscow branch of Writers' Union.

(+) I. Rodnjanskaja's distinction between propagandistic and esthetic literature in "On Belles Lettres and 'Severe' Art" (*Novyj mir*) — "'The writer's main idea is not a final truth but a question which,

[24] Vickery, 70.

[25] Priscilla Johnson, "New Heretics in Soviet Writing", *Saturday Review*, XLV (May 5, 1962), 8.

Date	Event
	by means of the actualization of the esthetic idea, he attempts to answer' ".[26]
	(−) *Junost'* editor Polevoj's critique, at the Fourteenth Komsomol Congress, of young writers' bourgeois attitude.
August, 1962	(+) L. Anninskij's avowal of "genuine talent as guarantee of artistic truth" in debate intended by editors to expose his point of view in "Essence of the Search — A Dialogue about the Prose of Young Writers" (*Oktjabr'*).[27]
	(−) Special decree of Central Committee against 'free thinking' in art, particularly in film.[28]

Fall, 1962	Sensitivity about world, especially Chinese reaction to Soviet policy during Cuban crisis.

September, 1962	(+) Favorable reaction toward young liberals and praise of *Ticket to the Stars* by board of Moscow branch of Writers' Union in meeting devoted to young writers.
October 21, 1962	(+) Evtušenko's "Stalin's Heirs" (*Pravda*).
November, 1962	(+) A. Solženicyn's *One Day in the Life of Ivan Denisovič* (*Novyj mir*).
November, 16, 1962	(+) G. Šelest's "The Nugget" (*Izvestja*), preceding appearance of *One Day ...* as first account in Soviet fiction of life in concentration camps.
November 23, 1962	(+) Xruščev's announcement before Central Committee of his advance approval for "The Heirs of Stalin" and *One Day ....*
November 30, 1962	(+) Public readings by poets Voznesenskij, Axmadulina, and Sluckij at Lužnikij Stadium before audience of 14,000.
December, 1962	(−) Liberals' loss of control over *Literaturnaja gazeta*.
December 1, 1962	(−) Xruščev's visit to art exhibit of Beljutin circle at Manež and subsequent denunciation of 'formalism': "'Judging by these experiments, I am entitled to think that you are pederasts, and for that you can get ten years. You've gone out of your minds, and now you want to deflect us from the proper course. No, you won't get away with it. ... Gentlemen, we are declaring war on you.' "[29]
December 17, 1962	(−) Speech by L. Il'ičev, head of Ideological Commission of Central Committee, before writers and artists denouncing innovators, labeling U. of Moscow mathematician and poet A. Esenin-Volpin

---

[26] Bode, *Osteuropa*, XII (September, 1963), 633.
[27] *Ibid.*, 632.
[28] Yuri Marin, "The Revival of 'Freethinking' by Young Soviet Writers", *Analysis of Current Developments in the Soviet Union*, No. 247 (November 13, 1962), 6.
[29] Blum, *The New Yorker*, XLI (August 28, 1965), 54.

Date   Event

	as insane (causing latter's subsequent commitment to an institution), and urging audience not to give interviews to Western press.
December 18, 1962	(−) Snubbing by Party officials of premier of Šostakovič's Thirteenth Symphony with text from Evtušenko's "Babi Jar".
December 24, 1962	(−) Evtušenko's revisions of text for Šostakovič's symphony.
December 24,26, 1962	(−) Il'ičev's meetings with deviant writers and artists, attacking Neizvestnij, Nekrasov, Kazakov, and Solženicyn.
December, 1962	(+) Appointment of Evtušenko and Aksenov to editorial board of *Junost'*.
	(+) Xruščev's lifting of ban on suppressed *Pages from Tarusa* during first part of year.
	(+) Recognition of early Russian symbolists and neglect of previously favored socialist realists in *All-world History, IX*, co-edited by L. Anninskij.
January, 1963	(−) Negative press reviews of *One Day...*, Nekrasov's *On Both Sides of the Ocean*, Èrenburg's memoirs, Tvardovskij, and Paustovskij.

Spring, 1963	Chinese rift and ensuing Soviet sensitivity to unorthodox ideological expression.

March 7,8, 1963	(−) Attack upon Èrenburg by Xruščev and Il'ičev before over six hundred intellectuals and Party workers at special meeting in Kremlin for 'silence' during early purges; further attacks upon Evtušenko circle, including Aksenov, Nekrasov, Voznesenskij, and sculptor Neizvestnij, (subsequent assignment of Evtušenko to factory work lists); condemnation of film *The Gates of Il'ič*, which poses conflict between the generations; labeling of so-called 'lunatic' writers.
March, 1963	(+) Cessation of campaign against Èrenburg and continuation of his memoirs in *Novyj mir*.
	(−) Declaration of adherence to Party directives at Fourth Writers' Conference.
March 15, 1963	(−) Neizvestnij's recantation.
March 25, 1963	(−) Display of dossiers to correspondents of foreign communist newspapers condemning liberal artists and writers.
March 28, 1963	(−) Evtušenko's recantation at meeting of Writers' Union for publication of *A Precocious Autobiography* in Paris *L'Express* on 2/21/63: consequent cancellation of public readings and trips abroad by poets, including Evtušenko's pending trip to the USA.
	(−) Voznesenskij's ironical recantation, promising to serve Soviet cause even more faithfully than in the past.

Date	Event
April, 1963	(+) Defense of *One Day...* by editors of *Novyj mir* as criterion for further writing in socialist realist vein: "For Idea Content and Socialist Realism".
April 3, 1963	(−) Aksenov's apology in *Pravda*, upon being accused of "inciting *stiljažestvo*",[30] for granting interview to Polish *Polityka* and berating older generation.
May, 1963	(−) 'Exile' of Voznesenskij to factory in Vladimir and Aksenov to construction project in Siberia to be closer to real life. (+) Removal of Frol Kozlov, opponent of liberals, from Presidium due to heart attack.
May, 7, 1963	Trial and sentencing of Wynne and Penkovskij, provoking tightened controls.
May, 7-10, 1963	(−) Restriction of discussion and policy making at Fourth All-Union Conference of Young Writers.
May, June, 1963	(+) Articles by B. Sučkov titled "Contemporaneousness and Realism" (*Znamja*) acquainting Soviet readers with hitherto unfamiliar Western writers and philosophers, including Mauriac, Böll, Proust, Joyce, Kafka, Faulkner, Huxley, Elliot, Sartre, Camus, Bergson, Jaspers, Heiddeger, Whitehead, and W. James.
June 18, 1963	(−) Il'ičev's proposal for a single Artists' Union at plenum of Central Committee, intended "to reimpose the ideological straitjacket of the Stalin era".[31]
August, 1963	Signing of the Atomic Test Ban Treaty.
August, 1963	(+) Tvardovskij's reading of satirical anti-Stalinist poem "Terkin in the Other World" at Xruščev's villa and its subsequent publication in both *Izvestija* (8/18/66) and *Novyj mir*.
August, 5-8, 1963	(+) Meeting of European Association of Writers in Leningrad: Èrenburg's speech defending 'modernism' and pleading for Soviet recognition of Joyce, Proust, and Kafka, apparently with Xruščev's approval and with favorable treatment in *Izvestija*.
December, 1963	(+) Discussion of Gor'kij's correspondence, recently printed in volume 70 of *Literaturnoe nasledstvo*, by Ju. Jusovskij in "Gor'kij and His Conversants" (*Novyj mir*), viewing Gor'kij as defender of and sympathizer with liberal writers and with references to his disparagement of *Mother* to Gladkov, Babel''s framing and persecution, Fedin's confession to Gor'kij of discontent with prevailing conditions, *etc*.

[30] Whitney, 41.
[31] Karavaev, *Bulletin, Institute for the Study of the USSR*, 29.

Date	Event
1963	(+) *Izvestija*'s defense of liberals under editorship of Xruščev's son-in-law, Adžubej. (+) Replacement of conservative *Literatura i žizn'* by *Literaturnaja Rossija* in early 1963. (+) Xruščev's cordial reception of Èrenburg in summer. (+) Reprinting of suppressed nineteenth-century writers — Baratynskij, Slučevskij, Tjutčev, and A. K. Tolstoj. (−) A. Čaxovskij's replacement of liberal Kosolapov as editor-in-chief of *Literaturnaja gazeta*.
January, 1964	(+) Publication of first work by Kafka to appear in Soviet Union, "In the Penal Colony", in *Inostrannaja literatura*.
March 13, 1964	(−) Exile of poet Iosip Brodskij to five years' forced labor at Archangelsk.
February 21, 1965	(+) Appeal of *Pravda's* new editor, S. Rumjancev, to intellectuals in editorial "The Party and the Intelligentsia" with references to liberal policy on literature during NÈP.
March 24, 1965	(+) Replacement of Il'ičev by moderate, P. Demičev, as Secretary of Central Committee and head of Ideological Commission.
September, 1965	(−) Arrest of 'underground' writers A. Sinjavskij and Ju. Danièl' followed by house search and confiscation of manuscripts by Solženicyn.
1965	(+) Continued agitation by Evtušenko for more artistic freedom for youth: reading of unauthorized poem on television, *etc.*
February 10, 1966	(−) Beginning of Sinjavskij-Danièl' trial, ending in severe sentences.
March, 1966	(−) Brežnev's indictment of underground writers and Šoloxov's defamation of Sinjavskij and Danièl' at Twenty-third Party Congress.
September, 1967	(−) Accusation by Solženicyn before Writers' Union of KGB's stealing his manuscripts and implicating him in smuggling his work to the West.
January, 1968	(−) Sentencing of poet Aleksandr Ginzburg and other intellectuals for underground literary activity. (+) Public protest of Ginzburg trial by wife of Julij Danièl', Larisa, and former Foreign Minister's grandson, Pavel Litvinov.
March, 1968	(−) Convictions of various intellectuals and expulsions from Writers' Union on charges of conspiracy.
April, 1968	(−) Mass arrests of those protesting previous sentences. (−) Solženicyn's letter to *Literaturnaja gazeta* denying he authorized foreign publication of *Cancer Ward*.
August, 1968	(−) Arrest of Pavel Litvinov, Larisa Danièl', and others protesting invasion of Czechoslovakia.

Date	Event
March, 1969	(+) Unexpected serialization in *Pravda* of Šoloxov's novel, *They Fought for Their Country*, with mild anti-Stalinist overtones.
Summer, 1969	(−) Renewed campaign attacking A. Tvardovskij for promoting cosmopolitan writers and publishing anti-Soviet material. Rumors of his forthcoming expulsion as Editor of *Novyj mir*.
July, 1969	(−) Expulsion of Evtušenko, Aksenov, and Rozov from editorial board of *Junost'*.
	(−) Defection of Anatolij Kuznecov in London.
August, 1969	(+) Unexpected publication in conservative *Oktjabr'* of Jurij Bondarev's anti-Stalinist novelette, *The Relatives*.
	(−) Re-sentencing of author Anatolij Marčenko soon after appearance in the West of his autobiographical memoirs as a political prisoner, "I Witness", ostensibly for slanderous remarks.
	(−) Kuznecov's expose in London *Sunday Telegraph* and on Western television of Soviet regime's continuing manipulation of writers. His renunciation of membership in the Writers' Union and the Communist Party and rejection of all his previously published works.
November, 1969	(−) Solženicyn's expulsion from Writers' Union.
	(+) Solženicyn's letter of rebuttal to Writers' Union: "Wipe the dust off your watches. They are running centuries behind the times."
	(−) Šoloxov's villification of Solženicyn — a "Colorado beetle" — at congress of collective farmers in Moscow.
	(−) Report by Writers' Union further villifying Solženicyn as "a weapon in the hands of our class enemies" and recommending his emigration.
	(+) Protest against Solženicyn's expulsion by Evtušenko, Okudžava, and other liberal writers.
December, 1969	(−) Removal of Jurij Rybakov as editor of journal *Teatr*.

ANALYSIS

The trend of literary events in the Soviet period is, as the foregoing evidences, strikingly erratic and unpredictable. Their pattern becomes more meaningful, however, when related to accompanying political phenomena. Thus, with the ascendancy of Stalin and the advent of collectivization and Five-Year Plans in the thirties, artistic freedom undergoes a noticeable decline. Maurice Friedberg does observe, however, that,

artistically, the late 1930's were a marked improvement over the preceding period of RAPP, but markedly inferior to the 1920's. Nevertheless, some significant works did appear in the late 1930's. Thus, these years marked the completion of Sholokhov's *The Silent Don*, perhaps the finest Soviet novel.

In Soviet literature, the late 1930's were marked by the reappearance of the historical novel, lyric poetry, and a great revival of the classics of Russian literature of the nineteenth century. The latter was particularly noticeable in connection with the observances of the centennial of Pushkin's death in 1937, when the poet's works were reprinted in tens of millions of copies.

The liberalization of the state's literary policy was carried further during World War II.[32]

All critics tend to agree, however, that "at no time has the quality of Soviet writing been as low as in the years 1947 to 1953".[33] Max Hayward calls them "years of utter sterility",[34] while Gleb Struve asserts that these "seven years before the death of Stalin had been the most barren period in the history of Soviet literature".[35]

The radical change of climate which follows the death of Stalin is itself marked by "sharp shifts in policy" which, as the preceding table indicates, ensue, at least during the 1953-1963 decade, with an almost 'cyclical regularity'.[36] Close scrutiny reveals that the 'thaws' which alternately occur between such shifts tend to last for periods of roughly three years. The spring of 1953 (Stalin's death) initiates a period of cautious hope and relative relaxation which continues through the spring of 1956 (Twentieth Party Congress), when it receives an almost official sanction. "Since the twenties", says Brown, "Soviet writers had never been as free of official directions as they were during that year."[37] Friedberg observes that at this time especially writers endeavored "to create for their readers according to the dictates of their conscience",[38] while H. T. Willets, writing in 1963, adds that "there is nothing in recently published Soviet literature resembling 'the demagogic outbursts' after the 20th congress. No Soviet writer is as boldly outspoken as were some of the contributors to the second *Literaturnaya Moskva* (1956)".[39] Other manifestations

---

[32] Friedberg, *Bulletin of the Institute for the Study of the USSR*, 34.

[33] *Ibid.*, 35.

[34] Hayward, *Dissonant Voices in Soviet Literature*, viii.

[35] Struve, *The New Leader*, 16. Walter Vickery suggests the following works, however, which — unlike S. Babaevskij's *Cavalier of the Golden Star* (1947-1948), B. Polevoj's *The Story of a Real Man* (1947), or P. Pavlenko's *Happiness* (1947) — afford perhaps a modicum of literary merit: I. Èrenburg's *The Storm* (1948); K. Fedin's *Unusual Summer* (1948); V. Kataev's *For the Power of the Soviets* (1949); E. Kazakevič's *Star* (1947); A. Koptjaeva's *Ivan Ivanovič* (1949); V. Panova's *Kružilixa* (1948); V. Panova's *Sputniks* (1947) (Vickery, 10).

[36] Blum, *The New Yorker*, XLI (August 28, 1965), 54.

[37] Brown, 259.

[38] Friedberg, *Bulletin of the Institute for the Study of the USSR*, 40.

[39] H. T. Willets, "New Directions?" *Survey*, No. 46 (January, 1963), 7.

include the appearance of *Not by Bread Alone* and the fact that Pasternak should have chosen the year 1956 in which to submit his *Doctor Živago* for editorial consideration. Criticism of both novels in the same year, however, rejection of the one, and a subsequent attack upon *Literaturnaja Moskva, II* betoken a decided reversal in the formerly permissive atmosphere.

All of these events are to a great extent politically explainable: as is generally recognized, the Twentieth Party Congress was intended to divert any responsibility for the regime's past transgressions from the shoulders of the living to those of its most suitable scapegoat — the deceased Stalin. Hence, the existence of an oppressive bureaucracy (as in *Not by Bread Alone*) could be openly admitted yet directly attributed to Stalin's still extant legacy. Some suggest in fact that on this and subsequent occasions Xruščev "thought he might galvanize his sluggish bureaucracy by identifying inefficiency with 'Stalinism'".[40] Though writers may have intended the present, they generously subscribed to the officially endorsed anti-Stalin myth in venting social criticism.

The ensuing reaction was doubtless in order that the myth should not backfire or get out of hand. The universal implications in Pasternak's manuscript as well as the bold critical impact of *Literaturnaja Moskva, II* probably helped provoke this reaction, while less literary phenomena, like the Hungarian revolt, made the leadership especially uneasy about further protest, in whatever form. The glory of Sputnik in turn commanded increased devotion and sacrifice from the Russian nation, while it "seemed to weaken the case of those writers who had attacked the bureaucracy as hostile to new ideas and an impediment to progress".[41] Struve therefore concludes that the 'thaw' — or, as herein defined, the first 'thaw' — had indeed ended by 1957, but with several ostensibly permanent gains: in its "break with the Zhdanov era", it had rather conclusively rejected "the absurd, wholesale vilification of everything Western, and the withdrawal from ... complacent cultural self-isolation" as well as "the open and shameless falsification of history, including literary history".[42]

Again, with the Third Congress of the Union of Soviet Writers in May, 1959, after a two- to three-year period of reaction which made the name Pasternak a national byword, a new era of quite opposite temperament and of equal length ensued. Blum calls this second major 'thaw' "the

[40]   Hayward, *Slavic Review*, 434.
[41]   Brown, 267.
[42]   Struve, *The New Leader*, 20.

most relaxed and optimistic period in Soviet cultural life since the nine-teen-twenties".[43] Characteristic are the period's bold liberal criticism, the general defiance of its numerous young writers, the appointment of at least a token number of prominent liberals to various boards of the Union of Soviet Writers, and the appearance of the artistically successful film, *Ballad of a Soldier*, in 1959, described by Klaus Mehnert as a "conquest of the past... . Indicative of the Russians' irrepressible hunger for truth is the fact that, up and down the land, hundreds of thousands, even millions stand in line in order for a few hours to witness Soviet defeats and difficulties."[44]

No critical political developments attend this period, but one does conclude it: the Cuban crisis and the Soviet leadership's concern about its consequent world image, particularly in the eyes of the Chinese and other communist peoples. This development in the fall of 1962 comes just before Xruščev's obviously staged indictment of abstract and formal-ist art in conjunction with his much publicized visit to the Manež art exhibit on December 1. The aftermath — a solid half year or more of further official reaction — is in turn lessened by the regime's gradual recognition of its failure either to placate Peking or to subdue the liberals, as well as by its apparent desire once more to woo Western confidence during the August, 1963, Test Ban Treaty negotiations and the accom-panying conference of the European Association of Writers in Leningrad. Anticipating some such outcome, the variously oriented literary groups align themselves and wage fierce war during the same year — "the die-hards, led by Kochetov, barricaded themselves in the literary journal *Oktjabr'* .... The liberals found their chief outlet in *Novyj mir*".[45] Burg observes that "during the spring and summer of 1962, the articles and literary works in *Novy mir* became more and more daring. The magazine *Znamya* shifted considerably to the 'left'. The 'cold war' was now conducted in the pages of *Novy mir, Literaturnaya gazeta*, and *Literatura i zhizn*."[46] *Izvestija* also returns, later the same year, to the defense of the liberals.

There follows a third two-and-one-half to three-year period of relative relaxation of controls, which is interrupted if not altogether terminated by the sensational trial and sentencing of the 'underground' writers, A. Sinjavskij (A. Terc) and Ju. Danièl' (N. Aržak) in February, 1966.

[43] Blum, *The New Yorker*, XLI (August 28, 1965), 59.
[44] Mehnert, *Osteuropa*, 436.
[45] Erlich, *Slavic Review*, 409.
[46] Burg, *Problems of Communism*, XII (January-February, 1963), 56.

This third period — which begins approximately where the present investigation leaves off (in late 1963) — is more of a quasi-'thaw', however. The true extent of its freedom is often uncertain and difficult to assess. Discussing trends in 1963, Gaev indicates that "quite unexpectedly a considerate attitude was adopted toward the exponents of freedom. Works by Yevtushenko, Voznesensky, Rozhdestvensky, Slutsky, and other intellectual leaders of progressive youth began to be printed in the central Party organ .... The object of this 'carrot' policy was clear. It was hoped ... that the condescension of the Party leaders would transform them into active defenders of the regime."[47] Gaev calls this appeal to the liberals "a judas' kiss" intended to serve the "mass Party against free thinking".[48] Bode nonetheless points to the conscious failure of most of the Soviet press in this period to discuss A. Solženicyn's *One Day in the Life of Ivan Denisovič* until as late as November, 1965.[49] One who does so — V. Lakšin (*Novyj mir*, January, 1964) — himself alludes to the period's prevailing ambiguity and tenuous atmosphere when he proposes that the Soviet reader's ultimate loyalty can be ascertained by the view he takes toward Solženicyn's prisoner-hero.[50]

The interpretation of this period is not without its optimism, however. In his review of the 1964 film, *The Living and the Dead* (based on the novel by K. Simonov), Mehnert contends that

in it [this film] the war — by contrast with earlier films, particularly those about the Stalin period — is depicted not as a triumph of glorious heroism and victories but, at least in its initial phase, as a horrible national and personal catastrophe. It is just eight years since a young Soviet author (Dudintsev) was bitterly attacked in the Party press because he had maintained that in the first months of the war the Soviet air force's deficiencies had shattered his faith in the superiority of the Soviet system .... Because the attack against Stalin is underplayed, the film is in effect an attack against the whole system under which the Soviet Union waged war in 1941.[51]

In his discussion of the year 1965 and in an even more optimistic vein, Victor Frank remarks that "perhaps the most spectacular thing about the post-Khrushchevian skyscrape in Russia is the fact that it contains so few spectacular features, that politics have come to matter so much less, that so very few people now care to pay attention to speeches at

---

[47] Gaev, *Soviet Literature in the Sixties*, 47.
[48] *Ibid.*, 47.
[49] Barbara Bode, "Die Diskussion um Solshenizyn (II)", *Osteuropa*, XV (November-December, 1965), 796.
[50] Lakshin, *Novyj mir*, 223-245.
[51] Mehnert, *Osteuropa*, 423.

writers' congresses and to articles in party journals. It is a healthy sign."[52]

Still others warn that, "unfortunately, so long as the Soviet regime remains what it is — a one-party totalitarian tyranny — this kind of spring, with alternating spells of *ottepel'* (thaw) and *zamoroski* (freeze-up), is the most one can expect; it will remain a sort of permanent climatic feature, the thaw spells being determined, as a rule, by policy considerations which have nothing to do with the arts".[53] The view of an anonymous ambassador is even less encouraging: "'The victories won by the intellectual left are not too reliable an indication of how dead Stalin really is. As long as "civic obedience" and submission to Party controls are required of the artist, the punishments administered in times of reaction will be the truest indication. By all means, watch the prize lists. But watch the pillories, too.'"[54]

CRITICAL ASSESSMENT OF HISTORICAL TRENDS

In its assessment of Soviet literature in still other respects, critical opinion is often divided. A number of reviewers, for instance, equate Soviet literature with the nineteenth-century classical tradition:

The tradition of literature as social commentary continues in Russia.[55]

Great moral zeal is a trait shared by all the Soviet writers. Their books aim at a moral revolution in their readers. ... This rather old-fashioned, eager, touchingly uncynical, unskeptical nineteenth-century idealism of the Soviet authors is one of their most surprising characteristics.[56]

Russia is now as earlier true to its nineteenth-century tradition: The writer must simultaneously be a philosopher, prophet, and a teacher of life — in short: he must be the spiritual and moral authority of the land.[57]

The main contribution which the intellectuals of today, like their predecessors, make to the establishment of freedom in Russia is to uphold and spread liberty as an ideal.[58]

Bode alludes to the obligation of writers both then and now to express their views on society and the state by means of indirection,[59] and

---

[52] Victor S. Frank, "The Literary Climate", *Survey*, No. 56 (July, 1965), 53.

[53] Gleb Struve, "Soviet Literature in Perspective: Some Unorthodox Reflections", *Soviet Literature in the Sixties*, (ed.) Max Hayward and Edward Crowley (New York, Frederick A. Praeger, 1964), p. 141.

[54] Cited by Blum, *The New Yorker*, XLI (September 11, 1965), 172.

[55] Brown, 294-195.

[56] Gibian, *Interval of Freedom*, 164.

[57] Barbara Bode, "Die Diskussion um Solzhenizyn als Zentrum der Auseinandersetzungen in der Sowjetliteratur", *Osteuropa*, XV (October, 1965), 679.

[58] Pipes, *Encounter*, 84.

[59] Bode, *Osteuropa*, XV (January-February, 1965), 55.

Whitney poses a rhetorical question which also recalls the former role of literature as a kind of social forum:

Where else in the world would 25,000 people or so turn out for an outdoor poetry recitation — as eagerly seeking admittance as if it were the decisive football game for the championship? Where else could a set of literary memoirs cause tremors in a government or a poem fan the flames of national emotion? Where else, indeed, is literature and art a matter of national policy and national concern quite on a par with foreign policy or national economic development?[60]

Yet others stress significant differences. Mathewson describes the Soviet resemblance to nineteenth-century classicism as "more imitation than creative repossession",[61] while Struve contends that the "dual tendency to assert the essential novelty and originality of Soviet literature and yet to assimilate the best of the Russian nineteenth-century to Soviet culture results ... in inevitable distortions which ... are the blight of Soviet literary scholarship. ... There is no need ... to accept the view of the continuity of cultural and literary tradition ...".[62] A frequent argument is that, unlike the mainstream of Soviet writing, Russian classical literature was essentially non-political, *i.e.* non-doctrinal. Even Whitney concedes this distinction: "In general, Russian classical writing did not have a political or ideological platform as mainspring of its being. ... Russian classical literature is outstanding for its deep insights, through art, into human beings and history."[63] Mathewson adds that

on the whole the Soviet outsider is not asked to carry the burden of protest of his famous predecessors, the scoundrels, criminals, and rebels against the order of the universe. There is no Chichikov wriggling out of the law, forever beyond redemption, no Huck Finn, heading for the frontier, leaving behind a civilization he has learned to despise, no Julien Sorel going to his death in calm defiance of the contemptible society he has invaded and conquered. The Soviet outsider is not an instrument of radical inquiry or protest.[64]

Hence, according to still others:

unlike in the Nineteenth Century, Neo-slavophiles and Neo-westernizers no longer oppose each other but complement and intermingle with each other.[65] Despite the wide preoccupation with the theme of youth in the fiction and drama of recent years, no writer has succeeded in creating a typical image of the young contemporary with even a remote degree of the artistic vitality

---

[60]   Whitney, 57.
[61]   Mathewson, *Soviet Literature in the Sixties*, 15.
[62]   Struve, *Soviet Literature in the Sixties*, 132.
[63]   Whitney, 4.
[64]   Mathewson, *Soviet Literature in the Sixties*, 13-14.
[65]   Bode, *Osteuropa*, XII (September, 1963), 641.

inherent in Griboyedov's Chatsky, Pushkin's Yevgeny Onegin, or Lermontov's Pechorin. But though it lacks literary stature, the portrait is revealing.[66]

'In socialist-realist art the purpose is crucial and the positive hero stands at the center of the stage, but in the 19th century it was the negative hero who predominated.'[67]

Muchnic in turn suggests why even the occasional work of protest, like those of the NÈP period, is, as literature, in some respects still deficient: "The spirit of the age itself — its apparent freedom notwithstanding — was a stifling one. ... It was an age of fighters. And the fighter is not free, his hand is forced by the enemy. It is a rare individual, maybe only a genius, who driven into and fixed in the posture of defense, can still maintain the freedom of his mind and heart."[68] Her reservation is reminiscent of Paustovskij's remark just prior to the 1959 Third Writers' Conference: "'Perhaps we shout so much about truth in literature just because we lack it.'"[69]

Others contrast the nineteenth century with the Soviet period in terms of the relatively greater "freedom of choice in artistic expression"[70] during the former. "Under Tsarism writers ... did not have to adhere to a particular style or literary doctrine, nor did they have to compose tributes to the Tsar."[71] Gibian, who elsewhere recognizes lines of continuity between traditions, also makes this qualification:

Negatively, under the tenets of socialist realism, Soviet authors are enjoined to avoid a number of practices: subjectivism, delving into individual psychology and dissecting motives, which constituted one of the glories of nineteenth-century Russian literature; experimentation with literary forms — any kind of innovation or avant-gardism; dwelling on the role of the individual instead of the group, the social class; departures from realism by the use of symbolism or any other technique suggestive of the modern and radical. ... They are to remember that the trend of Soviet development is upward; therefore, it is more realistic to stress the positive elements in the present situation because they are going to be the dominant forces in the future and hence are more 'typical' even today, whereas the negative elements should be played down because they belong to the past and are doomed to extinction. ...[72]

[66] Alexandrova, A History of Soviet Literature, 258.
[67] A. Sinjavskij, The New York Times Magazine, 120.
[68] Helen Muchnic, "Literature in the NÈP Period", Literature and Revolution in Soviet Russia 1917-1962 (ed.) Max Hayward and Leopold Labedz (London, Oxford University Press, 1963), 42.
[69] Quoted in Ernest J. Simmons, "Recent Trends in Soviet Literature", Modern Age, VII (Fall, 1963), 397.
[70] Ibid., 393.
[71] Howe, The New Republic, 19.
[72] Gibian, Interval of Freedom, 4.

Rubin makes the same distinction with his most devastating assessment of Soviet literary theory: "Viewed philosophically, the concept of history that lies at the center of Socialist Realism is a particularly pernicious example of the 'tyranny of abstractions'. Viewed politically, it represents a maneuver by an arbitrary political power to defend its authority from the challenge of the critical artistic imagination."[73]

Within the Soviet period itself, however, literature under Stalin is often differentiated from that which comes before and after. Both Kobetz[74] and Hayward[75] allude to Stalin's singular and almost total suppression of free thought and creative expression, which, says Hayward, became even more intensified and restrictive after 1946. Brown in turn attributes to literature of all but the Stalinist period as a "major theme ... the fate of the individual human being in a mass state".[76] Vickery also distinguishes the distortion of facts, the idealization of Stalin, the unwarranted optimism, and the depersonalization of characters so typical of and peculiar in degree to the same period.[77] Such writing is elsewhere contrasted to the post-Stalin trend of "'accusatory' (oblichitelnaya) literature, whose primary aim is to expose various social shortcomings"[78]: "After the death of Stalin, one of the main ways in which Soviet writers reacted to their expanded freedom was by creating a series of 'villains' or 'negative characters' such as they would not have dared to include in a work intended for publication in Stalinist Russia."[79]

Further distinctions are also made, however, between the earliest Soviet works and those which followed the death of Stalin:

What were the principal factors which determined literary developments in the earliest period in Soviet literature? The most important of them, the crucial one, was the almost overwhelmingly hostile attitude of the Russian intelligentsia, including the writers, to the new regime.[80]

The earlier debate had arisen on the subsoil of lively controversy over the relationship between art and philosophy. The philosophical grounding of art was not in 1956 a subject of dispute. ... Secondly, the significance of the two debates in terms of literary politics was altogether different. The first debate took place before the theoretical issue had been authoritatively 'settled', while

---

[73] Rubin, *Soviet Literature in the Sixties*, 96.
[74] Kobetz, *Sowjet-Studien*, 47.
[75] Hayward, *Dissonant Voices in Soviet Literature*, xix.
[76] Brown, 239.
[77] Vickery, 163-164.
[78] Struve, *The New Leader*, 18.
[79] Gibian, *Interval of Freedom*, 109.
[80] Gleb Struve, "The Transition from Russian to Soviet Literature", *Literature and Revolution in Soviet Russia 1917-1962* (ed.) Max Hayward and Leopold Labedz (London, Oxford University Press, 1963), 10.

rival factions were still jockeying for position; whereas the second 'debate' ... took place twenty years later. ... In the earlier debate we see lawyers pleading a cause, whereas in the later debate we see them appealing the judge's ruling. ... What took place in 1956 was not, strictly speaking, a debate. ... It consisted rather of a number of liberally oriented articles which reached, if not a climax, at least a crescendo of outspokenness toward the end of the year. Before the Hungarian and Polish events these articles did not encounter really threatening opposition.[81]

The foregoing distinctions between the literature after 1953 and that which precedes it (both Soviet and pre-Soviet) should correlate, where valid, with the comparison of 'Thaw' heroes and their predecessors in Chapter VII. Whatever its conclusions, however, the latter should provide a more sure basis of judgment, relying as it does on internal literary evidence, *per se.*

Other distinctive aspects of the post-Stalin 'Thaw' include, according to the critics:

(1) "Tolerance of disagreement and debate"[82]: Brown suggests that the Twentieth Party Congress (1956) was the first occasion since 1930 "that two opposing viewpoints in literature had been represented at a Party Congress".[83] Bode maintains that the basic opposition between the Tvardovskij and Kočetov circles in fact reflects a similar conflict within the Party's Central Committee,[84] while, according to Ronald Hingley, writing in 1962, a careful balance is maintained between the two factions, as evidenced by the presence on the Committee of the 'hard' line Gribačov, the 'soft' line Tvardovskij, and the moderate Šoloxov.[85] The following — Bode,[86] Burg,[87] and Johnson[88] — each affirm the aggressive, often daring character of Tvardovskij's defense of liberal writers. Though he confesses when compelled to, he immediately resumes his line, which he wages even more offensively than do Kočetov and others of the opposition: "Tvardovskij's camp fights offensively, though in a relatively more pacifist and reticent manner, while the Kochetov group, despite its outwardly bold aggressiveness, remains on the defensive."[89] As of 1962, Johnson posits the following typical alignment —

[81] Vickery, 100.
[82] Brown, 277.
[83] *Ibid.*
[84] Bode, *Osteuropa*, XV (January-February, 1965), 57.
[85] Ronald Hingley, "Soviet Literary Attitudes", *Survey*, No. 40 (January, 1962), 48.
[86] Bode, *Osteuropa*, XV (January-February, 1965), 57.
[87] Burg, *Problems of Communism*, XI (September-October, 1962), 35.
[88] Johnson, *Saturday Review*, 10.
[89] Bode, *Osteuropa*, XV (January-February, 1965), 57.

liberal organs *Novyj mir, Junost', Znamja,* and *Literaturnaja gazeta* opposed to the conservative *Neva, Oktjabr',* and *Literatura i žizn'*; liberals dominating the USSR Union of Soviet Writers, with conservatives controlling that of the Russian Republic; *etc.*[90] Evtušenko presents a slightly different phenomenon. He has, according to his autobiography, "taken on the burden of compromise for his entire generation. Partly by virtue of his compromises, of the split between poet and politician in his personality, the party had been able to keep the entire youth movement under control."[91]

(2) The following restrictions:

Although the boundaries are more fluid than they used to be, and the hierarchy more vulnerable to societal pressures than it was under Stalin, the regime seems determined to block (a) explicit criticism of the bureaucratic Establishment, (b) a search for new, nonrealistic modes of expression, and (c) any literary movement or ferment which is likely to develop into an autonomous source of moral authority.[92]

(3) The appearance, nonetheless, of numerous Soviet villains, the implication of which is suggested by the following statements:

Clearly the Marxist view of human nature imposes on the writer very definite restrictions. He is expected to castigate the old and affirm the new. And this he fails in some measure to do if he represents a negative character as being in any degree typical of Soviet man or as a product of Soviet society.[93]

. . . .

Insincerity usually expresses itself in the cynical manipulation of Party ideology for selfish ends. And this manipulation, in recent commentaries, is almost invariably the work of a member of the privileged class, so that the attack on moral evil becomes at the same time an attack on a specific class — or caste.[94]

. . . .

Behind the criticism of 'bad' Party workers and dead-letter Party activity may well lurk a more fundamental opposition to the Party, a rejection of Party values and of the Party's guiding role in Soviet life.[95]

. . . .

The worst among the negative characters are those who are prominent and admirable by the criteria of Soviet life. The fact that people like them are villains puts into doubt the whole structure of outward appearances by which the Russian people have been encouraged to judge a man's success or failure.[96]

[90]   Johnson, *Saturday Review*, 10-11.
[91]   Priscilla Johnson, "The Regime and the Intellectuals: A Window on Party Politics (Winter 1962-Summer 1963)", *Problems of Communism*, XII (July-August, 1963), xviii.
[92]   Erlich, *Slavic Review*, 414.
[93]   Vickery, 119.
[94]   *Ibid.*, p. 142.
[95]   *Ibid.*, p. 141.
[96]   Gibian, *Interval of Freedom*, 142.

Especially for the pleiad of young writers and young poets, the investigation by the Party of the crimes committed under Stalin has served as the point of departure for an ulterior offensive.[97]

(4) A frequent variety and originality which disappeared after the early thirties and which as such intrinsically register a kind of non-conformist protest — as suggested by Hayward's introduction to the anthology, *Dissonant Voices in Soviet Literature*:

Most of the voices represented here are dissonant, not in any political sense, but in that they do not speak in that trite and monotonous accent which, owing to the long and bitter years of Stalin's dictatorship, is still regarded by many people in the West as the sole voice of Soviet literature.[98]

(5) A general reforming intent in the liberal esthetic reaction toward the regime (rather than any urge to undermine or even reconstruct) — as eloquently expressed by Victor Erlich:

It may be argued that literary nonconformism of the first post-Stalin decade is both more and less than a consistent opposition to the regime. More, since at its deeper levels it seems to represent a moral uneasiness, a spiritual ferment which some day may call into question the entire Soviet world-view. Less, since for obvious reasons, the 'thaw' writers are not capable of effective political action. ... Their ostensible objective is not to change it (the system) but, if possible, to humanize it — to make it less monolithic and bureaucratic, more egalitarian and more responsive to individual needs. ... With the partial exception of the best of Solzhenitsyn, Kazakov and Voznesensky, the major literary products of the 'thaw' have been heartening moral symptoms rather than significant literary achievements.[99]

(6) The substantial body of 'underground' literature which is either circulated in unpublished form or clandestinely exported. "The most important developments in the spiritual life of Russia are being suppressed or ignored", according to Mihajlov.[100] "I happen to know of several important unpublished (and in some cases at present still unpublishable) works by well-known Soviet writers, both living and dead. There are probably many more in existence", writes Struve in 1964.[101] Bode, writing in early 1965, lists V. Tarsis, A. Esenin-Volpin, M. Narica, and the poet contributors to the underground journal *Phoenix* among the known 'underground' Soviet writers. "Their works enable us to

[97]   M. Slavinsky, "Le rôle de la literature en URSS dans la 'de-stalinisation'", *Est et Ouest*, XVII (November 1-15, 1965), 14.
[98]   Hayward, *Dissonant Voices in Soviet Literature*, vii.
[99]   Erlich, *Slavic Review*, 417.
[100]   Mihajlo Mihajlov, *The New Leader*, XLVIII (March 29, 1965), 34.
[101]   Struve, *Soviet Literature in the Sixties*, 135.

recognize the true state of affairs and the nation's mood", she argues.[102]

(7) Regarding genre, a "decline of the novel" and a preference for shorter forms — novelettes, short stories, poetry — for the following suggested reasons:

A large work of fiction was more open to criticism because it was expected to present all sorts of things according to official requirements — an epic panorama of social life, positive heroes, a happy ending, and other cliches of socialist realism. The shorter literary form was naturally more limited in scope, and therefore presented a reduced surface for criticism.[103]

[102] Bode, *Osteuropa*, XV (January-February, 1965), 56.
[103] Slonim, *Soviet Russian Literature: Writers and Problems*, 321.

VII

CONCLUDING ANALYSIS

THE HERO COMPARED WITH SIMILAR FIGURES IN THE PRIOR RUSSIAN LITERARY TRADITION

HEROES. — Based on the analyses in Chapter V, the following table classifies the hero of each of the fifty discussed plot situations according to the ten pairs of opposite characteristics which earlier served as criteria for the comparison of nineteenth-century heroes (Table 1, page 53). These characteristics are correspondingly numbered and represent, again, the following contrasts:

(1) opposition to *vs.* support of status quo;

(2) laudability *vs.* unjustifiability of hero's protest (whether or not his protest represents a realistic criticism of an either deceptive or deluded society and/or universe);

(3) self-understanding *vs.* self-delusion;

(4) resignation *vs.* engagement (a silent sufferer or unwitting victim *vs.* a hero whose action itself elicits or aggravates his alienation);

(5) rejection by the woman *vs.* the hero's own fickle behavior in a love situation;

(6) consistent resistance to the source of alienation *vs.* ultimate escapism;

(7) defense of others *vs.* exploitation of others as a means of retaliation;

(8) moral superiority *vs.* moral inferiority to foil (foils);

(9) minority protest *vs.* socially conditioned majority behavior or viewpoint;

(10) ultimate defeat *vs.* ultimate victory.

Plus and minus symbols are as previously used under the heading "Criteria" in Table 13, p. 236. Barred lines indicate the alternation of political 'freeze-thaw' intervals as previously discussed in Chapter VI (pages 256-261):

TABLE 16

Comparison of 'Thaw' Heroes According to Criteria Previously Used in Comparison of Nineteenth-Century Heroes

Plot #	1 +	1 −	2 +	2 −	3 +	3 −	4 +	4 −	5 +	5 −	6 +	6 −	7 +	7 −	8 +	8 −	9 +	9 −	10 +	10 −
1	+			−		−		−		−		−		−		−	+			−
2		−		−		−		−	±			−		−	+		+		+	
3	+		+		+		+				+				+			−		−
4	+		+			−	+			−		−			+			−		−
5	+		+			−		−				−		−		−		−		−
6	+		+		+		+		±		+				+		+			−
7	+		+		+			−			+		+		+			−		−
8	+			−		−	+					−			+			−		−
9	+		+		+		+		+								+			−
10		−		−		−		−	=			−		−		−		−	+	
11	+		+		+		+		± =		+				+		+		+	
12	+		+		+		+		±		+		+		+		+		+	
13		−		−		−	+					−		−	+			−	+	
14	+		+		+		+				+				+		+			−
15	+		+		+		+		+			−								−
16		−		−	+			−	±			−		−	+		+		+	
17	+		+		+			−	±		+				+		+			−
18		−		−		−		−				−		−			+			−
19	+		+		+		+		=			−			+		+			
20		−		−		−		−				−		−		−		−	+	
21	+			−		−		−				−			+		+			−
22	+				+			−				−					+			−
23	+				+			−				−					+			−
24	+		+		+		+		=			−			+		+		+	
25		−		−		−		−	±			−		−		−		−		−
26	+		+		+		+		±				+		+		+		+	
27		−		−		−		−	=			−				−		−	+	
28	+			−		−		−				−					+			−
29		−	+		+			−			+		+		+			−		−
30		−	+			−		−	=			−				−	+		+	
31	+		+		+		+						+		+		+		+	
32	+			−		−		−	±			−				−		−		−
33	+		+		+		+				+				+		+			−
34		−		−		−		−	± =			−				−		−		−
35	+		+	−		−		−	=			−				−	+			−
36	+		+		+			−			+				+		+		+	
37	+		+		+		+		±											−
38	+		+		+		+										+		+	
39	+		+		+		+		±									−		−
40		−		−		−		−	=			−		−						−
41	+		+		+		+		±		+				+					−
42	+				+			−				−			+		+			−
43	+		+		+		+										+		+	
44	+		+		+													−	+	

Plot #	1 +	1 −	2 +	2 −	3 +	3 −	4 +	4 −	5 +	5 −	6 +	6 −	7 +	7 −	8 +	8 −	9 +	9 −	10 +	10 −
45	+		+		+			−	±		+				+					−
46		−		−		−		−	=			−				−			+	
47	+		+		+		+												+	
48	+		+		+		+		±						+		+		+	
49		−		−		−		−	=			−		−		−		−		−
50	+		+		+		+								+			−	+	
Totals	+36	−14	+30	−18	+30	−20	+24	−26	+17	−14	+12	−27	+5	−12	+24	−14	+26	−17	+20	−30

As the totals of Table 16 indicate, the protagonists in question over-whelmingly oppose the status quo (and are, in all but three such cases,[1] supported in doing so by their authors) (column 1). The protests of well more than half are also endorsed by their authors (2), and an equivalent ratio of protagonists are favorably compared with foils (8) and find themselves opposed by a majority of adversaries (9). However, less than half to whom the criteria apply resist rather than escape[2] (6) or defend rather than exploit others (7). Conclusions which either dispel or dismiss the hero's alienation occur in an overwhelming number of plot situations (10).

These same findings, when contrasted to those for nineteenth-century heroes, indicate that, like the latter, heroes of the 'Thaw' period tend strongly to oppose the status quo and also to show an essentially domi-nant inclination to retaliate, to escape, to exploit rather than defend, to compare favorably with foils, however, and to be in the minority. On the whole, the heroes of neither period evidence an appreciably marked tendency to endure rather than actively oppose their opposition (4) or themselves be rejected rather than inconstant in a love situation[3] (5).

The trends for both periods nevertheless tend to differ in a number of important respects: The 'Thaw' hero's protest is more frequently endorsed by his author, and, on occasion, the same hero openly resists his opposi-tion rather than evades it — which never occurs in the nineteenth century

[1] In the works by Kazakov, who manages, generally, to view his heroes' predicaments with pure detachment.
[2] The connotations of 'escape' are here broadened to include a character's apathy or failure, in general, to assume or recognize his obligations or responsibilities, as posited by the author.
[3] Love situations in Table 16 also include (a) instances of alienated friendship and (b) cases involving the protagonists but not necessarily the situations cited and analyzed in Chapter V. Such additional instances are indicated in Column 5 by underscores.

(in the cases sampled). He is, therefore, often more tenacious (or else has less opportunity to escape his misfortune and is thus compelled to face it!). Unlike most nineteenth-century heroes, there are also indeed a number who, in the 'Thaw' period, neither escape nor resist, but merely endure the onslaught of their misery and torture. There are also proportionately greater numbers who are victimized rather than retaliate or otherwise provoke their opposition, who ruthlessly exploit rather than defend other people, yet who show considerable insight into their own motives (3). Though mostly still superior, protagonists are more frequently inferior to their foils and more often in the majority than in the nineteenth century. Unlike those of the preceding century, 'Thaw' protagonists DO NOT UNANIMOUSLY oppose the status quo, escape their offenders, or identify with a minority. Finally, and most significant, three fifths of the 'Thaw' heroes sampled experience victory or reconciliation in their story's outcome — quite the opposite of nineteenth-century heroes, four fifths of whom (of those sampled) end in failure.

'Thaw' heroes are equally distinguished from essentially pre-Stalinist 'underground' types of both the Soviet and pre-Soviet twentieth century, who, like nineteenth-century protagonists, are invariably in a minority and whose outcome is mostly tragic and fraught with violent escapism. The latter also markedly differ from 'thaw' heroes in that their comparison with peers is mostly unfavorable — the 'disillusioned idealist' of the first Soviet period being the lone exception. 'Thaw' heroes have perhaps even less in common, moreover, with the alienated types of the next three Soviet periods,[4] who become increasingly rare[5] and unfavorable and tend either (a) to express an unworthy protest, (b) to be in the majority, or (c) to enjoy a fortunate outcome. Only slightly more than half of the 'Thaw' heroes exhibit this third tendency, while the majority show quite opposite patterns to the first two.

There are still strong traces of the nineteenth century's oppressed 'little' people (*Bread, Silence, Short Circuit, One Day, Matrena, For the Good*) and of the early twentieth century's 'underground'-like informers and provocateurs, who hybridize with the Soviet period's 'incomplete' positive hero and bureaucratic villain[6] types as members, interestingly, of the establishment. These occur only infrequently, however, as the

---

[4]   See Van der Eng-Liedmeier's chronological breakdown, pages 64-65.
[5]   In a number of categories they altogether disappear in the periods immediately before and after World War II.
[6]   This type, it will be remembered, becomes increasingly rare and superficial until after the death of Stalin.

central character in a plot situation, *e.g.* Žuravlev (*Thaw*), Dremljuga (*Wings*), Minaev (*Opinion*), Drozdov (*Bread*), Party leaders (*Levers*), Kramov (*Quests*), Dononov (*Sonnet*), Varygin (*Journey*), Antipov (*Živago*), Globov (*Trial Begins*), Uvarov and Bykov (*Silence*), colleagues (*Bluebottle*), Xabalygin and Knorozov (*For the Good*).

Traces of more idealistically involved progenitors — the nineteenth century's 'antiheroic' nihilists and 'mock heroic' frustrated idealists; the twentieth century's 'hypersensitive intellectuals', including its distinctively Soviet manifestations ('disillusioned idealists' and 'vacillating intellectuals') — can be seen in a number of disenchanted and confused 'angry young man' types (Volodja, *Thaw*; Ven'ka, *Cruelty*; Tolja, *Legend*; Leksej, *Colleagues*; Dimka, *Ticket*; Volodja, *ABCDE*; Sergej, *Silence*) as well as in the cynically frustrated heroes of various 'underground' writers (Karlinskij, *Trial Begins*; Ioann, *Bluebottle*; Tolja, *Moscow*). Their disenchantment, however, is, for the most part, highly personal — as if what concerns them is less what others (people or institutions) do as that they, themselves, should not be tainted by association. Even Ven'ka Malyšev (*Cruelty*), one of the first (and whose setting is the period of War Communism) bemoans the fact that Lazar', *etc.* will feel that "I have deceived them! Deceived them in the name of the Soviet government!"[7] while Tolja, one of the last, exclaims: "I'll go onto the street and shout, 'Citizens, don't kill one another! Love your fellowman!' And what will come of it? Whom can I help? Whom save? I don't know, I know nothing ... Perhaps I will only save myself. If it isn't too late."[8] Such ethical discrimination is also obviously central to the character of Jurij Živago.

The only immediately recognizable remnant of the later nineteenth century's artistically rounded and philosophically 'complex' superfluous hero — *e.g.* one for whom life is both to some degree perplexing, but also a meaningful discovery and vision (Dostoevskij, Tolstoj) — is again, despite all that makes him unique to both centuries, Jurij Živago. Conceivable remnants of the earlier Soviet 'anarchists' are perhaps the heroes of such as Kazakov, *e.g.* Egor (*Renegade*) and Ageev (*Adam*). The only figures in the sample who directly resemble the nineteenth-century aristocrat alienated from the masses are Varygin (*Journey*) and again Živago, both however far less conscience-struck than their nineteenth-century predecessors. Pure Dostoevskian morbidity is by now quite diluted and mostly imputed to villainous foils. There are no more

---

[7] Nilin, *Znamja*, XXVI (December, 1956), 67.
[8] Aržak, 45.

'interim' martyrs, and, if, finally, there are still conformists who through cowardice nonetheless bungle the cause they serve, they are, like Tendrjakov's Leška (*Three, Seven, Ace*) and Stoljarskij (*Short Circuit*), cast in non-political guise and fairly infrequent.

THEMES. — With respect to themes, as such, Gibian,[9] Kersten,[10] Levitzky,[11] Mathewson,[12] and Vickery,[13] have all commented on thematic resemblances in nineteenth-century and Soviet fiction. Gibian discusses the topic with particular astuteness, while Pipes adds some provocative qualifications:

As we have moved from the Stalinist and near-Stalinist images of villains to those which the Party found more and more disturbing, a curious change took place in the stories we were looking at. The works became more and more similar to nineteenth-century Russian literature, to negative, critical realism. ... Again the writer is praising the lone hero who is going against the system; again he is revealing the iniquities of the rulers and of the social structure of the country. The writers find themselves in the curious position of implicitly calling for another revolution. ... As in nineteenth-century literature, the nonconformist and the outcast again stand for justice and humanity, the man in power for tyranny and dehumanization.[14]

The greatest contrast between the contemporary Soviet intellectual and his predecessor lies in their respective attitude toward politics. The old intelligentsia had a thorough commitment to politics; the modern one seems to shun and even despise it. The whole burden of the 'liberal' literature of the past several years is to assert the writer's right to an apolitical existence.[15]

. . . .

Like his 19th Century predecessor, the contemporary Soviet intellectual may feel that he has a particularly important role to play; but the role which he envisages for himself is vastly different. He is no longer the social and political reformer. Rather, he appears as the near relative of the 'alienated' intellectual of the West, about whom so much has been written. ... Intellectually, the roots of the contemporary intellectual rebels in Russia go back not to the *obshchestvennoe dvizhenie* (the movement of oppositional public opinion in the 19th Century), but to the religious tradition and to the whole 'modernist' movement, whose impressive development had been cut short by the Revolution, and which they are now attempting to resuscitate.[16]

Alexandrova adds a further reservation: "The literary pioneers of the early '20s hurried to show the details of the new revolutionary life,

---

[9] Gibian, *Soviet Survey*, 52.
[10] Kersten, *Politische Meinung*, 89.
[11] Levitzky, *Mosty*, 226.
[12] Mathewson, *Soviet Literature in the Sixties*, 15.
[13] Vickery, 156.
[14] Gibian, *Interval of Freedom*, 29.
[15] Pipes, *Encounter*, 82.
[16] *Ibid.*, 83.

avoiding a look into the inner lives of their heroes. The younger writers of today center all their attention on man in his unique individuality."[17] The argument seems to be that, while asserting a kind of individual social protest reminiscent of previous periods, this is done nonetheless in a manner unique to the 'Thaw' period, a manner which is both 'a-political' and profoundly introspective. This argument is, indeed, confirmed by the study at hand.

Two of the 'Thaw' period's three predominant themes — alienation in love and friendship and 'incomplete' positive heroes (mostly 'bureau-cratic villains') — find precedents in the prior Russian literary tradition, both pre-Soviet and Soviet. However, the third predominant theme, involving practical ethical dilemmas — conflicts of integrity *vs.* duplicity and apathy *vs.* responsibility — appears, in many respects, unique to the 'Thaw' period. Two other themes which occur in over half of the works sampled — the conflict between generations and criticism of the bureau-cracy and social injustice — again echo, in a general sense, similar themes in the nineteenth and earlier twentieth centuries.

The yearning for the pre-Revolutionary past (as in Pil'njak) can be faintly construed as occurring in the minds of Kazakov's heroes, par-ticularly Egor. However, other themes characteristic of the pre-Soviet and early Soviet twentieth century — atavism, self-destructive nihilism, the theoretician's envy of the practical man, *etc.* — no longer occur. Instead, there is a tendency to judge the practical person, the man in power, and generally find him wanting; to reject prescribed norms of behavior as inadequate when applied in the concrete instance and in the 'moment of truth'; to seek a sense of purpose in the freely individual, uncommitted life; and to find one's worth, one's essential dignity in one's relationship to others.

The 'incomplete' positive heroes thus serve, in their way, to point up what is no longer acceptable to those they oppose, while the arena of love and friendship — like that of father and son relations — proves to be the frequent testing ground of a man's true character and the moral dilemma which confronts him becomes his ultimate touchstone. In a very real sense, man is again his own measure. The collective order is, as such, no longer resisted and but seldom questioned, nor are group solutions generally entertained. Anti-utopianism is evident only in 'underground' works (*Trial Begins, Bluebottle,* and *Moscow*). Even here, however, or whenever the bureaucracy is indicted, writers seem more to emphasize

[17]   Alexandrova, *A History of Soviet Literature,* 347.

the cowardly conformity and opportunism of petty individuals rather than their ultimate threat to others. Perhaps this is why it is, after all, not so crucial that the endings of some works are less than satisfactory. Perhaps they have to be as a concession for publication.

Although the confusion of truth and logic (another early twentieth-century legacy — Andreev, *etc.*) can likewise be attributed to a number of insensitive bureaucratic villains, few of these are central heroes and a number are rendered not only despicable but also pathetic in their dereliction. Their own insecurity and uneasy conscience is, however, frequently emphasized (*e.g.* Bortaševič, *Seasons*; Minaev, *Opinion*; Party officials, *Levers*; Vasilij Petrovič, *Light*; Ivan Sokovin, *Short Circuit*). The nineteenth-century legacy of abstract social protest and the early Soviet emphasis upon individualism and non-conformity remain, but with a refreshing plea, in many instances, for ethical sensitivity and a return to absolute moral values. This lends the literature of the period increased universality and additional appeal for the general reader.

BIASES. — In general, twentieth-century Russian writers appear far less ambivalent and, by the same token, both less objective and less profound in their approval and/or disapproval of alienated protagonists than were their nineteenth-century predecessors. While in the earlier twentieth century, writers tend to be in full sympathy with their heroes' rebellious individualism, an unfavorable bias becomes increasingly dominant in the Soviet period, particularly under Stalin. 'Thaw' writers therefore more nearly resemble their early twentieth-century predecessors in this one respect — showing sympathy or even identifying with their heroes in some seventy per cent of the cases sampled and commiserating with their alienation, as such (with their rejection of the status quo), to an even greater degree. In this latter respect, however, they are again on common ground with the nineteenth-century writers who, more than they approve of their protagonists, *per se*, generally favor manifestations of social protest. If Turgenev's is the only truly non-polemical approach and the most objective for his century, moreover, he has, in this respect, a suitable and perhaps lone successor in the writer Kazakov.[18]

Authors' biases overwhelmingly favor 'Thaw' protagonists who (a) assert their free will or urge universal protest, (b) oppose the bureaucracy, or (c) are alienated in love and friendship. They also favor, though less overwhelmingly, protagonists challenged to think independently or

---

[18] Critics have also likened Nagibin's subject matter, lyrical detachment, *etc.* to Turgenev's, *e.g.* Gibian, *Soviet Survey*, 52.

confronted with ethical dilemmas, a number of whom are discredited for failing their challenge or rejecting a difficult but moral choice. Least favored are the 'incomplete' positive heroes. In few instances are the bias and its accompanying expectations so extremely optimistic (in only one of those sampled) as to be unconvincing or so restrained (in three cases sampled — all by the same author) as to be undetectable.

THE HERO SEEN IN TERMS OF POLITICAL EVENTS OF THE 'THAW' PERIOD

Reconsideration of the political matrix which underlies these same years will help account for what sets the 'Thaw' period apart, what makes it, despite its resemblances to the prior literary tradition, distinctive as well. One is immediately struck, for instance, by the realization that in the two substantial intervals of 'freeze' occurring in this same period, only FOUR of the thirty works sampled make their appearance — one of which, moreover,[19] is rejected in the USSR and published abroad. During the nearly three-year period which begins with the Hungarian uprising in November, 1956, and ends only at the time of the Third Writers' Congress in May, 1959, there appears in the Soviet Union only one such work, Kuznecov's *Continuation of a Legend*, whose mildly disillusioned young hero only rebels in his thoughts and then not forever and whose protest is never, in fact, ostensibly supported by the author.

Solženicyn's *Matrena's Home* and *For the Good of the Cause* both appear, ironically, during the period of critical reaction which begins with Xruščev's tirade at the Manež on December 1, 1962, and ends only in August, 1963, during the signing of the Atomic Test Ban Treaty. It is noteworthy that, in this same period, the editors of *Novyj mir* come to the defense of Solženicyn's *One Day in the Life of Ivan Denisovič* (April, 1963), but that — except for their courageous crusade in his behalf — he is subjected to an increasingly harsh polemical tirade with each succeeding publication.

Generally speaking, then, the most prominent literature of the 'Thaw' period (that herein sampled) is essentially the product of those alternating seasons of relatively relaxed controls when writers are encouraged, if deceptively, to hope for a renewed and continuing climate of full and free expression. What they then write about is instructive[20] as is the particular year and the wave of 'thaw' in which they write.

[19] *Doctor Živago.*
[20] See *Themes*, page 274.

Table 16 (page 270) indicates the following chronological trends with respect to heroes, as such, and Table 13 (page 236) with respect to themes and author bias: At the 'Thaw''s very outset heroes are predominately passive victims who, in general, neither aggravate their opposition nor in any way retaliate. They are mostly superior to their foils, and their outcome is victorious. The first of these trends reverses itself in 1956, heroes remaining basically more aggressive until 1962, when they become again more submissive. Comparison with foils remains favorable until 1957, being thereafter neither more nor less favorable to the hero. Victorious or compromised tragic endings are less regular by 1956 but recur as the dominant type of conclusion from 1961 until, in 1962, this trend is essentially reversed. In addition, a strong escapist tendency is seen in many characters between 1956 and 1962.

These findings immediately point out that two years in particular — 1956 and 1962 — are the focus of a number of radical reversals in total characterization. Both years, it is worth noting, come at the end of a primary wave of 'Thaw' and account for the largest concentration of works in the sample. If, next, the decade's two major periods of 'Thaw' — 1953-1956 (Stalin's death to the Hungarian revolt) and 1959-1962 (the Third Writers' Congress to the Manež affair) are contrasted to each other, the following significant differences also become apparent: heroes of the second wave are less often members of a majority and tend, rather more often, to end in defeat. In addition, more bureaucratic villains are central characters in the earlier period, serving, for instance, as the heroes in four of eight plot situations appearing in 1956, but in only one of twelve in 1962.

As for themes, during the first wave of 'Thaw' a greater number of works treat the bureaucracy, during the second both universal rebellion and idealistic disillusion. If anything, the conflict of generations is more prominent during the second wave. Authors in this second period also tend to identify more with their protagonists than those in the first. Four do so in 1956, eight in 1962.

The overriding distinction to which these several differences lead is partially explained by the fact that the second wave of 'Thaw' is dominated by an influx of new and younger writers. The following table contrasts the twenty-four writers sampled in sequence of age and according to (a) protagonists' characteristics, (b) thematic categories, and (c) author bias, as evidenced in the fifty sampled plot situations. (A plus sign in parentheses under the heading "Hero Characteristics" indicates that a given hero reflects both characteristics of the pair so signified.

Numbers and symbols are otherwise as previously used in preceding tables.)

TABLE 17

Comparison of Plot Situations Sampled in Terms of Authors' Ages and According to (a) Kinds of Protagonists, (b) Thematic Categories, and (c) Author Bias

Author	Yr. of Birth	Plot #	Hero Characteristics										Themes	Author Bias
			1	2	3	4	5	6	7	8	9	10		
Pasternak	1890	19	+	+	+	+	=	−		+	+	−	1 2 8	1
Pasternak	1890	20	−	−	−	−		−	−	−	−	+	6	4
Èrenburg	1891	4	+	+	−	+	−	−		+	+	−	4 10	1
Èrenburg	1891	5	+	+	−	−		−	−	−	−	−	3 10	2
Èrenburg	1891	6	+	+	+	+	±	+		+	+	−	8	1
Pogodin	1900	17	+	+	+	−	+	+		+	+	−	1	1
Tarsis	1900	45	+	+	+	−	±	+		+		−	7	1
Kaverin	1902	14	+	+	+	+		+		+	+	−	8	1
Kaverin	1902	15	+	+	+	+	+	−				−	4	2
Kornejčuk	1905	7	+	+	+	−		+	+	+	−	−	8	6
Kornejčuk	1905	8	+	−	−	+		−		+	−	−	10	2
Kornejčuk	1905	9	+	+	+	+	+				+	+	4	1
Panova	1905	1	+	−	−	−	−	−	−	−	+	−	4 5 10	2
Panova	1905	2	−	−	−	−	±	−	−	+	+	+	10	4
Nilin	1908	12	+	+	+	+	±	+	+	+	+	+	7 10	1
Ždanov	1909	18	−	−	=	−		−	−		+	−	6	5
Nekrasov	1911	34	−	−	−	−	(+)	−		−	−	−	3 6 10	4
Jašin	1913	13	−	−	−	+		−	−	+	−	+	3 4	4
Rozov	1913	35	+	(+)	−	−	=	−		−	+	−	2 7 10	2
Dudincev	1918	11	+	+	+	+	(+)	+		+	+	+	3 8	1
Solženicyn	1918	44	+	+	+	+					−	+	8	1
Solženicyn	1918	48	+	+	+	+	+			+	+	+	2 4	1
Solženicyn	1918	49	−	−	−	=	−	−	−	−	−	−	6	5
Solženicyn	1918	50	+	+	+	+				+	−	+	8	1
Granin	1919	10	−	−	−	−	=	−	−	−	−	+	6 10	4
Nagibin	1920	16	−	−	+	−	=	−	−	+	+	+	9 10	2
Tendrjakov	1923	26	+	+	+	+	±		+	+	+	+	4 8	1
Tendrjakov	1923	27	−	−	−	−	=	−		−	−	+	7 10	4
Tendrjakov	1923	30	−	−	−	−	=	−		−	+	+	10	4
Tendrjakov	1923	31	+	+	+	+			+	+	+	+	7	1
Tendrjakov	1923	39	+	+	+	+	±			−	−	−	4	1
Tendrjakov	1923	40	−	−	−	−	=	−		−	−	−	6	4
Tendrjakov	1923	41	+	+	+	+	±	+		+		−	5	1
Bondarev	1924	36	+	+	+	−		+		+	+	+	8	1
Bondarev	1924	37	+	+	+	+	±					−	5	1
Bondarev	1924	38	+	+	+	+					+	+	3	1
Zorin	1924	3	+	+	+	+	=	−		+	+	+	8	1
Aržak	1925	46	−	−	−	−	=	−	−	−		+	10	5

Author	Yr. of Birth	Plot #	Hero Characteristics 1	2	3	4	5	6	7	8	9	10	Themes	Author Bias
Aržak	1925	47	+	+	+	+					+		3	2
Terc	1925	24	+	+	+	+	=	−		+	+	+	1 2 4	1
Terc	1925	25	−	−	−	−	±	−	−	−	−	−	6	5
Kazakov	1927	22	+		+	−		−			+	−	1	3
Kazakov	1927	23	+		+	−		−			+	−	10	3
Kazakov	1927	42	+		+	−	−	−		−	+	−	4	3
Kazakov	1927	43	+	+	+						+	+	3	1
Kuznecov	1930	21	+	−	−	−		−		+	+	−	2 10	2
Aksenov	1932	28	+	−	−	−		−			+	−	2 7 10	2
Aksenov	1932	29	−	+	+	−		+	+	+	−	−	4	1
Aksenov	1932	32	+	−	−	−	±	−		−	−	−	1 10	2
Aksenov	1932	33	+	+	+	+		+		+	+	−	3 10	1

The barred lines in the foregoing table distinguish between three groups of writers: those old enough to have meaningfully experienced the purges of the thirties, nine in all representing sixteen of the plot situations sampled; those too young for the purges but old enough to serve in World War II, thirteen in all representing twenty-nine plot situations; and those too young to serve in the War, many of whom were evacuated to the East and never witnessed the ensuing battle, two authors representing five situations. The above table permits a number of useful generalizations about the heroes of these three groups of writers, shown in Table 18, below:

TABLE 18

Comparison of 'Thaw' Writers by Age

	Older Group	Middle Group	Younger Group
Heroes:	Mostly victorious (two times out of three!)	Resist adversaries the least.	Protest is less laudable.
		Less superior to foils.	Show least self-understanding.
		Usually defeated (one time out of two!)	More actively oppose adversaries.
			Exploit others least.
			Never defeated — *always* victorious!

	Older Group	Middle Group	Younger Group
Themes:			
	Least universal rebellion. Less artistic and scientific protest.		Six times the rebellion of first group. No 'incomplete' positive heroes.
Author Bias:			
	Identify but show least detached sympathy.		Most sympathetic — no harsh judgments.

In several respects the foregoing observations (Table 18) correlate with the literary-political tendencies noted in connection with the two major periods of 'Thaw' (1953-1956 and 1959-1962): It is older writers, obviously, who dominate the first period with its numerous bureaucratic villains and passive victims, most of whom emerge nonetheless victorious. Èrenburg's characters are an apt example. The fact that more aggressive characters and victorious endings return to vogue by the year 1962, then diminish, is indicative of the appearance at this time of Aksenov's novelettes and of works on similar themes by such as Rozov. Young writers would definitely appear, then, to usher in the second major wave of 'Thaw', but to default rather quickly in the establishment of trends to middle-aged writers of a less agitated, less cheery point of view, like Solženicyn. The fact that the second wave is, as a whole, less given to happy outcomes suggests its ultimate domination by writers of this middle group.

A number of critics have attempted to explain why so striking a difference in the works of authors who, though of diverse ages, write in the same decade. According to Bode, writers of the middle generation, now generally in their forties,

experienced with full awareness the last important steps in Russia's development: collectivization, the 'purges', the Second World War, the renewed terror after the War's end, the death of Stalin and its whole aftermath. ... In their artistic work they draw primarily upon their own experience, but by contrast with the older generation they have not been broken by the 'purges' of the pre-War years, because they were too young. And, by contrast with the youth who did not experience the War as men, they managed to free themselves from a number of myths and fictions and thus endured the events of the fifties as developed men with mature understanding. For this reason their world view is healthier, more constant and often enveloped in national Russian nuances ....[21]

[21] Barbara Bode, "Sowjetliteratur 1962-1963 (II)", *Osteuropa*, XIII (November-December, 1963), 826.

Whitney tries to suggest, however, wherein the younger generation, in its urge for emancipation, differs from the middle, as such:

The 'fathers' were, many of them, indoctrinated under Stalin, and many of them in different ways are still addicted to dictatorial, high-handed methods, though it is also they who exposed, of their own free will, some evils of the Stalin epoch. The 'fathers' are men who bore the cruel sacrifices of World War II. The 'fathers' expect to be respected and obeyed for their sacrifices — but the Russian 'sons' of today have their own view. They have been told so much about 'sacrifice' and 'duty' they are sick of hearing 'high' words. Brought up in days when as children they were taught to worship Stalin as a god they suffered a keen disillusionment when it turned out Stalin was guilty of horrible crimes. If the 'fathers' are impressed with accomplishments of Soviet society the 'sons' are more impressed with imperfections and faults. Born too late to take part in the war they are tired of hearing endlessly about the 'heroism' of those who did ....[22]

An anonymously quoted "Russian writer known in the West by another name" further characterizes this younger group as "a strange generation: knowledgable and understanding, but without much understanding. ... Authors a bit older fail to react at all and know only that they have to be careful; they became familiar with the world at the worst possible moment and are not surprised by anything."[23] Another Russian, the critic, Aninskij, adds that, in the evacuation during the War, young people's idealism was "'protected'", so that, fifteen years later, as they began to write, "'a sense of citizenship, high flown dreams, and Communist doctrine had entered their consciousness for a lifetime'". The fact, however, that they had not yet experienced real life forced them, in view of their idealism, to learn "'late and with difficulty to think realistically and independently'". Lacking a sense of the practical, they thus compromised themselves, despite their "'inability to be compromised'". And thus, says Aninskij, they acquired the "'spirit of inquiry and dissatisfaction with one's self'".[24]

The immediate impetus for the younger authors' widespread disillusion and its frequent articulation in their writing is again due to the unmasking of Stalinism, in which the older writers had already taken the initiative. It is noteworthy that the latter concentrate their attack more than any others upon the bureaucratic apparatus, often in settings following the War but preceding Stalin's death: "This makes it easier for the author to

---

[22]   Whitney, 106.
[23]   Gavrilov, *The New Leader*, 16.
[24]   Lev Anninskij, *Oktjabr'*, XXXIX (August, 1962), quoted in Bode, *Osteuropa*, XIII (November-December, 1963), 827.

deal with social ills that can be ascribed solely to the discredited dictator."[25]

A number of critics actually regard the literary 'de-Stalinization' as having become, unwittingly or otherwise, a castigation of the system in general in both the past and present. *Not by Bread Alone*, though the work of a middle-aged writer, is a case in point:

Unlike other negative characters in Soviet fiction, Drozdov and the whole clique he represents are neither villains nor paid agents of American imperialism. They are Party members, solid citizens, and first-class business men. ... By depicting Drozdov as the end result of the Communist regime, the novel goes beyond the 'little defects of the mechanism.' Within limits of this kind of criticism permissible in the USSR, Dudintsev indirectly questions the whole system.[26]

It is more likely that the new trend in literature is a reaction against the long reign of lies, deceit, bureaucracy, bootlicking and other abuses that continued after Stalin.[27]

The question arises as to whether one man alone could have committed so much evil without the cooperation of the Party. ... As a result a paradoxical situation has arisen in which literary works on the subject of de-Stalinization are boomeranging.[28]

These first 'Thaw' writers were doubtless aware of the new regime's tacit support and that it was, in fact, to the advantage of Stalin's heirs to turn him into a scapegoat. As the preceding tables suggest, furthermore, these earlier writers take particular care to create heroes who, though maligned, are of sterling character and in no sense rebellious; who, under no circumstances, think to take the law into their own hands. Nor do these writers seriously venture into themes asserting individual freedom in any universally abstract or intellectual manner. They make a further concession to the status quo by satisfactorily resolving things in the present.

The reversal of several trends in 1956 — more aggressive heroes, greater escapism, greater minority leanings, fewer reconciled conclusions — points, in turn, both to a more marked and impatient individualism and also to a more sober kind of general expectation. The authors who initiate this change are essentially middle-agers who, in 1959, are overtaken by newcomers whose poet-contemporary has accurately observed that "'in a political sense we are the children of the XX. and the XXII. Party

---

[25] Gaev, *Studies on the Soviet Union*, No. 4 (1965), 229.
[26] Slonim, *Soviet Russian Literature: Writers and Problems*, 305.
[27] Gaev, *Studies on the Soviet Union*, No. 4 (1965), 229.
[28] Gaev, *Soviet Literature in the Sixties*, 49.

Congresses, a generation which finds much in common with the revolutionaries of the twenties'".[29] As Bode observes, however, "the young writers strongly differ from the ambitious heroes of socialist labor, from the models of the twenties and thirties, from Pavlik Morozov or Pavka Korchagin. They indeed declare their loyalty to the Revolution, to the tradition of Lenin ... [but] the young writers seek something for themselves, including their own identity."[30]

The co-occurrence of themes treating idealistic disillusion, universal rebellion, and the conflict of generations as well as the author's increased identity with his often confused and aggressive protagonist in the second period of 'Thaw' strongly evidence the presence of these new young writers — as does the increased tendency in 1961 and the first half of 1962 to resolve the hero's conflicts in a harmonious manner (usually by rehabilitation). However, like the final and peak year of the first wave of 'Thaw', that of the second is likewise subject to a number of shifts which in turn reflect the ascendancy of a particular group of writers — in this case, those of middle age.

Heroes are again more passive. The situation temporarily resembles that of the 'Thaw''s beginning until, still in 1962, heroes' outcomes become for the first time predominately tragic or unresolved, remaining thus through the last work sampled. Especially prominent among the writers of this final phase are Kazakov and Solženicyn. By contrast with both preceding groups of writers, these latter — by holding to a more neutral line in terms of the bias with which they view their characters and by resorting less often to an optimistic resolution — evidence a certain objectivity which seems lacking in the others. Moreover, while their heroes are again highly victimized, these are invested, for all their surrounding gloom, with a definite and provocative transcendence. It is no longer so much the hero's circumstances as how he copes with them that invites the author's attention. As Gibian astutely observes, the period's truly significant literature is "the product of writers who emerged during and after the war".[31] Moreover, as he much earlier surmised,

when the Party permitted a liberalization in literature, it presumably aimed at promoting writing critical of bureaucratic abuses, exerting a corrective effect on the industrial and technological conditions. The writers went far beyond that aim. In fact, the material side of the evils they criticize seems to interest

---

[29]   Andrej Voznesenskij, *Literaturnaja gazeta* (March 30, 1963), quoted in Bode *Osteuropa*, XIII (November-December, 1963), 828.

[30]   Bode, *Osteuropa*, XIII (November-December, 1963), 830.

[31]   Gibian, *Literature and Revolution in Soviet Russia 1917-1962*, 131.

them far less than the intangible side; the poverty of goods pains them less than the poverty of spirit. They are crying out against a spiritual degradation.[32]

The seven[33] subplots by four 'underground' writers nevertheless reveal, despite their similar ethical transcendence, a vivid departure from the pattern of most middle-aged writers (to whose age group both Terc and Aržak belong). Instead, these authors display certain affinities, to the older group of writers, *e.g.* in their opposition of a highly favored protagonist with whom the author generally identifies to a despicable, deeply deluded, or extremely unsympathetic foil. Their point of view also resembles the somewhat anti-utopian striving of younger writers, but their heroes are generally more cognizant of their predicament and — with the exception of Pasternak's Živago and Tarsis' Sinemuxov, who through their written legacies achieve a certain sense of fulfillment — meet a sorry end. Their extreme bias for or against various characters can be explained by their satirical intent and their penchant for caricature.

'SCHOOLS' OF THE 'THAW' PERIOD: LITERARY VIEWPOINTS

The foregoing considerations permit, finally, a kind of grouping of the various writers sampled according to subject matter, style, and point of view: While the dominant trend in Soviet literature remains that of 'positive' heroes who experience "no genuine tragedy, no inevitability, no real desperation", who conquer "the remnants of their private-ownership instincts", or who re-enact "the classic theme of socialist realism, 'boy loves girl, girl loves tractor'",[34] and while no writers have evidenced the imaginative perception of the Silver Age and the twenties[35] — still what does emerge in this phlegmatic and tension-filled decade are, as Burg contends, "a whole number of diverse and mutually opposed literary tendencies".[36]

---

[32]   Gibian, *The New Leader*, 20.
[33]   'Underground' plots thus constitute a seventh of those sampled.
[34]   David Burg, "Die Partei und die Schniftsteller: Chronik eines Jahres in der Sowjetunion", *Der Monat*, XVI, No. 183 (November, 1963), 46.
[35]   Writing in 1960 and speaking particularly of the period, 1954-1957, Gibian observes "no revival of the symbolism of an Olesha, the modernism of a Pilnyak, the Maupassantesque precision and *mot juste* of an Isaac Babel". Gibian, *Interval of Freedom*, 159. As late as 1964, in fact, Mathewson renders a similar judgment: "They [Soviet 'Thaw' writers] have bypassed their own experimental writers of the period between the wars, most notably Babel and Olesha. ... Nor does one feel the presence of the Symbolist movement...". Mathewson, *Soviet Literature in the Sixties*, 15.
[36]   Burg, *Osteuropa*, XII (February-March, 1963), 128.

There are — besides the works written in strictly socialist realist vein or those by several older, accomplished, ostensibly neutral and non-programmatic writers[37] — a number of works which suggest a tenuous revival of the tradition of classical psychological realism. These works are "based on a direct rendering of experience, unadorned, unvarnished, brutal, such as could rarely be found in Stalinist literature" and which accurately reveal "psychological states seldom studied in Soviet literature of the preceding years".[38] Gibian cites Nekrasov in this connection.

In addition, there occur a number of movements to which Rzhevsky applies the collective label, 'emancipatory realism',[39] whose writers he views as 'literary innovators'[40] having in common "their striving for the maximum 'liberation' of their creative 'egos' and their search for new linguistic and stylistic forms".[41]

TABLE 19

'Thaw' Writers by School

A. *Traditionalists*

Socialist Realists	Neutral Stylists and Social Polemicists	Neo-Psychological Realists
Kornejčuk	Bondarev	Granin
	Dudincev	Jašin
	Èrenburg	Nagibin
	Kaverin	Nekrasov
	Panova	Nilin
	Zorin	Ždanov

B. *Innovators*

Avant-gardists and Mannerists	Naturalist-Romantic Lyricists	Philosophical Moralists	Poetic and Satiric 'Fantasists'
Aksenov	Kazakov	Solženicyn	Aržak
Kuznecov		Tendrjakov	Pasternak
Rozov			Pogodin
			Tarsis
			Terc

[37] Rzhevsky mentions the later Fedin, Leonov, Paustovskij, Kaverin, and Šoloxov, for whom, he argues, writing has become "a linguistic activity which is an end in itself and in which the criterion of the creative method is the *word as a vehicle of expression,* the work chosen for its expressiveness, precision, sound, imagery and 'uniqueness'. The search for the poetically striking expression, the absence of verbiage, and affinity with the traditions of classical Russian writing...". Rzhevsky, *Soviet Literature in the Sixties*, 67.

[38] Gibian, *Literature and Revolution in Soviet Russia 1917-1962*, 128

[39] Rzhevsky, *Soviet Literature in the Sixties*, 75.

[40] *Ibid.*, 77.

[41] *Ibid.*, 75.

Rzhevsky mentions as spearheading such diverse but related 'schools'
Kazakov, Solženicyn, and Aksenov.[42] These three names nicely coincide,
in fact, with three of four such categories suggested by the works sampled
in the present investigation. The fourth category is represented chiefly
by 'underground' writers whose genre is, in the main, what one might
call poetic or surrealist-satiric fantasy. The distribution of the twenty-
four authors in question in terms of this and the other aforementioned
literary movements is indicated in the preceding table and briefly discussed, as follows:

SOCIALIST REALISTS: By virtue of his facile cardboard 'superman'
hero, Romodan, Kornejčuk magically satisfies the needs of his play's
peasant populace and brings forward the glorious socialist cause.
Wings is a typically schematic study in the ascendancy of light over
dark, with no intermediate shading.[43]

NEUTRAL STYLISTS AND SOCIAL POLEMICISTS: Consisting equally of
older and middle-aged writers, this movement evinces a strong righteous
indignation toward bureaucratic injustice, which it tends to attack by
association with the evils of Stalinism. Its characters are made extremely
pathetic by the laboriously contrived circumstances in which they find
themselves. They are mostly uncomplicated personalities with whom
their authors strongly identify and are contrasted to correspondingly
unsympathetic (usually bureaucratic) villains. Their substance and appeal
greatly depend upon a plot whose artful twists and turns produce a
mostly fortuitous and pleasant outcome. Their authors are generally
skilled literary craftsmen with few stylistic pretensions who tend to be
unduly verbose.

NEO-PSYCHOLOGICAL REALISTS: With the exception of Nilin and
Ždanov, who are among the youngest of the older generation, this
group consists of middle-agers who sensitively explore the process of
guilt and the theme of conscience in characters whose social function is
not unlike that of the bureaucratic villains so villified by the foregoing
school. Their writing is, by contrast, subtle and short, almost sketchy.
They mostly view their heroes, whose character is constant and who for
the most part do little improving, with disapproval or regretful disdain.[44]

---

[42] *Ibid.*
[43] In an incisive essay on Soviet dramaturgy, the Soviet critic Mark Ščeglov classes
Wings with works in which "propaganda of communist ideas ... fails to become
propaganda by artistic means". Mark Ščeglov, "Realizm sovremennoj dramy",
Literaturnaja Moskva, II (Moscow, Gosudarstvennoe izdatel'stvo xudožestvennoj
literatury, 1956), 691.
[44] Nilin, whose hero is nonetheless exemplary, is the one exception.

Their works appear almost exclusively in the year 1956, at the peak of the first wave of 'Thaw'. It is as if the older generation's villification of certain formerly irreproachable 'positive' types has at last encouraged these writers to identify the tyrant mentality as a recognizable everyday phenomenon and as occurring in the lives of average, three-dimensional human beings whose malice and lack of feeling reflect a socially conditioned insecurity and cowardice. This makes these 'villains' even more tragic than their victims.

AVANT-GARDISTS AND MANNERISTS: Appearing after the first 'Thaw' Wave and before the peak of the second, the works of these writers treat youthful heroes of a mildly anarchistic inclination who, like the heroes of the second school, decry social abuse, particularly their elders' hypocrisy, but do so with a perhaps too strident voice and use their disillusion as an excuse for spurning others and evading social obligations. Their chief virtue is forthright honesty, which does not, however, prevent their ultimate capitulation to conformity. Their authors view them with detached, almost condescending sympathy. Burg attributes this genre to a number of playwrights besides Rozov, whose dramas, he contends, "advance the tradition of the 'bourgeois' drama of manners".[45] Younger writers, particularly Aksenov, display daring effects with colorful colloquial jargon reminiscent of various Western contemporaries like Hemingway and Salinger. Though their heroes' protest verges on

skepticism akin to that of underground literature. ... [they] do not challenge Communist doctrine but rather speak up against the hypocritical *misuse* of ideology ... while representing themselves as defenders of its true meaning. ... Nor can the avant-gardists be called skeptics in the broader sense. ... On the contrary their aspirations are quite positive: self-assertion, self-revelation, self-exploration."[46]

Moreover, their reconciliation with the status quo makes them into useful models of instruction reminiscent of Savva Grudcyn, Gore-Zločastie and other traditional prodigal sons.

NATURALIST-ROMANTIC LYRICISTS: Kazakov and his circle stand alone in their attractive, arresting manner. They are variously characterized by a number of critics. Perhaps most closely resembling the style and essentially detached viewpoint of Turgenev, Čexov, and Bunin (in this respect he is also something of a traditionalist), Kazakov appears (as herein sampled) during the second wave of 'Thaw'. Unlike Turgenev's characters, Kazakov's are completely divorced from the discussion of

[45] Burg, *Problems of Communism*, XI (September-October, 1962), 40.
[46] *Ibid.*, 39-40.

immediate social issues. Kazakov protests instead by ignoring what is not universally personal and subjective and by adopting a mood of 'simplicity' and 'ideological naivete'.[47] His stories are "unadorned, almost plotless renderings of love and parting, of contrasts between youth and old age, of daily joys and sorrows" which are depicted "without making a judgement or drawing a moral conclusion".[48] In common with other innovators, "the important thing is the individual experience of love, pain or fear" as presented through the "narrowing ... of focus to the frame of a single mind — or to a succession of these"[49] and the impressionistic recreation "in precise and realistic detail of all changes and nuances of feeling".[50] If, as stylists, writers of the second group are neutral, those like Kazakov are essentially 'neutral'[51] in point of view but also 'lyrical'[52] in an often minor key.

PHILOSOPHICAL MORALISTS: Continuing the trend of "'neutral' literature, in which Soviet writers treat the private lives of individuals without taking up any explicit or implied political position",[53] Tendrjakov's significant writing, like that of Solženicyn, begins in the second 'Thaw' period. If Tendrjakov's setting again suggests the atmosphere of Turgenev (e.g. Sportsman's Sketches), his tone, which registers "the barely audible echo of other worlds, or irrational primitive forces", is at least "quite new to Soviet literature".[54] Tendrjakov, as Burg observes, "stands somewhat apart. His contes-philosophiques combine social criticism with an interest in moral paradoxes and human emotions", and he is deeply "haunted by the inevitability of evil" which he finds "deep-rooted in man himself".[55] Bode also affirms this view.[56] It is, in a sense, their search for difficult but universal human truth which unites Tendrjakov and Solženicyn. The latter is often epitomized as a disciple of Dostoevskij[57] for his idealization of suffering and his evocation of the 'higher realities'. By favoring the meek and downtrodden 'little' people, whose "personal 'righteousness'" and "unagressive goodness"[58] he extolls, he clearly

[47] Brown, 291.
[48] Slonim, Soviet Russian Literature: Writers and Problems, 321.
[49] Brown, 291.
[50] Burg, Problems of Communism, XI (September-October, 1962), 42.
[51] Ibid.
[52] Ibid., 41.
[53] Hingley, Survey, 46.
[54] Bode, Osteuropa, X (September, 1960), 623.
[55] Burg, Problems of Communism, XI (September-October, 1962), 42-43.
[56] Bode, Osteuropa, X (September, 1960), 624.
[57] Bode, Osteuropa, XIII (October, 1963), 709. Johnson, Khrushchev and the Arts: The Politics of Soviet Culture (1962-1964), 272.
[58] Erlich, Slavic Review, 411.

exemplifies "the relatively recent emergence of a strong Christian movement within the literary community".[59]

POETIC AND SATIRIC 'FANTASISTS': These writers have in common their very eccentricity. Their antecedents have been traced to Gogol', Dostoevskij, Sologub, Blok, Majakovskij, and Zamjatin in the Russian tradition and elsewhere to such as Hoffmann, Poe, and Kafka. The works of the 'underground' writers (with the exception of Pasternak) are indeed richly imbued with "macabre fantasy and eroticism".[60] The fact that three of them are, nonetheless, of the older generation and the other two younger middle-agers and that their works occur sporadically during 'freeze' as well as 'Thaw' is also indicative of their capriciousness and diversity. (Sinjavskij, at least, is one of Pasternak's long admirers, entrusted in fact with editing the latter's first posthumous edition of selected verse.) Their affinity, of course, includes their common tendency toward the experimental, the symbolic and presentational in form (well characterized in Sinjavskij-Terc's celebrated essay, On Socialist Realism, as 'phantasmagoric art'); their spitefully satirical aversion to soul-stifling conformity and the status quo (Pasternak is much less a stone thrower than the others); their "humanistic affirmation of human dignity"; and therefore the essentially "religious humanism"[61] each of the rest shares with the author of Doctor Živago. If it is true that "one will find more about the problems of contemporary Soviet reality, even the purely human, in Dudintsev's Not by Bread Alone or in Granin's Own Opinion than in Doctor Zhivago",[62] it is also true that nowhere in the twentieth century can one find a more impassioned literary statement about the sacredness and worth of the individual private life than in the writing of this last group of writers. As Sinjavskij has declared, Aržak's Moscow is "'one long cry of: "Thou shalt not kill!" The hero says, "I cannot and do not wish to kill — a human being must remain human in all circumstances"'", while, among other things, Sinjavskij's own Trial Begins is clearly AGAINST "'anti-Semitism'".[63] Pogodin is grouped with the others for his comparable insistence on individuality and personal freedom and his employment of an expressionistic symbolic technique.

[59] Hingley, Survey, 46.
[60] Hayward, Dissonant Voices in Soviet Literature, xxxv.
[61] Levitzky, Mosty, II (1959), 228.
[62] Neander, Osteuropa, 786.
[63] Sinjavskij, The New York Times Magazine, 123.

SUMMATION

The foregoing categories represent this study's culminating generalization. The distribution of the authors in question in some seven philosophical-stylistic schools closely reflects the impact of Soviet history — particularly of Stalinism — on each of them according, mostly, to the ages at which they were subjected to its influence. The 'underground' writers, however, constitute an exception to this statement.

Except for these same 'underground' authors, the oldest and very youngest writers appear, in the long run, the most cautious and the least willing to entertain either a truly independent or profoundly tragic view of the alienated individual's predicament and its causes. Though their highly vocal indignation sounds the loudest, its ring is also more hollow and monotonous than the perceptive analysis of middle-aged writers who appear around 1956; the carefully selected, subtle nuances of Kazakov; or the provocative speculation and the truly spiritual affirmation of Tendrjakov and Solženicyn. Together with Pasternak, Tendrjakov and Solženicyn constitute the period's actual and not unimpressive literary-philosophical achievement.

These last mentioned 'schools' — the neo-psychological realists, naturalist-romantic lyricists, philosophical moralists, and poetic and satiric 'fantasists' — reveal, furthermore — by their less radical bias toward protagonists and by their protagonists' tendency toward greater minority leanings, more tragic endings, and less frequent reformation — far closer resemblances to the authors of nineteenth-century alienated heroes. Their world view, in other words, is similarly stark and objective — permitting their principal heroes, particularly when these are villains, to be viewed in a merciless but nonetheless sympathetic light and providing them with a lifelike roundness and complexity which are elsewhere lacking in the later Soviet twentieth century.

Though they evidence the stamp of their literary predecessors (particularly those of the nineteenth century), these same predominantly middle-aged writers are for the most part, however, far more original in their own right than other writers of a more conservatively Soviet caste. They have, as it were, assimilated the nineteenth-century legacy and made it again their own, while their less imaginative, less endowed contemporaries are more 'traditional' in that they are less free-thinking or genuinely creative. At the time one might have thought it an encouraging sign that these same middle-aged 'innovators' tend to appear first in 1956 and, thereafter, during the second major wave of 'thaw' —

i.e. toward the end rather than at the beginning of the period in question. Time and subsequent developments have unfortunately dispelled the hope that this second 'Thaw' would persist or at least be succeeded by a third after a similar two- to three-year interval of 'freeze'.

While, like the general issue of freedom and individuality, the theme of alienation in love and friendship tends to pervade writing during the whole decade — it is criticism of the bureaucracy which, as found in the works of older socialist realists and social polemicists, initiates the period; concern with 'incomplete' positive heroes which mainly interests the mostly middle-aged neo-psychological realists in 1956; and both idealistic disillusion and conflict between the generations (superficially reminiscent of Turgenev and also of writers in the earliest Soviet period) which is treated by the young avant-gardists and mannerists who appear in 1959.

Thematically, however, it is underground writers, such as Pasternak, and later philosophical moralists, like Solženicyn, who pose the most arresting ethical issues. In this regard, they again more nearly resemble certain later nineteenth-century writers, particularly Dostoevskij and Tolstoj. The problems they pose do of course reflect their heroes' peculiar collectivist milieu. They therefore tend to emphasize the lone individual's aspiration to a clear conscience and the priority he places upon personal wisdom, integrity, or goodness — in spite of the opposition to these values of the society in which he resides. These writers' most fitting parallel is, if at all, that of the medieval Russian hagiographer.

Finally, what almost all 'Thaw' writers have in common, in varying degree, is, as Burg contends, their "attempt to scrutinize — more or less independently, more or less honestly — *les conditiones humaines*".[64] Their almost overwhelming approval of their heroes' opposition to the status quo is indicative and affirms their substantial tie with the prior Russian literary tradition.

[64]   Burg, *Der Monat*, XVI No. 183, (November, 1963), 43.

APPENDICES

CRITICAL REVIEWS OF PROSE IN THE 'THAW' PERIOD

(1) Aleksandrov, K., "Revisionism as Reflected in Soviet Literature", *Bulletin of the Institute for the Study of the USSR* (April, 1958).

(2) Alexandrova, Vera, "Soviet Literature since Stalin", *Problems of Communism* (July-August, 1954).

(3) ——, "Voices of Youth", *Soviet Survey* (April-June, 1961).

(4) ——, "Youth and Life in New Soviet Literature", *Studies on the Soviet Union* (March, 1962).

(5) ——, *A History of Soviet Literature* (Garden City, Doubleday & Co., 1963).

(6) Blake, Patricia, "New Voices in Russian Writing", *Encounter* (April, 1963).

(7) Blum, Ralph, "A Reporter at Large. Freeze and Thaw: The Artist in Russia", *The New Yorker* (August 28, 1965).

(8) ——, "A Reporter at Large. Freeze and Thaw: The Artist in Russia", *The New Yorker* (September 4, 1965).

(9) Bode, Barbara, "Sowjetliteratur 1959", *Osteuropa* (December, 1959)

(10) ——, "Sowjetliteratur im Winterhalbjahr 1959-1960", *Osteuropa* (September, 1960)

(11) ——, "Sowjetliteratur im Sommerhalbjahr 1960", *Osteuropa* (January, 1961)

(12) ——, "1960: The Literary Harvest", *Soviet Survey* (April-June, 1961)

(13) ——, "Sowjetliteratur im Winterhalbjahr 1960-1961", *Osteuropa* (November-December, 1961).

(14) ——, "Sowjetliteratur im Winterhalbjahr 1960-1961 (II)", *Osteuropa* (January-February, 1962).

(15) ——, "Sowjetliteratur 1961-1962", *Osteuropa* (November-December, 1962).

(16) ——, "Sowjetliteratur 1961-1962 (II)", *Osteuropa* (January, 1963).

(17) ——, "Russlands jüngste Dichtergeneration", *Osteuropa* (April, 1963).

(18) ——, "Über Ästhetik, Ethik und ähnliche Nutzlosigkeiten", *Osteuropa*

(September, 1963).

(19) ——, "Sowjetliteratur 1962-1963", *Osteuropa* (October, 1963).

(20) ——, "Sowjetliteratur 1962-1963 (II)", *Osteuropa* (November-December, 1963).

(21) ——, "Die Auseinandersetzungen in der Sowjetliteratur als Spiegel der politischen Strömungen", *Osteuropa* (January-February, 1965).

(22) ——, "Die Diskussion um Solshenizyn als Zentrum der Auseinandersetzungen in der Sowjetliteratur", *Osteuropa* (October, 1965).

(23) ——, "Die Diskussion um Solshenizyn (II)", *Osteuropa* (November-December, 1965).

(24) Brown, Edward J., *Russian Literature since the Revolution* (New York, Collier Books, 1963).

(25) Burg, David, "The 'Cold War' on the Literary Front", *Problems of Communism* (July-August, 1962).

(26) ——, "The 'Cold War' on the Literary Front, II", *Problems of Communism* (September-October, 1962).

(27) ——, "Der moralische Bankrott des Nachstalinismus (über Nekrassows Roman 'Kyra Georgijewna')", *Osteuropa* (February-March, 1963).

(28) ——, "Die Partei und die Schriftsteller, Chronik eines Jahres in der Sowjetunion", *Der Monat*, No. 182 (November, 1963).

(29) ——, "Die Partei und die Schriftsteller, Chronik eines Jahres in der Sowjetunion", *Der Monat*, No. 183 (November, 1963).

(30) ——, "Um Pasternaks Platz in der Sowjetliteratur", *Osteuropa* (September, 1964).

(31) ——, "Ein Jahr nach Chruschtschows Sturz — Nachwirkungen und Reaktionen im geistigen Leben der UdSSR", *Osteuropa* (October, 1965).

(32) Campbell, A. J. C., "Plays and Playwrights", *Survey* (January, 1963).

(33) Clements, Robert J., "The European Literary Scene", *Saturday Review* (March 26, 1966).

(34) Dalton, Margaret, "Nikolai Arzhak", *The New Leader* (November 8, 1965).

(35) Erlich, Victor, "Post-Stalin Trends in Russian Literature", *Slavic Review* (September, 1964).

(36) F., F. "The Dilemma of Soviet Writers: Inspiration or Conformity", *World Today* (April, 1955).

(37) Field, Andrew, "Abram Tertz's Ordeal by Mirror", *The New Leader* (July 19, 1965).

(38) ——, "Prisoner in Fantasy", *The New Leader* (February 14, 1966).

(39) Folejewski, Zbigniew," Notes on the Problem of Individual vs. Collective

in Russian and Polish Literature, 1954-1957", *Indiana Slavic Studies* (1963).

(40) Frank, Victor S., "The Literary Climate", *Survey* (July, 1965).

(41) Frankland, Mark, "The Current Season", *Survey* (January, 1963).

(42) Friedberg, Maurice, "The Background to the Third Congress of the Union of Soviet Writers", *Bulletin of the Institute for the Study of the USSR* (December, 1958).

(43) ——, "Broken Laws of the Jungle", *Saturday Review* (September 28, 1963).

(44) Gaev, Arkadii, "Soviet Literature after the Last Attacks", *Analysis of Current Developments in the Soviet Union*, No. 3 (1963-1964).

(45) ——, "Banned Young Rebels Creeping Back into Soviet Literature", *Analysis of Current Developments in the Soviet Union*, No. 24 (1963-1964).

(46) ——, "A Party Blockade on Freedom of Expression", *Analysis of Current Developments in the Soviet Union*, No. 38 (1963-1964).

(47) ——, "The Father-and-Son Problem Becomes More Acute in the USSR", *Analysis of Current Developments in the Soviet Union*, No. 257 (January 22, 1963).

(48) ——, "The Decade since Stalin", *Soviet Literature in the Sixties*, ed. Hayward, Crowley (New York, Frederick A. Praeger, 1964).

(49) ——, "Soviet Writers Present a Distorted Picture of Stalin's Personality Cult", *Analysis of Current Developments in the Soviet Union*, No. 4 (1964-1965).

(50) ——, "Soviet Literature at the Beginning of the Second Stage of De-Stalinization", *Studies on the Soviet Union*, No. 4 (1965).

(51) ——, "The Disappearance of the Positive Hero from Soviet Literature", *Analysis of Current Developments in the Soviet Union*, No. 4 (1965-1966).

(52) ——, "Intellectual Opposition to Party Takes New Turn", *Analysis of Current Developments in the Soviet Union*, No. 26 (1965-1966).

(53) Garrard, J. G., "Vladimir Tendrjakov", *The Slavic and East European Journal* (January, 1965).

(54) Gibian, George, "The Revolt of the Moscow Writers", *The New Leader* (August 26, 1957).

(55) ——, *Interval of Freedom: Soviet Literature during the Thaw 1954-1957* (Minneapolis, University of Minnesota Press, 1960).

(56) ——, "New Trends in the Novel: Kazakov, Nagibin, Voronin", *Soviet Survey* (April-June, 1961).

(57) ——, "Soviet Literature during the Thaw", *Literature and Revolution in*

Soviet Russia 1917-1962, ed. Hayward, Labedz (London, Oxford University Press, 1963).

(58) ——, "Themes in Recent Soviet Russian Literature", *Slavic Review* (September, 1964).

(59) Guerney, Bernard Guilbert, "Voices in the Soviet Wilderness", *Saturday Review* (September 28, 1963).

(60) Hayward, Max, "Soviet Literature in the Doldrums", *Problems of Communism* (July-August, 1959).

(61) ——, "Introduction", *Dissonant Voices in Soviet Literature*, ed. Blake, Hayward (New York, Pantheon Books, 1962).

(62) ——, "Conflict and Change in Literature", *Survey* (January, 1963).

(63) ——, "Solzhenitsyn's Place in Contemporary Soviet Literature", *Slavic Review* (September, 1964).

(64) Howe, Irving, "Predicaments of Soviet Writing", *The New Republic* (May 11, 1963).

(65) ——, "Predicaments of Soviet Writing", *The New Republic* (May 18, 1963).

(66) J., M., "Literaturnaja Moskva, Sbornik II, 1956", *Soviet Studies* (January, 1958).

(67) Johnson, Priscilla, "New Heretics in Soviet Writing", *Saturday Review* (May 5, 1962).

(68) ——, *Krushchev and the Arts: The Politics of Soviet Culture, 1962-1964* (Cambridge, Mass., The MIT Press, 1965).

(69) Karavaev, A., "Between Thaw and Freeze in Soviet Literature", *Bulletin, Institute for the Study of the USSR* (March, 1964).

(70) Kersten, Heinz, "Die Sowjetische 'Tauwetter-Literatur'", *Politische Meinung* (January, 1959).

(71) Kobetz, Johann, "Die Sowjetrussische Literatur in Kraftfeld der Wandlungen und Spannungen zwischen dem XX. und XXI. Parteitag der KPdSU", *Sowjet-Studien* (July, 1959).

(72) Kramer, Karl D., "Jurij Kazakov: The Pleasures of Isolation", *The Slavic and East European Journal* (Spring, 1966).

(73) Laber, Jeri, "The Soviet Writer's Search for New Values", *Problems of Communism* (January-February, 1956).

(74) ——, "The Trial Ends", *The New Republic* (March 19, 1966).

(75) Levitzky, Sergey, "Svoboda i bessmertie. O romane Pasternaka 'Doktor Živago'", *Mosty*, II (1950).

(76) Marin, Yu, "The Revival of 'Freethinking' by Young Soviet Writers", *Analysis of Current Developments in the Soviet Union*, No. 247 (November 13, 1962).

(77) Mathewson, Rufus, "The Novel in Russia and the West", *Soviet Literature in the Sixties*, ed. Hayward, Crowley (New York, Frederick A. Praeger, 1964).

(78) Mehnert, Klaus, *Humanismus in der jüngsten Sowjetliteratur?* (Mainz, Verlag der Akademie der Wissenschaften und der Literatur, 1963).

(79) ——, "Moskauer Theater und Kino, Frühjahr 1964", *Osteuropa* (June, 1964).

(80) Meray, Tibor, "Three, Seven, Ace", *Soviet Survey* (April-June, 1961).

(81) Mihajlov, Mihajlo, "Moscow Summer 1964", *The New Leader* (March 29, 1965).

(82) Muchnic, Helen, "Boris Pasternak and the Poems of Yuri Zhivago", *From Gorky to Pasternak: Six Writers in Soviet Russia* (New York, Random House, 1961).

(83) Neander, Irene, "Pasternaks Neuer Roman", *Osteuropa* (December, 1958).

(84) (*The New Republic*), "Writers in the Soviet Union", *The New Republic* (December 11, 1965).

(85) (*The New York Times Magazine*), "The Trial of Sinyavsky and Daniel", *The New York Times Magazine*, trans.- ed. Max Hayward (April 17, 1966).

(86) Rubin, Burtin, "The Shock of Recognition", *Survey* (April, 1963).

(87) ——, "Highlights of the 1962-1963 Thaw", *Soviet Literature in the Sixties*, ed. Hayward, Crowley (New York, Frederick A. Praeger, 1964).

(88) Ruge, Gerd, "Zu Besuch bei sowjetischen Schriftstellern", *Der Monat* (September, 1958).

(89) Scriven, Tom, "The 'Literary Opposition'", *Problems of Communism* (January-February, 1958).

(90) Seduro, Vladimir, "Das Trauma der älteren Generation", *Osteuropa* (January-February, 1958).

(91) Simmons, Ernest J., "Recent Trends in Soviet Literature", *Modern Age* (Fall, 1963).

(92) Slavinsky, M., "Le role de la litterature en URSS dans la 'de-stalinasi-tion'", *Est et Ouest* (November 1-15, 1965).

(93) Slonim, Marc, *Soviet Russian Literature: Writers and Problems* (New York, Oxford University Press, 1964).

(94) (*Soviet Affairs Analysis Service*), "Soviet Youth Breathes Life into the Arts", *Soviet Affairs Analysis Service*, No. 14 (1961-1962).

(95) Steininger, A., "Die Wundertätige", *Osteuropa* (May-June, 1959).

(96) Struve, Gleb, "The Second Congress of Writers", *Problems of Com-*

munism (March-April, 1955).

(97) ——, "Russia Five Years After Stalin", *The New Leader* (April 7, 1958).

(98) ——, "After the Coffee-Break", *The New Republic* (February 2, 1963).

(99) ——, "Soviet Literature in Perspective: Some Unorthodox Reflections", *Soviet Literature in the Sixties*, ed. Hayward, Crowley (New York, Frederick A. Praeger, 1964).

(100) Swayze, Harold, *Political Control of Literature in the USSR, 1946-1959* (Cambridge, Mass., Harvard University Press, 1962).

(101) Szasz, Thomas S., "Toward the Therapeutic State", *The New Republic* (December 11, 1965).

(102) Tesch, Darrel D., *From Soviet to Socialist Patriotism: A Summary of Postwar Literary Developments.* (Oberammergau, Germany, US Army Field Detachment "R" Office of the Ass't. Chief of Staff, Intell. Dept. of the Army, the Army's Institute of Advanced Russian Studies, 1962).

(103) Tikos, Laszlo, "Die andere 'unbewältigte Vergangenheit'", *Osteuropa* (January-February, 1965).

(104) Turkevich, Ludmilla, "Soviet Propaganda and the Rebellious Artist", *Russian Review* (January, 1956).

(105) Vickery, Walter, "The Cult of Optimism", *Political and Ideological Problems of Recent Soviet Literature* (Bloomington, Indiana University Press, 1963).

(106) Whitney, Thomas P., *The New Writing in Russia* (Ann Arbor, University of Michigan Press, 1963).

(107) Wilson, Edmund, "Doctor Life and His Guardian Angel", *The New Yorker* (November 15, 1958).

(108) ——, "Legend and Symbol in 'Doctor Zhivago'", *Encounter* (June, 1959).

(109) Zekulin, Gleb, "Solzhenitsyn's Four Stories", *Soviet Studies* (July, 1964).

TITLES OF 'THAW' WORKS WITH ALIENATED PROTAGONISTS

Abramov, F., *Children of the Pines* (*Zv.*, April, 1962): 19 (1).
——, *Around and About* (*Ne.*, January, 1963): 19, 48 (2).
Agranenko, S., *Under One of the Roofs*: 79 (1).
Aksenov, V., *Colleagues* (*Ju.*, June-July, 1960): 3, 8, 26, 57, 94, 106 (6).
——, *Halfway to the Moon* (*Nim.*, July, 1962): 20, 58, 106, (3).
——, *It's Time, Friend, It's Time* (*M.g.*, April, 1964): 46 (1).
——, *Oranges from Morocco* (*Ju.*, January, 1963): 48 (1).
——, *Papa, What Does That Spell?* (*Nim.*, July, 1962): 20, 28, 106 (3).
——, *Ticket to the Stars* (*Ju.*, June-July, 1961): 8, 16, 24, 26, 35, 48, 57, 67, 76, 78, 93, 94, 106 (13).
——, *When the Bridges Rise*: 8 (1).
——, *The Wild One* (*Ju.*, December, 1964): 31 (1).
Alekin, A., *Butterfly* (*Ju.*, May, 1960): 11 (1).
Alekseev, N., *The Heirs*: 42 (1).
Alešin, S., *Alone* (*Te.*, August, 1956): 55, 100 (2).
——, *The Ward* (*Te.*, November, 1962): 58 (1).
Andreev, A., *Urge for Life* (*Ok.*, January-February, 1958): 1 (1).
Antonov, S., *The Empty Race*: 94 (1).
——, *The Questionnaire*: 70 (1).
Arbuzov, A., *Somewhere They Are Waiting for Us* (*Te.*, January, 1963) 48 (1).
Aržak, N., (pseudonym for Julij Danièl') *Hands* (1963): 34, 85 (2).
——, *The Man from MINAP* (1963): 34, 93 (2).
——, *This Is Moscow Speaking* (1962): 34, 35, 65, 85, 93 (5).
Baklanov, G., *An Inch of Land* (*N.m.*, May-June, 1959): 48 (1).
Balter, B., *Goodbye, Boys* (*Ju.*, August, 1962): 45 (1).
Bednyj, B., *The Girls* (*Zn.*, July-September, 1961): 24 (1).
Belenskij, G., *You Aren't Alone* (*Mo.*, November, 1960): 24 (1).
Berggol'c, O., *Day Stars*: 50 (1).
Bondarev, Ju., *Forget Who You Are*: 77 (1).

——, *Silence* (*N.m.*, March·May, 1962): 15, 28, 44, 76, 79, 81, 86, 92, 93, 98 (10).

Bubennov, M., *Eagle Steppe* (*Ok.*, July-October, 1959): 4 (1).

Čerepaxova, E., *Public Favorite*: 94 (1).

Davydova, N., *The Love of Engineer Izatov* (*N.m.*, January-March, 1960): 4, 10 (2).

Dementev, Ju., *I Enter Life*: 102 (1).

Dombrovskij, Ju., *Preserver of the Past* (*N.m.*) 49 (1).

Doroš, E., *Arid Summer*: 26 (1).

Dubov, N., *A Hard Test* (*N.m.*, September-October, 1960): 3, 11 (2).

Dudincev, V., *A New Year's Tale* (*N.m.*, January, 1960): 5, 10, 24, 35 (4).

——, *Not by Bread Alone* (*N.m.*, August-November, 1956): 1, 5, 7, 24, 35, 39, 42, 48, 55, 61, 70, 71, 81, 88, 89, 92, 93, 97, 100, 105 (20).

——, *The Unknown Soldier* (unpublished): 31, 81 (2).

Èrenburg, I., *The Thaw* (*Zn.*, May, 1954 and April, 1956): 5, 24, 26, 36, 39, 42, 55, 60, 73, 93, 96, 100, 104, 105 (14).

Evdokinov, N., *The Sinner* (*Zn.*, December, 1960): 13 (1).

Gladilin, A., *The First Day of the New Year* (*Ju.*, February, 1963): 45, 58 (2).

——, *Smoke in the Eyes* (*Ju.*, December, 1959): 10, 94 (2).

Golosovskij, I., *I Want to Believe*: 81 (1).

Gorbunov, N., *The Mistake*: 55 (1).

Gorodeckij, S., *Man of Action*: 48 (1).

Granin, D., *After the Wedding* (*Ok.*, July-September, 1958): 71 (1).

——, *I Go into the Storm* (*Zn.*, August-October, 1962): 18, 48 (2).

——, *One's Own Opinion* (*N.m.*, August, 1956): 1, 24, 26, 55, 70, 71, 77, 93, 97, 100, 105 (11).

——, *Those Who Seek*: 51 (1).

Grekova, I., *Summer in the City* (*N.m.*, August, 1965): 51 (1).

Grossman, V., *The Elk*: 69 (1).

Gulia, G., *The Chestnut House* (*Ok.*, September, 1960): 11 (1).

Issakov, I., *The Wager of the Flying Hollander*: 15 (1).

Ivanter, N., *It's August Again* (*N.m.*, August-September, 1959): 4, 9, 26, 100, (4).

Jampol'skij, B., *Tales of Beasts and Birds* (*L.M. II*, 1956): 66 (1).

Jašin, A., *Levers* (*L.M. II* 1956): 24, 35, 42, 48, 54, 67, 71, 93, 97, 100, 105 (11).

——, *Wedding at Vologda* (*N.m.*, December, 1963): 19, 48, (2).

Kabo, L., *On a Difficult March* (*N.m.*, November-December, 70, 71, 100 (3).

Kalinin, A., *Harsh Field* (*M.g.*): 10 (1).

Karpov, E., *The Blue Winds* (*Ne.*, June, 1962): 69 (1).

Kaverin, V., *A Piece of Glass* (*N.m.*, August, 1960): 11 (1).

——, *Quests and Hopes* (*L.M. II*, 1956): 26, 42, 54, 55, 66, 70, 71, 89, 97 (9).

——, *Seven Unclean Pairs* (*N.m.*, February, 1962: 15 (1).

Kazakevič, E., *By Daylight* (*N.m.*, July, 1961): 15 (1).

——, *The House on the Square*: 42, 48, 93 (3).

Kazakov, Ju., *Adam and Eve* (*Mo.*, August, 1962): 35, 58, 72, 77, 106 (5).

——, *Along the Road*: 72 (1).

——, *Antlers* (1958): 24, 72, (2).

——, *Arcturus* (*Mo.*, August, 1957): 3, 106 (2).

——, *At the Station*: 11, 58, 106 (3).

——, *Autumn in the Oak Woods* (*Zn.*, September, 1961): 72 (1).

——, *Blue and Green* (1956): 24, 56, 72 (3).

——, *A House under a Precipice* (*Zn.*, April, 1957): 5, 56, 93, 106 (4).

——, *Kabiasy* (*Zn.*, September, 1961): 72 (1).

——, *Manka*: 56, 72, 93, 106 (4).

——, *Morning Calm*: 72 (1).

——, *Night*: 5 (1).

——, *The Old Men*: 72 (1).

——, *On the Island*: 56, 72, 93, 106 (4).

——, *Pomorka*: 72 (1).

——, *The Renegade* (*Ok.*, July, 1959): 5, 9, 35, 58, 61, 72, 77, 102, 106 (9).

——, *The Smell of Bread* (*T.s.*, 1961): 70, 72 (2).

——, *Teddy*: 72 (1).

——, *There Goes a Dog* (*Zn.*, September, 1961): 16, 72, 92 (3).

——, *To the City* (*T.s.*, 1961): 16, 26, 72, 93 (4).

——, *The Wanderer*: 72 (1).

Koneckij, V., *Tomorrow's Cares* (*Zn.*, February, 1961): 14 (1).

Konovalov, V., *Sources* (*Ok.*, January-March, 1959): 9 (1).

Kornejčuk, A., *Why the Stars Smiled* (*Zn.*, January, 1958): 52 (1).

——, *Wings* (*N.m.*, November, 1954): 36, 55, 61, 73, 102, 105 (6).

Koževnikov, A., *The Vision* (*N.m.*, July, 1960): 11 (1).

Koževnikov, V., *Be Acquainted, Baluev!* (*Zn.*, April-May, 1960): 4, 11 (2).

Kozlov, V., *An Awkward Fellow* (*Ne.*, July, 1962): 48 (1).

Kuprijanov, I., *My Brother* (*Ok.*, November, 1961): 50 (1).

Kuznecov, A., *Continuation of a Legend* (*Ju.*, July, 1957): 11, 48, 57, 71, 94 (5).

——, *The Girls* (*Ju.*, August, 1960): 11, 94 (2).

Leonov, L., *The Russian Forest* (1953): 55, 100, 104 (3).

Lipatov, V., *The Mainstream* (*N.m.*, April-May, 1961): 14 (1).

L'vov, S., *Save Our Souls* (*Ju.*, February, 1960): 12 (1).

L'vova, K., *Elena* (*Al.*, No. 19, 1955): 105 (1).

Maksimov, V., *A Man Survives*: 43 (1).

Mal'cev, E., *Enter Every Home* (*Mo.*, October-December, 1960): 13 (1).

Mariengov, A., *The Crown Prince*: 46 (1).

Mdivani, G., *Alarming Night* (*Te.*, December, 1958): 26 (1).

Medynskij, G., *Honor* (*Mo.*, April-May and October-November, 1959):
4, 9, 100 (3).

Metter, I., *Two Days* (*Mo.*, June, 1960): 4 (1).

Mixalkov, S., *The Forgotten Trench*: 79 (1).

Mikulina, E., *Dupljanka* (*N.s.*, June, 1963): 45 (1).

Moskovkin, V., *How Are You, Semen?*: 71 (1).

——, *Varik Barks at the Moon* (*Ju.*, May, 1960): 11 (1).

Nagibin, Ju., *Before the Holiday*: 102 (1).

——, *The Conversation*: 56, 102 (2).

——, *Echoes*: 24 (1).

——, *The Xazar Ornament* (*L.M. II*, 1956): 54, 71, 89 (3).

——, *Light in the Window* (*L.M. II*, 1956): 54, 66, 100, 105, 106 (5).

——, *The Man and the Road* (*Zn.*, December, 1958): 5 (1).

——, *The Old Turtle*: 1 (1).

——, *The Rocky Threshold*: 56 (1).

——, *The Winter Oak* (1953): 5 (1).

Narymov, M. (pseudonym for Mixail Aleksandrovič Narica-Nary-
mov), *The Unsung Song* (Gr., No. 48, 1960): 25, 78, 93 (3).

Nekrasov, V., *In the Native City* (*N.m.*, November-December, 1954):
5, 55, 93 (3).

——, *Kira Georgievna* (*N.m.*, July, 1961): 5, 7, 15, 24, 26, 35, 48, 77, 78,
93 (10).

——, *The Second Night* (*N.m.*, May, 1960): 11, 24 (2).

Nikitin, V., *The Melting Earth*: 94 (1).

Nikolaeva, G., *Battle on the Way* (*Ok.*, March, May, July, 1957): 55,
71, 92 (3).

Nikulin, L., *With New Happiness* (*Mo.*, October, 1961): 50 (1).

Nilin, P., *Cruelty* (*Zn.*, November-December, 1956): 1, 24, 70, 71, 93 (5).

——, *Probation*: 93 (1).

Obuxova, L., *The Splinter* (*Ne.*, January-March, 1961): 13 (1).

Okudžava, B., *Good Luck, Schoolboy!* (*T.s.*, 1961): 6, 8, 15, 26 (4).

Ovečkin, V., *A Difficult Spring*: 5, 57, 102 (3).

——, *District Workdays* (*N.m.*, September, 1952): 5, 93, 102 (3).

Palman, V., *Skirmish* (*S.R.*, December 2, 1962): 47 (1).

Panferov, F., *In the Name of the Young* (*Ok.*, July-August, 1960): 5, 11 (2).

——, *Reflections*: 71 (1).

——, *Volga Mother River* (August-September, 1953): 93 (1).

Panova, V., *How Are You, Fellow?*: 21 (1).

——, *Seasons of the Year* (*N.m.*, November-December, 1953): 5, 24, 70, 73, 93, 97, 100, 104, 105 (9).

Pasternak, B., *Doctor Živago* (1957): 24, 39, 55, 75, 78, 82, 83, 105, 107, 108 (10).

Pogodin, N., *Living Flowers*: 32, 93 (2).

——, *Loyalty* (*Ok.*, August, 1963): 69 (1).

——, *Petrarch's Sonnet* (*L.M. II*, 1956): 26, 55, 66, 70, 100, 105 (6).

Poluxin, O., *Whirlpool*: 12 (1).

Rozen, A., *Happy Age* (*Zv.*, September, 1959): 9 (1).

Rozov, V., *ABCDE* (*Ju.*, September, 1961): 16, 26, 41, 48, 94 (5).

——, *Before Supper* (*Te.*, January, 1963): 21, 79, 106 (3).

——, *Good Luck*: 53 (1).

——, *In Good Time*: 106 (1).

——, *The Immortals*: 106 (1).

——, *In Search of Happiness*: 106 (1).

——, *On the Wedding Day* (*N.m.*, March, 1964): 79 (1).

——, *Unequal Struggle* (*Ju.*, March, 1960): 10, 32 (2).

Rybakov, A., *The Adventures of Kroš* (*Te.*, September, 1961): 48 (1).

——, *The Last Two Weeks* (*Zv.*, January, 1965): 88 (1).

Saltykova, A., *Maša is Twenty-Seven Years Old* (*Ok.*, April-June, 1959): 4 (1).

Salynskij, A., *The Forgotten Friend*: 70 (1).

Sartakov, S., *Don't Give Up the Queen* (*Ok.*, December, 1960): 4 (1).

Semenov, Ju., ... *In Fulfillment of One's Professional Duty* (*Ju.*, January-February, 1962): 16 (1).

Semin, L., *One Against One* (*Ne.*, March, 1963): 48, 92 (2).

Šestov, M., *The Golden Ring*: 71 (1).

Ševkunenko, Ju., *Serežka from Malaja Bronnaja*: 48 (1).

Šoloxov, M., *Virgin Soil Upturned* (*Zv.*, 1959-1960): 81 (1).

Štolikov, G., *The Gates of Il'ič* (film, 1962): 58, 81, 103 (3).

Simanko, M., *The Temptation of Fragi* (*N.m.*, September, 1960): 11 (1).

Simonov, K., *The Living and the Dead*: 10, 93 (2).

Snegov, S., *Go to the End* (*Zn.*, April-May, 1962): 15, (1).

Sofronov, A., *Integrity* (*Mo.*, October, 1961): 50 (1).

Solženicyn, A., *For the Good of the Cause* (*N.m.*, July, 1963): 23, 29, 40, 44, 63, 68, 87, 93, 109 (9).

——, *Incident at Krečetovka Station* (*N.m.*, January, 1963): 19, 40, 48, 109 (4).

——, *Matrena's Home* (*N.m.*, January, 1963): 19, 24, 35, 40, 44, 63, 68, 87, 93, 109 (10).

——, *One Day in the Life of Ivan Denisovič* (November, 1962): 5, 7, 17, 24, 28, 35, 40, 44, 58, 63, 64, 68, 77, 78, 81, 86, 90, 92, 93, 103, 109 (21).

Stukalov, O., *Wide-open Windows* (*Te.*, September, 1962): 47 (1).

Tarsis, V., *Red and Black*: 59, 93 (2).

——, *Tale of a Bluebottle Fly* (*Gr.*, December, 1962): 35, 59, 93, 99, 101, 103 (6).

Tendrjakov, V., *An Extraordinary Event* (*N.iR.*, July, August, October, 1961): 16, 48, 78 (3).

——, *The Fall of Ivan Čuprova* (1955): 26 (1).

——, *The Miracle Worker* (*Zn.*, May, 1958): 71, 95 (2).

——, *On the Heels of Time* (*M.g.*, October-December, 1959): 10, 53 (2).

——, *Potholes* (1956): 53 (1).

——, *Rainy Weather* (1954): 53 (1).

——, *Short Circuit* (*Zn.*, March, 1962): 16, 48, 78, 91, 106 (5).

——, *Three, Seven, Ace* (*N.m.*, March, 1960): 10, 24, 26, 53, 61, 80, 81, 93 (8).

——, *The Trial* (*N.m.*, March, 1961): 14, 24, 48, 53, 77, 94 (6).

——, *A Tight Knot*: 81 (1).

——, *Unsuited* (1954): 53, 57 (2).

——, *The White Flag* (*M.g.*, December, 1962: collaboration with Ikramov): 19 (1).

Terc, A. (pseudonym for Andrej Sinjavskij), *Fantastic Stories* (1961): 25, 35, 64, 93 (4).

——, *The Trial Begins* (*Ku.*, May, 1960): 24, 25, 35, 64, 74, 84, 85, 91, 93 (9).

Tevekelian, V., *Beyond the River Moskva* (*Mo.*, February-April, 1959): 4, 9 (2).

——, *Granite Does Not Melt* (*Mo.*, February-April, 1962): 48 (1).

Uspenskaja, ——, *Our Summer*: 104 (1).

Val'ceva, A., *Apartment No. 13* (Mo., January, 1957): 1, 42, 70 (3).

Vasilevskij, V., *The Knot*: 5 (1).

Vojnovič, V., *Here We Live* (*N.m.*, January, 1961): 14, (1).

——, *I Want to Be Honest* (*N.m.*, February, 1963): 20, 48, 93 (3).

Volodin, A., *The Elder Sister*: 41 (1).

——, *Factory Girl*: 57, 71, 93 (3).

Voronin, S., *The Blue Danube*: 56 (1).

——, *Futile Honor*: 71 (1).

——, *On Native Ground* (*Ne.*, September, 1959): 10, 48, 100 (3).

——, *Nocturnal Fears* (*L.R.*, May, 1963): 90 (1).

——, *Return Home*: 56 (1).

——, *Two Lives* (*Ne.*, October, 1961): 50 (1).

Zeleranskij, N., *Miška, Sereža, and I* (*Ju.*, July-August, 1959: collaboration with B. Larin): 94 (1).

Ždanov, N., *Journey Home* (*L.M. II*, 1956): 24, 48, 54, 66, 71, 93, 104 (7).

Žestev, M., *Tat'jana Tarxanova* (*Zn.*, January, 1962): 44, 81 (2).

Zlatogorov, M., *He Who Stands Alongside* (*Ju.*, October, 1961): 50 (1).

Zorin, L., *Guests* (*Te.*, February, 1954): 5, 24, 36, 42, 48, 55, 61, 70, 73, 93, 100, 105 (12).

SYNOPSES OF SELECTED PLOTS SHOWING
CHARACTER ALIENATION

V. Panova, *Seasons of the Year*

Gennadij Kuprijanov: Sense of fulfillment through work (2).

Gennadij Leonidovič Kuprijanov moves from job to job. None seems to satisfy him. He didn't like school and trained to be a chauffeur after his grammar school education. He served as such under a general while in the military service, then performed various jobs after his discharge. Though none of them appealed to him, he still wanted his own car, a good salary, and an important position. He nonetheless expected them to come to him without effort and did whatever he pleased. When things didn't turn out as he wished, he came to resent life, which he felt was deceptive.

Gennadij Kuprijanov: Trust and approval of society and employers, trustworthy friends and associates (4, 10).

While visiting his mother on New Year's Eve, the same Gennadij has appropriated a car belonging to his employer and driven it some 200 kilometers. For this he is subsequently discharged. As a youth he had almost been excluded from the *Komsomol* for failure to perform certain services. His mother had interceded, however, and helped him write a statement which enabled him to remain in the organization. He has meanwhile acquired friends who change jobs frequently and do nothing when unemployed. As the tenant of Zinaida Ljubimova and her son, Saša, he discovers that they have won ten thousand rubles in government bonds bequeathed to them by Zinaida's deceased husband. He and an acquaintance, Cycarkin, subsequently visit Saša and ask to see the bonds, for which they offer him 15,000 rubles. They finally prevail upon Saša, Who then takes their money to the police and reports the transaction. The bonds have been purchased for more than their value so that Cycarkin, as the director of a government base, can have a pretext for spending money he has embezzled. Cycarkin, who is something of a benefactor to Gennadij, has already given him money and provided him with his present job as the director of an auto pool. When Gennadij reports that Saša has gone to the police, Cycarkin seems undisturbed. However, he requires Gennadij to sign a receipt for the money he next lends him. At first Gennadij decides not to spend the money, but then does so. While on an unearned vacation Gennadij runs out of funds and wires Cycarkin, who finances his return trip. After Gennadij returns, Cycarkin's accomplice, a young boy, asks that Gennadij come to them. He is then told that he owes them an additional service — that he must serve a ten-year prison sentence in order to cover their crimes, for which they will pay him. Gennadij refuses. He is then shown the receipt he had previously signed, since countersigned by another party now criminally implicated. He must go to prison in any event. They want him to confess to having burned a warehouse which was under Cycarkin's supervision. He protests, and they let him go. Just as he reaches his parents' home, however, Cycarkin's young accomplice, who has followed him, shoots him in the back.

Gennadij Kuprijanov: Members of Gennadij's family (4, 5).

As he pays a surprise visit to his mother on New Year's Eve, Gennadij is relieved to learn that his sister, Jul'ka, and his former wife, Larisa, are not at home. He does not inquire about them and speaks condescendingly to his mother even though she sends him part of her salary. He had married Larisa without receiving his father's permission, then soon grew disenchanted with her. Although expecting a child, she in turn threatened a divorce because of his abuse of her and his failure to live at home. She finally obtained an abortion, which caused Gennadij's family to sympathize with her. They even insisted that she stay with them and that Gennadij leave. Since that time he has not invited his mother to visit him and has begun an affair with his landlady, Ljubimova. He will not discuss the affair with his mother and only visits her at work. Prior to his vacation he again approaches his mother for money. She finally takes a stand against him, disapproving his way of life and accusing him of living off others. She reproaches him for addressing her in the polite form and tells him not to see her again until he becomes a man. On the same occasion he encounters Larisa and begins to flirt with her, thinking he can win her back. Instead she asks him to consent to a divorce and tells him he is stupid and crude, then leaves. His mother reluctantly sends him money during his vacation after he wires her that he has sold his watch.

Dorofea Kuprijanova: Her son, Gennadij (5).

On New Year's Eve Dorofea Kuprijanova observes her sleeping son, Gennadij, and realizes how incomprehensible he has become to her. Later that year as she hostesses an outstanding Bulgarian Communist patriot, Popova, she encounters Gennadij on the street. He and two other young men make disdainful comments about the young Bulgarian girl who is Popova's interpreter. Dorofea is shocked at his behavior and does not acknowledge him.

Larisa Kuprijanova: Her husband, Gennadij (4).

Larisa Kuprijanova has a date on New Year's Eve, which pleases Dorofea. Gennadij has ignored her since he was told to live elsewhere. Before then he had insulted her in front of others and spent his nights away from home. Later, when he again pays attention to her, she asks him for a divorce.

Zinaida Ljubimova: Her lover, Gennadij (4).

Saša has come to the Kuprijanovs, inquiring about Gennadij for his mother, Zinaida Ljubimova, whom Gennadij is obviously avoiding. Even when Dorofea later reminds Gennadij of his obligation to Zinaida, he remains indifferent. After going to live with Zinaida and forming an alliance with her, he had ceased to pay his rent and even scolded her for her inability to pay for the electricity. His attention to her then became erratic.

Saša Ljubimov: His mother, Zinaida (5).

In his protest against the liason between his mother and Gennadij, Saša Ljubimov leaves school and becomes a construction worker. Saša resents the manner in which Gennadij has, from the very first, appropriated their rooms, making them clean up after him and waking them when he returns home at night. His mother has begun to dress better in order to please Gennadij and even saves him the best food. Saša finally avoids being at home, while Gennadij, learning that Saša has reported the bond transaction, insists that Zinaida choose between them. She is obviously tormented to lose Gennadij, and Saša leaves.

Bortaševič: Integrity, conscience, social responsibility, self-respect (10).

A certain Red'kovskij is being expelled from the Party. As director of a building trust he had constructed his own *dacha*. A mason who had refused to cooperate and a plasterer who had complained were both subsequently dismissed. Red'kovskij had also bribed various Party officials. At the trial, Bortaševič eloquently denounces the defendant, not so much for his appropriation of resources as for his corruption of others. Bortaševič himself had become an important official in a government trust after the war. His secretary, Nadežda, had helped him adapt to his new responsibilities. She had influenced him to salve his principles and do business with NÈP men. He finally succumbed to her wiles, divorced his plain wife, and married Nadežda instead. She then pressured him to become indebted in order to buy new furniture, clothes, *etc.* She induced him to sell government materials to private persons in order to obtain a large apartment. Then she suggested that he borrow from his chief accountant, who willingly complied. With this money they bought her a fur coat, *etc.*, while she pretended that her father had won money for them. The accountant refused to be repaid and even offered more money until it became impossible to pay him back. Meanwhile, Bortaševič was constrained to sign papers which his accountant brought him and to hire and fire people the accountant recommended, not realizing that behind the scene his employees were conducting shady business. He did not even question finding money in his desk drawer, in order not to admit to himself that he was implicated in plundering the state. Later he was transferred to another city, but brought his accountant with him. He continued to follow the latter's advice, even sending to trial a number of workers against whom the accountant testified. Eventually people begin to gossip about Bortaševič's betrayal of his workers. He is no longer able to sleep well and, since the trial of Red'kovskij, can no longer delude himself that he is a good communist. He is also aware that Cycarkin has burned a certain warehouse in order to destroy incriminating evidence. Now Bortaševič even longs for death. Finally, on the day of his daughter Katja's birthday, he learns that Cycarkin and others have been arrested. After returning home and as investigators arrive, he locks the door of his room and shoots himself. He is found wounded and taken to the hospital.

Bortaševič: Support of friends (4).

On the morning of the day he shoots himself, Bortaševič is puzzled both by the failure of a Party official to respond to his remarks and by the behavior of his friend Čurkin's secretary, who promises to connect him by phone then calls him back and says that Čurkin is out. After Bortaševič's death, his daughter is visited by an actress, Vera Zajceva, who requests his wife's new address in order to be cleared of scandal involving his name. When Katja says she is unable to provide the address, Zajceva, who has been Bortaševič's mistress, berates her and casts aspersions on both Katja and Katja's father.

Bortaševič: His wife, Nadežda (4).

After Bortaševič realizes how his wife has implicated him in others' crimes, he begins to resent her. He also senses that she could betray him. Meanwhile she has begun to live her own life, spending months away on cures, *etc.* In turn Bortaševič resorts to occasional intrigues with his secretaries. Finally, Nadežda herself spreads rumors about her unsuccessful marriage, and Bortaševič realizes that she is preparing for a separation in order to be found guiltless in case he is apprehended. This makes him all the more vengeful.

Sergej Bortaševič: Respect for his father (5).

Sergej Bortaševič has beat up a friend, Fedorčuk, who had imputed that his father is involved in a scandal. Sergej feels that his friend is dishonest but eventually discovers that he was telling the truth.

Nadežda Bortaševič: Her children (5).

Soon after Bortaševič's funeral, Nadežda goes to live with relatives. Her children, Katja and Sergej, refuse to attend her, arguing that she had not accompanied her husband to his grave on the day of his funeral.

Čurkin: Integrity, responsibility to society and friends (10).

Čurkin, who is in charge of housing, has promised friends and various important persons apartments under construction. Deserving people in real need are consequently overlooked. Dorofea discovers this and threatens to inform on Čurkin if he does not assign the apartments more equitably. He has found housing for a number of Bortaševič's friends, including Vera Zajceva. After Bortaševič's death, Dorofea shames Čurkin into visiting Bortaševič's children and looking after their needs.

Sergej Bortaševič: Success in love (4).

Sergej, who has a physical disability, meets an attractive girl and wonders if such a woman could love a man like himself without pitying him. He sees her infrequently thereafter.

Saša Ljubimov: Katja Bortaševič (4).

Saša Ljubimov is infatuated with Katja Bortaševič but is timid about making this known, fearing that she would not care for him. After her father's death, Katja quits school and works in construction under Saša. He is happy for her presence. He discovers however that another man waits for her after work each day. She eventually marries the latter and returns to her studies.

L. Zorin, *Guests*

Pokrovskij: Petr Kirpičev, the bureaucracy (8).

A journalist, Pavel Pavlovič Trubin, has arranged to meet with a local citizen, Mixail Aleksandrovič Pokrovskij, at the home of the elder Kirpičevs. Pokrovskij, who is originally from Voronezh, had heard of Trubin through journalist-relatives and has sought his help. He had been a member of the bar for thirty years at Voronezh and was asked in January to assist in the defense at an important trial, replacing a lawyer who had suddenly taken ill. As a number of perplexing facts came to his attention, he and two other defense lawyers were released from the case and were also incriminated with advising their defendant in such a way as to deceive the court and shed doubt upon the verdict. The case is that of Ekaterina Ševcova. Pokrovskij argues that he could not be implicated since he was only involved in the case in its final stages. He was nonetheless expelled from the bar. He then appealed to Krasnoščekov of the republic's ministry, who was unsympathetic and saw no reason for repealing the expulsion. He next turned to Petr Kirpičev in Moscow, who simply referred him back to Krasnoščekov. Pokrovskij suspects that the Ševcova case was manipulated from the beginning. Trubin then indicates that he is already acquainted with the case and has arranged for Pokrovskij to inform Aleksej Kirpičev about the affair. Aleksej, the elder Kirpičev, is a deputy of the Supreme Soviet and a famous revolutionary. Sergej — the school teacher son of Aleksej's son, Petr, and Trubin's former acquaintance — lives with his grandparents; at Trubin's urging, he prevails upon his father to grant Pokrovskij another interview. Pokrovskij then asks Petr to intercede for him. While Pokrovskij goes away satisfied and Sergej remains hopeful that his father will help, Trubin is skeptical of a favorable outcome. Finally, Pokrovskij obtains an interview with Aleksej. Meanwhile Petr is overheard on the telephone discussing a rumor that Krasnoščekov will be transferred to Union offices in Moscow. In order to curry the latter's favor, Petr advises the party with whom he is speaking to take care of Pokrovskij and his associates once and for all. The others then denounce him for his overheard remarks, while he vindictively vows that Pokrovskij's cause is futile.

Petr Kirpičev: Social justice (10).

In his confrontation with Trubin, Petr makes snide allusions to irresponsible, sensation-seeking journalists. He cites as a case in point a particular journalist named Pticyn who tried to make trouble over a certain affair. Trubin responds that he knows Pticyn and surmises that the affair in question is probably the Ševcova case. He affirms that Pticyn is a very just individual, whereas the Ševcova case is one of the dirtiest, involving arbitrary interference on both local and higher levels. He then describes the case and accuses Petr's associates of being more interested in the dignity of their position than in the fate of individuals. Later — thinking they are alone — Petr, his wife, and son, Tema, exult in the prospect of their materialistic future.

Elder Kirpičevs and their daughter, Varvara: Their son and brother, Petr (4, 5).

Aleksej Kirpičev is a famous revolutionary, a patriot of socialist society, whose wife and daughter share his altruistic idealism. When they learn of the true circumstances surrounding Pokrovskij, they turn against Petr. They also realize that, self-sacrificing as they themselves have always been, they have overindulged Petr and thus contributed to his corruption. Varvara becomes attracted to Trubin for the very qualities so absent in her brother.

Nina Konstantinovna Kirpičeva: Her husband, Petr (4).

Soon after their arrival at his parents', Nina sarcastically remarks to Petr that he must be very fond of his youngest son, Tema, since he seemed even more eager than Tema himself to have Tema's girl friend, Nika, accompany them. Petr quickly explains that it was his prerogative, not Tema's, to invite her. Later Nika asks Tema if Petr really loves Nina. When they are finally alone, Petr becomes familiar with Nika, embraces her, on the pretext that he wants her to marry Tema. She tells him she is frightened of the way he looks at her. Nina then warns her to be wary of Petr and not end up as she has. Nika decides not to return to Moscow in their company, and Petr prevents Tema from going to her to find out why.

Sergej Kirpičev: His father, Petr (5).

Sergej tells Trubin that his mother died shortly before the end of the war and his father then married Nina, with whom he had been living for some time. Therefore Sergej did not return to live with them. Sergej later reprimands Petr for infidelity to his mother. They also disagree about Aleksej. Petr says that times have changed requiring new approaches, while Sergej rejoins that their goal is just the same. When he overhears Petr on the telephone, he expresses his disillusion in the latter.

Petr Kirpičev: His father, Aleksej (5).

After Pokrovskij speaks with Aleksej, Petr also asks to see him, but Aleksej excuses himself as not feeling well. Having overheard Petr's telephone conversation, Aleksej then denounces Petr for betraying a man whose good character he (Aleksej) has just confirmed.

Tema Kirpičev: His girlfriend, Nika (4).

As Nika becomes disillusioned with Petr, she also becomes indifferent to Tema.

I. Èrenburg, *The Thaw*[1]

Dmitrij Koroteev: Truth, integrity (10).

At a club meeting of local factory workers in a Volga industrial town, Dmitrij Koroteev is asked to comment on a particular novel. He expresses a conservative opinion, appearing critical of an incident in the novel involving an extra-marital love affair. A young girl refutes his view, maintaining that the novel conveys genuine emotional experiences. In his mind he regrets having been so platitudinous. After the meeting he still muses about the hypocrisy of his remarks, then dismisses them. In Part Two, after he is married to Lena, he gives them both concern about his tendency to become confused and to conform to the expectations of others. They have since discussed his remarks at the club meeting, where Lena had been present. She reminds him that he denied the reality of the hero's feelings, although they were his own at the time. He cannot explain why he had spoken that way. Grigorij Savčenko, a fellow engineer, has begun to wonder if Dmitrij is not a coward for not defending Evgenij Sokolovskij, the factory's chief designer, before the management and not voting against the latter's reprimand. When Savčenko accosts

---

[1] Only the first part of this work was referred to by as many as five critics in the foregoing survey (Appendix B). The second part was generally ignored or disparaged as inferior to the first. Since there is considerable continuity between both parts and both involve essentially the same characters however, the accompanying synopses cover the action in both.

Dmitrij, the latter is evasive, and Savčenko thinks Dmitrij must have feared being in the minority. Later Dmitrij tells Lena not to worry about some of the things he says, that he hasn't gotten used to his work since returning from a recent cure.

Dmitrij Koroteev: Emotional self-confidence, trust in others (4).

After speaking at the readers' club, Dmitrij reflects about his step-father's arrest in 1936 and how he (Dmitrij) was then ousted from the Komsomol and avoided by his friends. He recalls the young girl whom he loved during the war and who was unexpectedly killed at its end during the occupation of Leipzig. This had soured him on marriage. After his graduation from an engineering institute he had been promised a position there, but another man had pulled strings and got the job himself. On a later occasion he meets Lena Žuravleva at the theatre and begins to reveal his feelings for her, but she discourages him and he decides to repress himself thereafter. Even after they have married (Part Two), Lena senses a barrier between them.

Lena Žuravleva: Her husband, Ivan (4).

Lena Žuravleva becomes emotionally estranged from her husband, Ivan, when he reacts unkindly to a Jewish physician, Vera Šerer. He continues thereafter to disillusion her. She stays with him only for the sake of their daughter, Šura, until they finally separate. After marrying Dmitrij (Part Two), Lena receives letters from Ivan, who has since been transferred elsewhere, asking to have their daughter, Šura, for the summer. She fears he will alienate Šura's affection and puts him off. Finally Ivan announces that he is coming for Šura.

Lena Žuravleva: Emotional Integrity (4, 10).

Lena becomes disturbed when she first realizes that she is in love with Dmitrij, who in the past had been a frequent guest in her and Ivan's home. She becomes aware of her feelings after the readers' club meeting. Intending to tell Ivan, she long procrastinates doing so, finding one pretext or another. She also vists Vera, betraying her anxiety without disclosing her problem. At last she tells Ivan, who agrees to a separation. She nonetheless avoids revealing her true feelings to Dmitrij.

Lena Žuravleva: Her mother, Antonina Pavlovna Kalašnikova (5).

While perplexed about her relationship to Ivan, Lena dares not write her mother about it, fearing this would disappoint the latter, who is also a *kolkhoz* chairman. Although she has always admired her mother, Lena has never been able to confide in her. Later a young alcoholic factory worker is sent to her mother's *kolkhoz* and informs his mother of Lena's separation. The other woman maliciously informs Antonina, Lena's mother, who then visits Lena and reproaches her for not confiding.

Lena Žuravleva: Ekaterina Alekseeva Dmitrieva (8).

In Part II, Lena, who is a school teacher, clashes with her new principal, Ekaterina Alekseeva Dmitrieva, who herself has had a tragic personal life and been abandoned by her husband. She in turn criticizes Lena for the latter's unsuccessful first marriage and accuses her of not having adequate control in her classes. At a teachers' meeting she alludes to the case of a student who has carved initials in a desk top. Lena then discovers that the offender is one of her own precocious students. He expresses his regret, and she promises not to divulge his confidence. Word reaches Dmitrieva, however, who then publicly chastizes Lena for condescending to the students and vows to complain to the school board.

Ivan Žuravlev: Unpleasant reality, genuine emotional values (6).

Ivan Žuravlev is always optimistic about the unpleasant lot of others. When the chief engineer reported that his wife was dying of cancer, Ivan told him not to grieve, that she would get better. Whenever his workers' inadequate housing is brought to his attention, he argues that it is better than he has seen in Moscow, *etc.* and speaks encouragingly without doing anything to improve the situation. He has never regarded Dmitrij as a rival, presuming that he can trust Lena's good sense. He remains fairly indifferent even after Lena announces her intention to leave him. It is only after his own position is in jeopardy that he becomes worried about the problems that have been bothering others. When Dmitrij fails to endorse his denunciation of Sokolovskij, he begins to think that Dmitrij and Sokolovskij are plotting against him and for the first time suspects Dmitrij's interest in Lena. After a storm destroys much of the workers' housing and he becomes liable, he imagines that the forces of nature are opposing him personally.

Andrej Puxov: His son, Volodja, and his daughter, Sonja (5).

Andrej Ivanonovič Puxov was forced by his wife to retire from school teaching for the sake of his health. He has worked effectively with other youth but cannot influence his own son, Volodja, who mocks him. He is also unable to communicate with his daughter, Sonja. He is distressed that Volodja gives lip service to the ideological line in art but ridicules it in private. While Sonja reprimands him for risking his health to assist his past students, Andrej vainly urges her to lead a more assertive life of her own.

Volodja Puxov: Artistic integrity (3, 10).

After leaving art school Volodja had been assigned a studio, which was then taken from him when at an artists' meeting he failed to win an award and became abusive. This taught him to fawn before his superiors. Now he only paints propagandistic works, which he himself disdains, for the money they bring. In Part II, he is bothered by the contrast between his own work and that of his friend, Saburov, a true esthete. He rationalizes however that genuine art is not rewarded in the artist's lifetime and that his art is therefore more satisfying. Still he envies Saburov's creative freedom and personal accomplishment. Finally he attends a discussion of both his and Saburov's paintings. He is angered by praise of Saburov and publicly castigates Saburov's art. When he then tries to apologize, Saburov only pities him. However, Saburov's wife tells him never to see them again.

Tanečka: Self-confidence, sense of purpose, artistic success (3, 4).

Tanečka, Volodja's actress friend, decides that she has no talent. She has been disappointed in love on a number of occasions. She forms an alliance with Volodja out of loneliness, rather than affection. She resents the role she was required to play in K. Simonov's inartistic, polemical play, *Someone Else's Shadow*, but later she feels that her portrayal of Ophelia has also been a failure.

Sonja Puxova: Emotional integrity (4, 10).

Sonja Puxova loves Grigorij Savčenko but will not encourage him. She feels insecure about the future — where they will be assigned to work, the availability of an apartment, *etc.* She therefore concludes that a good citizen must suppress his feelings. When Grigorij takes her for a walk, she rejects his advances but is later distressed that she has done so. When she is assigned to work in a Penza factory, she pretends that nothing else interests her. As Grigorij sees her off at the train their conversation betrays a mutual misunderstanding. In Part Two, she avoids writing Grigorij and gives the impression that she is interested in another man in Penza. While home on leave, however, she becomes resentful when she learns that Grigorij is going to Paris with a delegation and has not told her. She wishes he would visit her even though she has not invited him to and regrets that she has been so detached. She attributes his apparent aloofness to his love for someone else and resolves in turn to hide her own feelings.

Grigorij Evdokimovič Savčenko: Sonja Puxova (4).

Grigorij Savčenko is consistently led to believe that Sonja does not care for him. She has not replied to his passionate letters, despite the time they had kissed in the woods. He decides not to disturb her with the news that he is going to Paris.

Vera Grigor'evna Šerer: Others' 'good will' (4).

Dr. Vera Šerer is sensitive to people's opinions, due to the arrest of Jewish doctors charged with plotting to poison Soviet leaders. While Lena commiserates in her behalf, Ivan avoids doing so.

Vera Grigor'evna Šerer: Emotional integrity (4, 10).

The death of Vera's husband in the war has emotionally numbed her. As a doctor she becomes distressed at her inability to save a number of patients but will not let Sokolovskij console her. In Part II, she is, for a while, ignorant of his difficulties. The real source of their misunderstanding is said to be that they are both so tired.

Evgenij Vladimirovič Sokolovskij: Vera (4).

In Part II, Sokolovskij fights depression. In addition to his censure by the Party, Vera tells him they should not see each other again.

Evgenij Vladimirovič Sokolovskij: Žuravlev, the bureaucracy (8).

In Part I, Sokolovskij speaks out against administrative negligence, causing people like Žuravlev both to hate and fear him. The latter viciously slanders him in turn, taking advantage of the fact that Sokolovskij's wife had earlier left him and defected to the West. Others spread and compound Žuravlev's rumors. The resulting suspicion and need for further explanations so depress Sokolovskij that he becomes ill and must go to bed. In Part II, he is charged at a meeting of the Party bureau with refusing to submit to instructions. He was provoked when others criticized his new scheme for making metal cutting tools. Those who approved his idea were too timid to support it, being unsure of their superior's viewpoint. Sokolovskij also resented the arbitrary revision of his project and has walked out on his colleagues. His failure to return to work is in fact due to his ensuing illness, but misinterpreted. The Party bureau consequently reprimands him. He then becomes all the more misanthropic and cynical about his former friendships.

Evgenij Vladimirovič Sokolovskij: His daughter, Maša; Western culture (2, 5).

Sokolovskij has a grown daughter, Maša, who was taken as a child to Belgium by her mother. In Part II, Maša writes him that she is coming on a visit. When he meets her in Moscow, he is bewildered by her criticism of Soviet culture: she calls his hotel old-fashioned and the Bolshoj Ballet nineteenth-century. He is equally perplexed by her abstract art. He feels that they are strangers. Maša refuses to stay with him for an extended visit. He is disappointed that she has commented about externals but has failed to notice the people as such and does not appreciate their many accomplishments.

Trifonov: Free thought, toleration (6).

Trifonov is a local conservative bureaucrat who feels insecure under the new management since it requires officials to solve their own problems rather than defer to Moscow for answers. He opposed Dmitrij's agitation for the annullment of Sokolovskij's reprimand and is generally distressed at the new management's concern for individuals. When the reprimand is annulled, he goes home irritated and upset.

A. Kornejčuk, *Wings*

Petr Aleksandrovič Romodan: Dremljuga, the bureaucracy (8).

Petr Aleksandrovič Romodan, the newly arrived secretary of the district Party committee, is shown his new country house and comments that it is larger than necessary since he lives alone. He is told that his predecessors have not lasted long, which gives the president of the district executive committee, Gordej Afanasevič Dremljuga, undue authority. Romodan and Dremljuga eventually clash when the latter refers to himself as a general and Romodan reminds him that there are no generals in the Party. Romodan also accuses Dremljuga of deceptive speeches and suggests that they render active assistance to various district officials rather than remain at the office. Finally Romodan reprimands Dremljuga for relying on his seniority and not properly fulfilling his job. Each threatens to register complaints about the other.

Dremljuga and other bureaucrats: Social justice, service, confidence in others, the people (8, 9).

Dremljuga's wife and those of other officials vie to take credit for any local achievements, while constantly flattering each other. Dremljuga relies on the memory of an assistant to recall important facts. He says he cannot take a vacation because he would not trust anyone else with his responsibilities. He also blames the district's bad livestock situation on the war, its poor milk production on the fact that the cows are not hybrid, *etc.* One of Dremljuga's assistants had earlier served a prison sentence — ostensibly a victim of Dremljuga's slander when Dremljuga had been his superior officer in the army. The director of a machine tractor station, Soxa, arrives by chance at a Party meeting which had been called while he was away hunting. He is at first annoyed, then argues that his statistics are relative and that he himself lacks the necessary technical background for his position.

Dremljuga and other bureaucrats: Unpleasant reality (6).

Dremljuga relies on his district's statistical superiority despite its poor productivity. His assistant, Ovčarenko, theorizes about dairy problems in terms of Pavlovian psychology, the subject of his doctor's dissertation. Romodan suggests that he leave practical problems to the technicians and make better use of his own nervous system. Romodan also chides other bureaucrats for enjoying agricultural products without helping to produce them. Dremljuga insists that all agronomists prefer to live in town. He has established thirty-six speeches as the respectable norm for a forthcoming district conference and arranges for everyone's speeches to be edited in positive terms. Romodan compares the edited versions with the originals, which are generally negative and filled with criticism of Dremljuga. Later, at a meeting of collective farmers, Ovčarenko delivers a long, dry pedantic speech filled with drawn-out quotations and quotations of quotations, evading the farmers' questions and complaints with pat phrases about the realization of communism, *etc.* He argues that their questions are irrelevant to his speech, while Romodan reverses the argument to show how irrelevant Ovčarenko's remarks are both to the problems at hand and to the eventual building of communism.

People: The bureaucracy (9).

Romodan is urged to acquire material for the completion of a new hospital wing which has been in process for four years. His predecessors have failed to do so. He also observes that there is very little produce since the collective farmers have no incentive for raising it. He is later prevailed upon by his old school teacher to petition for a new structure for housing the local historical museum and to requisition garden tools.

People: Truth, integrity in their relationship to the bureaucracy, self-respect (10).

Dremljuga's wife is embarrassed when Romodan is told that she had thought he would be young and handsome, but he replies that he likes people to speak the truth. He is then told that the people only speak the 'holy untruth' before their bosses. When he complains to a subordinate about the dirth of summer vegetables in Ukrainian cities the latter agrees and thanks him for his advice, saying this is the first time he has been summoned to the district office in years. Dremljuga castigates another obsequious subordinate for not reporting to him, even though he (Dremljuga) was away at the time.

Romodan: His wife, Anna, and daughter, Lida (4, 5).

A local doctor, Anna Andreevna, is Romodan's former wife. When he first encounters her, he says that in the past he had tried to reach her by mail, *etc.*, while she changes the subject. He inquires about their daughter, Lida. Anna says Lida is no longer his daughter and uses her mother's maiden name instead. She advises him not to mention their past to others and not to visit her. When he finally does so, Lida tells him he must not sit down, expresses her shame of him, and leaves.

Anna Andreevna Romodan: Her husband, Romodan (4).

When Romodan and Anna finally come to an understanding, she reveals that she was imprisoned, accused in an anonymous letter of having ties with the Germans during the war. She cannot forgive Romodan for going to Kiev instead of standing by her. He explains that he was summoned by the Central Committee before he knew she had been arrested, then was put off when he tried to inquire about her. She replies that she holds nothing against him but that her heart has petrified just the same. They both comment about the deceit, self-deception, and lack of faith which they experienced under Stalin. Anna learns only later from another source that Romodan had been severely wounded during the War.

Lida Romodan: Love (4).

Lida pretends to be interested only in music and not love; she hopes to enroll in the conservatory at Odessa. She plays Beethoven's Moonlight Sonata, however, and otherwise betrays a romantic nostalgia.

Katerina Stepanovna Remez: Love (4).

Katerina Stepanovna Remez, another doctor and Anna's superior, sings a song which Romodan had himself sung earlier. She has forced him to undergo an operation for the removal of shrapnel. As he thanks her she avoids the physical contact of shaking hands and asks for a cigarette instead, although, as Romodan knows, she does not smoke. Still later, she serves as intermediary between Romodan and his family and is instrumental in reuniting them despite indications that she is secretly in love with him.

D. Granin, *One's Own Opinion*

Ol'xovskij: His supervisor, Minaev (3).

Ol'xovskij, a young engineer, has submitted an article to his superior, Minaev. His self-assured arrogance both aggravates and attracts Minaev.

Minaev: His subordinate, Engineer Ol'xovskij (4).

After Minaev has betrayed Ol'xovskij by innuendo, he wishes to have a heart to heart talk with him, urge patience, and be of some help at the proper moment, but senses that Ol'xovskij would not understand and would only reject him. He still badly wants to prove to Ol'xovskij that he (Minaev) is not to blame.

Minaev: Ethical responsibility (10).

Minaev replies unfavorably to a letter of inquiry about Ol'xovskij from the latter's instructor, Loktev. This arouses Loktev's suspicions about the slanderous nature of Ol'xovskij's article. The resulting suspicion seems all the more convincing for its lack of substantiation. On another occasion, as a Ministry official is visiting their laboratory, Minaev turns on a motor to prevent Ol'xovskij from effectively communicating with the official. When asked by the official about Ol'xovskij's manuscript, Minaev avoids committing himself, which reinforces the impression that Ol'xovskij is a scandal monger. Both Minaev and his assistant make innuendoes to impress the official, who then entrusts Minaev with rendering judgment upon Ol'xovskij. This both pleases Minaev and makes him feel guilty. He now pities Ol'xovskij and senses the injustice of condemning another for simply speaking the truth without tact. Minaev thereupon becomes a director and forgets about the case until he is sent another inquiry regarding a tactless letter in which Ol'xovskij argues the inefficiency of new motors designed by a famous academician and naively attacks the system of scientific publication. Since the letter is scrawled by hand on notebook paper, Minaev concludes that no one else would ever read it to the end. He hopes to find a way to help Ol'xovskij. At a Party meeting, however, Ol'xovskij criticizes Loktev for his professional and intellectual incompetence. Minaev knows that this is, again, the truth but that Loktev will avenge himself. Minaev thereupon refers the inquiry about Ol'xovskij to his assistant. Despite its damning innuendoes, the assistant's answer is too charitably worded to be contended.

Minaev and Assistant: Intellectual integrity, courage, self-respect (6, 10).

Ol'xovskij's article mostly disturbs Minaev because it attacks the contribution of a famous academician. When he tries to discourage Ol'xovskij, the latter asks him if he has himself reached the point where he can freely speak out on principle. Minaev's reply is indirect and condescending. He refuses to endorse Ol'xovskij's article, arguing to himself that one must sometimes protect one's position by not stating an opinion. He behaves toward the visiting official in a fawning and hypocritical way and feels he can no longer intervene for Ol'xovskij, especially after the latter attacks Loktev, without antagonizing a number of important people. He forces his assistant to admit that he writes what Minaev wants him to so that some day he can express his own opinion. Minaev in turn implies that this is wishful thinking. When summoned to the city council to discuss Loktev's demand for Ol'xovskij's dismissal, Minaev intends to stand up to Loktev but fears to be caught in duplicity. He senses how his hesitation has strengthened Loktev's hand, but, as his resentment grows, he speaks ever softer. Finally he asks that the decision be postponed. He recalls his youth when, in his first job, he and others had similarly protested the construction of a certain motor. He capitulated in time, however, and became an assistant shop foreman while the others were fired. He realizes now that he has been compromising ever since. Meanwhile, his institute has not fulfilled its plan. The forementioned academician places the blame on Minaev's predecessor, however. Thus it becomes doubly difficult for him to defend Ol'xovskij. While on an intervening vacation, he is confronted by the figure of his youth, which scolds him for still delaying the time when he will act with integrity.

V. Dudincev, *Not by Bread Alone*

Lopatkin: Drozdov, the bureaucracy (8).

Dmitrij Alekseevič Lopatkin learns that Moscow has overlooked his new invention. Leonid Ivanovič Drozdov, the local factory manager in Muzga, was supposed to hand Dmitrij's letter to a minister and make further inquiries in his behalf while in Moscow, but did not do so. Meanwhile a machine proposed by Professor Avdiev and similar to Lopatkin's has been accepted instead. Lopatkin had originally been summoned to Moscow to build his machine, but was then rebuffed at Avdiev's urging. He had previously resigned his job as a school teacher and now fights a paper war in behalf of his invention. The Ministry finally responds, requesting that he proceed with the design of a prototype. While working on the prototype at the district capitol, he apprehends an assistant, Maksjutenko, who has adapted his machine to Maksjutenko's own design and also neglected a previously discussed correction. Urjupin, head of the design section, also schemes against Lopatkin. A draftsman and former inventor, Araxovskij, warns Lopatkin and lends him technical literature to study in order not to be deceived. Lopatkin then discovers and corrects a number of defects before his design is completed. Returning to Muzga, he learns that Avdiev's machine, while inefficient, is being built with funds originally assigned to his own project. Lopatkin's machine would permit the casting of pipes with interchangeable molds. At the Central Scientific Institute of Foundry Research he explains that his device would enable all auxiliary operations to be performed simultaneously with those of the casting machine, insuring an increase of five times the present productivity yet requiring only one fourth the present space. Such a machine would lead to full automatization. It is nonetheless voted down after a number of prejudiced experts raise objections. Lopatkin thereupon files complaints, which Minister Šutikov in turn rejects. Lopatkin nevertheless continues to write accusatory letters to various committees and newspaper offices. Meanwhile he modifies his design to accommodate a universal machine capable of casting iron pipes of any shape. He also learns that a machine is being built at Muzga according to the design stolen by Maksjutenko. He is next summoned before a deputy prosecutor who accuses him of libeling various bureaucrats. He defends himself by asking how many people have been prosecuted for suppressing technical data, but is required to write an explanation. Finally he manages to inform Šutikov that the machine presently being built was lifted from his design and receives approval for further work on his own plan. He wonders why both Drozdov, who is by now a Ministry official, and Avdiev are now so cooperative. A sympathetic official, Galickij, hints that they will still try to sabotage him. Later he observes workmen bringing centrifugally cast iron pipes to the Ministry building. Although these have been water-cooled, he realizes that pleading for his own machine will now be ascribed to personal ambition, jealousy, *etc.* The new pipes are indeed used as a pretext for stopping work on his machine. Šutikov now taunts him to ask the Ministry for funds. If he appears ungrateful, he will look like a typical loser. He nonetheless realizes that his machine could also make two-layer pipes and is consequently summoned before a general who engages him to adapt his machine for the construction of hollow rotary bodies in a secret project. Lopatkin requests that Nadja Drozdova be included as his partner in the project order. His rivals suddenly prove to be fearful and desperate opponents. Urjupin and Maksjutenko visit the project and on one occasion notice that Nadja has signed various drawings as co-originator. They then denounce Lopatkin to Šutikov for criminal infringement of procedure in connection with official secrets, referring to Nadja's involvement. Lopatkin is consequently suspected of working on Drozdov through his wife and is called before a military prosecutor, although the fact that several scientists have brought charges unwittingly establishes that there is no official secret after all. In order to protect Nadja, Lopatkin denies that they have had relations together. Nadja is interrogated separately and claims not to be a co-inventor in order to glorify Lopatkin but does not deny their intimacies in order to reveal how much she admires him. During his subsequent trial, Lopatkin is not informed of what he is charged with disclosing to Nadja. He does, however, manage to tell Nadja to save his drawings at all cost. Despite numerous discrepancies in his favor, Lopatkin is sentenced to eight years in a labor reformatory camp. A commission is then appointed to open his office and confiscate his documents. Urjupin heads the commission, which includes Maksjutenko, and is told that any documents not marked secret can be given to Nadja. The commission deposits relevant documents in the Institute archives and marks the rest for burning. Antonovič, one of Lopatkin's subordinates, manages to rescue the drawings by subterfuge. Nadja's authorized request for non-secret documents meanwhile arrives too late and Urjupin, thinking they are burned, replies that all the documents were secret and none can be given her.

Lopatkin: Intellectual conformity (3).

In Muzga Drozdov chides Lopatkin for not promoting his invention more collectively. Drozdov then offers Lopatkin the services of a local tailor, but Lopatkin declines. This gives Drozdov further cause to resent Lopatkin for appearing superior. At the district capitol, Urjupin belittles Lopatkin for his too general knowledge. In Moscow at the C.S.I.F.R., Lopatkin argues in behalf of the individualist *vs.* collective approach, for which Drozdov once again reproaches him. He takes rooms with a Professor Busko, who was also an independent and persecuted inventor. They share views about the individual *vs.* the herd, *etc.* During the intermission of a concert, Lopatkin notices a group of colleagues, apparently from some institute, and momentarily yearns to be part of a group like them rather than a lonely individualist. Šutikov several times offers Lopatkin the chance to head a department in his institute, which he always declines. Both Lopatkin and Busko agree that the combination of integrity, courage, and intelligence is missing in most scientists. After returning from Siberia, Lopatkin shows Nadja a further refinement in his machine, which converts it into an automatic foundry. Lopatkin's achievement while in prison suggests that he who still thinks for himself remains free. Galickij later tells Lopatkin how once Avdiev also diverted him as a competitor by encouraging him to pursue an insignificant topic for the doctor's degree.

People: Affluent bureaucrats (9).

Returning from Moscow, Drozdov peels an orange and throws the peelings on the snow. Children, who have never seen an orange, grab them up. He lives in a converted two-apartment house, and his wife, Nadja, wears a new mink coat. As a school teacher she later visits the large, poor family of one of her students, Sima S'janova, who must work hard and has little time to study. Nadja discovers that Lopatkin is their roomer. The S'janovs are described as simple people of the heart who stand behind Lopatkin. As Drozdov proposes celebrating their two-year wedding anniversary, he discourages Nadja from inviting her friends so they won't be jealous of her possessions. When Nadja goes to the hospital, other patients are cleared out to give her a private room, which she protests. Drozdov reprimands her, however, for her egalitarianism. While living with Busko, on the other hand, Lopatkin continues to lead an improvised existence — resorting at times to a diet of black bread and fish oil. Both of them attribute Nadja's anonymous help to the kindness of their simple neighbors. Busko describes the private enterprises to which average Soviet citizens must often resort.

Leonid Ivanovič Drozdov: Other people (6).

Leonid Ivanovič Drozdov espouses a theory of managerial isolation. When he learns of Lopatkin's and Nadja's partnership, he becomes mostly concerned about quieting gossip, even to the extent of helping them out, and only becomes vindictive when he discovers that the proceedings against them will in any event be in secret. He is envious of his superior, Šutikov, who is invited to all the receptions, goes on all the foreign tours, and has ghost writers. When the machine approved by Šutikov proves inferior and jeopardizes Šutikov's position, Drozdov rejoices.

Scientists: Truth, integrity (6).

After Šutikov first snubs Lopatkin, Lopatkin reads a ghost-written article attributed to Šutikov pleading for opportunities in behalf of inventors. After the machine endorsed by Šutikov proves ineffective, Avdiev urges that a new standard be devised which will show off the machine to better advantage. Šutikov also enlists the support of an academician, Saratovcev, in approving a temporary increase in the weight of the machine's pipes. Avdiev then warns Šutikov that Lopatkin is back and that they must not request a new standard. Šutikov manages to retrieve his request just in time but, realizing that the excess cast iron in their pipes is no longer justifiable, suffers a mild heart attack. Meanwhile, Drozdov assembles papers suggesting he has supported Lopatkin's project all along, then asks staff members to determine who is to blame for its suppression. He carefully implicates Urjupin, Maksjutenko, and the C.S.I.F.R. officials who tried to conceal the overexpenditures on their own machine and to change the state standard for pipes. Finally, the Ministry publishes an order condemning the C.S.I.F.R. machine and blaming Urjupin and Maksjutenko, but sparing Saratovcev and Avdiev. The monetary waste is not mentioned so as not to upset the public. Trite statements are made in support of inventors.

Lopatkin: Nadja's love (4).

In Muzga, Lopatkin feels that Nadja is snubbing him and considers her stupid. She informs him by letter, however, that Avdiev's machine is being built at the Muzga factory. In Moscow she also sells her fur coat to provide Lopatkin and Busko with necessities and money and brings Lopatkin information on the manufacture of the machine stolen from his plan. After separating from Drozdov, she begins to handle Lopatkin's correspondence, *etc.* When after Lopatkin's interview with the deputy prosecutor he is nearly brought to tears in her presence, she decides she loves him, though she expects only friendship in return. Soon after, Busko finds an excuse for leaving them alone in his apartment, which encourages them to go to bed together. Busko does not return until morning. At their next meeting, however, Lopatkin, confused about his true feelings, tells Nadja they must not continue their affair. She agrees, meanwhile continuing to serve as his secretary. She thereafter avoids his presence except for business purposes. After his return from Siberia, she embraces and kisses him, but he fails to respond. She even gives him Žanna Ganičeva's photograph, but he shows no interest in either woman.

Lopatkin: Žanna (4).

In Muzga, Lopatkin receives a letter from Žanna registering her disappointment that he has not been successful and explaining that she can no longer wait for him to be recognized. He writes her in turn, wishing her well and saying she need no longer wait for him. In Moscow he encounters her on the street, however, and feels that, were he to return to teaching, she would come back to him. When he recontacts her, she urges him to give up his invention. He refuses, but lies to her to reassure her about its progress. After his affair with Nadja, he feels that he has betrayed Žanna.

Nadežda (Nadja) Sergeevna Drozdova: Her husband, Drozdov (4).

Nadja, for whom Drozdov abandoned his first wife, is considerably younger than he. She had come to Siberia looking for a man who was an outstanding leader and thus became Drozdov's unofficial wife. He has nonetheless managed to obtain a passport for her as Mrs. Drozdov. She grows melancholy in his company and is disturbed by his crude utilitarian philosophy. In trying to justify him to herself, she castigates Lopatkin before the other teachers. When she returns from the hospital, she insists on sleeping in a separate room, using doctor's orders as a pretext. After her affair with Lopatkin in Moscow, Drozdov's mother, who lives with them, reproaches her for staying away all night. Nadja blatantly raises the issue of Drozdov's first wife instead.

Nadežda (Nadja) Sergeevna Drozdova: Love for Lopatkin (4).

In Muzga, Nadja has avoided noticing Lopatkin because of her

attraction to him in the past. In reviling him before the teachers, she has
secretly hoped that someone would disprove her argument. Lopatkin
comes by and overhears her. When she discovers this, she is mortified,
becomes ill, and is rushed to the hospital. In Moscow she sacrifices her
reputation and material possessions in his behalf without expecting him
to return her affection. Later, however, when he mentions visiting
Žanna, Nadja becomes disconsolate and ails physically.

Žanna Ganičeva: Lopatkin (4).

Žanna has always been attracted to Lopatkin, but is unwilling to make
the necessary sacrifices while he is working on his invention. After he
returns from prison and is finally successful in promoting his machine,
she is especially attracted to him. When he visits her, he notices the fur
coat which her mother had bought from Nadja. When he does not
declare his love, she bids him go and holds the door against his reentry.
Later she comes to his office in his absence requesting a job. Nadja
mentions another woman, Valentina, who had sacrificed everything for
Lopatkin. Žanna then leaves, realizing she is unworthy.

Valentina Pavlovna: Love for Lopatkin (4).

Another school teacher in Muzga, Valentina Pavlovna, has left her
husband and taken her daughter with her because of her love for Lopatkin, who doesn't even notice her. She supplies him with writing materials
before he goes to Moscow and delivers him Nadja's letter about Avdiev's
machine when he returns again to Muzga. When they say goodby, she
insists on kissing him, then quickly walks away.

P. Nilin, *Cruelty*

Venjamin (Ven'ka) Malyšev: Others' inhumanity, injustice, utilitarian
morality (7, 10).

Venjamin (Ven'ka) Malyšev works as a district communist detective
in the small Siberian town, Dudari, during the period of War Communism. He is angered when he learns that another detective has, in
rounding up a gang of bandits, killed a young boy. One of the bandits,
Bukin Lazar', is insolent to the detectives, but Ven'ka cultivates his
acquaintance even though Lazar' had wounded him in the roundup.
Ven'ka regards the opponents of Soviet power as deluded by White
officers but not intrinsically evil. Lazar' finally tells him that he is a close

acquaintance of the notorious bandit chief, Kostja Voroncov. Later, after Lazar' has escaped and while on an expedition, Ven'ka and his detective companion, the narrator, are intercepted but not harmed by Lazar' and others. They hold a private conference with Ven'ka directing him in fact to the dwelling of Voroncov's former mistress, Klan'ka Zvaina. Voroncov has abandoned her for another, and Ven'ka manages to win her confidence. Back in Dudari, a certain *Komsomol* member, Egerov, is chastised at a special meeting for his participation in religious ceremonies — which he denies. Sensing Egerov's honesty, Ven'ka manages to speak in his defense, which keeps Egerov from being expelled from the *Komsomol*. A newspaper correspondent, Uzelkov, chides Ven'ka for adhering to Christian morality. Ven'ka, however, effectively refutes him and forces Uzelkov to admit that Egerov did not deserve to be expelled. Confronted by Ven'ka, Uzelkov is also unable to defend applying punishment to deter others. Ven'ka, on the other hand, asserts his faith in instinctive morality as opposed to self-contradictory theses. In the Spring, Ven'ka precedes, then returns and accompanies another roundup, intended to apprehend Voroncov. During the earlier trip he lives with Lazar' and completely wins him over to the communist cause by his humane conduct and strong convictions. Voroncov is captured, with the assistance of Lazar' and Klan'ka. Lazar' then decides to return with the detectives to Dudari and be reconciled to the authorities. As Ven'ka's chief joins them, Lazar' is forced to ride ahead of the rest like a prisoner and is then arrested. Ven'ka becomes disturbed that Lazar' is not rewarded for his assistance and that he, Ven'ka, has unwittingly deceived him.

Venjamin (Ven'ka) Malyšev: Love of Julja Mal'ceva (4).

Ven'ka and the narrator are attracted to a new cashier, Julja Mal'ceva, at the local grocery store. They frequently visit the store on the pretext of making small purchases, but are too timid to attract her attention. They try to attend the play rehearsals in which she takes part but are not admitted, whereas Uzelkov manages to escort her to and from them. Uzelkov also professes to discuss difficult books with her, which causes them to take these same books from the library and study them. Ven'ka reveals his infatuation with her to the narrator. At the *Komsomol* meeting she supports Ven'ka's defense of Egerov and is about to speak with him when Egerov intervenes to thank him. As Ven'ka suffers from Lazar''s wound, he hallucinates and calls to her. The narrator and another interested friend finally bring the two together. After their date,

Ven'ka tells the narrator he would marry Julja if she would accept, but he is too timid to ask her. He feels guilty about an affair which he had when he was younger that gave him a venereal disease, although he has since been cured. He meets with Julja a time or two later and resolves that, after Voroncov's capture, he will continue his education and come to an understanding with her. Before the expedition Ven'ka writes her a love letter, but receives no reply. After returning from the expedition, Uzelkov shows him the same letter, which he says was in a book he had lent Julja and which she has just returned to him. Ven'ka presumes that he has been unlucky with Julja, which adds to his general depression. He is unaware that his letter reached Uzelkov by accident and that Julja was hoping to see him again.

Uzelkov and communist officials: Others' private lives, loyalty to truth (6).

Uzelkov arrives in Dudari to cover the activities of the local detectives. Although an unimportant person, he boldly asserts himself by showing off his book knowledge, conversing freely with prisoners and witnesses, and making the detectives feel inferior. In turn, the detectives' chief cultivates Uzelkov so that their work will be well publicized. Uzelkov tends to exaggerate their exploits in the press. Ven'ka's chief also takes credit for the expedition against Vorontsov after it is accomplished. This is justified as raising their authority in the eyes of the populace. Some of the detectives, however, dispute the promotion of Soviet power by deception. After Ven'ka's suicide, some nevertheless criticize him for spoiling their image as Komsomol members and communists. Even the narrator feels such resentment during the burial. On the same occasion, Uzelkov, with his usual bravado, tries to persuade the detectives' chief that Ven'ka was guilty of a political offense in taking his own life.

A. Jašin, *Levers*

People: Bureaucracy, voice in government, social justice (8, 9).

One evening four men sit indoors on a collective farm. Petr Kuzmič complains that the district consults with them but never approves their plan and that the district's plan is also probably handed down from above. He concludes that they are not trusted. Ščukin adds that justice is only talked of but never applied. Cipišev suggests that justice blinds those who should promote it. Kuzmič says that he recently approached the District First Secretary, suggesting how the *kolkhoz* might meet its norm and produce to capacity, but the Secretary insisted they overfulfill their plan immediately and urged him to persuade the farmers accordingly and to act as a kind of lever. Cipišev complains that it is a defect of the bureaucracy that people are regarded only as levers and suggests that the Secretary ought to talk with them openly, as people, not like a dictator and condescendingly. Konoplev concurs that their district leaders are unable to talk to the peasants and are interested only in statistics. He argues that since the collective farm has transformed the peasant, the peasant ought to be trusted and consulted. Instead, everything is dictated from above. Kuzmič observes that, although the district officials pretend to advise them, they in fact give orders which have to be complied with.

Citizens: Integrity, social responsibility (10).

Later, as they conduct a Party executive meeting, Kuzmič, who is in fact the *kolkhoz* chairman, observes that since the district has not accepted their plan they must themselves be at fault, particularly in failing to convince their workers. He reminds the others that their function is that of levers. Cipišev, who is the secretary of the *kolkhoz* organization, proposes that they find a way to reward one or two workers and fine others so as to provide more incentive and stimulate competition. They agree on the number to be selected for awards and fines. Since they have no time to draw up a resolution, however, Kuzmič suggests they leave this to Cipišev, who knows how to work such things. Before their Party meeting the same group had discussed instances of graft and influence in which they themselves were involved. Ščukin, for instance, became the warehouseman by arguing that all important posts should be filled by communists. He also received communal sugar from his predecessor, for whom he obtained another job at the warehouse. During the Party meeting, all are in agreement, as before, but now support the other side of the questions they had discussed previously. As they leave the meeting, all are slightly dissatisfied with themselves.

Citizens: Mutual trust, freedom of thought (3-4).

After their exchange of remarks and before the meeting, Konoplev discovers Marfa, the cleaning woman, who had been sitting all the time behind the stove. All are suddenly concerned about her presence and ask why she is there: in order, she answers, to prevent their starting a fire with their cigarette butts. Their conversation immediately terminates, and they become uneasy. They continue to smoke in silence, then exchange insignificant remarks. They now view Marfa as they would a suspicious stranger. Finally Ščukin laughs and exclaims that they have all been frightend by an old woman. Then the others join in the laughter and Konoplev admits that he was afraid they had been caught by the 'big man'. Kuzmič observes that they are so insecure they even fear themselves. Although Konoplev is later amused at Kuzmič's transformation as the latter speaks to them in a formal, authoritarian manner, Konoplev restrains his smile and is far more conscious of his coughing than previously. All agree with Kuzmič's proposal that they correct their plan to meet the requirements of the district, since there is no alternative. By contrast, the schoolteacher, Akulina Semenovna, who arrived late, removes her kerchief and becomes more natural after the meeting has ended and people her own age have entered the building. Kuzmič is also more sympathetic about her request for firewood after the meeting. He and Konoplev again discuss everyday affairs as they go into the street.

Bureaucrats: Unpleasant reality, sense of dedication to and rapport with others (6).

The District Secretary has boasted of their increased achievement, which contradicts the facts. During the local Party meeting, Cipišev begins to speak in a more stern and authoritative manner, sounding exactly like the District Secretary even in his tone of voice. He fulfills all directives to the letter in order not to make a mistake, but postpones the one practical problem — that of firewood for the school house — until after the meeting. He imitates the District Secretary because he has only recently been appointed and is unsure of himself. When he turns the meeting over to Kuzmič, the latter continues in a similar vein.

V. Kaverin, *Quests and Hopes*

Tat'jana Petrovna Vlasenkova: Kramov, the bureaucracy (8).

Tat'jana Petrovna Vlasenkova, a research M.D., has developed a substance out of fungus which has curbed the growth of various bacilli and is now being experimented with on human patients. As she is interviewed by a Ministry official, she reproaches both him and her former superior, Kramov, for minimizing the significance of her work. Kramov is agitating for the purchase of a British formula instead. She accuses him of having interferred with her research in the past. After she receives permission to continue with her discovery, she senses that Kramov is hoping she will fail, even though he pretends to be helpful. As she approaches the Ministry for further assistance, she is put off. Then unfounded rumors circulate that her preparation will be withdrawn from use, that she will have to go to court, *etc.* Some of her colleagues begin to doubt the value of her work. Various bureaucrats, including Kramov, who holds a chair in microbiology at the Institute and Skrypačenko, Kramov's former pupil and now director of the Institute of Preventive Medicine, have used their influence to obstruct her request for a factory, *etc.* Even after she has demonstrated success, the committee on Stalin awards passes over her achievement. Finally when a British scientist, Norcross, comes to Moscow, Kramov suggests a test to determine which nation's penicillin is the stronger. Tat'jana must submit in order not to lose face. After her preparation proves superior and following her husband Andrej's arrest, an ally, the chief surgeon of the Red army, suggests a connection between the arrest and the effort of her enemies to disparage her work. This is confirmed by others. She is increasingly avoided by acquaintances, while her best friends must bear insults on her account. Even her membership in the Party is disputed because of Andrej.

Andrej Vlasenkov: Social justice, the bureaucracy, others' good will (4, 8).

Andrej Vlasenkov, director of the Institute of Preventive Medicine, is distressed that, despite his success with a typhus vaccine, two of his staff and a foreign visitor have become infected with the disease. The fact that the Institute is now a source of infection gives him a bad reputation. The Institute had long been in administrative turmoil and was traditionally exploited as a stepping stone by former officials. Andrej has made enemies in his effort to improve its organization, and Skrypačenko, who would like to see him fail, spreads rumors against him. Skrypačenko's anonymous letters create suspicion even when they are not believed. Unexpectedly, Skrypačenko visits Andrej, offering to suppress the rumors if Andrej will make him his assistant. Andrej responds by beating him up and throwing him out of his apartment. There are no immediate repercussions, except that Andrej's colleagues begin to avoid him and he is criticized in a journal. After Andrej's brother, Mitja, determines that infection had been spread at the Institute through its ventilating system — Skrypačenko still blames Andrej for not being better informed. Skrypačenko replaces Andrej as director of the Institute, after which various staff members are arrested. In his disillusion Andrej has written a novel about his profession, which is well received by those who have read it. Suddenly he too is imprisoned. Tat'jana pleads with various officials to intercede for him but receives only excuses. She is not allowed to see him. Later she discovers that false charges have been made against him by her own enemies. His manuscript is also returned by the publisher after his arrest. Tat'jana vows that, if there is any justice on earth, Andrej will return to her or she would prefer to die.

Tat'jana Petrovna Vlasenkova: Her husband, Andrej (4).

After Tat'jana's return to Moscow from work in the field, Andrej seems like a stranger and appears dissatisfied with her. Before she can say goodbye to him she is suddenly transferred to Stalingrad to forestall a cholera epidemic. In Stalingrad she encounters an acquaintance of her youth, Volodja Lukaševič. As they reminisce together, he indicates he would have been more interested in her in the past had he known she would settle for Andrej. His remarks disturb her sleep. Later in Moscow, during Andrej's absence, she discovers Volodja near death in a hospital. He is suffering from blood poisoning, which she miraculously cures with an unprecedentedly large dose of her penicillin preparation. Volodja has written a letter to her confessing his love and becomes despondent as he recovers. Tat'jana recalls that he had previously told her she could only be happy with him. He reproaches her for trying to cheer him while not really caring for him. She is suddenly aroused by his affection, but tells herself that the problem will be cleared up when she speaks with Andrej. She hesitates to explain to him what has transpired, however. During a social gathering, Volodja arrives and, by innuendo, reveals that something has transpired between him and Tat'jana. He tactlessly refers to their meeting in Stalingrad, then acts awkward and guilty, which implicates Tat'jana as well. Sensing that Andrej now suspects her, she is overcome by a malicious urge to deny everything. In turn, Andrej reproaches her for never having loved him and for marrying him out of pity. He again seems to her like a complete stranger.

Tat'jana Petrovna Vlasenkova: Integrity toward her son, Pavlik (5, 10).

Pavlik Vlasenkov, Tat'jana's schoolboy son, is staying with Tat'jana's mother in her home town, Lopakin. As she becomes torn between Volodja and Andrej, Tat'jana longs to see Pavlik. After Andrej's arrest, she brings Pavlik to Moscow, but is distraught to know how she can tell him about his father since he has been taught to believe that no cruelty or injustice ever transpires in Soviet society. His father has also always been an example to him. She decides not to tell Pavlik though she later realizes that he suspects something since he never asks about his father. Finally, in Pavlik's hearing, Tat'jana inadvertently alludes to Andrej's imprisonment.

Elizaveta Sergeevna Gordeeva: Mitja Vlasenkov (4).

While recovering from an injury in a Stalingrad hospital, Tat'jana makes the acquaintance of another female patient, also a medical doctor, Elizaveta Sergeevna Gordeevna, who worked with Andrej's brother, Mitja, in Rostov. Although married, she befriended him and then separated from her husband, but did not encourage him further because of a basic difference in their personalities. Although realizing that he loves her more than he does Glafira Sergeevna, his former wife, Elizaveta is nonetheless jealous of the latter. When Mitja returns to Moscow and encounters Elizaveta, he arranges accommodations for her at a hotel and requests that she be included in his forthcoming expedition. Elizaveta is momentarily piqued, however, that he has recontacted Glafira. Mitja persuades Tat'jana to visit Elizaveta and reconcile him to her. Elizaveta in turn feels that she would torment him and he be too demanding were she to go on the expedition. Tat'jana agrees, although she senses that Elizaveta would like to be persuaded otherwise. Elizaveta decides not to accompany him.

Glafira Sergeevna Kramova: Her second husband, Kramov; free existence, acknowledgment of truth (4, 10).

Glafira Sergeevna Kramova fears her husband, even when he travels abroad. Although she wants children, he will not allow her to have any. After Andrej's arrest, she visits Tat'jana, declaring that she wants to do a good thing for once in her life and that one should learn how not to hate even if one cannot learn to love. She tells Tat'jana that her own husband, Kramov, is Tat'jana's avowed enemy. She confirms that Andrej's arrest was arranged in order to destroy Tat'jana and that Skrypačenko and others have conspired with Kramov. Tat'jana realizes that Glafira has confided in her because, although living in a large city, she has no other friends. She seems like a foreigner in her own community. Her relationship with Kramov attests to extreme mental cruelty on his part. Finally, she authenticates his treachery against Andrej, providing the original copy of denunciatory letters he and others have written. She says that Tat'jana should feel free to name her as the source of this information and asks that Tat'jana convey to Mitja that he is the only one she ever loved.

Kramov and scientific bureaucrats: Integrity (6, 10).

Valentin Sergeevič Kramov has been an unsuccessful theoretician and is now trying to save his position. He will do anything to acquire a reputation in science and is supported by other self-seeking individuals who depend upon his recognition for their own — which makes him all the more dangerous. He had, for instance, written a letter to Stalin, published in *Pravda*, pledging a hundred thousand rubles to the war effort. The letter had subtly credited himself rather than his group for the contribution. In like manner, he endeavors to take credit for every scientific advance. Were he to convince the government they should acquire the British penicillin patent, he would be honored for a great service. He is peeved that a similar formula, Tat'jana's, has long been in his archives and that he has done nothing about it. Tat'jana notices how hypocritically confident he now is of her discovery, while five years ago he was equally confident that it would be forgotten as a curiosity. She sarcastically congratulates him for being bold enough to endorse it at such a late moment when he had opposed it for so long. His wife observes that there are hundreds, even thousands like him, no better than thieves, and that Kramov is not the ringleader, though he appears to be. He was different when she married him, however, not yet afraid he might be discovered a fraud. After his wife's suicide, he asks Tat'jana to visit him. While she pretends to be ignorant of his designs, he trains his lamp on her, hoping to detect what she knows in her eyes. He assures her that he believes in Andrej's innocence and even blames Andrej's arrest on malicious slanderers. When he asks her what his wife told her, she recounts all the neutral details in her conversation with Glafira, lying as accurately as possible in order to counteract his deceit. He inquires why she has not asked him to endorse Andrej, since he would gladly do so. He also mentions an official of his acquaintance through whose influence Andrej can doubtless be freed. He finally offers her a position as head of an institute of antibiotics where her work can be to his credit. This is the price he is asking. She realizes that he cannot be satisfied with past acclaim but must strive for power and recognition all his life. Later, in the post-war years, Tat'jana notes that scientists are required to espouse the superiority of Soviet achievements and, in doing so, have fallen behind. Although Kramov is now dead, clever artificers still make careers for themselves in science.

Ju. Nagibin, *Light in the Window*

Vasilij Petrovič: Fellow citizens (10, 9).

When he first became the director of a rest home, Vasilij Petrovič's predecessor had shown him a special apartment in a certain bungalow, elaborately furnished with television, billiards, *etc.* which was to be kept vacant for 'him himself'. Vasilij is troubled, however, about always keeping the apartment empty and feels guilty for having already assigned a pair of newlyweds to separate dormitories and for failing to offer the apartment earlier to the family of a stone mason who had helped build the rest home. He is also troubled that his waitresses must watch television over the heads of vacationeers, through the windows of the television room. After he scolds Nastja and Stepan for using the apartment, he experiences a feeling of self-revulsion.

Vasilij Petrovič: Nastja, idolatry of leaders (4, 7).

Nastja, the charwoman, is critical of Vasilij's guilt about the apartment. When he confesses it to her, she censures him instead of being sympathetic.

Nastja and Stepan: Idolatry of leaders (7).

Nastja has been assigned to clean the special apartment every day and Stepan, the porter, to keep ice from the steps and supply logs for the fireplace. Nastja was widowed by the war and became bitter about life until assigned to care for the apartment, which has given her a purpose. She dreams of the magnificence of the person for whom it is intended and is incensed that anyone would dare use it. After a year, however, the apartment seems dead and dull without inhabitants. Nastja becomes depressed and feels deceived that the important person has never come to use his apartment. She is no longer excited about caring for it. Finally she invites Stepan and his children to share its facilities with her. Even when Vasilij apprehends and scolds them, they appear haughty and defiant.

N. Pogodin, *Petrarch's Sonnet*

Dmitrij Alekseevič Suxodolov: Conventional impersonality, insensitivity, conformity (1).

After Suxodolov tells his old musician acquaintance, Armando, of his love for a young girl, Maja, Armando comments that this signifies Suxodolov is again a human being. The latter adds that, since his infatuation, he has gotten along better with people and in his work. His only contact with Maja is through the letters he writes her — which seems to satisfy him. Armando likens his letters to the sonnets Petrarch wrote to Laura and advises him to keep writing Maja, to continue singing his song. Dononov, Suxodolov's colleague, criticizes Suxodolov's personal life, which he argues must be accounted for in his work. Suxodolov replies that his private life is his own affair and that such discussion is unworthy of them both. Both Dononov and Suxodolov's wife, Ksenija, are concerned about the effect of Suxodolov's private life on his reputation. Dononov argues that love is permissible in one's youth but has no place later on, while Suxodolov accuses Dononov of speaking malicious nonsense. Likewise, Pavel Mixajlovič, Suxodolov's superior, chastises Suxodolov for not confiding in him. Suxodolov again replies that there are aspects of life which are too sublime and complicated to be accounted for by convention. He refuses to write an explanation, quoting from Dostoevskij that there are some things relating to women that even a father and son cannot discuss together. Although Pavel implies that Suxodolov's unwillingness to explain himself will be viewed as disrespectful to the Party, Suxodolov says there are some things you don't even tell the Party if not of a political nature. He compares himself to a small molecule in the Party, which the Party dare not abuse.

Dmitrij Alekseevič Suxodolov: His wife, Ksenija Petrovna (4).

Suxodolov's house manager, Marina, tells him that, whereas his relationship with Ksenija is now considered comradely, it would have once been thought base. He realizes that he never loved his wife and that their attachment is merely one of habit. He also resolves not to let anyone interfere between him and Maja. Ksenija then confronts him about where he spends the nights and calls him a corrupter. He tells her to be quiet, but she vows to make trouble for him until he breaks off his affair. He refuses to do so.

Dmitrij Alekseevič Suxodolov: Loyalty of friend, Armando, and colleague, Dononov (4).

When Suxodolov meets Armando, he accuses Armando of having cuckolded various women's husbands, including himself. He then confesses to Armando his love for Maja. Although encouraging, Armando imputes impure motives to their relationship, while Suxodolov warns him to say nothing of it to anyone else. Armando thereupon informs Ksenija. Dononov likewise protests about Suxodolov's affair to Pavel and others and, together with Ksenija, registers a formal complaint against him.

Ksenija Petrovna: Her husband, Suxodolov (4).

Ksenija demands that Suxodolov curse and insult her in order to prove he loves her; she also accuses him of treating her like a slave. After she reads one of his letters to Maja in which he expresses the hope that Maja will fall in love and raise a family, Ksenija declares that she and others have themselves been responsible for pushing him into another woman's arms. She weeps, expecting that he will not return and realizing that he is a great person.

Armando: Personal ethics, Suxodolov's friendship, achievement (4, 10).

Armando eventually visits Pavel, pleading in behalf of Suxodolov and expressing regret that he himself has betrayed the latter's confidence. Later, when confronted by Suxodolov, Armando asks him if he has come to kill him, but Suxodolov replies that everything has been dead between them for a long time, then reproaches Armando for making things so difficult for him. Armando argues that there never was a Laura, but Suxodolov replies he knew that already. Armando then reveals that a second woman came into his own life and kept him from being a skilled musician. He warns Suxodolov to avoid a similar fate. Suxodolov views Armando as ill, pays for his drinks, and buys him a train ticket. After Suxodolov leaves, Armando raises his violin, weeping and invoking his muse.

Maja: Loyalty of friend, Klara (4).

While at a concert, Klara notices that her girlfriend, Maja, is looking for someone, but Maja will not say for whom. Klara insists that, as a friend, Maja should confess everything to her. Later Klara offers Pavel copies of Suxodolov's letters to Maja. When he refuses to accept them she decides to send them in the mail so that he will have to read them anyway.

Klara and Dononov: Personal ethics, free thought, humanitarian values (6).

When Pavel refuses to read Klara's copies of Suxodolov's letters and tells her she needn't feel obligated to have people read them, she asks if he has given her an order. After she forces the letters on him through the mail, he asks her if she finds Suxodolov's comparison of Maja to a song unseemly; he tells her she should also view Raphael's Sistine Madonna as offensive religious propaganda. He then asks her if communists' lives really have to be deprived of all poetry. She still laments that he will not give her orders. He then observes that they have different viewpoints about the creation of the new communist morality and that it is a long and difficult process, whereas she thought it had already been worked out. He tells her she must learn to think independently rather than live by the thoughts of others. She replies that she will go mad without direction for her emotions. Likewise, Pavel accuses Dononov of adopting philistine virtues. Dononov asserts that if a person is devious in his private life he will also deceive the Party. Such logic, says Pavel, would also brand such a person a traitor. Dononov agrees. Pavel then accuses Dononov of seeing everything in black and white and of adhering to a dogma which sent decent people to prison in the past and would make a saintly person like Suxodolov appear dishonest. Both Klara and Dononov pretend to be motivated by high principles.

N. Ždanov, *Journey Home*

Pavel Alekseevič Varygin: Unpleasant reality, the people (6).

Having returned to his home village after a long absence to attend his mother's funeral, Pavel Alekseevič Varygin visits their old home and speaks with the midwife who roomed with his mother. She shows him his mother's ragged bed and makes him aware of her impoverished circumstances. A farmer's wife comes to complain about the size of her private plot of land. A soldier's wife complains that their life is one of work and little reward and asks if it is right for the government to control their hemp crop and undermine their chance for profit. He replies that this is a political question. Another indicates that they are impoverished because not motivated to work without pay and that they would be better off if there were fewer bureaucrats for them to support. Hearing everyone's complaints Varygin becomes anxious to return home. As he leaves, he thinks that he should have told them that, whereas people like himself govern, the rest of them have to do the work. He eagerly anticipates returning to his comfortable office but is disturbed by a vague feeling of guilt.

Pavel Alekseevič Varygin: Devotion to his mother (5, 10).

Varygin had not seen his mother for six years, though he had occasionally received letters suggesting her poor circumstances. The soldier's wife suggests how happy Varygin's mother would have been, had she lived to see him again, alluding to the fact that he had promised to see her the year before but had not come.

B. Pasternak, *Doctor Živago*

Jurij Andreevič Živago: Sense of purpose and self-determination, political power, the regime, political inhumanity, regimentation (1, 2, 8).

When, after World War I and the Revolution, Dr. Jurij Andreevič Živago returns to Moscow, he soon feels that the Communist Party is itself a betrayal. He also senses that he can no longer control his future and that, though he would gladly sacrifice himself for the general good, it would accomplish nothing. In Siberia, after he is abducted to render medical service to communist partisans, he makes three abortive escape attempts. He is meanwhile forced into a society which he detests but cannot avoid. He is further disillusioned by having to witness mutual atrocities perpetrated by both Whites and Reds. Finally escaping, he reaches Jurjatin, where he is repelled by the political decrees, texts of speeches, *etc.* posted by the officials and concludes that his life is enslaved to a meaningless, impractical jargon. After returning to Moscow from Jurjatin, he remains indifferent to society, unambitious, and unproductive.

Jurij Andreevič Živago: Ties of friendship (4).

After returning from the War, Jurij is disappointed to discover the distance between himself and his old friends, Gordon and Dudorov. When he comes to Moscow for the last time, he is further disillusioned by their shallow lives.

Jurij Andreevič Živago: Family ties (4).

Jurij's parents both died during his boyhood. His father had been irresponsible and dissolute, his mother sickly. As he completes his medical studies, he is steered into a marriage to Tonja Gromeko at the urging of her dying mother. Upon returning from the War he has a traumatic encounter with his young son, Šura, who slaps him in the face. This leaves a foreboding impression upon both Jurij and Tonja. After bringing his family to Varykino, he re-encounters Lara Antipova, with whom he establishes an alliance. He suffers a bad conscience, however, and decides to end the affair and confess his deception to Tonja, but postpones doing so until his capture by the partisans makes it impossible. After fleeing from his captors, he momentarily thinks of

Tonja and their two children, realizing that he is never available when they need him. He promptly forgets them again as the sight of a rowan tree reminds him of Lara, whom he thereupon vows to find again and love. When he learns that his family is safely established in Moscow, he feels that he and they are fated to remain apart. After returning to Moscow for the last time, he makes only half-hearted efforts to rejoin them in Paris.

Tonja Živago: Her husband Jurij's love (4).

Before he returns home from the War, Jurij writes Tonja about meeting and working with Lara Antipova in a hospital at the front. Sensing his attachment to Lara, Tonja writes him not to bother returning home but to remain with the nurse he has described and with whom she feels she cannot compete. In Jurjatin he deceives Tonja with Lara. Later, instead of rejoining Tonja, he remains in Moscow and lives with Marina, the daughter of the Gromeko's former servant, Markel. Marina bears him two children. He later leaves her and lives by himself.

Paša Antipov: Social injustice (8, 9).

Before the Revolution, Paša Antipov witnesses the routing of demonstrators protesting the Tsar's manifesto. His father had been banished to Siberia for leading a railroad strike.

Paša Antipov: Human values, human life (6).

After the Revolution, Paša Antipov becomes the red commander, Strel'nikov, who unfeelingly murders and destroys to establish the new order. His lawless brutality finally turns upon him and he shoots himself to avoid capture and execution.

Lara Gišar (later Antipova):   Komarovskij (4).

Lara Gišar is seduced by Komarovskij, her mother's lover, who has become genuinely infatuated with Lara instead. In order to pay a debt incurred by her prodigal brother, Lara later vows to extract money at gunpoint from Komarovskij. Locating him at a Christmas party, she shoots instead at a certain Kornakov, who had previously prosecuted the father of Paša Antipov. Later in Varykino she chooses to accompany Komarovskij to safety under the illusion that Jurij will join them.

Paša Antipov: His wife, Lara's love (4).

After their wedding, Lara reveals to Paša the story of her affair with

Komarovskij. This shocks Paša but confirms his suspicions about her. After they move to the Urals, their life together becomes onerous and artificial. He finally enlists in the army, thinking that she does not love him and imagining that she has married him as a means of atoning for her past. Lara later tells Jurij that her broken marriage resulted from the evils of the times but that Paša thought the cause was personal.

A. Kuznecov, *Continuation of a Legend*

Tolja: Sense of purpose, self-understanding (2).

As he completes school, Tolja, the narrator, feels lost and helpless. He indicts his teachers, who have failed to teach him about life. Because he did not cram consistently enough, he must work rather than continue his education. He finally joins a group of enlistees who are traveling from Moscow to Vladivostok. On the train he feels alone and useless and wonders why he ever left. Again he laments that he never received advice in school about how to live and must still read the 'book' about life. Later, in Irkutsk, a companion, Miška, rebuffs him for insisting on his right to exciting experience.

Tolja: Injustice (8).

While on the train, Tolja becomes incensed when several of his colleagues intercede for another, Vasek, who has been robbed, then proceed to drink up the recovered money. While working at Irkutsk, Tolja is bothered by certain truck drivers who demand that he credit them with additional trips. He later tells Miška that he becomes especially discouraged when he encounters parasites.

Tolja: Self-sacrifice (10).

The father of Tolja's Moscow friend, Vit'ka, had earlier mocked the boys' idealism and said that one day they would worry only about earning money. Vit'ka has reacted by becoming a kind of beatnik, but Tolja resists his cynicism. After leaving Moscow, however, he is frequently tempted to amass money in order to return and buy a car with which to impress his girl friend, Juna. Both she and Vit'ka are well provided for, and the prospect of their pleasures impels him on one occasion to pack his suitcase, but a fellow worker discourages him from leaving. He is nonetheless uncertain as to whose is the better way of life, Vit'ka's or that of a Siberian industrial worker. He even asks his Siberian girl friend, Tonja, if they are not just material for building the future.

When he goes fishing with another comrade, Len'ka, he becomes almost hysterical and tries to borrow money with which to return to Moscow.

Tolja: His mother (5).

Tolja feels he may have come to Siberia as a reaction to his mother's urging to adopt a common, mundane, familiar way of life. He also feels that he has disappointed her.

Ju. Kazakov, *The Renegade*

Egor: Reality, the external world (1).

Egor, a young buoy-keeper, is an inveterate drunkard like his wife, who drowned when, in an inebriated condition, she fell through the river's ice the winter before. He now enjoys the company of Alen'ka, a young girl who visits him for two to three days at a time. He avoids associating with the people in his village, even on holidays. He is only occasionally discontent with his life, particularly when he recalls his days in the navy or views a passing ship, which incites him to wander and seek a new life.

Egor: Responsibility, conscientiousness, ambition, sense of duty (10).

Egor takes pleasure in his own languor. He is even too lazy to bail out the water that seeps into his boat. He is indifferent about his work and avoids exploiting his sideline as a ferryman, in which capacity he could earn a good income without undue effort. Even Alen'ka tries to persuade him to stop drinking, marry, and find a more challenging, more respectable job — but in vain.

Egor and Alen'ka: Traditional mundane, sensible, unfeeling existence (1).

When travelers occasionally spend the night at Egor's lodge and after he imbibes their liquor, Alen'ka feels ashamed for him, aware of the rude and ludicrous impression he makes upon his guests. In her embarrassment, she nonetheless awaits the moment when he will amaze them — which he does as soon as he suddenly begins to sing. Impressed as they are by his gift, he never completely shares it with them. Perhaps twice a month, when he is especially bored and restless, he drinks all day until, at the right moment, usually toward evening, he and Alen'ka excitedly walk to a favorite outdoor spot where they sing together. Now he sings, not as before the guests, but in full voice and under the sway of his emotions.

Both rapture in their music's sweetness and sorrow. Alen'ka yearns to have lived with Egor at an earlier time in just such a state of drunken innocence, while Egor moans and cries as if lamenting the transiency of their ecstasy. Together they experience extreme happiness and torment. They sing and fall on the grass; then she kisses him and declares her love, while he lies nearly insensible.

A. Terc, *The Trial Begins*

Karlinskij: Regimentation, impersonality, de-humanization, extinction, insignificance, personal satisfactions (1, 2, 4).

Karlinskij is repulsed by an allusion to neo-Mathusianism and abortions, then cynically reflects that perhaps someday human embryos will be sold in tin cans to supplement the fish reserves — an enlightened kind of cannibalism. He fears his death and cannot understand how communism can possibly replace people's faith in an after life or how there can be any real meaning outside the individual. He realizes that he can confide his apprehension to no one else, because others would only pity themselves for having to die — which he thinks accounts for their self-deception, *e.g.* Globov's in politics and Marina's physical vanity, etc. He decides to make Marina the means of curing his insomnia and apprehension by turning her own power against her. As, later at a planetarium, Karlinskij and Marina attend a lecture intended to prove that there is no God in the heavens, he becomes depressed by a feeling of insignificance and purposelessness. Marina's presence reassures him about his own existence however, and he continues to make love to her as planned. His strategy is to flatter her that she is the cause of his suffering and thereby win her gratitude. On another occasion as they tour an art gallery, he expounds on the relationship between sex and knowledge. He indicates that animals propogate but do not philosophize since they have no shame, which is the essence of love and knowledge. Neither gods nor animals apparently experience the special self-awareness which produces shame. Shame is in turn pleasurable because forbidden. During a military celebration Karlinskij listens to Radio Free Europe on his short wave set, then turns it off as the program is jammed with music from the local celebration. When Katja shows him Serezha's seditious notebook, he resents their attempt to involve him as a free-thinking person in their plan. That same night two plain-clothes men discuss the desirability of trapping written material which people flush down toilets and even of detecting people's thoughts and feelings with a 'psychoscope'.

After Karlinskij manages to seduce Marina, he is disappointed to discover that he does not desire her and is only anxious for her to leave.

Vladimir Petrovič Globov and Colleagues: Truth; humanitarian values; concern for son, Sereža (6, 5).

Vladimir Petrovič Globov lectures his son Sereža that their leaders have all the answers and that everything is subordinate to their great purpose, for which millions have died. He cites the example of a commander who, by mistakenly shooting one of his men for insubordination, inspired respect in his other men and thus won a battle. At a soccer game he castigates a losing player for not using brutal means to reach his goal, resorting to political analogies and invoking anti-Semitism. Late that night in an empty courtroom he rehearses his speech prosecuting Rabinovič, an abortionist, and associating the latter's crime with sabotage. He imagines that the defense lawyer produces Marina and Sereža as evidence against the prosecution and insists that they be tried also. He then imagines that his indictment of Rabinovič will be the beginning of a series of trials exposing a whole world conspiracy. He later dreams that Rabinovič guides him through a museum and shows him a thinking machine, a human brain in a glass jar, which may blow up the universe with its thought. The brain has concluded that, like Christianity, Socialism will also become corrupt and be superceded. Rabinovič adds that the doctrine of ends justifying means results in impermanent systems. Globov orders him to stop the machine. During a military celebration Globov urges Sereža to look at their Leader in a crowd of people, even though no one person is distinguishable from the rest. When Sereža protests that he cannot identify their leader, Globov accuses him of being blind. Speaking with Sereža's grandmother, Globov proudly asserts that with his two hands he has both plowed the soil and sent people to their death. He acquaints her with various rumors about foreign infiltration, *etc.* His ears are described as flushed with blood, suggesting the need for a bloodletting. Although the grandmother observes that innocent people are thus persecuted, he justifies this by the analogy of a tank in battle which must sometimes run over its own wounded. She agrees that their purpose justifies everything, but that nothing else would. Later, at a celebration in his honor, Globov is praised for his prosecution of Rabinovič. His colleagues, who are described as kindly and innocent people who yet terrify the world, allude to a nation-wide conspiracy among Jewish doctors. After Sereža's arrest, Globov is warned not to protest in order to avoid casting suspicion upon himself. He is advised to have another son instead. The grandmother insists, however, that he intervene and accuses him of denouncing Sereža. Globov tells her to leave, then orders a cleaning woman to wash up the puddles left by the grandmother's wet feet. After destroying the furnishings in his room in a fit of rage, Globov addresses the bust of his Master, as would a soldier his commanding officer after a victorious battle. During a stampede of people, pressing to view the Master's bier, Globov's own body strikes and wounds a number of them as if he were an instrument controlled by the Master's gigantic hand. When he overhears that a little girl has been crushed by a truck, he argues to himself that victims are necessary to the general purpose and that this would be true even if she were his own child.

Vladimir Petrovič Globov: His wife, Marina; progeny (4).

Marina Globov deceives her husband with Karlinskij, offering excuses for not returning home in the evening. When Globov is toasted on the birth of a prospective daughter, he replies regretfully that there are no grounds for such a toast. He is proud that he himself came from a large family and is himself eager for offspring. Finally Marina spitefully reveals that she has submitted to an abortion to prevent their having a child. Globov feels betrayed both as husband and public prosecutor. He thus becomes indifferent to her, locks her out of his room, and even suspects her of kidnapping the baby he longs for and of plotting with the doctors to kill it again. This leads him to suspect that someone is hiding in his cupboard, which causes him to destroy all of his furnishings with a Caucasian sword.

Marina Globova: Everything and everybody but herself, non-carnal values (6).

Marina Globova's beauty is an end of its own, not the means to money or clothes, which are used only to enhance her beauty. She objects to the presence of the Master's bust because it does not suit her surroundings. She enjoys posing in the nude before her bedroom mirror, requiring Globov to view her through the keyhole, meanwhile examining herself for sags and wrinkles. During her birthday dinner she surrenders her body to various guests while dancing. Incensed that Globov has interfered by knocking over the phonograph, she later castigates him, then vengefully discloses her abortion. When he slaps her, she is concerned only about the appearance of her cheek. Karlinskij has noticed that, like an animal or a goddess and unlike other people, she has neither shame nor curiosity, while Globov himself senses that he is a means to her end. After Globov avoids her, she craves his attention and even manipulates his hands upon her body in order to arouse him.

Sereža Globov and Katja: Soviet ideology, the regime, the older generation (7, 5).

Globov warns Sereža not to ask his teacher awkward questions about history and philosophy, particularly about the justice of certain wars or that of the Revolution itself. Karlinskij has meanwhile made Sereža suspect that justice is relative. Globov tries to convince him that he is too young to understand affairs of state and should rely instead on the utterances of their leaders. His grandmother also warns him that he is talking like the enemy and avoids showing him her true sympathy. While she urges faith in their ultimate goal, Sereža remarks that only the World Revolution can help them. He arranges a rendevous with a young girl, Katja, at the zoo, where they will not be overheard. There they discuss plans for a new, equitable world order. Later Katja brings Sereža's notebook to Karlinskij, who, though sympathetic, warns her to destroy it. She in turn feels she has betrayed their cause and retrieves the notebook from him.

People: Established values, freedom (6).

After a lecture at the Planetarium and to everyone else's amusement, an old man still insists that there is a God, while a little boy bursts into tears, unable to believe that the earth revolves around the sun and that the sun is larger than the earth. When the Master dies, the people react as would dogs who have lost their owners, as if they want him to return to kick and beat them. They prefer a Master to freedom.

Rabinovič: Christianity (7).

After his conviction and while working as a prisoner, Rabinovič unearths an ancient dagger with a crucifix-shaped handle and philosophizes about the way men have turned the cross into the handle of a deadly weapon, thus making God, who was intended to be the end, into the means. He points the dagger into the air, both invoking and at the same time reproaching Deity.

V. Tendrjakov, *Three, Seven, Ace*

Nikolaj Petrovič Bušuev: Scruples, fellow men (4, 6).

Nikolaj Petrovič Bušuev, a former prison inmate, is rescued from drowning by a lumber worker, Leška Malinkin, then hired as a wood floater by Malinkin's supervisor, Dubinin. Bušuev soon encourages the other workers to join him in gambling at cards. At first they play for very low stakes, and Bušuev allows the others to win. Finally he entices the miserly Egor to join them, then raises the stakes and eventually wins from the latter the equivalent of several months' wages. When, next morning, Bušuev refuses to return the money, the two become violent but are separated. However, the excitement of playing induces all of them, including Egor, to gamble again with Bušuev. Once more they lose to him, which convinces them that he is cheating. Egor rushes Bušuev, but Bušuev knocks him to the floor, then holds the others at bay with his axe until they are cowed and he can safely conceal his winnings.

Aleksandr (Saša) Dubinin: His men's loyalty, justice (4, 8).

Saša Dubinin, manager of the lumber floating point, invites Bušuev to join them as a worker, not because he trusts him but because he does not fear him. Although aware of Bušuev's card playing, he feels helpless to intervene. He realizes that, where cards begin, drinking bouts and scandals follow, but he cannot dictate to his men in what is not directly related to their work. After Bušuev's final confrontation with the other workers, Dubinin apprehends him searching for his passport in Dubinin's office. Bušuev next leads Dubinin to the river, pretending by a ruse to show him where he has buried his winnings, but then demanding that Dubinin return his passport, which he presumes must be in Dubinin's pocket. Dubinin draws his knife, successfully defending himself against Bušuev's axe and finally felling Bušuev, who, in falling, crushes his skull against a rock and dies. Dubinin then reports the incident to the police, who the next day send an investigator. The latter quickly presumes that Dubinin has killed Bušuev for his money. Dubinin realizes that the investigator will not be satisfied before he can accuse someone and that he was himself equally thoughtless and insensitive at the same age. If the money cannot be found, Dubinin must be arrested. Although he has a clear conscience and knows that if he had not stabbed Bušuev he would himself have been killed, Dubinin also realizes that there will be no forgiveness if he is accused of murder. Unable to locate Bušuev's winnings, one of his men sorrowfully observes that they have gambled away another human being.

Lumberjacks: Courage (10).

After he knocks Egor to the floor and wields his axe, Bušuev threatens to kill the first one who opposes him and tells them he has nothing to lose. Even though the others are stronger than he, have axes in the corridor, and outnumber him twenty to one, no one moves.

Leška Malinkin: Courage, conscience, integrity, illusions, loyalty (7, 10).

After Bušuev has cowed the other workers and all have retired to their bunks, he whispers to Leška to go outside and wait for him. While waiting outdoors, Leška is tempted to visit Dubinin in the office but waits too long. When Bušuev appears, he tells Leška that the winnings — ten thousand rubles — are hidden beneath Leška's pillow and that Leška is to take them to his native village, where he is then to await Bušuev. Bušuev threatens to kill him if he does not cooperate. Returning to his bunk, Leška is tempted to reveal the plot but fears Bušuev's reprisal. He realizes how unrealistic his concept of the world had been until now and feels helpless and stupid before the life that surrounds him. As Egor goes to Bušuev's bunk and searches it in his absence, Leška fears that he will discover the money under Leška's pillow and even strangle him. Egor, an old companion, suddenly seems an incomprehensible stranger. After the inspector's arrival, Leška further fears to produce the money since he did not do so earlier. He imagines that they would now suspect him of conspiring with Bušuev. He is perplexed to think that Dubinin is viewed as a murderer and wishes he had not saved Bušuev from the rapids. If he reveals the money, he thinks even Dubinin will turn from him and expel him from the settlement, and he will be known as a thief in his native village. He considers hiding the money where Egor can find it but is too frightened and throws it into the river instead. Each of the men is interrogated in turn. As Leška is questioned he feels that the interrogator is now his superior and not Dubinin. Fearing this new authority, he resolves that nobody will get the truth from him and answers that he does not know where Bušuev put his money. That night the others are surprised to find him sobbing in his pillow.

V. Aksenov, *Colleagues*

Aleksej (Leksej) Maksimov: Mundane life, the uneventful future, socialist self-sacrifice (2, 7, 10).

Leksej Maksimov, a young medical intern, complains about the possibility of receiving an appointment in a provincial area where he might culturally deteriorate. He is attracted by the offer to serve as a ship's doctor. He opposes the notion of self-sacrifice and the propaganda that encourages it. His fellow student, Saša, has been assigned to a rural center, and Leksej urges him to feign illness in order not to have to leave so soon, generally mocking Saša's decision to go there because the area is in need of a doctor. Leksej is himself at first assigned to inspect ships and keep records, which bores him. He is critical of those who seek an easy life, while what he seeks is an exciting one.

Aleksej (Leksej) Maksimov: Swindlers, hypocritical self-seekers (8).

While checking food stuffs in a sea port warehouse, Leksej discovers that a shipment of contaminated flour has not been destroyed as required but has instead been sold at private gain for consumption by a ship's crew. When he confronts the warehouse manager, he is first bribed, then threatened. He is told that if he persists he will be prevented from ever serving on a ship. Others then advise him not to get involved. He becomes concerned that such people still operate within communism. He is disillusioned by those who, while professing glib patriotism, serve their own purposes instead.

Aleksandr (Saša) Dmitrievič: Fedor Bugrov (4).

Saša Dmitrievič first encounters the anarchistic Fedor Bugrov when he examines a bull dozer crew afflicted with influenza and notes that Bugrov, unlike the others, is feigning illness. Bugrov boldly admits that he has no physical complaint but boasts that he is in love and that Saša will have to favor him because they are interested in the same girl, Daša. His stare suggests to Saša that he is a killer. Saša refuses to declare him ill, however, despite Bugrov's attempted blackmail. As he leaves, Bugrov shakes a threatening fist at him. Later, at a village dance, Bugrov appears with a gang and, after being refused by Daša, seizes her anyway. When no one else intervenes, Saša confronts him and tells him to leave. Bugrov advances toward him but Saša ducks, then delivers a blow to his head which sends Bugrov to the floor. The others then oust both Bugrov and his gang. Bugrov consequently loses prestige with his cronies and, in order to gain their respect, vows vengeance upon Saša. As, still later, Saša calls upon Daša to assist him in a medical call, he discovers Bugrov and the matchmakers negotiating with Daša's mother. The others restrain Bugrov while Saša and Daša leave. Then Bugrov rushes after them, groping for his knife, as the two leave the scene in a helicopter. While on a subsequent call, Saša encounters Bugrov robbing a warehouse. They fight and Bugrov knifes Saša in the back.

Aleksandr (Saša) Dmitrievič: His eventual wife, Ina (4).

Before leaving for his assignment, Saša has become acquainted with Ina, a student at the University of Moscow, who then sees him off. Later, realizing that he will be away from civilization for most of the year, he becomes interested in local girls and is attracted to Daša Gurianova, an efficient and loyal nurse. Daša reminds him of Ina, however, and he becomes confused as to which of them he ought to encourage. He begins to worry that he cannot remember Ina well and that Daša is becoming more attractive to him. Later he is convinced that he is in love with Ina and tries to maintain a distance with Daša, yet remains concerned that Bugrov might take advantage of her. Finally Ina announces that she is coming to visit him. He becomes uneasy, fearing that they no longer know each other.

Daša Gurijanova: Saša's love (4).

Daša Gurijanova tells herself that she only admires Saša and does not love him, even though she prefers him to the unpleasant Bugrov. She tries to convince herself that Saša is too comical to be taken seriously. Later, as Saša makes preparations for Ina's visit, she tries not to take notice. When Bugrov arrives with the matchmakers, she tells herself that she is really in love with Saša and will end up an old maid. That same evening, as she and Saša spend the night with a patient in the country, the patient's wife, thinking they are a married couple, wishes them a good life together, which embarrasses them both. Then, before they retire, Saša asks her to keep him company. Fearing he will become involved with her she rushes off.

Fedor Bugrov: Sense of purpose and accomplishment (2).

Fedor Bugrov undermines one of Saša's patients, who is undergoing a treatment for ulcers, by making him drunk. When Saša apprehends them and reprimands the patient, Ibraxin, the latter then turns on Bugrov and tells him not to come back. Bugrov thus feels completely alienated. Daša has spurned him, and the members of his gang are now reformed and trying to be exemplary workers. He is conscious of his unsuccessful life, suffers from insomnia, and wants to hide.

Vladislav (Vladka) Karpov: Vera Velesina (4).

A third intern, Vladka Karpov, is anxious not to be sent away from his ex-girl friend, Vera, even though she has since married Velesin, one of their professors. His two ideals — to have Vera as his wife and pursue a career in surgery — have both passed him by. Vera, who is really interested in Leksej, arranges a clandestine meeting with the latter without Vladka's knowledge.

Vera Velesina: Leksej's love (4).

Vera Velesina is concerned about giving up her husband, who is also her graduate mentor, and losing her career by following Leksej. She also wants to avoid upsetting her father, who has suffered a stroke.

The generations: One another (5).

After graduation and before receiving their assignments, Leksej and Saša encounter two half-drunk older men. One, who has lost a leg and introduces himself as Sergej Egorov, taunts them for being less idealistic and certain of their goals than his own generation. He also accuses them of loafing. Leksej accosts him, while Egorov's friend reprimands Leksej for abusing a war hero. Leksej then replies that Sergej probably lost his leg as a drunkard under a streetcar.

V. Tendrjakov, *The Trial*

Semen Teterin: Truth, integrity, courage, loyalty, conscience, self-respect (10).

An experienced hunter, Semen Teterin, escorts a medical assistant and neighbor, Mitjagin, and an industrial manager, Dudyrev on a bear hunt. Having wounded their prey and cornered it on a bridge which begins to give way under its weight, Mitjagin and Dudyrev simultaneously fire. At the same moment Teterin hears the accordian of a young boy who had earlier crossed their path. He shouts to the others to refrain their fire, but it is too late. The bear is felled, as is the young boy, whose body they find in the water by the bridge. Meanwhile Teterin's hunting dog, Kalinka, chews at the bear's withers to avenge the death of her daughter, whom the bear had killed earlier the same night. After investigators arrive, the bullets are sought in order to establish which hunter killed the boy and which shot the bear. One bullet passed through the boy's body, however, and the other, which presumably lodged in the bear's withers, cannot be found due to Kalinka's mauling. The investigators conclude that this bullet entered the bear's mouth, then passed through its throat and out of its body through the withers causing the blood flow which attracted Kalinka. As, later, villagers assist Teterin in removing the bear, he complains to them about Mitjagin, who had obviously never shot a rifle before but pretended otherwise; he thus presumes that Mitjagin is responsible for the boy's death. While skinning the bear, however, Teterin discovers the used bullet, which, in order to determine its calibre, he heats and reshapes. He then sizes it in his own gun, which has the same calibre as Dudyrev's, but discovers to his surprise that it does not fit his gun, thus proving that Mitjagin's rifle shot the bear and Dudyrev's killed the boy. After Dudyrev advises Teterin to bring the bullet to an investigator's attention, Teterin is in turn questioned about his acquaintance with Mitjagin and warned that he might be suspected of trying to protect his friend at Dudyrev's expense and that false evidence is also punishable. He is also told that no one will believe his evidence in view of the fact that the investigators have ruled that the bullet passed through the bear. Moreover, the bullet he showed them has been perfectly re-formed, and no one can now prove that it has ever been fired. Other circumstances further favor Dudyrev: the fact that he is a more experienced hunter and that, in the position where they were standing when they fired, Mitjagin had a less obstructed view of the bridge. Teterin is further warned not to complicate the affair since he too might be tried for negligence for permitting Mitjagin to join them in the hunt, *etc*. As he leaves the investigator, Teterin sees Dudyrev's car drive up and immediately suspects that the two are in collusion. After this, he is tempted to put the bullet with his others so that it will be indistinguishable but is restrained by thoughts of Mitjagin's children. He finally consults with his good friend, the local *kolkhoz* manager, Borovikov. The latter advises that he not discuss his evidence with anyone else. When Teterin asks him if this means he should hide the truth, Borovikov cites the example of a subordinate whom he had to dismiss for inefficiency, though loyal. By acting as he did, Borovikov saved money and served the interest of the *kolkhoz*. He had acted according to his own truth, not that of his subordinate. He then suggests the relativity of truth with respect to the boy's death, that the law would condemn Dudyrev and remove him from his position but that his successor might well be inferior, thus jeopardizing the general welfare. If Dudyrev's forest industry is successful, for instance, his workers will remain steady clients of the *kolkhoz* and the *kolkhoz* workers themselves will have a better income. Teterin remains dissatisfied, however, realizing that, according to Borovikov's theory, an innocent person could be ground into meal to feed the rest. He in fact asks Borovikov if, for the general good, Borovikov would shove Teterin into a pit along with Mitjagin. Borovikov answers that he would push himself into a pit for the general good, to which Teterin replies that he should feel free to do so but to ask permission of Teterin before doing the same with him. Teterin then rationalizes, reflecting on Borovikov, who is just as guilty as he but does not worry about it, and on Duryrev, who is even more directly involved in the affair but appears to have forgotten about it as he conducts his business. Teterin asks himself why he should be a suffering Christ and better than the rest, takes the bullet from his pocket, and finally throws it away where it can never be found again. At Dudyrev's urging, the investigators agree to interrogate Teterin once more without partiality. This time, however, he replies that there is no bullet and tells them to consider that he had never found one. He tells himself that they would merely accuse him again of trying to defend Mitjagin. For the first time in his life, he senses that he has been motivated by fear. Later, at the trial, he continues to lie, sensing that his argument would be even weaker now that he has thrown away the bullet and fearing the complicated questions that might ensue. He pretends to have brought the investigator an unused bullet in order to protect Mitjagin. Only after his own testimony does Teterin hear Dudyrev ask to be considered equally guilty in the crime. Teterin now realizes that Dudyrev did not act in his own self-interest and that he (Teterin) can no longer use this as a justification for himself. He later realizes that he did not have to defer to other people and wonders if it is too late for him to change. He tormentedly concludes that there is no worse trial than that of one's conscience.

Semen Teterin: Encroaching civilization, Dudyrev (9).

Teterin is the most famous of local hunters. The forest is his whole life, and numerous shelters which he himself has built have been named after him. The newly arrived Dudyrev is fated eventually to destroy Teterin's forest realm. The latter has directed the construction of a large woodworking combine and has procured an extensive transportation network for the whole area. His combine will serve a number of forest industries and lead to numerous lumber camps in the area. When the noise of tractors, *etc.* intrudes on the forest, Teterin's enterprise will be ended. After the accident, while on his way to consult with Dudyrev, Teterin is perplexed by the presence of bulldozers, dumptrucks, new housing, *etc.* He asks one worker to leave a certain old woman in her hut until she dies, feeling as ancient as she. Although told where to find Dudyrev, he loses himself in the maze of structures, even though he is never lost in the forest. He senses Dudyrev's great power and contrasts to this the latter's respect for him and the forest as well as an earlier occasion when he had scolded Dudyrev during the hunt. He now recalls

Kalinka's hesitation to cross the bridge and identifies with her insecurity. His consequent hatred for Dudyrev becomes aggravated by the general respect of everyone else for whom Dudyrev is constructing improved housing.

Vasilij Maksimovič Mitjagin: Teterin's loyalty (4).

After the accident, Mitjagin's wife accuses Teterin of placing the blame on her husband. She laments that she and her children will have no breadwinner. Thereafter, every time he leaves his home, Teterin anticipates encountering Mitjagin or his wife and having them accost him with questions. Mitjagin avoids him, however. On one occasion they meet by accident, and Teterin blinks and stands aside. Teterin realizes that Mitjagin believes he is himself the murderer, and Teterin is tempted to reassure him but dare not since Mitjagin would then require him to take action in his defense.

Konstantin Sergeevič Dudyrev: Privilege, personal advantage, pragmatic officials (8, 10).

When Teterin confronts Dudyrev with his evidence, Dudyrev asks him if he expects Dudyrev to condemn himself as a murderer in order to protect Mitjagin. Teterin replies that Dudyrev must act according to his conscience and that Teterin does not wish to advise him because Dudyrev has better judgment. Dudyrev then tells Teterin to report his findings to the investigator. Dudyrev is inclined to think that Mitjagin is the murderer but decides to share Mitjagin's fate and not protect himself. Out of conscience, he will assume half the guilt himself. The inspectors assure him however that they are not literalists and understand both his and Mitjagin's obvious innocence. He argues that he does not wish to be an exception to the law and points out that Teterin may not have been very convincing simply because he is not accustomed to speaking with other men. He also recites an anecdote about a drunkard who looked for his missing purse under the light, even though he lost it on the dark side of the street, suggesting that the inspectors fear complications. He senses that they want to avoid friction with other officials. He tells himself that truth and happiness are inseparable and cannot be acquired by looking only in the light. At a subsequent meeting he offers additional reasons why the inspectors should believe Teterin: had Teterin intended to deceive them, he could have rendered the bullet into any imperfect form and not reshaped it, nor would he have taken it to Dudyrev first. The tree which had obstructed Dudyrev's sight, furthermore, had not blocked the whole bridge, and there was no direct evidence that the boy had fallen into the water from the bridge's middle. He realizes that the inspectors do not care to consider his arguments and that he is only making things awkward for them. His very name has forced them to search for truth under the light, but he finally convinces them that he is serious and does not wish their special consideration. At the trial he consistently maintains that, in the absence of more definite evidence, he is equally guilty with Mitjagin. He does not consider either of them a criminal, but, if the court disagrees, it must punish them equally.

Konstantin Sergeevič Dudyrev: Faith in Teterin and the people (7).

After the trial, Dudyrev becomes suspicious of Teterin's denial, realizing that Teterin has lied on one of two occasions and told the truth on the other. As a hunter, furthermore, Teterin had been, for Dudyrev, a personification of the simple and honest people (*narod*). Dudyrev had therefore expected more of Teterin than of even himself. Since Teterin acts from natural impulses, while Dudyrev has been conditioned as one of the intelligentsia, Dudyrev is forced to conclude that people change more slowly than outward life, that while he can build his industry in three or four years, human chraacter is only formed over decades. He decides that it is more important to teach people how to live and that blind dedication is not the same thing as the true love of a doer.

V. Aksenov, *Ticket to the Stars*

Dimka Denisov: Tradition, conformity, responsibility, vocation (1, 10).

Dimka Denisov refuses to go to college in order not to imitate his brother, Viktor. He would rather be a tramp than do what everybody else expects of him. When Viktor offers him and his friends a job at his plant to discourage their making a trip to the Baltic, Dimka tosses a coin to avoid having to choose, tossing it however in such a way that he controls the outcome. He and his friends have no use for theories and profess not to believe in love. They consider people with mundane occupations bourgeois. When asked about his life plans, Dimka replies that that is the concern of parents, who have to pay for one's education. He is not anxious to enter college immediately and is willing that he and his friends sell their possessions to finance their trip. Once underway, he becomes homesick. Eventually he signs onto a ship's crew in Estonia and experiences the rigors and discomforts of sailing. While his friends have already decided on a career without tossing coins, he is still unsure of his future and is inclined to continue drifting.

Parents and Viktor Denisov: Dimka, the younger generation (5).

Viktor Denisov realizes that he has ignored his younger brother Dimka and no longer understands him. Dimka seems to him a complete stranger. They argue the wisdom of Dimka's trip but finally agree to correspond, and Viktor agrees to conciliate their mother. Dimka and his friends have left their parents notes informing them of the trip. The latter are mystified and blame themselves for not being more strict.

Galja Bodorova: Realistic life role (10).

Before Galja Bodorova leaves for the Baltic with Dimka and two other boys, her mother intervenes as she dances and wipes off her lipstick. Galja insists on joining the boys, even though their trip will disturb her plans to train as an actress. They joke with her about her dream for a screen test. She too becomes homesick after leaving. On a beach in Estonia she envisions herself as a leading actress. She imagines being photographed and contended for by movie directors. An actor, Grigorij Dolgov, invites her and Dimka to a party, encourages her aspirations, and tries to buy off Dimka so that he can be alone with her. Dolgov and Galja finally disappear in a cab. When she returns the next day she protests that Dolgov has not compromised her but really loves her and is helping prepare her for an actors' institute. They will soon leave for Leningrad, where she will begin her studies. She intends to achieve on her own merit, however, and not rely on connections.

Dimka Denisov: Galja Bodorova (4).

In Moscow Galja suggests to the boys that they attend a light romantic movie, but Dimka ridicules the idea, and she implies that he is not grown up to love. Viktor notices that Dimka is unsure of himself in her presence. It is unclear whether her attachment to the boys is romantic or merely a childhood friendship. On the beach in Estonia young men gather around her, while she pretends not to notice. Her pose pains Dimka. He and his friends tease the young Estonians by stealing their ball, finally inducing a response from Galja. Then, in her presence, they discuss her figure, which shocks her and incites her to slap Dimka. He is in turn puzzled and confused by her reaction. Later, as he watches her, she seems especially attractive. She becomes aware of his attention and is pleased that he is looking at her. They flirt and experience intimate contact. He confesses his love for her. They remain for a long time on the sand, oblivious to all else. Later, when she is distracted by Dolgov, Dimka chases the two of them in a truck as they drive off in a cab. He then tries to break into the hotel, is arrested by the police, but released the next morning. When they next meet, Galja is conscience-struck and wishes Dimka would reproach her, but dare not reveal her experience of the night before. He accuses her of lying about it, and they argue. She refuses to go with him and the others to a fishing cooperative, even when he begs and weeps for her to come. Later he ignores her when he sees her on the street. Although she maintains that she loves another, she would still like his friendship. Dimka resolves to kill Dolgov with an underwater speargun, but is restrained by his comrades. At the fishing co-op, Dimka becomes interested in other girls, particularly one Ulvi. Ulvi eventually intercedes for Galja, who later appears at the co-op in work clothes and with a mop. She tells Dimka she failed her acting exam and asks him to visit her. In spite, he proposes to Ulvi, then to a waitress, but is rebuffed. He realizes, however, that he is still in love with Galja, who asks him to forgive her. Still suspecting her motives, he writes her a cynical, condescending note before going to sea again. Meanwhile, Galja has run along the beach in a distraught condition, caught cold, and been hospitalized.

Viktor Denisov: Compromise, materialism, self-seeking (3, 10).

Viktor Denisov secretly envies his brother Dimka's disdain for conformity and social pressure. Viktor himself dares to perform an experiment which, if it fails, would render his past work in vain and jeopardize his professional status. He openly admits that the experiment disproves his own dissertation. His superior advises him not to publish the results until his dissertation is finished, that his dissertation will have no practical application, and that the results of his experiment can be published instead. Viktor refuses to muzzle his thought for a degree. He also realizes that his experiment will alienate his colleagues by disproving their work too. He has already displeased an important official whose initials are V. V. and who had earlier disparaged cybernetics but is now one of its champions. Viktor must face the latter before other scientists and defend his experiment. He is even unsure of his own superior's support and is tempted, like Dimka, to flip a coin but chooses instead to face his opponents. As he does so he draws a pointed analogy about W formations in soccer, which is also a play on V. V.'s initials in Latin letters. Although he successfully defends his experiment, he fails the defense of his dissertation. When he visits Dimka, he expresses his admiration for the boldness, courage and self-confidence of the younger generation, by contrast with his own.

V. Nekrasov, *Kira Georgievna*

Vadim (Dimka) Kudrjavcev: His wife, Kira Georgievna (4).

When they married in 1936, Kira Georgievna was impressed with her husband Dimka's avant-garde poetic gift. A year later he was arrested on false charges, but she was unsuccessful in intervening for him with the bureaucracy. Years later, after his unexpected return from a concentration camp, they have difficulty communicating. Then they achieve a moment of understanding in which she desires Dimka and no one else. Later she joins him at the home of his mother in the Ukraine. His mother and sister do not approve his returning to her, however. She mocks Dimka's frequent references to his exile, sensing he has rejected everything that preceded it. Finally his sister urges her to leave, without offering an explanation. Dimka also becomes critical of Kira. He feels that she is too optimistic and does not appreciate the difficulty of his adjustment. He finally concludes that, as an artist, she has substituted the artificial and pleasantly superficial for the real. He is also concerned about the woman he lived with in exile and their young son. The two women eventually confront each other in a Kiev hotel, where the little boy fails to respond to Kira. Dimka forgets their appointment when Kira calls again. The sight of his sleeping child persuades him to stay with the boy and his mother. After her return to Moscow, Kira writes Dimka that she is staying with her second husband, Nikolaj, and suggests that they not see one another again.

Vadim (Dimka) Kudrjavcev: Artistic conformity (3).

When he returns to Kiev, Dimka becomes frustrated because, though he would prefer to treat the people he got to know in Siberia, the newspapers only want him to write about collective farms. His contract with a movie studio is similarly for a scenario on the life of fishermen. He concludes that his second twenty years were more meaningful than the first because of the people he met and the thinking and learning he was forced to do.

Kira Georgievna: Her first husband, Dimka (4).

In the Ukraine Kira perceives that Dimka has rejected everything in their past and is no longer nostalgic about poetry or involved in esthetic discussions. He does, however, object to the lack of realism and the over-idealization in contemporary art. This makes him seem to her a kind of dogmatic reactionary. After she writes him that they should not see each other again, she receives no reply.

Nikolaj Ivanovič Obolenskij: His wife, Kira Georgievna (4).

After returning from a party with friends, Kira's young model and chaperone, Juročka, impulsively kisses her. She debates whether or not to reproach him for it but instead proposes at their next meeting that they take a trip to the country. Before leaving, she phones her current husband, Nikolaj, to say she has met a girl friend at whose *dacha* she is spending the night. Later, she joins Dimka in Kiev, giving Nikolaj the excuse that she needs to go away for a rest. She is aware that in her absence he will be lonely, not eat or take pills, *etc.*, and she feels guilty about paying him so little attention. She resolves to send him a telegram from the train but fails to do so and again procrastinates writing him from the station. During her whole trip she manages only to send him a brief post card. She reasons that it would be better to speak to him in person than write him any more lies. Returning to Kiev from the home of Dimka's mother, she is handed a telegram, already a week old, which informs her that Nikolaj has had a heart attack and is in serious condition.

Kira Georgievna: Ethical values, conscience (10).

In 1940 Kira had met Nikolaj, a professor at her art institute, and accompanied him to Moscow the next year. The author suggests, by innuendo, that she may have married him for his means and influence. As she begins her affair with Juročka, she avoids facing the implications of her behavior and even encourages Juročka to keep visiting her and Nikolaj so that the latter won't become suspicious. She rationalizes her new relationship as being of a different order, since Nikolaj is so much older than she. She forgets that she is just as much older than Juročka. Although intending before she leaves for Kiev to inform Nikolaj of Dimka's return and her feelings for him, she delays doing so, telling herself she does not want to upset his work, *etc.* In Kiev, Kira encounters an old school friend who is living with an invalid mother and small daughter. Their poverty saddens Kira and makes her feel guilty by contrast. As, after her return to Moscow, Kira waits for Juročka, she somehow realizes that she is again taking advantage of a situation and that this has been her custom ever since she long ago received a letter from Dimka allowing her her freedom.

Juročka: Kira Georgievna, Nikolaj Ivanovič (4, 5).

After becoming intimate with Kira, Juročka feels guilty toward Nikolaj and is inclined to avoid him. Kira questions him about his girl friend, Tonja, asking to meet her and encouraging them to get married, while, under the circumstances, Juročka is reticent to have them meet. He becomes disillusioned in Kira after meeting Dimka, whose conversation goes beyond art, touching upon life itself. After Kira's departure, Nikolaj graciously offers to entertain Juročka, who reminds him of his own deceased son by a former wife. Conscience struck, Juročka resolves to avoid Nikolaj and realizes he would prefer being with Dimka. After Kira's return to Moscow, she arranges another rendezvous with Juročka, but finally decides not to meet him. When he does not call, she assumes he has been offended when, in fact, he has forgotten.

Nikolaj Ivanovič and Kira Georgievna: Truth, artistic excellence, personal satisfaction (3, 6, 10).

While Kira is in Kiev, Nikolaj finishes a commissioned portrait, which is praised, but feels himself that it is superficial. He assesses his own artistry as mediocre. Before returning to Moscow and after meeting Dimka's mistress, Kira sees a young mother wheeling a carriage and becomes regretful for the first time in her life that she has had no children. Later she reviews her work as a sculptress and is disappointed.

V. Rozov, *ABCDE*

Volodja: Parents; his uncle, Vasilij (5).

Volodja's parents discuss their mistakes in rearing him. His mother thinks he should have material security, while his father says they have spoiled him and left him nothing to strive for. When he arrives home late, his father calls to him, but he says he is going to bed instead. They then reproach him, while he protests that he owes nothing to anybody and has not even asked his parents to help him. His mother invites him to go with them for a cure, but he refuses, preferring to be by himself. His father then suggests he visit his uncle, Vasilij, who was a famous partisan and lives in the Urals. Arriving at Vasilij's he scoffs at the latter's provincial interests and calls him prehistoric.

Volodja: Society; his cousin, Sima (8, 4).

When he first meets his cousin, Sima, Volodja knocks her over, then kisses her. He perversely knocks a pie on the floor, mocks his relatives, spills the contents of his suitcase, and resolves to return home. At his uncle's bidding, Sima pursues him. When she catches up, he pushes her away. Later he puts her on a train and continues walking. She leaves the train and pursues him further, while he retaliates by throwing her shoe away and putting her on another train, which she again leaves. He then throws sticks at her, hides, and tries to hitch a ride in a truck without her. Sima makes a scene, however, protesting that Volodja is her husband and is leaving her with a child — vowing to report the driver if he fails to cooperate. Later, at a station, they try to sell Volodja's jacket for food, but they lose it as the crowd pushes forward to board a train. At a bakery he calls a woman's attention to a five ruble note protruding from her purse. The woman regards him suspiciously and counts her money. He drops his last remaining coin when someone rushes him, and cannot find it. Finally he picks up dirty scraps which have fallen from a little boy's purchase and shares them with Sima. An old man engages them to saw fire wood for their supper, but keeps delaying the meal in order to make them work longer, then feeds them a skimpy supper and turns his dog on them when they protest. They finally get a ride in a truck; all the riders sing songs, except for Volodja, who scowls.

Volodja: Sense of purpose, vocation (2, 10).

Returning to Moscow as the flagman on a train, Volodja enters the dispatcher's office and, when asked how he likes his work, says he is quitting. He doesn't want to become a physicist, like his mother, because, he says, science cannot make people more honest or happier. He tells his father he does not know what he will do next and his uncle that he does not want to be a student and live off his parents. He later tells Sima that he is concerned about his place in the world, realizing that, without ambition, human beings are insects. He is attracted to a young industrial worker, Palčikov, who yearns to go to Africa to see giraffes and ostriches. Still later, as he and Sima shovel rubble into a wheel barrow, he scoffs at the nobility of their labor.

Volodja: Conformity, compromise, dogmatism, world conditions (7, 2, 10).

While in Moscow, Volodja complains to a girlfriend about the imperfect world. He tells his mother he does not want to be a physicist in order not to think as she does. Likewise, he no longer does his schoolwork, despite his ability. He accuses his parents of settling for both the good and the bad, while he loves only the good. He rejects as sentimental the sacrifices they made for him during the War. When his mother lectures him that only one road leads to the truth but many roads lead to error, he replies that maybe that is not true either. When she accuses him of cynicism he asks her to be patient until he is "broken". She objects that she does not want him "broken", but he insists that everyone else is. He tells his cousins that he dreams of unmasking all hypocrites, but since this is impossible he would like to destroy the earth instead and have life begin anew. He has learned all the fundamentals — the A, B, C's — until he is sick of them. When his uncle declares that Volodja's parents have asked him to make Volodja into a human being, the latter protests becoming as dull and mediocre as the rest of them. A kindly railroad man invites him and Sima home for a meal but becomes incensed when Volodja argues that people deserve to be punished by war. The railroad man's wife explains that her husband had been shell-shocked in battle. Volodja protests that there is nothing one can do to avoid war, though, if there were, he would gladly be cut into a hundred thousand pieces to avoid it. He insists that all people want money and glory and are hypocritical if they pretend otherwise. He is delighted to learn that Sima is adopted and of unknown nationality. This means that she is simply a human being, without a name or a country. The fact that they have made her into a Russian, he suggests, shows the way people want to be certain about everything. He prefers uncertainty. He wants to rise above the universal rubble, so that others will not suffer. They encounter a drunken traveling official who does his work without questioning what the state decides. When a woman objects to the man's loose talk, the official insults her, and Volodja retaliates by throwing a pickle at him. He is offered work by another railway man, who tells him to sign a receipt for an amount larger than he is to receive. Volodja refuses and is then accused of trying to extort more money than was agreed upon.

Sima: Her cousin, Volodja (4).

When Volodja tries to leave Sima by hitching a ride with a truck driver, she is hurt by his betrayal and momentarily resolves to return home.

Ju. Bondarev, *Silence*

Sergej and Nikolaj Voxmincev: Social injustice, Uvarov, Bykov, slanderers (8).

After his return from the service and while dancing at a restaurant,

Sergej Voxmincev is distracted by the sight of his former battery commander, Captain Uvarov. Sergej approaches him and, recalling a battle in which Uvarov betrayed his men, suggests that they talk. As he reminds Uvarov of the incident, the latter calls for the head waiter but Sergej warns him not to persist or he will announce to everyone that Uvarov is a murderer. He also accuses Uvarov of pinning his guilt on a subordinate, who was court-martialed and later died in prison. Uvarov still tries to force his friendship on Sergej, arguing that they should forget the past. Sergej remains belligerent, however, whereupon Uvarov threatens to destroy him if he stands in his way. Sergej finally strikes Uvarov, who falls to the floor. The crowd is generally sympathetic to Uvarov and critical of Sergej, who notes how people tend to judge by appearances. When a policeman arrives, Uvarov tries to minimize their disagreement, while Sergej vainly seeks to expose him. Later, Sergej recalls his father's angry refusal to provide a neighbor, Bykov, with a reference, denouncing the latter as a disloyal communist. Bykov, who manages a large factory and was a major in the army, has also threatened to have another neighbor, the eccentric painter, Mukomolov, jailed. Sergej is finally summoned to the police because of his encounter with Uvarov at the restaurant. He welcomes this as an opportunity to reveal Uvarov's crime, but is instead charged a modest fine and told that his victim does not want to take the case to court. Although warned to watch his reputation, he is still determined to settle accounts with Uvarov. At a New Year's Eve party to which he has been invited by his girl friend, Nina, Sergej again encounters Uvarov, who still sollicits Sergej's friendship. They will soon be fellow students at a mining institute. However, Sergej still feels compromised and intimidated by Uvarov's persistent overtures and by the fact that he must sit with him at the same table. When, at midnight, Uvarov proposes a toast to Stalin, Sergej refuses to drink with him and accuses Uvarov of being unworthy to speak for other soldiers. With a smile, Uvarov passes off Sergej's outburst as a nervous complaint. Sergej returns the smile, then leaves in order not to spoil the occasion for others. Meanwhile, Sergej's friend, Konstantin Korabel'nikov, has unwittingly assisted Bykov in a black market operation and accosts the latter. Bykov immediately counter-charges that he is being slandered, while Sergej's father urges Konstantin to say no more, but to bring everything to the attention of the authorities as soon as possible. Sergej is later upset to learn that Mukomolov has been attacked by the press and wants to believe that there has been a mistake. Finally Sergej's father, Nikolaj Grigor'evič, is visited late at night by men in raincoats and placed under arrest. The investigators rifle through their personal effects, commenting rudely upon a love letter from Sergej's mistress and forcing Sergej to help them locate his father's alleged Trotskyist literature in a wood shed. They also confiscate Sergej's notebooks. As they work he senses fear and mutual aversion among the investigators themselves. Sergej becomes incensed by the machine which has so brutally intruded into their lives. Bykov becomes strongly suspect of having denounced Sergej's father. After the arrest, Sergej suffers hallucinations. Mukomolov urges Sergej to report the affair to his Party committee and not conceal it, but Sergej insists it is a mistake and that his father will return. When he visits the information office of the Ministry of State Security, he notices many other people there who appear as distraught and lost as he. He is neither told of the charge against his father nor where his father is being held and is himself dismissed with a warning. He then considers whether or not to compromise with the truth and acquiesce to social pressure. He finally decides to inform the Institute that he cannot leave for practical work because his sister is ill and his father is not free to assist her — which corresponds to the truth, though vaguely. He is thereupon accused of lying and failing to report his father's arrest. He suspects Uvarov's part in the denunciation and exclaims that only fascists would so suspect their own people, while Uvarov maintains that Sergej is no longer a loyal communist, *etc.* Sergej in turn chides the Party bureau for believing a traitor and refuses to write a declaration for them. At a later meeting, Uvarov explains the battle incident, blaming the loss of his men on Sergej. Sergej then accuses Uvarov of reversing roles and gives his side of the story. The rest prefer not to consider their private controversy, and a bare majority vote for Sergej's expulsion. Sergej is unwilling to admit his mistakes, which might have softened their judgment. He tells his superior, Svidirov, that he did not expect to find such compromising people in the Party and immediately writes a letter of resignation in order to avoid being expelled from the Institute. He begins to wonder how human villainy can so persist in the Party and even extracts an admission from his former teacher, Morozov, that no one really believed Uvarov. Morozov says he himself supported Uvarov with his silence for reasons that are in Sergej's best interest, implying that he can be more helpful by speaking out later. (What he has in mind is never clarified.) Learning that Sergej is leaving the Institute, his fellow students try to persuade him that things will improve and not to be rash. They offer to petition the other students in his behalf, arguing that the Party is the people, *etc.* Sergej thinks differently, however, and cannot be deterred. He considers himself wiser than they in view of his recent experiences.

Sergej Voxmincev: Aftermath of World War II and Stalinism, sense of purpose, vocation (2).

After his return from the service, Sergej has nightmares in which he is pursued by cross-shaped airplanes and figures made of planks. Like other veterans, he is worried about finding work. Ever since discovering the corpse of a soldier from his own neighborhood, he has been uncomfortable about dead people. He refuses to buy a second-hand suit formerly owned by a soldier killed in the War. While Konstantin argues that they must take no more risks but make the most of their lives, Sergej maintains that during the War he took risks for a purpose but now has none. The sight of Uvarov and the reminder of his dead comrades intensifies his loneliness, as does the news that his former friend, the Mukomolov's son, had disappeared in action. When Mukomolov asks him if he thinks Stalin knew about everything that happened during the War, Sergej is uncertain. He first enrolls in a driving school, intending to become a chauffeur, then is encouraged to take a preparatory course at the Institute of Mines. Like many of the other applicants who are also veterans, he feels uncertain of himself and of what he really wants.

Sergej Voxmincev: Nina's love (4).

After the incident with Uvarov at the restaurant, Sergej makes a phone call and observes the girl with whom he was dancing in an adjoining booth. He reflects on their physical estrangement as they make their separate calls. They miss the last subway train, and he offers to accompany her home. She is suspicious and physically aloof until he stops to rub her foot for frostbite. Finally she invites him to her apartment, where he awakens the next morning. Her name is Nina. He eventually asks her to marry him, but she refuses, explaining that she has a husband elsewhere. They continue their relationship, and she even consents to break with her friends, among them Uvarov, in order to appease him. He later sees her on the street with another man, presumably her husband, and despairs. After his father's arrest, she contacts him by phone, but he refuses to speak to her.

Nikolaj Grigor'evič Voxmincev: His son, Sergej (5).

After returning from the service, Sergej is aloof toward his father. Sergej had heard from friends that his father had had an affair with an army nurse. Sergej had then written him that he no longer considered himself his son. Irritated by his father's apparent weakness, Sergej finally asks him why he puts up with Bykov. His father points out that Bykov has committed no evident crime and that it is difficult to prove anything against him, then alludes to an incident in his own career that has left him with a blemished reputation. They openly clash about their relationship, for which Sergej now feels guilty. When Nikolaj urges Konstantin to bring Bykov's operation to the attention of the authorities, Sergej again berates him for his cowardly caution. When Nikolaj is consequently arrested, he tells Sergej he knows the latter does not love him, but urges him to go on living as he should.

Konstantin Korobel'nikov: Integrity, industry (10).

Sergej questions why Konstantin cultivates Bykov's acquaintance, but Konstantin reminds him he drives a truck for the factory Bykov manages. Konstantin becomes increasingly dissatisfied with his way of life. On one occasion he approaches Bykov for money and comments that Bykov seems especially well off, upon which Bykov warns him against slander. Konstantin then leaves, glad he did not take any money. After Konstantin and Sergej have attended the Institute for three years, Konstantin becomes restless and considers leaving.

Konstantin Korobel'nikov: Assja's love (4).

Sergej's sister, Assja, criticizes Konstantin for his cynicism, for having so much money to spend, and for doing underhanded business with Bykov. When she offers to clean his messy apartment, she insists that he not look at her in the mirror as he shaves off his sideburns, which he does hoping to please her. When he kisses her hand, she scolds him and leaves. He finally reproaches her for her coldness, while she upbraids him for being dirty-minded. She is upset that she attracts him, slaps herself, wishes she were a man. When he finally confides his love for her to Sergej, he is advised to seek someone of his own generation.

Painter, Fedor Mukomolov, and poet, Xomin: Critical toleration, artistic freedom (3).

Fedor Mukomolov's art is defamed by the critics, and he is unable to sell his pictures. Later he is attacked for defending a liberal art critic and favoring Western influences. His wife predicts that he will be expelled from the Painters' Union. Although he vows to fight his critics and avoid being expelled, his bravado seems superficial. In turn, Uvarov has exposed a fellow student, Xomin, for writing antipatriotic verse. Although he writes harmless nature poetry, Uvarov had enticed him to read it, then denounced him as a counterrevolutionary. The poet's bedding and personal effects are also searched in the night.

Uvarov: Principles, integrity (6).

The students at the Institute allude to the hypocrisy of Uvarov, who, though bored by Party meetings, is always affable and gets ahead. Although himself a traitor, he accuses others of disloyalty.

V. Tendrjakov, *Short Circuit*

Vasilij Vasil'evič Stoljarskij and other subordinates (Boris Evgen'evič Šackix): Ivan Sokovin, confidence, initiative, self-fulfillment (4).

Vasilij Vasil'evič Stoljarskij has worked in the same power plant control room for thirty years. He is now frustrated, sensing that his potential has not been fully utilized. He could, for instance, have designed the power system so as to avoid excessive reductions in power load during emergencies, but his superior, Ivan Sokovin, never asks for his advice. He once discovered an error in planning and reported it to Ivan, who then took it to the higher authorities and himself received credit for saving millions of rubles. A power failure suddenly results from the shorting of two high voltage cables. Vasilij immediately refers to the authorized emergency plan and accordingly cuts off two nearby towns, but spares a chemical factory and a restaurant which is hosting a distinguished foreign guest. Meanwhile, subsidiary power stations become depleted and cut themselves off in self-defense. The whole power system is about to collapse. Ivan arrives and Vasilij reminds him that the plan forbids reducing the load any further. Ivan announces, however, that he will take upon himself Vasilij's responsibility — an infraction of protocol when another is already at the control panel. Ivan then deprives the entire city of power for fifteen minutes. As they wait, Vasilij becomes concerned that Ivan has not spoken to him. He realizes that the entire city had to be cut off but could not bring himself to do it. The emergency plan bore Ivan's signature, and Vasilij had always been cowed by orders, papers, and Ivan in particular. Suddenly Ivan turns and verbally abuses him, which is especially painful because he has already reproached himself. He meekly replies that it has become impossible to act independently after working with Ivan for so many years. In Ivan's apartment, meanwhile, another subordinate, Šackix, is reprimanded on the phone by the director of the chemical factory, who threatens to take the power authorities to court. Šackix protests his own innocence in the affair, then observes, half to himself, that he was much more content before Ivan, whom he also fears, elevated him to his present position. Meanwhile, Vasilij remains confused as to whether or not he is to blame. He reflects that he could only have coped with such an emergency, had he asserted himself long ago against Ivan. When Ivan finally orders him to sit down and continue his job, he explains that he is ill and leaves. His behavior perplexes Ivan, who does not sympathize but considers him insubordinate and thereupon decides to demote him.

Vadim Sokovin: His father, Ivan; impersonality, pragmatism (5, 10).

In view of a recent reconciliation with his son, Vadim, Ivan Sokovin has declined attending the reception for a foreign guest in order to celebrate the New Year with his own family. Ivan had opposed the installation of a turbine in the local chemical plant, which would have provided it with an independent source of power, while Vadim, the plant's chief electrical engineer, had argued against his father. The authorities deferred to Ivan because of his powerful position. During the power failure, acids discharge at the same plant, creating poisonous gas. One of the workers, Vadim's boyhood acquaintance, San'ka, is overcome by the gas, suffers a concussion when he falls, and later dies. Although Vadim realizes that his father had, if need be, inadvertently to kill someone to save the city, he likens the situation to that of a worshipper appeasing a god and also recalls that his father earlier prohibited the plant's acquiring its own turbine. After Ivan is mistakenly led to believe that Vadim was his victim, he contrasts Vadim's youth with his own and concludes that, where his son had everything given to him, he was himself a self-made man. As he gradually learned about electricity he began to worship power and machines for what they can give man and concluded that man must also serve machines. He recalls that Vadim had opposed this view, but tells himself that he would still have cut off the power, even if he had known it would kill someone and even if the victim were his own son. When, later, Vadim rejoins the family and is informed of the birth of his new daughter, he can only speak about San'ka. The women feel that his remarks have ruined the glad news and argue that, since one cannot help others' suffering, one should try to preserve one's own happiness. Vadim then pleases the women by toasting his wife's health, but fails to share their viewpoint.

Ivan Kapitonovič Sokovin: Human values (6).

Ivan Sokovin rhapsodizes about time as about a powerful deity whom men worship. He also invokes a second god, energy. Vadim sarcastically mocks his father's worship of the nonhuman, which revives their old grudge. Ivan had opposed the installation of a turbine at the chemical plant, arguing that, in a year and a half, the city would have adequate power from additional systems. During the power failure, he places professional priorities before the consideration of individual human lives. At the apartment, Šackix praises Ivan for always managing to face and deal with the unexpected and unpredictable in life. Ivan's wife objects, however, declaring that Ivan can also be vain and narrow-minded. She says that Šackix has made Ivan into a god, but he cannot do everything, while Šackix admits that, since Ivan always assumes the responsibility, no one else can be like him.

Automobile-owning couple: People (4).

As, learning of the power failure, he rushes to the chemical plant, Vadim prevails on a couple in an automobile to give him a ride. They hesitate, but he argues that it could be a matter of life and death, and they finally relent. As they drive, the couple seem concerned mostly about a knock in their engine. After they deliver Vadim at the plant, the wife urges her husband to turn around and leave, fearing an explosion. They are described as simple people who live for their own amusement and are too preoccupied with their own interests to be concerned about others.

Ju. Kazakov, *Adam and Eve*

Ageev: Vika, other people (4).

After the painter, Ageev, comes to a northern town and sends for a female acquaintance, Vika, he gets drunk and locks himself in his room, although he knows this will upset her. After they board the boat which will take them to a remote island, he is again disturbed by the smells coming from the boat's restaurant and by the people's noise and joviality. He feels momentarily close to Vika, however, recalling when he had first kissed her in Moscow at a party and confessed his love to her. They have yet to spend a night together. On the island, she prepares a meal and ecstatically calls him her Adam. He scowls and leaves. He later regrets his rudeness and even thinks of his mother, who loved him more than anyone else and for whom he also showed a lack of feeling. Vika calls him again and, though he loves her, he still does not respond, even deigning to reply to her questions. That evening he gets into his own bed, mentally defying her to come to him. When she speaks, he tells her to be quiet. She calls him a selfish egoist and vows to leave on the next boat. She now regrets that she plead illness to her dean and family in order to join him. He tells her to be quiet and to leave as soon as she can, although he feels like crying. The next day he remains in bed, facing the wall and refusing to respond when he is called to lunch and dinner. That evening he rows to another island, converses with a fisherman, then returns, still ignoring Vika, who stands on the shore. She has already packed her suitcases, and he goes to sleep. Before her departure, they have another silent meal together, during which he feels affectionately disposed but realizes that they must say goodbye.

Ageev: Criticism, artistic freedom (3).

After Vika's arrival, Ageev asks her about a certain picture from his own exhibit. Her reaction suggests that she does not especially care for it, and this angers him. He complains about the criticism his paintings receive because they are nonconformist and tells her of his ambitions while at art school, which were quickly berated by the critics. He wonders if, like Van Gogh, he will have to die before he is recognized. He has painted illustrations for three years to earn his living and still has no studio. He decries the reviewers' hypocrisy and castigates the idealistic school of painting, which emphasizes the mass rather than the individual. Although he senses his need for Vika, he is impatient for her love and understanding and hates having to argue and prove things. If she would only agree with his opinions, he would paint her and perhaps become inspired. He regrets what he has said to her and determines to work instead of talking. Meanwhile, he thinks of the critics in Moscow who make lofty remarks to the girls in restaurants in order to entice them to bed. None of them believe what they write. These thoughts comfort him but he still wonders if the critics are not right and he wrong, if, despite his talent, his life has not lacked an essential idea.

Ageev: Mediocrity, compromise, mundane existence (10).

Ageev shows critical taste about a landscape which hangs in his hotel. He also dislikes the music of local youths and seeks relief from his surroundings through alcohol. Later, on the island, he shows genuine appreciation for the view of a sunset from a bell tower.

A. Solženicyn, *One Day in the Life of Ivan Denisovič*

Prisoners: Inhumanity, injustice (8).

The inmates of a Siberian prison camp are subjected to numerous unjust abuses. After they have warmly dressed for a day's work, they must sometimes strip outdoors and be checked for extra garments or secret letters. Bujnovskij, an ex-naval captain, protests that such treatment is not communistic and violates the criminal code, for which he is promptly sentenced to ten days in the guard house. His sentence is set for that evening so that another day's labor can be extracted from him. It is unlikely that he will survive his punishment. Another prisoner, Der, serves as foreman and mistreats the others. In order to avoid extra work, the prison cook allows additional portions to prisoners who assist him, thus decreasing the amount available to everyone else. His assistants include bowl watchers, and bowl gatherers. Due to the failure of a mechanical lift, the men must raise cement blocks by hand. In order to repair a cement trough they must dismantle the rail on a stairway, which makes their work doubly dangerous. After a crew of prisoners has stolen roofing paper in order to close off an open window and make their work bearable, Der threatens them. When the prisoners are recounted on their way back to the barracks, they are further deprived of their free evening time. They always gather firewood as they return, knowing that a certain number will have to give theirs up to the guards. They usually have to work two Sundays out of five. Prisoners with skills are given special preference, such as standing first in line. The barracks commander strikes only the meekest when he calls them outdoors for a count. Ivan Šuxov even questions the justice of their imprisonment: because of their country's inadequate preparation before the War, many of them were captured by the enemy and all such were consequently suspected of being defectors. Ivan too was forced to testify to treason in surrendering to the Germans. Others have been arrested for the following misdemeanors: feeding the men of a deserting general, receiving a souvenir from a British admiral, belonging to a pious religious sect, and being the son of a kulak. After 1949, prison sentences were arbitrarily increased from ten to twenty-five years; nor are prisoners always released on schedule.

Ivan Denisovič Šuxov and fellow prisoners: Loyalty to the system, absolute integrity (7, 10).

Ivan's squad leader, Tjurin, bribes the officials with salt pork in order to receive a less arduous work assignment. When Ivan is forced to clean the guard room floor as a minor punishment, he intentionally uses too much water in order to annoy the officers and thus be excused from the task. He rushes about the prison grounds avoiding contact with guards who might punish him for being alone or failing to remove his hat at a certain distance. Whenever possible, the prisoners steal materials and tools in order to do better work and thus more satisfactorily fulfill their work quotas. The squad leader uses the utmost ingenuity in writing his work report, irrespective of the slight accomplishment it represents. In order not to be late for the afterwork roll call, the prisoners conceal excess mortar instead of using it up. At such camps they are permitted relative freedom of expression in political matters, and their remarks about Stalin, *etc.* are generally disrespectful.

Ivan Denisovič Šuxov and fellow prisoners: Spontaneous gratification, contemplation of the future (10).

Though Ivan has a borderline temperature, he is yet fearful that the doctor may declare him well and that he will be put in the guard house for being late to his work assignment. He therefore decides to avoid being examined. He carefully weighs his bread ration, sewing part of it in his jacket and another part in his mattress. For Tjurin's services in bribing the officials, the other squad members share with him their gift packages. Ivan avoids staring at other prisoners when they smoke in order not to antagonize those who might otherwise share their butts with him. He no longer plans his future, since the authorities do this for him. He always saves a crust of bread in order to scrape his bowl clean at a later meal. He watches his squad's bowls so that they are not stolen and confuses the cook when he counts them in order to acquire an extra one. The men go back to work before the afternoon whistle is sounded in order to complete their work assignment. Ivan offers to stand in line for other prisoners in order to share in their packages. He risks punishment in order to salvage a broken hack saw blade, which he can make into a knife and use for tailoring and other skills that will earn him extra money. He must calculate how to join his squad in the mess hall after they have already entered without the mess chief's knowledge. He must also bargain for trays, free tables, extra bowls of food, *etc.* He assists one prisoner in protecting a parcel as they leave the barracks for a count and is again rewarded with a portion of the contents.

Fetjukov and Others: Caution, fellow-feeling, restraint (10).

Ivan Šuxov has always remembered the advice of his first squad leader that you will not survive if you try to get by on other people's leftovers, rely on doctors, or betray your comrades. He feels that tattlers do sometimes manage to survive, although at others' expense. The work squads are so organized that if one man lets down, he will jeopardize the food rations of the whole group. Hence they all push one another. Fetjukov, a slacker, fears the possibility of having his throat cut, but is reminded that this happens only to informers. Because he is more circumspect and less greedy, Ivan is awarded extra bowls and cigarette butts while Fetjukov goes without. Another slacker in another squad goes to sleep on the job and makes the men late by forcing them to wait for a recount when he cannot be located. The men "boo" him, and his own squad beats him up before a guard can do so.

V. Tarsis, *Tale of a Bluebottle Fly*

Ioann Sinemuxov and Rozalija Zags: Rational self-discipline, socialist discipline, theories, collectivist idealism (7).

While concluding that the discipline of a socialist society should even keep people from hurting flies, the philosopher Ioann Sinemuxov is suddenly annoyed by a fly which lands on his bald head according to its own guiding principle. It persists in annoying him until he finally smashes it with the twelfth volume of his work on rational self-discipline. Thus begins Ioann's tragedy: he had always placed priority on the consistency of human behavior but is now forced to consider that his uncontrollable caprice might lead him to murder his own wife or his department head, both of whom have troubled him far more than the fly. Philosophy seems no longer meaningful. He thereafter lives like the fly, purging his mind of all ideas. He vows to become completely guileless, believing that convictions, however genuine, are both ephemeral and transient. If idealism is relative, he concludes, collectivism can never work either. He now realizes that his treatises have promoted the tyranny of the few over the many. When he discusses his transformation with Leonid Ostankin, deputy secretary of his Party cell, the latter agrees with him about the discrepancy between the Soviet state and true socialism. They liken their society's pseudo-socialism to astrology as distinct from astronomy. The fact that Arxangelov, their fanatic leader, prohibits Ioann's further publication also proves their corruption, since Ioann has written only to help his fellows. Later, Ioann is offered a position as a housing inspector in order to become reconciled to Soviet life. He accepts the offer, but in order to view conditions as they really are. He thereupon makes ironic allusions to those who decry negro lynchings in America, but overlook anti-Semitism and genocide under the Soviets, and who deplore the poverty of American writers, while ignoring similar conditions in the USSR. He also observes the farce of Soviet elections. Some of his colleagues try to reform him, while others secretly sympathize with his views. He concludes that contradiction is an inevitable quality of life; hence, their social dialectic can have no synthesis. One of his colleagues, Rozalija Zags, makes capital from her affairs with men. She opposes property, except in her own instance, and declares that life's only value is what one gets out of the process of life. She concurs that all socialism is false.

Ioann Sinemuxov: Orthodox colleagues, conformity, officials, bureaucracy, wife and son (4, 5, 8).

After the Twentieth Party Congress, Ioann wrote an article castigating philosophers who equate socialist discipline with freedom, equality, and justice. His colleagues — Akaciev, Dubov, and Osinovatyj — then suppressed his writing. He had already been chided for not attending Party meetings and was told he was not well and would require treatment. Ioann was their enemy because he was not a conformist and could therefore make a more meaningful contribution to the cause. The others in fact deter communism by their bureaucratic mentality. Ioann's solution is to reduce the bureaucracy; abolish patronage, trade, and money; and consolidate all organizations into one. His wife is indifferent to his ideas and fears retaliation because of them, while their son, Oleg, is a corrupt member of the *komsomol*. Ioann is warned that he will be purged from the Party, which leads him to observe that today's politicians are as corrupt as yesterday's priests, while the church has become increasingly liberal, and that tyranny is unavoidable under a one-party system. He is now avoided by his colleagues, but vows to defy his foes and not submit to them nor leave his country, which he dearly loves. He is urged to speak at a Party meeting where they will debunk him. He is also dismissed from his Institute, for which his wife reproaches him. His colleagues are concerned, however, that he may become popular with the students and even be publicized in America. Although ailing, he decides to write a confession, which seems to improve his condition, thus distressing his wife, who was looking forward to his death. In his diary he indicates that he avoids other people because they are false and might influence him to be the same way. He witnesses, in his new job, the tremendous waste of human energy in the bureaucracy: even his superior admits that their cleaning women could distribute living space more judiciously, since they know everyone on the list. Ioann concludes his remarks with a requiem: people are like flies, both in quantity and quality.

Ioann Sinemuxov: Satisfaction in love (4).

Love has always frustrated Ioann. He cannot decide if it is physical or spiritual. The more he hated a woman the more he loved her. His sister-in-law, Zina, denies herself to him because he might expect too much and become infatuated with her. Rozalija explains that it is her nature to be physically transient, whereas he needs eternal values.

Afanasij Zags: Truth, his wife Rozalija's fidelity, involvement (4, 6).

Rozalija's husband, Afanasij Zags, is a documentary film editor who prides himself in never revealing the truth. He says that, under socialist realism, they would make over *The Brothers Karamazov* and *War and Peace* into Panferov's *Bruski* and Babaevskij's *Cavalier of the Golden Star*. Rozalija openly deceives him with other men. When they encounter him in the living room, he merely asks, having overheard her moaning, if she has had her pain again. She tells Ioann that Afanasij only resents the fact that she does not moan for him as she does for others. She and her lovers usually send him to the drug-store for toothache medicine, though he has no toothache, so that they can continue their amours.

N. Aržak, *This is Moscow Speaking*

Anatolij (Tolja) Nikolaevič Karcev: Official ideology (7).

A radio announcement, prefaced "This is Moscow Speaking", broadcasts a decree of the Supreme Soviet that Sunday, August 10, 1960, will be declared Public Murder Day and that, with certain exceptions, anyone may kill anyone else from 6 a.m. until midnight. The narrator, Tolja, is with a group of friends when they learn of the announcement. They quickly break up, no longer able to enjoy themselves. After an editorial appears in *Izvestija*, extolling the decree with trite, idealistic political phrases, Tolja suspects that people have become reassured because of its familiar language and because they already have an Artillery Day and a Soviet Press Day, *etc.* When, on the day in question, he joins a crowd which surrounds the corpse of a young boy, he hears an old man protest about conscience. Another man refutes him, however, insinuating that conscience and a governmental decree are not one and the same; but Tolja feels that Lenin would not have wanted it this way. Later, he is himself almost killed by an assailant who wants to murder him for the motherland.

Anatolij (Tolja) Nikolaevič Karcev: People's duplicity, mutual fear, mistrust (10).
(*People*: Duplicity, mutual fear, mistrust (4)).

The anticipation of Public Murder Day forces Tolja to know himself all over again. Unlike his friends, he is, by nature, direct and honest. If he wishes to have an affair but does not intend to marry the woman, he tells her so. By contrast, his friend, Volodja, declares that if there is a Jewish pogrom on Murder Day, he will himself fight. After Volodja leaves, Tolja is still unsure with whom Volodja intends to fight. In general, people become especially polite and obsequious to one another, while Tolja begins to fear that his enemies may wish to kill him. He decides to stock up on provisions and barricade himself at home on the fatal day, but then becomes disgusted with himself for being so cowardly. Instead, he will go out of doors and tell people not to kill each other. Perhaps in this way he will at least save his own soul. On August 10, he sees no one in either the kitchen or lavatory. As he descends the stairs, however, he encounters an old neighbor woman who screams and throws her shopping bag, breaking bottles of yogurt. When he attempts to help her, she screams all the more, objecting that she had held him in her arms when he was a baby. After Murder Day, he rejoins his friends, who suddenly begin to discuss their experiences on that occasion. His date, Svetlana, observes that they are all victims of terror, and he agrees.

Anatolij (Tolja) Nikolaevič Karcev: Peoples' gullibility, inhumanity, lack of values (10).
(*People*: Gullibility, inhumanity, lack of values (6)).

After the announcement, people sing in the streets, declaim poetry, and publish verse dedicated to the forthcoming event. Even jokes are made about it. Volodja accuses a mutual friend of being a careerist for having delivered a speech at school in favor of the decree, but Tolja replies that any Party member would have to do the same, if prevailed upon, and reminds Volodja that he had spoken against nationalism at his own school during the Doctors' Plot. Volodja expresses his regret at having believed the newspapers on that occasion. Next, a neighbor justifies the decree to Tolja in terms of experimentation and the democratization of power. He argues that society's undesirable elements will be eliminated in this fashion, at the hands of the people. The neighbor's wife orders her husband to his room, while Tolja observes that life in a concentration camp didn't improve his neighbor. As Tolja makes love to his mistress, Zoja, she suggests that they kill her husband on Murder Day, then marry. He tells her to get out and go to hell. She calls him a sissy. He reflects that, if he really hated certain persons, he would perhaps want to kill them too — and with even better justification. He is thinking of several of his former professors and employers, the writer K (Vsevolod Kočetov) and those who were responsible for 1937 and the reactionary post-War policies. Volodja sarcastically suggests that in 1937 they had the same freedom to kill, but that it was organized then and will now be a kind of self-service. On Murder Day, as Tolja wrestles with an assailant before Lenin's tomb, he does so at the very feet of oblivious sentries. Among the atrocities committed on that day is the battle at Peredelkino between mercenaries hired by Kočetov to protect him and assassins hired by the other writers to kill him.

Artist, Saša Čuprov, and poet, Arbatov: Conventional Soviet art, absence of genuine realism or artistic freedom (3).

An artist friend, Saša Čuprov, complains that he is not only unable to sell his avant-garde pictures but that a nonconformist poster which he designed for Public Murder Day was recently rejected. He shows Tolja the poster, which depicts a morbid corpse. Čuprov agrees that the poster should have been less realistic and more conventional. They later visit an old poet, Arbatov, who refuses to read his poetry until they have drunk and he has tested Tolja. As they drink, Arbatov becomes more candid, declaring that to reveal one's innermost feelings is more dangerous than removing one's clothes in public, since it might provoke someone to kill you. He then pulls a curtain, disclosing his collection of nonconformist pessimistic and philosophical books. The corpse which Tolja later views on Murder Day looks exactly like the one in Čuprov's poster.

A. Solženicyn, *Matrena's Home*

Matrena Vasil'evna Grigor'eva: Bureaucratic indifference, social injustice (8).

An old peasant woman, Matrena Vasil'evna, has not worked for a long time because of her health, and has received no pension from her *kolkhoz* and very little help from her family. A neighbor urged her to claim a military pension for the loss of her husband, who had been missing for twelve years. She went back and forth to various offices in the district, encountering constant red tape, which wore her out. Like the other women, she steals peat, which is delivered free to the officials but is unavailable to the people. She has to carry some 400 full bags a great distance in order to be supplied for the winter. She also forages for her goat by cutting grass along the edges of fields. One bag full of grass makes a forkful of hay. Her garden plot has been cut back to one third of an acre, despite much idle ground near by. She is still called on to help out when the workers are short-handed but receives no pay. She only complains that the regular workers waste time and do not really work at all. She assists the other women to plow their gardens, refusing to be paid, and takes her turn feeding two herdsmen every six weeks. She also helps her relatives whenever they need assistance, without resenting it. The accident which later claims her life results in part because the railroad authorities had left a crossing unguarded and the engines involved had no lights.

Matrena Vasil'evna Grigor'eva: Compassion of relatives and neighbors (2, 4).

Matrena nearly married Faddej Mironovič, but he did not return immediately from the First World War, so she married his brother instead. That winter Faddej returned home and almost killed both Matrena and his brother. He refused to marry any of the village girls and looked instead for a girl from elsewhere with Matrena's same name, whom he then married. While Faddej's Matrena bore him six children, the heroine's all died in infancy. The village concluded that Matrena was cursed. Her husband did not return from the Second World War. She then reared her brother-in-law's youngest daughter, Kira. In her will, she has bequeathed her top storey to Kira. Her sisters hope to receive the rest of the house. At Faddej's insistence, she finally consents to give her upper room to Kira in advance of her death so that Kira and her husband can qualify for a plot of land to put it on. Her sisters denounce her for this action, saying they do not want to see her again, and her cat even strays off. On the day that Faddej and his family take apart the room and remove the lumber, Matrena insists on helping them. Unwittingly, she has put on the narrator's jacket, and he scolds her for getting it dirty. She also accompanies the movers, who had been too stingy to bring two tractors and have instead constructed two sledges.

The second sledge falls apart at a railroad crossing and Matrena assists the men to free it when she and two others are struck by two oncoming engines and killed. Soon after the news of Matrena's death, a neighbor, Maša, comes by requesting Matrena's gray shawl, which she said was promised her daughter and will be taken by Matrena's sisters. The narrator imagines Faddej standing in the doorway, threatening to chop up Matrena and his brother, and realizes that the threat has materialized forty years later. At the traditional ritual lament, Matrena's sisters blame her death on the room's untimely bequest, indirectly accusing Faddej's family and suggesting that the room is all they will receive. The women in the other family blame Matrena for not taking care of herself and bringing blame on them, suggesting that they will still discuss the inheritance of the house. The few women who sincerely mourn are not allowed to tarry. At the funeral supper, the mourners become drunk and, thus, less sorrowful. Faddej only comes later for discussions with the sisters. They dare not take the case to court for fear the house will go to the state. Finally, they reach a settlement. Later, one of the sisters-in-law tells the narrator that Matrena's husband did not love her because she dressed so simply and was not pretentious. He spent his money on himself instead and had a mistress in town. All her remarks about Matrena are critical: she disapproves of her helping people without pay, *etc.*

Matrena Vasil'evna Grigor'eva and Narrator: Materialism, personal satisfaction (10).

Matrena's menus are invariably plain, but the narrator, who is her boarder, finds no fault with them. When he thanks her for food, she replies that it is already his. The narrator himself no longer looks for life's meaning in physical satiety and is more intrigued by Matrena's smile, which he would like to photograph. In all, Matrena bore and lost six children. Although she believes her husband is dead, the narrator suspects that he purposely did not return to her. She was in no way obligated to assist the men with the broken sledge when she and two others were killed.

Matrena's neighbors: Fellow-feeling (6).

Both Faddej and the tractor driver insisted on hauling the lumber in one trip by using two sledges, since the driver was being paid for the job and Faddej was anxious to have the room moved quickly. All the men drank bootlegged liquor before leaving the house. Kira's husband, himself a train engineer, should have known enough to warn the station about the tractor. Their greed has almost caused the death of 1,000 people who were riding in an express train which was halted just before reaching the site of the accident. Despite the death of his own son, Faddej seems only interested, in the aftermath, in salvaging the lumber and bargaining for a share in the remaining estate.

A. Solženicyn, *For the Good of the Cause*

Teachers and students,
Fedor Mixeevič, Ivan Gračikov: The bureaucracy (8).

The teachers and students at an electronics institute have struggled to build a new classroom building which was promised for the current school year. The students worked during the preceding year both before and after classes, on Sundays and during vacations. The new structure will free their present classroom building for conversion to a badly needed student dormitory. Conditions in the present building are also trying, with classes held in the corridor, several labs in one room, *etc.* Because no one at the school was qualified to make a survey, the principal, Fedor Mixeevič, asked the building office of the local relay factory to serve as the contracting party. Vsevolod Xabalygin, the plant manager, must now sign over the deed of transfer, which he had promised to do by August but has procrastinated, arguing that everything must first be completed. When a number of Moscow officials accompany Xabalygin in an inspection of the building, Fedor explains, among other things, about the students' bad environment when living in town. He is then told that the new building is to be appropriated by an important research institute. When he next appeals to the sympathetic secretary of the town Party committee, Ivan Gračikov, the latter dissuades him from contacting the Council of Ministers in Moscow, since they would only refer the matter back to the district committee, whose supervisor, Knorozov, has likely already approved the transfer. The latter never changes his mind after a decision. Ananevič, secretary of the Party bureau, rejects the teachers' request for a general meeting on the subject and also dissuades the *Komsomol* from discussing it, which, he says, would be a political mistake. He argues that what is good for the state should please everyone. Finally, Gračikov asks Knorozov if the building was transferred with his knowledge. He abruptly answers "yes", as if ending the conversation. When Gračikov still argues that the students have been cheated and will become demoralized, expecting the same kind of treatment in the future, and that people are what count, not bricks and mortar, Knorozov becomes incensed and threatens Gračikov with his job. The appropriation of the building for the new institute will involve costly alterations, as will the conversion of a new dormitory, presently under construction, which will be left to the school for classrooms.

Bureaucrats: Integrity (6).

Although the school is under the jurisdiction of the local economic council, the officials who inspect it are from another ministry. They make innuendoes about how well off the school is, commenting that there is less space between the desks at their ministry, *etc.* One official sees a pin-up picture on the wall where instruments are stored and hints at wasted space. They have pat answers for all of Fedor's objections, insisting, for example, that the transfer is 'for the good of the cause'. Fedor receives only sympathetic assurances from the Department of Education of the Economic Council. Knorozov later admits that he had agitated to bring the research institute to their area, which will make them a more important industrial community. Fedor accepts Knorozov's decision without protesting, enamoured as he is by the latter's decisiveness. Knorozov's consequent conversation with Xabalygin also reveals that the latter expects to be awarded the new institute's directorship. Returning to the new school building, Fedor sees Xabalygin directing workman to place boundary stakes in a curve in order to claim as much land as possible for the institute and leave as little as possible for the school.

Students: Contemporary Soviet literature (3).

The students complain to one of their teachers about the plentitude of unpopular and excessively long contemporary books. Another brings up the uncommon subject of style, which they would like to discuss.

BIBLIOGRAPHY

ORIGINAL SOURCES

Novels

Aksenov, Vasilij, "Zvezdnyj bilet", *Junost'*, VII (June, 1961), 3-34.
——, "Zvezdnyj bilet", *Junost'*, VII (July, 1961), 33-66.
Bondarev, Jurij, "Tišina", *Novyj mir*, XXXVIII (March, 1962).
——, "Tišina", *Novyj mir*, XXXVIII (April, 1962).
——, "Tišina", *Novyj mir*, XXXVIII (May, 1962), 43-92.
Dudincev, Vladimir, "Ne xlebom edinym", *Novyj mir*, XXXII (August, 1956), 31-118.
——, "Ne xlebom edinym", *Novyj mir*, XXXII (September, 1956), 37-118.
——, "Ne xlebom edinym", *Novyj mir*, XXXII (October, 1956), 21-98.
Kaverin, Venjamin, "Poiski i nadeždy", *Literaturnaja Moskva II* (Moscow, Gosudarstvennoe izdatel'stvo xudožestvennoj literatury, 1956), 42-291.
Panova, Vera, "Vremena goda", *Novyj mir*, XXIX (November, 1953), 3-101.
——, "Vremena goda", *Novyj mir*, XXIX (December, 1953), 62-158.
Pasternak, Boris, *Doktor Živago* (Ann Arbor, The University of Michigan Press, 1959).

Novelettes

Aksenov, Vasilij, "Kollegi", *Junost'*, VI (June, 1960), 3-45.
——, "Kollegi", *Junost'*, VI (July, 1960), 54-80.
Aržak, Nikolaj, *Govorit Moskva* (Washington, B. Filippov, 1962).
Èrenburg, Il'ja, "Ottepel'", *Znamja*, XXIV (May, 1954), 14-87.
——, "Ottepel'", *Znamja*, XXVI (April, 1956), 23-90.
Kuznecov, Anatolij, "Prodolženie legendy", *Junost'*, III (July, 1957), 6-59.

Nekrasov, Viktor, "Kira Georgievna", *Novyj mir*, XXXVII (June, 1961), 70-126.

Nilin, Pavel, "Žestokost'", *Znamja*, XXVI (November, 1956), 3-61.

——, "Žestokost'", *Znamja*, XXVI (December, 1956), 7-75.

Solženicyn, Aleksandr, "Odin den' Ivana Denisoviča", *Novyj mir*, XXXVIII (November, 1962), 8-74.

Tarsis, Valerij, "Skazanie o sinej muxe", *Grani*, XVII (December, 1962), 5-85.

Tendrjakov, Vladimir, "Korotkoe zamykanie", *Znamja*, XXXII (March, 1962), 3-54.

——, "Sud", *Novyj mir*, XXVII (March, 1961), 15-60.

——, "Trojka, semerka, tuz", *Novyj mir*, XXXVI (March, 1960), 3-32.

Stories

Granin, Daniil, "Sobstvennoe mnenie", *Novyj mir*, XXXII (August, 1956), 129-136.

Jašin, Aleksandr, "Ryčagi", *Literaturnaja Moskva II* (Moscow, Gosudarstvennoe izdatel'stvo xudožestvennoj literatury, 1956), 502-513.

Kazakov, Jurij, "Adam i Eva", *Moskva*, VI (August, 1962), 142-157.

——, "Otščepenec", *Oktjabr'*, XXVI (July, 1959), 111-118.

Nagibin, Jurij, "Svet v okne", *Literaturnaja Moskva II* (Moscow, Gosudarstvennoe izdatel'stvo xudožestvennoj literatury, 1956), 396-403.

Solženicyn, Aleksandr, "Matrenin dvor", *Novyj mir*, XXXIX (January, 1963), 42-63.

——, "Dlja pol'zy dela", *Novyj mir*, XXXIX (July, 1963), 58-90.

Terc, Abram, "Sud idet", *Kultura*, special number (May, 1960), 62-130.

Ždanov, Nikolaj, "Poezdka na rodinu", *Literaturnaja Moskva*, *II* (Moscow, Gosudarstvennoe izdatel'stvo xudožestvennoj literatury, 1956), 404-414.

Plays

Kornejčuk, Aleksandr, "Kryl'ja", *Novyj mir*, XXX (November, 1954), 3-50.

Pogodin, Nikolaj, "Sonet Petrarki", *Literaturnaja Moskva*, *II* (Moscow, Gosudarstvennoe izdatel'stvo xudožestvennoj literatury, 1956), 300-351.

Zorin, Leonid, "Gosti", *Teatr*, XV (February, 1954), 3-45.

Literary Film Scenario

Rozov, Viktor, "ABCDE", *Junost'*, VII (September, 1961), 13-37.

LITERARY BACKGROUND SOURCES

Monographs

Bayley, John, *Tolstoy and the Novel* (New York, The Viking Press, 1966).
Belinskij, V. G., *Geroj našego vremeni, sočinenie M. Lermontova* (Moscow, Gosudarstvennoe izdatel'stvo xudožestvennoj literatury, 1958).
Berdjaev, Nikolaj, *Mirosozercanie Dostoevskago* (Paris, YMCA Press, 1968).
Bill, V. Tschebotarioff, *The Russian People* (Chicago, The University of Chicago Press, 1965).
Chizhevskij, Dmitrij, *On Romanticism in Slavic Literature* (The Hague, Mouton & Co., 1957).
Frye, Northrop, *Anatomy of Criticism* (Princeton, Princeton University Press, 1957).
Gifford, Henry, *The Hero of His Time* (London, Edward Arnold & Co., 1950).
Jackson, Robert Louis, *Dostoevsky's Underground Man in Russian Literature* (The Hague, Mouton & Co., 1958).
Lermontov, M. Ju., *Geroj našego vremeni* (Moscow, Gosudarstvennoe izdatel'stvo xudožestvennoj literatury, 1959).
Levin, Harry, *The Gates of Horn* (New York, Oxford University Press, 1966).
Mathewson, Rufus, Jr., *The Positive Hero in Russian Literature* (New York, Columbia University Press, 1958).
Mirsky, D. S., *A History of Russian Literature from its Beginnings to 1900* (New York, Vintage Books, Inc., 1958).
Moser, Charles, *Antinihilism in the Russian Novel of the 1860's* (The Hague, Mouton & Co., 1964).
Nabokov, Vladimir, *Nikolai Gogol* (New York, James Laughlin, 1944).
Puškin, A. S., *Evgenij Onegin (Sočinenija v trex tomax, II)* (Moscow, Gosudarstvennoe izdatel'stvo xudožestvennoj literatury, 1954).
Setchkarev, Vsevolod, *Gogol: His Life and Works* (New York, New York University Press, 1965).
Slonim, Marc, *The Epic of Russian Literature* (New York, Oxford University Press, 1964).

Spector, Ivan, *The Golden Age of Russian Literature* (Caldwell, Idaho, The Caxton Printers, Ltd., 1952).

Struve, Gleb, *Soviet Russian Literature 1917-1950* (Norman, University of Oklahoma Press, 1951).

Van der Eng-Liedmeier, A. M., *Soviet Literary Characters*, (trans.) B. Timmer (The Hague, Mouton & Co., 1953).

Wellek, René & Warren, Austin, *Theory of Literature* (New York, Harcourt, Brace & World, Inc., 1956).

Wimsatt, W. K., Jr. & Beardsley, Monroe C., *The Verbal Icon: Studies in the Meaning of Poetry* (Lexington, University of Kentucky Press, 1954).

Articles

Berdnikov, G., "Ivanov: An Analysis" (citing A. P. Skaftymov, *Stat'i o russkoj literature* (Leningrad-Moscow, 1957), 51-63, (trans.) Joyce Vining), *Chekhov*, (ed.) Robert Louis Jackson (Englewood Cliffs, N.J., Prentice-Hall, Inc., 1967), 88-98.

Davie, Donald, "Tolstoy, Lermontov, and Others", *Russian Literature and Modern English Fiction*, (ed.) Donald Davie (Chicago, University of Chicago Press, 1965), 164-199.

Dobroljubov, N. A., "Čto takoe Oblomovščina?", *Izbrannye filosofskie proizvedenija* (Moscow, Gosudarstvennoe izdatel'stvo političeskoj literatury, 1948), *I*, 501-543.

Dostoevskij, F. M., feuilleton of June 15, 1847, *Èpoxa* (Berlin, 1922), 69-75.

——, speech before the Society of Lovers of Russian Literature, June 8, 1880, *Sobranie sočinenij*, *X* (Moscow, Gosudarstvennoe izdatel'stvo xudožestvennoj literatury, 1958), 442-459.

du Bos, Charles, "The Chekhovian Sense of Life", (trans.) Leslie Jackson, *Chekhov* (ed.) Robert Louis Jackson (Englewood Cliffs, N.J., Prentice-Hall, Inc., 1967), 184-194.

Friedberg, Maurice, "The Background to the Third Congress of the Union of Soviet Writers", *Bulletin of the Institute for the Study of the USSR*, V (December, 1958), 30-40.

Gercen, A. I., "O romane iz narodnoj žizni v Rossii (Pis'mo k perevodčice 'Rybakov')", *Izbrannye proizvedenija* (Moscow, Izdatel'stvo 'Detskaja literatura', 1964), 366-376.

Gončarov, I. A., "Miljon terzanij", *Literaturno-kritičeskie stat'i i pis'ma* (Leningrad, Gosudarstvennoe izdatel'stvo 'xudožestvennaja literatura', 1938), 51-65.

Halliday, E. M., "Hemingway's Ambiguity: Symbolism and Irony", *American Literature*, XXVIII (March, 1956), 1-22.

Jackson, Robert Louis, "Chekhov's *Seagull*", *Chekhov*, (ed.) Robert Louis Jackson (Englewood Cliffs, N.J., Prentice-Hall, Inc., 1967), 99-111.

Lawrence, D. H., "Preface to Dostoevsky's *The Grand Inquisitor*", *Selected Criticism*, (ed.) Anthony Beal (New York, The Viking Press, Inc., 1956), 233-241.

Mathewson, Rufus, "The Novel in Russia and the West", *Soviet Literature in the Sixties*, (ed.) Max Hayward and Edward L. Crowley (New York, Frederick A. Praeger, 1964), 1-17.

Mirsky, D. S., "Chekhov and the English" (cited from *Monthly Criterion*, VI (October, 1927)), (ed.) Donald Davie, *Russian Literature and Modern English Fiction* (Chicago, University of Chicago Press, 1965), 203-213.

Muchnic, Helen, "Literature in the NEP Period", *Literature and Revolution in Soviet Russia 1917-1962*, (ed.) Max Hayward and Leopold Labedz (London, Oxford University Press, 1963), 28-43.

Rahv, Phillip, "Gogol as a Modern Instance" (cited from Philip Rahv, *Image and Idea* (New York, New Directions, 1949), *Russian Literature and Modern English Fiction*, (ed.) Donald Davie (Chicago, University of Chicago Press, 1965), 239-244.

Slonim, Marc, "The New Spirit in Russian Literature", *Soviet Literature: An Anthology*, (trans.) George Reavey (New York, Covici Friede Publishers, 1934), 13-48.

Stilman, Leon, "Oblomovka Revisited", *The American Slavic and East European Review*, VII (1948), 45-77.

——, "Problemy literaturnyx žanrov i tradicij v 'Evgenii Onegine' Puškina", *American Contributions to the Fourth International Congress of Slavicists* (The Hague, Mouton & Co., 1958), 321-367.

Turgenev, I. S., "Gamlet i Don-Kixot", *Sovremennik*, XXV (January, 1860), 239-258.

CRITICAL SOURCES

Monographs

Alexandrova, Vera, *A History of Soviet Literature* (Garden City, Doubleday & Co., 1963).

Brown, Edward J., *Russian Literature since the Revolution* (New York, Collier Books, 1963).

Gibian, George, *Interval of Freedom: Soviet Literature during the Thaw 1954-1957* (Minneapolis, University of Minnesota Press, 1960).

Johnson, Priscilla, *Krushchev and the Arts: The Politics of Soviet Culture, 1962-1964* (Cambridge, Mass., The MIT Press, 1965).

Mehnert, Klaus, *Humanismus in der jüngsten Sowjet-literatur?* (Mainz, Verlag der Akademie der Wissenschaften und der Literatur, 1963).

Muchnic, Helen, *From Gorky to Pasternak: Six Writers in Soviet Russia* (New York, Random House, 1961).

Rowland, Mary F. and Rowland, Paul, *Pasternak's 'Doctor Zhivago'* (Carbondale, Southern Illinois University Press, 1967).

Slonim, Marc, *Soviet Russian Literature: Writers and Problems* (New York, Oxford University Press, 1964).

Swayze, Harold, *Political Control of Literature in the USSR, 1946-1959* (Cambridge, Mass., Harvard University Press, 1962).

Vickery, Walter, *Political and Ideological Problems of Recent Soviet Literature* (Bloomington, Indiana University Press, 1963).

Whitney, Thomas P., *The New Writing in Russia* (Ann Arbor, University of Michigan Press, 1963).

Articles

Aleksandrov, K., "Revisionism as Reflected in Soviet Literature", *Bulletin of the Institute for the Study of the USSR*, V (April, 1958), 48-55.

Alexandrova, Vera, "Soviet Literature since Stalin", *Problems of Communism* (July-August, 1954), 11-14.

——, "Voices of Youth", *Soviet Survey*, No. 36 (April-June, 1961), 44-48.

——, "Youth and Life in New Soviet Literature", *Studies on the Soviet Union*, new series, II (March, 1962), 157-167.

Anatol', A., "Obraščenie A. Kuznecova k PEN" (cited from '*Russkaja mysl*'' (September 6, 1969)), *Novoe russkoe slovo* (October 5, 1969), 2.

Binyon, T. J., "Introduction", *Žestokost'* (Oxford, Pergamon Press, 1963), ix-xxvii.

Blake, Patricia, "New Voices in Russian Writing", *Encounter*, XX (April, 1963), 27-38.

Blum, Ralph, "A Reporter at Large. Freeze and Thaw: The Artist in Russia", *The New Yorker*, XLI (August 28, 1965), 40-100.

——, "A Reporter at Large. Freeze and Thaw: The Artist in Russia", *The New Yorker*, XLI (September 4, 1965), 32-85.

Bode, Barbara, "Die Auseinandersetzungen in der Sowjetliteratur als Spiegel der politischen Strömungen", *Osteuropa*, XV (January-February, 1965), 55-70.

——, "Die Diskussion um Solshenizyn als Zentrum der Auseinandersetzungen in der Sowjetliteratur", *Osteuropa*, XV (October, 1965), 679-694.

——, "Die Diskussion um Solshenizyn (II)", *Osteuropa*, XV (November-December, 1965), 784-796.

——, "1960: The Literary Harvest", *Soviet Survey*, No. 36 (April-June, 1961), 34-43.

——, "Sowjetliteratur 1959", *Osteuropa*, IX (December, 1959), 813-822.

——, "Sowjetliteratur im Winterhalbjahr 1959-1960", *Osteuropa*, X (September, 1960), 613-624.

——, "Sowjetliteratur 1961-1962", *Osteuropa*, XII (November-December, 1962), 793-812.

——, "Sowjetliteratur 1961-1962 (II)", *Osteuropa*, XIII (January, 1963), 16-32.

——, "Sowjetliteratur 1962-1963", *Osteuropa*, XIII (October, 1963), 702-717.

——, "Sowjetliteratur 1962-1963 (II)", *Osteuropa*, XIII (November-December, 1963), 821-835.

——, "Sowjetliteratur 1964", *Osteuropa*, XVI (January, 1966), 30-52.

——, "Über Ästhetik, Ethik und ähnliche Nutzlosigkeiten", *Osteuropa*, XII (September, 1963), 627-641.

Burg, David, "The 'Cold War' on the Literary Front", *Problems of Communism*, XI (September-October, 1962), 33-46.

——, "The 'Cold War' on the Literary Front, II", *Problems of Communism*, XI (July-August, 1962), 1-14.

——, "Der moralische Bankrott des Nachstalinismus (über Nekrassows Roman 'Kyra Georgijewna')", *Osteuropa*, XII (February-March, 1963), 128-135.

——, "Die Partei und die Schriftsteller: Chronik eines Jahres in der Sowjetunion", *Der Monat*, XVI, No. 183 (November, 1963), 33-48.

——, "Um Pasternaks Platz in der Sowjetliteratur", *Osteuropa*, XIV (September, 1964), 640-645.

Dalton, Margaret, "Nikolai Arzhak", *The New Leader*, CXLVIII (November 8, 1965), 17-18.

Erlich, Victor, "Post-Stalin Trends in Russian Literature", *Slavic Review*, XXIII (September, 1964), 405-419.

Field, Andrew, "Abram Tertz's Ordeal by Mirror", *The New Leader*, XLVIII, No. 15 (July 19, 1965), 9-15.

Folejewski, Zbigniew, "Notes on the Problem of Individual vs. Collective in Russian and Polish Literature, 1954-1957", *Indiana Slavic Studies*, III (1963), 26-34.

Frank, Victor S., "The Literary Climate", *Survey*, No. 56 (July, 1965), 46-53.

Friedberg, Maurice, "The Background to the Third Congress of the Union of Soviet Writers", *Bulletin of the Institute for the Study of the USSR*, V (December, 1958), 30-40.

Gaev, Arkadii, "The New Party Campaign for Ideological Control over Literature", *Analysis of Current Developments in the Soviet Union*, No. 215 (February 17, 1962).

——, "The Decade since Stalin", *Soviet Literature in the Sixties*, (ed.) Max Hayward & Edward L. Crowley (New York, Frederick A. Praeger, 1964), 18-54.

——, "The Father-and-Son Problem Becomes More Acute in the USSR", *Analysis of Current Developments in the Soviet Union*, No. 257 (January 22, 1963).

——, "Intellectual Opposition to Party Takes New Turn", *Analysis of Current Developments in the Soviet Union*, No. 26 (1965-1966).

——, "Soviet Literature after the Last Attacks", *Analysis of Current Developments in the Soviet Union*, No. 3 (1963-1964).

——, "Soviet Literature at the Beginning of the Second Stage of De-Stalinization", *Studies on the Soviet Union*, No. 4 (1965), 225-229.

Garrard, J. G., "Vladimir Tendrjakov", *The Slavic & East European Journal*, IX (Spring, 1965), 1-18.

Gibian, George, "New Trends in the Novel: Kazakov, Nagibin, Voronin", *Soviet Survey*, No. 36 (April-June, 1961), 49-55.

——, "The Revolt of the Moscow Writers", *The New Leader*, XL (August 26, 1957), 18-21.

——, "Soviet Literature during the Thaw", *Literature and Revolution in Soviet Russia 1917-1962*, (ed.) Max Hayward and Leopold Labedz (London, Oxford University Press, 1963), 125-149.

——, "Themes in Recent Soviet Russian Literature", *Slavic Review*, XXIII (September, 1964), 420-431.

Hampshire, Stuart, "'Doktor Zhivago' as from a Lost Culture", *Encounter*, IX (September, 1958), 3-5.

Hayward, Max, "Conflict and Change in Literature", *Survey*, No. 46 (January, 1963), 9-22.

——, "Introduction", *Dissonant Voices in Soviet Literature*, (ed.) Patricia Blake and Max Hayward (New York, Pantheon Books, 1962), vii-xlii.

——, "Solzhenitsyn's Place in Contemporary Soviet Literature", *Slavic Review*, XXIII (September, 1964), 432-436.

Howe, Irving, "Predicaments of Soviet Writing", *The New Republic*, CXLVII (May 11, 1963), 19-21.

J., M., "Literaturnaja Moskva, Sbornik II, 1956", *Soviet Studies*, IX (January, 1958), 322-345.

Johnson, Priscilla, "New Heretics in Soviet Writing", *Saturday Review*, XLV, No. 18 (May 5, 1962), 8-11.

Karavaev, A., "Between Thaw and Freeze in Soviet Literature", *Bulletin of the Institute for the Study of the USSR*, XI (March, 1964), 29-38.

Kersten, Heinz, "Die Sowjetische 'Tauwetter-Literatur'", *Politische Meinung*, IV, No. 32 (January, 1959), 84-91.

Kobetz, Johann, "Die Sowjetrussische Literatur in Kraftfeld der Wandlungen und Spannungen zwischen dem XX. und XXI. Parteitag der KPdSU", *Sowjet-Studien* (July, 1959), No. 7, 47-71.

Kramer, Karl D., "Jurij Kazakov: The Pleasures of Isolation", *The Slavic and East European Journal*, X (Spring, 1966), 22-31.

Laber, Jeri, "The Soviet Writer's Search for New Values", *Problems of Communism*, V (January-February, 1956), 14-20.

Lakšin, V., "Ivan Denisovič, ego druz'ja i nedrugi", *Novyj mir*, XL (January, 1964), 223-245.

Levitzky, Sergey, "Svoboda i bessmertie. O romane Pasternaka 'Doktor Živago'", *Mosty*, II (1950), 224-236.

Marin, Yury V., "A Reassessment of Values in Soviet Society", *Analysis of Current Developments in the Soviet Union*, No. 247 (November 13, 1962).

——, "The Revival of 'Freethinking' by Young Soviet Writers", *Analysis of Current Developments in the Soviet Union*, No. 247 (November 13, 1962).

Mathewson, Rufus, "The Novel in Russia and the West", *Soviet Literature in the Sixties*, (ed.) Max Hayward and Edward L. Crowley (New York, Frederick A. Praeger, 1964), 1-17.

Matlaw, Ralph E., "A Visit with Pasternak", *The Nation*, CLXXXIX, No. 7 (September 12, 1959), 134-135.

Mehnert, Klaus, "Moskauer Theater und Kino, Früjahr 1964", *Ost-europa*, XIV (June, 1964), 422-437.

Mihajlov, Mihajlo, "Moscow Summer 1964", *The New Leader*, XLVIII, No. 7 (March 29, 1965), 2-38.

Neander, Irene, "Pasternaks Neuer Roman", *Osteuropa*, VII (December, 1958), 781-786.

Rubin, Burtin, "Highlights of the 1962-1963 Thaw", *Soviet Literature in the Sixties*, (ed.) Max Hayward and Edward L. Crowley (New York, Frederick A. Praeger, 1964), 81-99.

——, "The Shock of Recognition", *Survey*, No. 47 (April, 1963), 160-171.

Ruge, Gerd, "Zu Besuch bei sowjetischen Schriftstellern", *Der Monat*, X (September, 1958), 25-41.

Rzhevsky, Leonid D., "The New Idiom", *Soviet Literature in the Sixties*, (ed.) Max Hayward and Edward L. Crowley (New York, Frederick A. Praeger, 1964), 55-80.

——, "O tajnopisi v romane 'Doktor Živago'", *Grani*, XV (October-December, 1960), 150-164.

Ščeglov, Mark, "Realizm sovremennoj dramy", *Literaturnaja Moskva, II* (Moscow, Gosudarstvennoe izdatel'stvo xudožestvennoj literatury, 1956), 681-708.

Scriven, Tom, "The 'Literary Opposition'", *Problems of Communism*, VII (January-February, 1958), 28-34.

Silbajoris, Rimvydas, "The Poetic Texture of Doktor Zhivago", *The Slavic and East European Journal*, IX (January, 1965), 19-27.

Simmons, Ernest J., "Recent Trends in Soviet Literature", *Modern Age*, VII, No. 4 (Fall, 1963), 393-406.

Sinjavskij, A., "The Trial of Sinyavsky and Daniel", (trans.-ed.) Max Hayward, *The New York Times Magazine* (April 17, 1966), 115-125.

Slavinsky, M., "Le rôle de la litterature en URSS dans la 'de-stalinisa-tion'", *Est et Ouest*, XVII, No. 350 (November 1-15, 1965), 14-18.

Solov'eva, Inna, "Problemy i proza (zametki o tvorčestve Vladimira Tendrjakova)", *Novyj mir*, XXXVIII (July, 1962), 235-249.

"Soviet Youth Breathes Life into the Arts", *Soviet Affairs Analysis Service*, No. 14 (1961-1962).

Steininger, Alexander, "Die Junge Sowjetische Dichtergeneration", *Ost-europa*, VIII (July-August, 1958), 459-478.

Struve, Gleb, "After the Coffee-Break", *The New Republic*, CXLVIII (February 2, 1963), 15-17.

——, "Russia Five Years After Stalin", *The New Leader*, XLI (April 7, 1958), 16-21.

——, "The Second Congress of Writers", *Problems of Communism*, IV (March-April, 1955), 3-11.

——, "Sense and Nonsense about *Doctor Zhivago*", *Studies in Russian and Polish Literature*, (ed.) Zbigniew Folejewski, *et al.* (The Hague, Mouton & Co., 1962), 229-250.

——, "Soviet Literature in Perspective: Some Unorthodox Reflections", *Soviet Literature in the Sixties*, (ed.) Max Hayward and Edward L. Crowley (New York, Frederick A. Praeger, 1964), 130-149.

Tikos, László, "Die andere 'unbewältigte Vergangenheit'", *Osteuropa*, XV (January-February, 1965), 71-78.

Wilson, Edmund, "Doctor Life and His Guardian Angel", *The New Yorker*, XXXIV (November 15, 1958), 201-226.

——, "Legend and Symbol in 'Doctor Zhivago'", *Encounter*, XII (June, 1959), 5-16.

Zekulin, Gleb, "Solzhenitsyn's Four Stories", *Soviet Studies*, XVI (July, 1964), 45-62.

POLITICAL BACKGROUND SOURCES

Monographs

Alexandrova, Vera, *A History of Soviet Literature* (Garden City, Doubleday & Co., 1963).

Brown, Edward J., *Russian Literature since the Revolution* (New York, Collier Books, 1963).

Gibian, George, *Interval of Freedom: Soviet Literature during the Thaw 1954-1957* (Minneapolis, University of Minnesota Press, 1960).

Mehnert, Klaus, *Humanismus in der jüngsten Sowjetliteratur?* (Mainz, Verlag der Akademie der Wissenschaften und der Literatur, 1963).

Slonim, Marc, *Soviet Russian Literature: Writers and Problems* (New York, Oxford University Press, 1964).

Vickery, Walter, *Political and Ideological Problems of Recent Soviet Literature* (Bloomington, Indiana University Press, 1963).

Whitney, Thomas P., *The New Writing in Russia* (Ann Arbor, University of Michigan Press, 1964).

Articles

Alexandrova, Vera, "Soviet Literature since Stalin", *Problems of Communism*, III (July-August, 1954), 11-14.

Blum, Ralph, "A Reporter at Large. Freeze and Thaw: The Artist in Russia", *The New Yorker*, XLI (August 28, 1965), 28-100.

——, "A Reporter at Large. Freeze and Thaw: The Artist in Russia", *The New Yorker*, XLI (September 11, 1965), 168-217.

Burg, David, "The Cold War on the Literary Front: III", *Problems of Communism*, XII (January-February, 1963), 44-58.

Feiffer, George, "Brodsky: Reactions in Moscow", *The New Leader*, XLVII (September 14, 1964), 11-13.

Friedberg, Maurice, "The Background of the Third Congress of the Union of Soviet Writers", *Bulletin of the Institute for the Study of the USSR*, V (December, 1958), 30-40.

Gavrilov, Nikolaj, "Letter from a Soviet Writer", *The New Leader*, XLVI (December 9, 1963), 14-18.

Gibian, George, "Soviet Literature during the Thaw", *Literature and Revolution in Soviet Russia 1917-1962*, (ed.) Max Hayward and Leopold Labedz (London, Oxford University Press, 1963), 125-149.

Hayward, Max, "Conflict and Change in Literature", *Survey*, No. 46 (January, 1963), 9-22.

——, "Introduction", *Dissonant Voices in Soviet Literature*, (ed.) Patricia Blake and Max Hayward (New York, Pantheon Books, 1962), vii-xlii.

——, "Solzhenitsyn's Place in Contemporary Soviet Literature", *Slavic Review*, XXIII (September, 1964), 432-436.

——, "Soviet Literature in the Doldrums", *Problems of Communism*, VIII (July-August, 1959), 11-16.

Hingley, Ronald, "Soviet Literary Attitudes", *Survey*, No. 40 (January, 1962), 42-48.

——, "Soviet Literary Attitudes", *Survey*, No. 46 (January, 1963), 3-8.

Howe, Irving, "Predicaments of Soviet Writing", *The New Republic*, CXLVII (May 11, 1963), 19-21.

Johnson, Priscilla, "New Heretics in Soviet Writing", *Saturday Review*, XLV (May 5, 1962), 8-11.

——, "The Regime and the Intellectuals: A Window on Party Politics (Winter 1962 — Summer 1963)", *Problems of Communism*, XII (July-August, 1963), ii-xxvii.

Karavaev, A., "Between Thaw and Freeze in Soviet Literature", *Bulletin of the Institute for the Study of the USSR*, XI (March, 1965), 29-38.

Kobetz, Johann, "Die Sowjetrussische Literatur in Kraftfeld der Wandlungen und Spannungen zwischen dem XX. und XXI. Parteitag der KPdSU", *Sowjet-Studien*, No. 7 (July, 1959), 47-71.

Lakšin, V., "Ivan Denisovič, ego druz'ja i nedrugi", *Novyj mir*, XL (January, 1964), 223-245.

Marin, Yuri, "The Revival of 'Freethinking' by Young Soviet Writers", *Analysis of Current Developments in the Soviet Union*, No. 247 (November 13, 1962).

Mathewson, Rufus, "The Novel in Russia and the West", *Soviet Literature in the Sixties*, (ed.) Max Hayward and Edward L. Crowley (New York, Frederick A. Praeger, 1964), 1-17.

Mehnert, Klaus, "Moskauer Theater und Kino, Frühjahr 1964", *Osteuropa*, XIV (June, 1964), 422-437.

Mihajlov, Mihajlo, "Moscow Summer 1964", *The New Leader*, XLVIII (March 29, 1965), 2-38.

——, "Moscow Summer 1964", *The New Leader*, XLVIII (June 7, 1965), 3-14.

——, "Why We Are Silent", *The New Leader*, XLVIII (August 30, 1965), 12-15.

Muchnic, Helen, "Literature in the NEP Period", *Literature and Revolution in Soviet Russia 1917-1962*, (ed.) Max Hayward and Leopold Labedz (London, Oxford University Press, 1963), 28-43.

Pipes, Richard, "Russia's Exigent Intellectuals: A Eulogy and Warning", *Encounter*, XXII (January, 1964), 79-84.

——, "The Soviet Jacobins", *The New Leader*, XLIX (April 25, 1966), 9-11.

Reeve, F. D., "Writer vs. Bureaucrat in the Soviet Union", *The Atlantic Monthly*, CCXIII (January, 1964), 69-74.

Rubin, Burtin, "Highlights of the 1962-1963 Thaw", *Soviet Literature in the Sixties*, (ed.) Max Hayward and Edward L. Crowley (New York, Frederick A. Praeger, 1964), 81-99.

Simmons, Ernest J., "Russia's Different Generation", *The National Observer*, V (February 28, 1966), 22.

Slavinsky, M., "Le rôle de la litterature en URSS dans la 'de-stalinisation'", *Est et Ouest*, XVII (November 1-15, 1965), 14-18.

Slonim, Marc, "The New Spirit in Russian Literature", *Soviet Literature: An Anthology*, (tr.) George Reavey (New York, Covici Friede Publishers, 1934), 13-48.

Sosin, Gene, "Talks with Soviet Writers", *Survey*, No. 36 (April-June, 1961), 3-12.

Struve, Gleb, "Russia Five Years after Stalin", *The New Leader*, XLI (April 7, 1958), 16-21.

——, "The Second Congress of Writers", *Problems of Communism*, IV (March-April, 1955), 3-11.

——, "Soviet Literature in Perspective: Some Unorthodox Reflections", *Soviet Literature in the Sixties*, (ed.) Max Hayward and Edward L. Crowley (New York, Frederick A. Praeger, 1964), 130-149.

——, "The Transition from Russian to Soviet Literature", *Literature and Revolution in Soviet Russia 1917-1962*, (ed.) Max Hayward and Leopold Labedz (London, Oxford University Press, 1963), 1-27.

——, "Western Writing in Soviet Literature", *Survey*, No. 50 (January, 1964), 137-145.

Willets, H. T., "New Directions?", *Survey*, No. 46 (January, 1963), 3-8.

INDEX OF AUTHORS, CRITICS AND TITLES OF FICTION*

---

* For additional references see Appendices A and B.